INFORMATION SYSTEMS IN BUSINESS

SECOND EDITION

Professor M J S Harry

Senior Visiting Fellow
University of Bradford Management Centre

PITMAN
PUBLISHING

London · Hong Kong · Johannesburg · Melbourne · Singapore · Washington DC

PITMAN PUBLISHING
128 Long Acre, London WC2E 9AN
Tel: +44 (0)171 447 2000
Fax: +44 (0)171 240 5771

A Division of Pearson Professional Limited

First published in Great Britain in 1994
Second edition published in 1997

© Pearson Professional 1997

The right of Mike Harry to be identified as Author
of this Work has been asserted by him in accordance
with the Copyright, Designs and Patents Act 1988.

ISBN 0 273 62567 5

British Library Cataloguing in Publication Data
A CIP catalogue record for this book can be obtained from the British Library

10 9 8 7 6 5 4 3 2 1

Typeset by Pantek Arts, Maidstone, Kent
Printed and bound in Great Britain by Clays Ltd, St Ives plc

The Publishers' policy is to use paper manufactured from sustainable forests.

CONTENTS

....

PREFACE

Imagine going to a travel agent to choose a holiday. You are interested in a cycling tour of Denmark. When you explain your idea to the travel agent, you find yourself being subjected to a lecture on tyre pressures by someone who is clearly a cycling enthusiast.

Making polite excuses, you go to another travel agent around the corner. After hearing what you want, the agent passes you a copy of 'European Transport Policy for the Year 2000' and discusses the various Danish opt-outs from the Treaty of Maasstricht.

Finally you come to an agent who has no opinions at all, and just hands you an untidy pile of brochures.When you get home you find that the only thing they have in common is that they contain either the word 'bicycle' or the word 'Denmark'.

Similar dangers seem to confront those business and management students who want to explore the world of information systems. There are many excellent books on computer hardware and software, but an explanation of disk file structures is no more a business information system than tyre pressures are a cycle tour of Denmark. There are some important books which take the 'higher', 'broader' or 'corporate' view of the impact of information technology on organizations, but for them the bicycle and its rider can hardly be seen from the god-like mountain top.

Unlike our two examples, real management and business information systems have to see the whole view of the country; which brings us to the untidy pile of brochures. If we are to see information, systems and management coming together to make things happen, then there has to be something which relates the choice of the computer disk to the nature of the organization, and the nature of the organization to the choice of computer disk.

As in the first edition of *Information Systems in Business*, I believe that what makes this relationship is the connexion between management and information through the concept of control. The word 'control' can be frightening, if we take it to mean a method or management style used by the strong to exploit the weak. But once we see that any form of management is about trying to make things happen, then control as a *concept* is as relevant to destroying tyranny as it is to imposing it. Fortunately, in most situations our aims are less dramatic but no less important. Selling a product, treating the hospital patient, protecting a woodland or making the trains run on time, are all about trying to make things happen.

This new edition contains extra material compared with the old. My main aim has been to include more examples from everyday business, organizational and political life to reinforce the understanding of concepts. Where I have made any improvements to the previous edition, it should be credited to my students.

As for my continuing eccentricities, 'connexion' and 'organization' show that I know some Latin and Greek and that I was born before 1945: not that I can't spell.

M.J.S Harry
March 1997

Hard:
When you can measure what you are speaking about, and express it in numbers, you know something about it. When you cannot measure it, when you cannot express it in numbers, your knowledge is of a meagre and unsatisfactory kind.
LORD KELVIN

Soft:
There's nothing I hate more than nothing;
Nothing keeps me up at night.
I toss and turn over nothing:
Nothing can cause a great big fight.
EDIE BRICKELL AND THE NEW BOHEMIANS

Uncertain:
All the business of war, and indeed all the business of life, is to endeavour to find out what you don't know from what you do; that's what I called 'guessing what was at the other side of the hill'.
ARTHUR WELLESLEY, DUKE OF WELLINGTON

CHAPTER 1
· · · · · · · · · · · · · · ·

The Approach and Structure of this Book

1.1 WHO THIS BOOK IS FOR

This is intended to be a *teaching* book and is designed for you, the reader, who wants to *learn* about information systems applied to the operation of businesses and organizations.

I've emphasized the two words *teaching* and *learning* because they will help to explain:

- the style used when writing this book
- the detailed structure of the book in terms of the variety of components to be found in each chapter.

The way I have dealt with both of these features comes from what I have learned from my own experience of teaching and thinking about the subject of *information systems in business* working with learners. To understand this background, I need to explain that some of the features of this book are different because I am trying to overcome certain unfriendly and negative trends which I think have come into teaching, learning and the books used to support them.

I have tried to be positive, and to avoid two distortions which can interfere with the main messages of any book which teaches *systems thinking*, with its emphasis on *holism*. The distortions which I am trying to avoid can be explained in terms of two stereotypes, which you may already have come across as a learner.

The first distortion focusses on the teaching process. I will call this the *hard stereotype*. Teachers, lecture rooms, teaching materials and assessment all cost money. Any institution which aims to make the teaching process more economic can apply the Henry Ford principle of economies of scale and mass production. Thus large-scale lecture theatres maximize student-to-staff ratios. Standard syllabi and fixed lecture schemes de-skill teaching and maximize staff interchangability. Standard presentation materials and student handouts cut library and materials costs. Mechanical assessment procedures like multiple choice questions streamline examinations and testing. I suppose I could parody this approach by saying, 'So just be quiet and listen to what you are told: it may be coming up in the exam'.

Many of my readers have probably experienced that kind of teaching. It is often found in subject areas like quantitative methods for business or statistics. Successful students can do things like calculate a standard deviation or carry out a test using chi-squared, but when asked what the standard deviation measures, or to explain the concept of statistical significance, they look blank. They have been successfully taught, but have learned very little.

The second distortion represents a reaction to this heavy teaching emphasis. I will call this the *soft stereotype*. The impersonal large lecture is replaced by small seminar discussion groups. Students are encouraged to set their own agenda to the point that the teacher will sit and say nothing until somebody is so agonized by the silence that they feel obliged to blurt out some platitude. The reading material for such a course is very 'open', which means nothing is given and everything is possible. The assessment is likely to take a very unstructured format like an embarrassing role play, keeping a diary or some kind of project, preferably of a personal nature.

I expect this kind of learning is also familiar to many of my readers. It can result in the development of a very high level of learning in terms of self-analysis, group political skills and guessing what the lecturer *really* wants you to say. It can also be very attractive to institutions who wish to pass off lack of management and poor teaching under the guise of 'student-centred learning'. Under this regime, students learn a lot about themselves and their teachers, but are taught very little about anything else.

At their best however, both structured teaching and open learning are not like these stereotypes and form vital ingredients of the teaching–learning partnership. There are times when students have the right to direction from a teacher and clear answers to questions. But having had that direction and having received those answers, students who have really learned something will be able to go on and use what they have learned by setting their own objectives and developing their own methods. They recognize that using something can often result in what is used being modified, added to, and eventually replaced.

Both the writing style and the structure of this book are based on the assumption that it is for those who want to be taught and to learn. If I am trying to *teach* the subject of information systems in business, then I need to present facts and answer questions in a structured framework whilst avoiding the rigidity of the hard stereotype. If you want to *learn*, I have to open up discussion of issues and show potential diversity whilst avoiding the universal 'definite maybe' of the soft stereotype.

Since this is a teaching–learning book, the writing style will be different from books which aim to be catalogues of facts or academic dissertations. As you have seen already, I often use the style of 'I think', 'you may find' or 'we discussed' rather than 'in the author's opinion', 'it may be found' or 'as was discussed'. This is because my aim is to develop a teaching–learning partnership rather than record for posterity what I think I know about the subject. For the same reason, I frequently use personal examples or illustrations with a strong human element rather than an impersonal catalogue of events.

The intimacy of the style does not mean however that this is an elementary book. 'Information systems' has a strong *conceptual* foundation. This means that, although *how* this book is written tries to avoid unnecessary difficulties, *what* it covers in terms of subject matter can often be quite advanced. You shouldn't be surprised if some parts look quite difficult the first time around. I have found that there is no substitute for time and thought for understanding concepts.

A final point before we finish this first section. Out of the 800 or so words I have written so far, over a dozen have been put into *italics*. My purpose when doing this is not just to emphasize the flow of words as we would use them when speaking, but identify *concepts* or *themes* which will be taken up and discussed further in the book. So even the emphasis on simple words like *what* and *how* above are already leading us into some important systems concepts which will be taken up later.

1.2 WHAT SUBJECTS ARE COVERED

Old names and new meanings

When we get into a train we go into a 'carriage'. The reason it is called a carriage is because people up to the early nineteenth century used to travel in carriages pulled by horses. After Richard Trevithick invented the steam engine and railways were created, the engine was regarded as an 'iron horse' and the things which it pulled were sufficiently similar to the old way of transporting people to be called 'carriages'.

Using old names to describe new things in this way can help us relate the new to the old. It also has the disadvantage that the new way can be limited by the old ideas. Unlike a horse, an 'iron horse' in the form of a modern electric locomotive can run equally well backwards and forwards. If we had kept thinking about the horse concept, we would never have got on to the idea of having power units at both ends of trains which could both push and pull, running forwards or backwards.

Information and information systems have gone through a similar change in the last years of the twentieth century that transport systems went through in the middle years of the nineteenth. Old words are still being used to describe new ways of doing things in order to help people make the adjustment to the changes. Besides being helpful however, these ways of describing things can prevent a realization of the important changes which are taking place and their practical implications.

To understand what subjects are covered in this book, we need first to understand how the words *information, systems* and *business* of the title are commonly used. We can then give some indication of how the whole book will develop and build on these uses.

Information and information systems

The term *information system* is commonly taken to imply a computer-based system which gathers data and produces the information which the user requires. In this context the term *information* is used to describe what the system either records via a keyboard, processes using software, prints out on paper, shows on a screen, or stores on a computer disk. We are not going to deliberately redefine the terms information and information system in this book in some new smart fashion that throws away this view, and with it, the learning and experience of the past. Much of what was developed between the 1960s and the 1980s, when computerized information systems made big advances, can be built on rather than thrown away.

What we will see however is that the more common uses of *information* and *information system* are particular examples of *how* these concepts have been applied. *What* they could be is something much wider; and something with much wider practical implications also.

Business

Similarly, the use of the word *business*, particularly following world political developments at the end of the 1980s, is narrower than the concept which it implies. The frequent use of the word to imply operations principally concerned with money and motivated by profit represents a reduction of its meaning. In this book the words *business* and *organization* will be often put together to show a resistance to this process. The word business in the title of this book is intended to mean the wider senses of 'task', 'duty', 'serious work', or 'what we are about' which can still be found in a good dictionary. When we talk of information systems 'in business' therefore, we recognize that commercial business is just one particular example of the wider subject of purposeful activity.

Subject areas for information, systems and business

If we look at the large number of existing books whose titles contain the words *information, system* and *business,* we find three common types of emphasis or subject area:

1 Books which consider *businesses* or *organizations* as *systems,* like Beer (1985) or the excellent Schoderbeck et al. (1990), but do not study information systems in particular detail. These use the principles of systems thinking which have been applied across a whole range of subjects, as in Beishon & Peters (1981), to take a systems view of businesses and their management. This represents a change from older views, where a business is thought of primarily in terms of departments and organization charts, and management is thought of as the name of a class of employees and what they do. A systems approach looks behind the names and labels for *how* things are done to see *what* is going on in a business.

2 Books which cover the subject of *information systems* applied to management and business, such as Curtis (1995). These interpret the terms information and information system in the mainly computer-based sense discussed above and do a thorough job relating such a view of an information system to a mainly conventional, organizational view of management. What they do not do to any great extent is to see businesses or organizations as systems.

3 Books which focus on the *analysis, design* and *development* of either the broad range of management systems, like Wilson (1990); or information systems in particular, like Flynn (1992). Such books have a strong emphasis on methodology.

In this book we shall be covering all three of these subject areas, but not by merely joining them together. I shall use a systems view from the first subject area above to establish the concept of a business as a system and the role of management as a component of that system. The second subject area is then covered by placing information and the information system as integral components of the management system, so that they are viewed in business and management terms. The third area of systems development methodology then studies systems development methods in terms of how they serve the needs of a business as a system, rather than as a predefined set of techniques. The overall unity of the three subject areas therefore comes from the key concept of a *system*, and in Chapter 3 I will develop a particular systems model for applying the concept.

1.3 HOW THE CONTENTS ARE ORGANIZED

The organization of the chapters

The organization of the chapters in this book is intended to reflect the view of its subject content laid out in Section 1.2. The structure of the individual chapters is intended to work with the view of teaching–learning argued out in Section 1.1.

Let us begin with the effect of the subject of the book on the organization of the chapters. This book aims to present and develop the subject of information systems in business, using a *systems* view to bring together the subject components of management in businesses, information systems, and systems analysis, design and development.

Any attempt to develop the subject in this way is unlikely to succeed unless we have some understanding of the key words which describe it. For us these words are *information, system* and *business.* Presenting and developing the subject of information systems in business will therefore require an explanation and understanding of the *concepts* of information and system, followed by study of their *application* to business. The chapters of this book are therefore grouped to reflect the sequence of concepts (Chapters 3–5), followed by applications (Chapters 6–8).

We also saw in Section 1.2 that concepts associated with a particular technology can take on new applied forms as that technology is developed. When this happens there is a danger that the new development becomes restricted by the older thinking. Since *information* is closely bound up with recent developments in information technology, we need to ensure that our understanding of this key concept does not get confined to a particular technological view. Chapter 2 is therefore designed to open up the concept of information, to show some of the variety of forms it can take, and to prepare for the detailed treatment in Chapters 3–5.

Concepts

The sequence of Chapters 3–5 then follows our aim of placing information systems in a business context using a systems approach. In Chapter 3 we establish the fundamentals of systems thinking and use these to build a systems view of businesses, their management, and the role of the information system as a component of management.

Once we understand the role of information systems in management, we are ready to say more about the nature of the product it delivers to management: namely information itself. Hence Chapter 4 covers the important concepts relating to information.

By the end of Chapter 4 the coverage of the key concepts of information and information systems will have explained the role of *data* as the building blocks we use to construct information. To understand the concepts behind the application of this principle to data processing, databases and database management, Chapter 5 therefore covers the data concepts relevant to these applications.

Our view of the subject of information systems in business not only leads to a sequence of concepts followed by applications; it is also reflected in the sequence of individual chapters. We set the systems context for business and information systems first in Chapter 3 before looking in detail at information in Chapter 4. Similarly we wait until we have some understanding of information as a whole before looking at the concepts behind the detailed data from which it is constructed. As we shall see in Chapter 3, this view which seeks to understand individual components in relation to their role in a greater whole, is an important aspect of systems thinking.

Applications

The same systems principle governs the sequence of the two applications chapters. We look first in Chapter 6 at what information systems have to do when applied to businesses. Once we know what they must do, we are in a position to consider what methods we might use for their development and implementation. Hence Chapters 7 and 8 look at systems development methodology.

The structure of the individual chapters

The organization of the chapters is based on the sequence of concepts before applications, and setting the whole picture before looking at the details. Such an approach, as we shall see in Chapter 3, can be described as *top-down*. For understanding and learning about a subject however, there is also a need for a *bottom-up* approach. When using this we start with a particular example as a first step towards understanding wider principles.

The structure of the chapters recognizes the need for both approaches. We will now look at each of the components to be found in Chapter 3–8 to see the roles they are intended to play in the teaching–learning process.

The mini-case

The purpose of the mini-case is to introduce the subject of the chapter in a way that shows some of the issues and questions that have to be sorted out for us to learn about the subject.

Some of the cases deal with large-scale events concerning companies or even whole nations. Others are quite intimate and personal. Some are about things which actually happened, whilst others are fictitious but true to life in that they are based on my own experience. What all the cases have in common is that they illustrate situations that actually happen, so the first section of every case is entitled 'What Happened'.

The style of the cases may seem less formal than those you are used to. This is deliberate, and reflects what they are trying to achieve. The essential point is to be able to read through a case and take in a feel for the atmosphere and the issues. The cases are not designed to be sources for detailed facts or technical points. Material of that type is found in the cases in the Appendices which I will deal with below.

Whilst it may be very relaxing and easy to just read through a case and 'take in a feel for the atmosphere', if all the cases stopped at this point we would be left in a soft stereotype position of wondering what we were trying to achieve. Each case therefore next includes a section which looks back at what happened and gives a viewpoint, comment or interpretation of the events. Once we have got past Chapter 3 and have begun to build some basic systems concepts, this second section of the case will take up what was covered in previous chapters as a basis for comment. Thus, for example, the case in Chapter 5 is interpreted from an information systems viewpoint and takes up aspects of systems thinking and information systems covered in Chapters 3 and 4.

Once you have read a case and seen some comment on it, I think you will be ready for a closing of the broad, unstructured consideration of the case and a clear statement of the issues. Each case finishes with a section entitled 'The Issues' which spells out in a more formal, serious way what the case was designed to introduce.

The learning objectives

The result of the mini-case section should be that you are beginning to understand what sorts of questions need to be answered by the main subject content of the chapter. The 'Learning Objectives' spell out the subject material that must be understood if we are to answer these questions. I have frequently prefaced objectives with the phrase 'To understand' because I believe that it is the real test of learning. Understanding implies that we not only know a fact or know how to do something, but we also know how one fact fits in with another or when it makes sense to use a skill that we have acquired.

I know that there is a currently fashionable school of thought which says that understanding cannot be directly observed and therefore cannot be an objective. Such a view is confusing *whats* and *hows*. The objectives of this book spell out *what* you should hope to learn from the chapters. *How* you show that you have acquired this understanding will be through everything from successfully answering STQs to producing a successful dissertation.

The subject content

This is the main part of every chapter which aims to deliver the subject material set up by the learning objectives. I have already explained why the writing style is the way it is and the significance of the use of italics. In addition, four other features need explaining:

1 The text is interspersed with STQs or self-testing questions. Their aim is to encourage you to pause after some important point has been made in the script and check to see if you have understood what has been said. You may feel that this interrupts your flow of reading; if so, ignore them and come back later. I've assumed from my own experience that pausing to check is a good idea because it prevents me from kidding myself that I've understood something. Consequently, the narrative following an STQ sometimes builds on the answers to them which are found at the end of the chapter.

2 Examples of principles in the text may refer to any of the mini-cases which you have studied so far, or to the ones in the appendices. If, like me, you are someone who does not read a book starting at page one and going through it one page at a time, you will need to check the names of the various cases so that you know what is being referred to.

3 The text contains many diagrams. In Chapter 3 we shall learn about *systems diagrams*, but the diagrams in this book cover other kinds of diagrams too. The diagrams include some explanation of what they show, but they are just one part of the whole presentation of the book, so do consider them in relation to what is said about them in the text.

4 The subject content of the text is divided into sections and subsections, which are numbered in relation to the chapter in which they occur. Thus the subject content of Chapter 3 is divided into Sections 3.1, 3.2, etc.; and a section like 3.1 is divided into 3.1.1, 3.1.2, etc. To avoid complexity I call all sections and subsections 'sections' for convenience.

Boxes

Chapters 2–8 contain various *boxes*. These are mainly extracts from very recent articles in *The Financial Times* and *Investors Chronicle*. My decision to include these comes from my experience of teaching *concepts*. Just as nourishment from food takes physical digestion and time, so concepts require their mental digestion period. Most students find the process a lot easier, however, if they can relate concepts to actual examples and experience. In the text I often use quite simple ideas to relate things to personal experience. This approach is user-friendly, but there is a danger that the link with the hard world of business will be missed if not enough factual material is included. So in this edition I have included the boxes to reinforce the message that concepts do relate to the real world.

Key words

Every subject has its own specialist vocabulary. The purpose of the key words section at the end of each chapter is designed to give you an opportunity to test that you have acquired the vocabulary you need to feel easy with its subject matter. Key words also act as a list of the important facts or concepts you should have learned.

Seminar agendas, exam questions and project/dissertation subjects

This section is intended to indicate how you can develop your learning in two different ways:

1 By suggesting how an issue or subject area which has come up in the text can be pursued in more depth.

2 By suggesting new 'by-product' or 'spin-off' subjects which are not part of the main chapter subject but could be developed from it.

Since this section is intended to open up further thinking rather than consolidate what we have covered, the suggestions are often very broad. Remember however that making the aims of a dissertation too broad is a common student fault. I remember when I was a young lecturer about to supervise my first dissertation. I asked my head of department for advice on how to start. He said, 'You make an appointment for the student to come and see you. When he comes in the door, and before he can say anything, you tell him it's too broad'. My subsequent experience suggests that this is not so absurd as it sounds.

If you are thinking of a dissertation topic it might be worth having an open seminar approach to a suggestion with a tutor, your peer group or a business contact at an early stage; but be prepared to narrow down to a specific issue or application from the general area considered.

References and bibliography

Books can be included in references and bibliographies for a range of very different reasons:

  a. As an authority or original book on the subject referred to.
  b. As a source of a quotation.

    c. As an illustration or example of some particular style or school of thought.

    d. As further or alternative reading on something already well covered in the text.

    e. As a reference book.

    f. As a book to avoid.

    g. To show that the person compiling the bibliography (or their assistant) has done their homework.

and so on.

It is important therefore to check why a book is in the bibliography and not assume that it constitutes either a reading list, a list of endorsements, or a recommendation to buy. When a book is referred to in the text, I normally explain why this is, and I often make comments on their style and difficulty. I can say that virtually all the books which I recommend are ones I own myself. I have avoided the indiscriminate listing of large numbers of books on the same subject, but I do refer to some very different types of book where I want to show the potential range of a subject.

Appendices

The mini-cases are mainly designed to be readable introductions to the issues and subject matter of the individual chapters. It is also useful to have cases which can be referred to for examples and issues for whole subject range. I have therefore included some additional short cases in the appendices for this purpose. Besides making these cases suitable for illustrating a range of subject content, I have also deliberately chosen very different kinds of organization in an attempt keep open a wide view of the term *business.*

In addition to the extra cases, I have used appendices for factual material which would block the flow of the main text.

The appendices are also designed to provide you with additional material for discussion and comparison throughout the book. You may find them useful seminar material for just about all the subjects which come up.

For all these reasons it is worth reading the appendices at an early stage in your studies so that you become familiar with them.

Chapter 2

The structure of Chapter 2 is a modified version of that found in the rest of the book. This is because Chapter 2 is designed to open up questions which subsequent chapters are intended to answer. Hence those sections of a normal chapter which are concerned with assessment or listing of concepts are absent.

1.4 TEACHING–LEARNING SUGGESTIONS

In the previous section we explained the teaching–learning material which is to be found in all the main chapters of this book. Besides this specific material, there are a number of general suggestions that you may apply throughout your reading:

1 Before reading the *Issues* section of the mini-cases, you could try to identify what you think the issues are. If you find that an issue you thought was present has not been picked up by me, it would be worth seeing if it is covered in the main body of the chapter. If it isn't, perhaps you've discovered a useful seminar agenda or dissertation topic.

2 When discussing the *Learning Objectives* I made the point that you as an individual learner are being guided on *what* you should understand. Those who test you will be concerned with *how* this understanding can be shown. If you are studying for a specific course which has a syllabus or some other official course documentation, it will be worth checking whether it has 'learning outcomes' or some similar statement of assessment policy. Worth checking also whether past assessment like exam or test papers take any notice of them: lecturers and teachers don't always follow the official line.

3 The STQs in the *Subject Content* usually refer to one particular mini-case or a case in the appendices. Relating the STQs to other cases in the book or to your own experience can be equally useful. Don't be too quick to downgrade your own experience if you are not in conventional employment. If you are involved in the business of working at home, looking for a job, or bringing up children; these are all potential sources of experience you can relate to. As a student at a college or university you are involved in the business of producing educated and qualified people. One of the major themes of this book, which distinguishes the *whats* and the *hows*, should continue to open up the idea that 'the word business in the title of this book is intended to mean the wider senses of "task", "duty", "serious work", or "what we are about"'.

4 The *Key Words* provide an agenda for testing and revision. The real test of whether you understand something is to explain it to someone else. Get an intelligent critical person to ask you to explain to them what the key words mean. If they understand your explanation, the chances are that you understand the word yourself.

5 Remember that books in the *Reference and Bibliography* themselves contain further references. Thus although I tend to recommend one or two good books on a specialist subject rather than list several indiscriminately, these books themselves have specialist references. If you don't understand the reference system of the library you use, find out about it.

BIBLIOGRAPHY

Beer, S. (1985). *Diagnosing the System.* Wiley.

Beishon, R.J. & Peters, G. (Eds). (1972), (1976), 2nd edn. (1981), 3rd edn. *Systems Behaviour.* Harper & Row.

Curtis, G.C. (1995). *Business Information Systems*, 2nd edn. Addison-Wesley Longman.

Davis, G.B. & Olson, M.H. (1984). *Management Information Systems.* McGraw-Hill.

Flynn, D.J. (1992). *Information Systems Requirements: Determination and Analysis.* McGraw-Hill.

Harry, M.J.S. (1990). *Information and Management Systems.* Pitman.

Schoderbeck, P.P., Schoderbeck, C.G. & Kefalas, A.G. (1990). *Management Systems.* Business Publications.

Wilson, B. (1990). *Systems Concepts, Methodologies and Applications.* Wiley.

BSW Windows

What happened

BSW Windows is a small firm which was created and is owned by one man: Harry Seaton. Whilst many people have not heard of BSW Windows, once they have heard of it they soon find out that Harry is the owner and founder of the company. Most things belonging to the company, from its vehicles to the headed notepaper, bear the legend 'BSW Windows – a Harry Seaton company'. Strictly speaking, Harry Seaton does own more than one company because he is also a director and the majority share-holder of the local football team, but BSW Windows is his real obsession.

Although Harry is an emotional, self-opinionated and larger-than-life character, the rationale behind BSW Windows has been thought through in a very calm and unemo-tional way. The area in the north of England where BSW Windows operates consists of former coal mining villages, hill-farming market towns, and one cathedral city which is the headquarters of local government. What all these very different towns and vil-lages have in common is a large proportion of old buildings. The coal mining villages are mainly nineteenth-century terraced houses, many of which now need renovation and have recently been 'listed'. A listed building is one which may not be either demolished or even have its appearance changed without special government permis-sion. Many of the centres of the market towns consist of groups of stone-built eighteenth-century houses which form 'conservation areas'. Like listed buildings, these are subject to special restrictions which control the form and appearance of any refurbishment or redevelopment. The cathedral city is so rich in old buildings that it is regarded as part of the European heritage, which has even wider implications for the care and maintenance of its old buildings.

The essential market opportunity behind BSW Windows, which Harry Seaton rec-ognized in the 1970s, was that these various restrictions controlling the repair and refurbishing of old buildings worked against most of the existing window replace-ment firms. Harry saw that the public had a stereotyped view of such 'cowboy' window firms who did very low priced work on the basis of hard selling and the eco-nomic efficiency that comes from repetitive production of a few popular products. These firms made most of their money by installing replacement windows on more recent housing developments where the dimensions of the windows were standard and the range of styles was limited. Since listed buildings and those in conservation areas were built before standard sizes and metrication, their windows did not conform to this modern mass production approach. Indeed, where such firms had been let loose on old buildings, they had changed dimensions and styles to conform to the modern ones that were conveniently available, usually with unsympathetic results. By the late 1970s the activities of these firms had resulted in reports headlined 'desecration of our heritage' in an important national broadsheet newspaper.

Harry recognized that BSW Windows could be different from most of these companies and therefore gain commercially. He set up a firm which designed individual windows for buildings in terms of their dimensions and style, but used standard materials and procedures for making them. In this way he could make a product that was close to the original in dimensions, appearance and style; but was made using economic modern methods and often cheaper materials. Although BSW Windows did not officially offer a set range of window designs, research into local historic traditions showed that there had been standard popular styles in the past just as there were today. Harry's firm classified these and used the results of this classification to bring an element of standardization which streamlined the measuring up, specification and manufacturing procedures.

The sales representatives of BSW Windows were contracted to the company as self-employed agents, not as employees. Consequently their earnings depended entirely on the commission they gained from their sales. This resulted in an aggressively motivated salesforce, and was an idea which Harry had copied from other, sometimes less respectable firms. He realized however that BSW Windows representatives fighting for the same contract would be confusing for the customer, and would frustrate his attempts to distance the company from the cowboy image; so representatives were alloted informal 'territories'. This decision worked very well for most sales representatives, since they could concentrate on understanding their own area and recognize property redevelopment or refurbishment opportunities that could be exploited to their own advantage.

Besides the actual selling, representatives also had control over the measuring up and pricing of the replacement windows. Their specification and measurements for individual windows were placed with the production department of BSW Windows and a cost negotiated for their manufacture. To place an order with the production department, sales representatives used a standard specification form for each job. The form exploited Harry's systematic classification of old window designs in terms of style, dimensions and finish.

The cost and timing of the installation was also negotiated with the fitting department of BSW Windows who were very much under Harry's personal control. This procedure ensured that whatever the sales representative may have promised, or whatever pressure may have been applied to the customer, people in vans with the legend 'BSW Windows – a Harry Seaton company' made sure that customers were, or were persuaded into being, 'satisfied'.

Since the commission for sales representatives was made up of the difference between the price they agreed with the buyer and the cost of manufacturing and fitting they negotiated with BSW Windows, there were pressures on both production and sales representatives to fine tune costs and prices. A similar tension existed between sales representatives and the fitting department with equivalent pressures on costs, but Harry's personal involvement in the fitting procedure ensured that quality as well as cost was a pressure on the final outcome of any deal between a customer and the sales representatives of BSW Windows.

From the introduction of the IBM Personal Computer and rival compatibles in the early 1980s, local computer sales people started to call on BSW Windows, and Harry in particular, to sell software which had been developed for window replacement firms. In the area of computers, Harry relied on a young recruit he had made to the firm in 1982 called Matthew Cope. Matthew had qualified at the local technical college in computer studies. Matthew was different from many of Harry's employees in that he was not afraid to speak his mind and even disagree with Harry when technical computing questions came up. The result was that a computer system was first introduced in 1986 to convert the order specifications of the sales representatives into a material and cost breakdown. By 1988 BSW Windows had such a heavy work load that Matthew convinced Harry to go a stage further and consider an extension to the software which would convert orders into job tickets and schedule the jobs through production and assembly.

The late 1980s saw Harry Seaton and BSW Windows as a local success story. Harry himself now became a personality in his own right. He became prominent in the local Conservative Party and was encouraged to stand as a district councillor, which he successfully did. He also sat on several charity committees, particularly those which encouraged young people in sport and outdoor activities. Consequently, newspaper pictures of Harry at charity events or his appearance on regional TV interviews made him even more famous.

Then in 1990 everything appeared to suddenly collapse. BSW Windows was affected by the big recession in the building and housing market. Harry himself was hit emotionally by the sudden death of his wife. For all his image as a tough businessman who sometimes sailed close to the wind, Harry had very traditional views on marriage and was very close to his wife. Local news media were now highlighting the job losses at the firm, 'Harry's tragic loss', and hints that worse was to come.

What did not make headlines was the sudden departure of Matthew Cope, although from the firm's point of view this was almost as serious. Harry had become so impressed with Matthew that he let him have most of his own way with the computing system. In terms of the system itself this confidence was justified. The software was developed to add production and assembly scheduling to cost and material breakdown; but Matthew did not stop there. Once the system had been running for eighteen months, enough data had been collected on all the jobs done in that period to enable some useful analysis. As a result of this, estimated figures, like job times or best ways of cutting up materials to reduce waste, became much more accurate. Unfortunately when Matthew left, much of the understanding of the special features of the software left with him. It took several months for one of Matthew's assistants to gain this understanding, and then only after several chaotic mistakes.

Despite all these troubles BSW Windows survived. Harry negotiated a merger with a sports facilities company which he found out about through his charity work contacts. His company then got through the recession by cashing in on the moves towards farm diversification. The recession in agriculture had led to farmers being encouraged to use their land for golf courses, tourism and other recreational activities. BSW Windows itself diversified to produce large sun lounges, swimming pool covers and other window-related constructions used in sport and recreation.

The merger meant that the legend 'a Harry Seaton company' continued to appear on vehicles and notepaper, and Harry remarried recently and the football team got promoted, so there might be more to come.

Opening up views of information

The BSW Windows mini-case is intended to be rather different in style from other textbook cases you may have read. I have included some details which seem to have very little to do with the apparently serious subject of information in business. Details of Harry Seaton's personal life, for example, or his political affiliations, may seem more like subjects for a tabloid newspaper than a serious academic textbook. In fact, the information about both Harry Seaton and his company was deliberately chosen to illustrate the *wide range* or *richness* of forms that information can take. Whilst some of these forms of information are not always relevant to business, we shall see that the subject of business information is much wider than is often found in conventional coverage of 'management information systems'.

Since any view of what constitutes an information system will depend on the view taken of information, our exploration of the question 'what is information?' will also affect our views on the question 'what is an information system?'. Indeed, we shall find that answering the two questions is a complementary process with each affecting the other, so we will begin our opening up of views of information by introducing three important themes that will recur throughout this book.

The first theme is that an information system is more than a collection of information technology equipment. Despite the fact that computer manufacturers often describe a computer system plus its supporting equipment as an 'information system', we shall find that real information systems only work if there is another vital set of components called human beings actively present. Unlike the machines, human beings do not work tirelessly and obediently; nor is their behaviour always logical, consistent or predictable like that of a machine. As components of an information system, *human beings* bring qualities to it which go beyond the calculated data processing of a machine. If we consider the role of Matthew Cope at BSW Windows, a view that the information system was just the computer system and the software would be very misleading. Harry Seaton did not have the same information system after Matthew left that he had had before. Any view of information in the context of real information systems will therefore need to take account of a wider range of information than that which is formally processed on a computer system.

The second theme is that an information system is not something detached and isolated with an existence and objectives all its own. Badly designed or implemented computerized information systems may sometimes give this impression, but the title of this book recognizes that information systems are to be studied in the context of their use in *business*. At BSW Windows the computer system which Matthew developed was successful because it was relevant both to the way that sales representatives worked and the way their activities had to be coordinated with production, assembly and fitting. This meant that the system had to take into account costing and payment as well as scheduling. Hence we shall later see that *management* will be an essential theme which helps us decide what information systems should do and what information they therefore need to use. As we consider the wide range of activities that can be involved in management, so our view of the range of information which may be relevant will also be widened. This will include a recognition that the way we view management and the role of information systems will be relevant both to businesses with a commercial motive and to organizations with other, non-profit-making objectives.

The third theme is that of *conceptualism* and particularly the distinction of 'whats' and 'hows'. Focussing on *who* does something, or *how* or *where* they do it, can often distract us from *what* is being done or is needed. To someone like Harry Seaton who saw business as primarily dealing with people it was very easy to focus exclusively on who did something rather than what was being done. This meant that Matthew almost became an embodiment of the computer system at BSW Windows, and when he left, the effectiveness of the system nearly went with him. The important thing for the company however was what the computer system did, not who did it. There was therefore a complex balance to be made between the needs of individuals, like the encouragement of Matthew, and the needs of the greater whole, like the longevity and reliability of the system. Since all answers to questions about who, how, where or what must be some form of information, understanding the conceptual distinctions between them will also enrich our understanding of the role of information and the design of information systems.

Identifying these three themes is just a beginning to our exploration of what information is and its role in the context of information systems in business. However these alone point to a wide ranging or *rich* view, and we shall look further at some of the different kinds of information which arose in the BSW Windows case later in this chapter. Our aim at this stage has been to open up the principal issues we shall have to face if we are to answer the question 'what is information?'

The issues raised

The potentially wide range or richness of the view of information that we have opened up implies two issues that have now to be resolved in order to answer the question 'what is information?' in the context of information systems in business:

Issue 1. What are we trying to find out when we ask the question 'What is information?'

Issue 2. How do we decide on an answer?

To someone who is very suspicious of anything that might bear the label 'academic' or 'theoretical', Issue 1 could look dangerous. Is it the beginning of a philisophical discussion that will have little to do with a practical subject like business? The quick answer to such a question is 'no', but I think we need to be careful not to be tricked into making false assumptions.

There is often a hidden implication in the use of words like 'academic' or 'theoretical' of a stereotyping view which I have frequently come across in both education and business. This view assumes that subjects which are 'academic' or 'theoretical' are separate from, and even opposed to, those which are 'real' or 'practical'. Where this destructive view takes root, people who believe it are then tempted to take sides according to how they stereotype both themselves and what they see as the other side. 'Academic' people see themselves as able to question assumptions and build a wider view of a subject which is not bogged down by irrelevant detail. They characterize the opposition as narrow minded and simplistic. 'Practical' people on the other side see themselves as being realistic and able to actually achieve things, with the 'academics' as an ineffectual talking shop.

The real danger of this stereotyping is that it actually distorts a view which is useful. In this book the chapters are grouped into the earlier ones on concepts and the later ones on *applications* and *development*. Concepts are ways of *thinking* about things, whilst application and development are concerned with *doing* them. In practice people are both thinkers and doers, and in this book we shall see that it is partnership of these two skills which makes for success.

If we are to answer the question 'what is information?' therefore, we can see that it could be approached from a 'thinking' or conceptual viewpoint, or from a 'doing' or application viewpoint. If we feel that both of these views have a part to play in a partnership, then it would be worth exploring both approaches to answering the question. In Section 2.1 we shall look at the question from both viewpoints and then see how they work together.

Issue 2 arises naturally from Issue 1. If a question can be approached in more than one way, it is very likely that different ways of asking the question will give different answers. If we are to avoid looking like an example of the 'academic' stereotype who cannot give straight answers to questions, then we need a yardstick that will enable us to choose between answers. In Section 2.2 we will consider a range of possible answers to the question 'what is information?' and then in Section 2.3 propose a yardstick for choosing between them.

LEARNING OBJECTIVES CHAPTER 2

1 **To identify the different approaches that can be made to answering the question 'what is information?'.**

2 **To establish an approach to answering the question which is appropriate in a business context.**

3 **To understand the answers that may be given to the question using such an approach.**

What is Information?

2.1 UNDERSTANDING THE QUESTION AND WAYS OF GIVING ANSWERS

So far we have used the BSW Windows case to open up the question 'What is information?' sufficiently to hint that a wide range of answers is possible. This has led us to understanding that choosing between this wide range of possible answers will depend on how we interpret the question. Two important ways in which the question can be interpreted are in terms of whether we approach the question from a 'thinking' or conceptual viewpoint, or from a 'doing' or application viewpoint.

To understand this distinction further we will take an apparently simple example before turning to the subject of information itself. Consider the question: what is 'blue'? A straight answer would be that it is a colour; but that in itself doesn't tell us too much. We might know more if we were told that it is the colour of the sky, a darker colour than yellow, and more often the favourite colour of men than of women.

If these answers look more informative but still rather mixed, we could call in a scientist to give us a definition. A scientist might say that blue is the description we give to a particular form of light, that all light is a form of electromagnetic radiation, and that differences which we call colours represent radiations of different wavelengths. If we look at the rainbow, the red end of the spectrum of colours is formed by radiation with a longer wavelength, and the blue end by radiation with a shorter wavelength. Thus the colour blue can be defined as light of a particular wavelength.

If we look at these various answers to our simple question we can see that they tell us two different sorts of things about the colour blue. Answers like 'it is a darker colour than yellow' or even just 'it is a colour' put it into place in relation to other things we know. If we know what we mean by the idea of a colour or the concept of light and dark colours, these sorts of answers help us fit the colour blue into our existing knowledge. Generally, we fit new things into our existing knowledge by identifying their characteristics, distinguishing them from other things, and classifying them in relation to other things in terms of these similarities and differences. This sort of answer considers that what we know can be explained in terms of *rational relationships* or the *structure* of our knowledge.

But what do we mean by 'similarities' and 'differences'? Answering this question leads into the second sort of answer that can be made to questions like 'what is blue?'. The answers 'more often the favourite colour of men than of women' or 'light of a particular wavelength' implied the idea of *experimental testing* or what *process* we have to go through to establish or confirm our knowledge. They imply that interviewing people or measuring the wavelength of electromagnetic radiation is the way we can establish our knowledge of what 'blue' is.

These two sorts of ways of answering questions have been talked and argued over for centuries. For us however, it is sufficient to realize they are two complementary ways to increase our knowledge of something. We often call the study of what things are, and what we know about them, to be some form of *science,* a word that comes from the Latin word *scientia* meaning *knowledge.* Names for many particular sciences often end in '-ology' which comes from a Greek word indicating a branch of knowledge or study. Given the way that the English language includes so many words which have been derived from Greek and Latin, it is not surprising to find two words which cover the science of answering questions and knowing about things:

1. *Epistemology* – from the Greek *episteme* = knowledge, which is the study of what we know and how we can know it.
2. *Methodology* – from the Greek *meta* = along and *odos* = a way, which is the study of method or the ways of doing things.

Thus the sort of answer to a question which explains things in terms of rational relationships or the structure of our knowledge is likely to be epistemological. An answer based on a method of experimental testing or some other process of finding out will be methodological in emphasis.

When answering the question 'what is information?' we shall use both approaches in this book. Sometimes we will try to understand what information is by looking at the characteristics of different kinds of information, and comparing how they differ as well as what they have in common. The result of answering the question in this way will be to focus on what information *is* and how it fits into the overall *structure* of our knowledge. In these situations the approach will be mainly epistemological.

At other times we shall be answering the question 'what is information?' by studying what it *does* or *process.* In these situations the approach will be methodological.

I have said that we will use both of these approaches and that they are complementary. This is not completely fair. You will notice a clear bias as we go through this book towards a methodological approach. My bias comes from a belief that it is very hard in a practical subject like business to completely separate what something *is* from what it *does.* Therefore although we will often answer the question 'what is information?' in an epistemological way, the structure of our knowledge, in terms of comparisons and classification, will depend ultimately on our experience of what the information does and what it is used for. Since this latter view is essentially methodological, I confess a methodological bias.

With this introduction to different ways of understanding the question 'what is information?', we will now consider some possible answers.

2.2 EXPLORING SOME POSSIBLE ANSWERS

The richness of information as a concept

The term *rich* is one we shall use several times in this book, and particularly in Chapter 8 when we consider *soft systems methodology*. For the moment we can recognize that the word has two meanings. The first meaning is the more common one of having lots of money; but the second one is of something rich being a full, productive or well-stocked source. It is this second meaning that we shall normally use, and it is the one being used in this section to describe views about information.

Given the Learning Objectives of this chapter we shall not attempt to produce a rigorous definition of the term information, nor try to produce an encyclopedic classification of meanings. Instead the paragraph headings of this section begin to explore some of the richness of the concept so that we can understand issues which arise when we try to answer the question 'what is information?'.

Structural views of information

If we consider most examples of something which we might call information, we shall find that it is likely to be made up of parts or *components*, which are put together in a particular *structure*. Thus information about the potential customers of BSW Windows and the windows that they wish to have installed would include such details as customers name and address, plus data about the windows in terms of their style and measurements, as in Fig 2.1. All of what we have referred to as 'details' or 'data' would consist of words and numbers like 'Customer Name: John Smith, Address: 23 Foxthorn Paddock, Torcross, Northumberland. Window: 25 paned 6x4 Regency'.

In this example the information is essentially constructed by putting together characters in a particular sequence or structure to form words; or individual figures to form numbers or measurements. These in turn can be arranged into a structure which forms sentences, records or some greater whole. If we take such a structural view of information, then we see it as *data*, like characters, figures or words, organized in a particular way to form *information*.

This simple example illustrates a major practically applied concept of information which forms the basis of *data* and *database management systems*, which we shall explore further in Chapter 5. If information is seen as data assembled into a particular structure, then designing a database to support an information system raises the issue of what sort of structure should be used.

It is also worth noting that this view of information is not confined to structures of words and numbers. Data about the occurrence and colour of pixels on a computer screen can be brought together in an overall structure to form the information conveyed by a diagram or a picture.

Processing views of information

A structural view of information leads naturally to the complementary processing view. We saw above that a structural view sees information as 'made up of parts or components which are put together in a particular structure'. To understand how this leads to a process view, we should look at the phrase 'put together'.

Anything that exists in a particular structural arrangement must have been put together in that way as a result of some *process*. If we look at the geometrical structure of bricks in a wall or the more sophisticated and subtle construction of our own bodies, they are like the way they are because some process such as bricklaying or biological growth has gathered the components and assembled them together in a particular sequence to create that structure.

If we see information as a structure of data components, as in Fig 2.1 for example, various processes will have to be carried out to construct both the individual components and then the whole. One component of the whole with its own particular structure is 'Customer Name'. To create this component and add it to the whole, some process like asking the customer and recording the name on the document must take

---

BSW Windows Ltd.

(A Harry Seaton Company)

ORDER ENQUIRY

Customer	**Enquiry**
Name: Mr. John Smith	Date: 16/5/88
Address: 23 Foxthorn Paddock	Sales Representative: K. Taylor
Torcross	
Northumberland	
Telephone: (01919) 102030	

Initial Job Specification (include quantity, size and style)

4 off. 25 paned 6x4 Regency

Fig 2.1 An Order Enquiry Document for BSW Windows

The *structure* of this document can be seen in two ways. One way is to see how the items are arranged on the page. The other is to consider how individual entries come together to make greater wholes, like all the details that make up the information about a customer. The first way sees the information in *physical* terms: *how* the document is arranged. The second way sees the information in *logical* terms: *what* the information shows.

place. For the result of this process to be successful, all those involved need to share a common view of what the output from the process will look like in terms of its own structure and how it fits into the structure of the whole. Without this common view, the sequence of operations needed to process the information can become confused, and the resulting output garbled. I know from my own experience that understanding the answer to a simple question like 'What is your name?' is not as obvious as it seems. Many cultures, e.g. Magyar or Chinese, put the surname first; and some British surnames (like mine) sound like first names anyway. Thus the structural arrangement of the forename and surname components that make up the information 'Customer Name' determines how the process of assembling those components is carried out. Similarly, the place of 'Customer Name' in the wider structure determines where the components are entered on the document: a correct customer name entered under 'Sales Representative' would be useless.

The structural view of information, which regards it as a particular logical arrange-ment or structure of data components, therefore implies a complementary process view that sees information almost as some form of substance which is gathered up, transmitted, transformed, assembled and recorded. This process view might see an information system as a kind of information 'factory' which produces a product called information from raw materials called data.

The complementary nature of the structure and process views of information will be developed further in several parts of this book. In Chapter 3 we shall see how a process view helps us put information systems into a management context; in Chapter 5 we shall look in depth at the way data structures can be accessed and processed as well as defined, and the practical implications for database management. In Chapter 7 we shall see how complementary structure and process views of information affect the nature of methods used for information systems development.

Information as communication

We often talk of things like books, documents or filing cabinets as 'containing' infor-mation. This idea of information being inside something is misleading however. At the beginning of *The Hitch Hiker's Guide to the Galaxy*, Adams (1979), vital information about the forthcoming demolition of planet Earth has been available 'on display in the bottom of a locked filing cabinet stuck in a disused lavatory with a sign on the door saying *Beware of the Leopard*'. Not surprisingly, the person who needed this informa-tion felt he had not been properly informed. If we consider information which is going to have any real use at all, it is not sufficient that it should be contained in something or recorded somewhere. We have to be aware of its existence, and we have to be able to positively access it or have it transmitted so that we can receive it. Information is not information until it has been communicated and understood.

Notice the addition of the word *understood* to the concept of communication. Seeing or hearing something alone does not make it information. It is possible to listen to a whole conversation in a language we do not understand and yet receive no informa-tion at all. Similarly, a complete electronic circuit diagram for a piece of equipment contains a lot of information; but only for someone who understands circuit diagrams. We can therefore identify one view of information which says that information is essentially the communication of understanding. In Chapter 4 we shall develop this view further and explore the concept of a *shared symbol set* as an essential of an information system which enables understanding.

Before leaving this view of information we can discover another important aspect of it by referring to the BSW Windows case. The potential departure of Matthew Cope was something about which Harry Seaton probably felt he had little information. At no time did Matthew say anything or put anything in writing to suggest that he was thinking of leaving. I suspect however that people close to Matthew would have known. People don't just communicate information by words, pictures or symbols. Tone of voice, so-called body language and other aspects of general behaviour can all communicate information too. I wonder if Harry had been observing more closely he might have 'read the signs' or 'picked up the vibes' or any of the many phrases we use to indicate that communication of information between human beings is more than speech and writing.

Information as an organized body of knowledge

The importance of understanding in relation to information can lead us to the broad consideration of 'what can we know, and how can we know it?' which we covered in the previous section. As we saw, study of such questions is the concern of epistemology.

There is however one particular way of viewing what we know which is widely used in relation to communication and understanding. If we consider an important ingredient of both our own understanding and our ability to communicate it to others, we find that we frequently use *ordering* and *classification* of information to help us relate things and build on our experience. The ability to make sense of things through ordering and classification comes from us being able to set *procedures* or define *rules*.

Particular examples of such organization of information can cover a wide range. There are formal, universal classification systems like those used by botanists to classify plants, or by mathematicians to define functions. Such information is usually set in the wider context of science and human knowledge. In business and management, less grandiose and universal ways of organizing information can still be of great practical importance. Being able to classify customers in markets or products on the basis of manufacturing methods can be important information for a business, without necessarily having any great universal significance. The success of BSW Windows was partly due to classification bringing an element of standardization which streamlined the measuring up, specification and manufacturing procedures.

As individuals, we also use informal, personal ways of grouping things according to our tastes and interests. If someone says that they do not like spicy food, we might guess that they would not like some Indian dishes, but we couldn't be sure. My mother's apple pie always had cloves in it: is that 'spicy'? We might feel that classification of this kind is not as rigorous or scientific as the kind done by mathematicians or biologists, but if we consider very practical issues like the user-friendliness of computer software, is classifying tastes in software that different from classifying tastes in food?

In subsequent chapters of this book we shall find that viewing information in terms of classifying and ordering is relevant to ways of constructing databases in Chapter 5 and object-oriented approaches to systems development in Chapter 8. Hence we shall also say more about this view in Chapter 4.

Information as clarification and the reduction of uncertainty

Many situations which we would describe as uncertain or confused are those where information is either lacking or is wrong. If you have ever been stuck at an airport or in a train, waiting for the explanation of a delay, you will probably understand how lack of information equates with uncertainty. The less information, the greater the uncertainty.

The reverse also seems to apply in the way that we use the word information and words related to it like being 'well informed'. Being well informed implies not just that we know something, but also that we know how to deal with things: that we are in control. Harry Seaton did well with BSW Windows whilst he was clear and certain about his firm, its market, his employees and his personal life; but when outside influences acted in a way he didn't notice and didn't have information about, he nearly lost control, and his world almost fell apart.

In Chapter 4 we shall look further into the relationship between information and certainty to see that information need not be seen in terms of the absolute distinction of knowing or not knowing. The concept of *entropy* will help us develop a view of how informative particular information can be. We shall prepare for this in Chapter 3 by distinguishing uncertainty which comes from lack of information from uncertainty which comes from differences in opinion.

Information as power

'Being well informed', which we have just discussed, leads on to 'being in the know', as one of many popular phrases implying that the possession of information means possession of power. The arch Nazi propagandist Joseph Göbbels is reputed to have said that whoever ran the information also ran the show. If we consider examples of the concept that possession of information gives power, we can see that different forms of information are often referred to, and that the power too takes different forms.

In BSW Windows, much of Harry Seaton's power came from having information about markets and the people in local government and industry. Matthew Cope's power came from the information he possessed on the workings of the computer system. We might say that Harry's power often came from knowing who and knowing what, whilst Matthew's came from knowing how. Other distinctions are possible, and when we come to formalizing the role of information and information systems in businesses and organizations in Chapter 3, we shall produce a model to relate the different forms of information.

For the moment it is worth considering that power could come from information about:

- facts and figures, like knowing how much commission a sales representative at BSW Windows had earned
- what someone was trying to do, like BSW's sales targets
- how something was done, like the workings of BSW's computer software
- policy, like BSW's decision to merge with another company
- beliefs and personal motivation, like being able to read Harry Seaton's mind and know what makes him tick.

Whatever the form of the information and the power that it brings, the fact that it does bring power can make it a desirable *commodity* or *resource*. As such, information takes on a value and can be something which is traded, exchanged and hoarded. Many of the attempts which are currently fashionable for 'open government' or 'the right to know' reflect the belief that since information gives power, in a democracy it should be shared. Whether it is sensible to expect the possessors of information to give it up willingly depends on your view of human nature. Although not a complete cynic, I am cautious enough to believe that voluntary sharing of power cannot always be relied on and that practical design of information systems will need to recognize this.

In Chapter 6 we shall see how a systems view of businesses and organizations enables us to see past how a particular business or organization works to the role of the information system within it. From this we can get a clearer view of what forms of power are present.

In Chapter 7 we shall see that technical development of information systems which does not take account of wider issues of power and politics is unlikely to succeed. We shall therefore consider how systems development methods can take account of these wider, non-technical issues.

Box 2.1

LEIGH INTERESTS: OUT OF A HOLE

(*Investors Chronicle* 21/6/96: all italics are mine)

Malcolm Wood, architect of Leigh Interests, selected outsider Sean Bowden as chief executive in October 1993. There was much to do. The culture created by Mr Wood during his 14 years at the top needed overhauling. Quite how Mr Bowden, due to report to Mr Wood as executive chairman, intended to achieve this was never revealed. Mr Wood died three weeks after hiring Mr Bowden. The overhaul has not left many skidmarks but it has been thorough. Last week, the fifth and last surviving member of the Wood team handed over to a Bowden man.

Mr Wood was a heavyweight character who took Leigh into waste management and made it an industry leader. In his last four years he spent twice current market capitalisation on capital expenditure and aquisitions. *But he was not a model of modern management practice. He is said to have taken much of Leigh's management information system to his grave as it only existed in his head.* There were other blemishes. Leigh was often considered at the sloppy end of waste-handling and three recent convictions under the Environmental Protection Act suggest that this may still be the case.

COMMENT

A Harry Seaton character? The concept of information systems which sees them as paperwork, procedures and information technology might see this as a critical report on Leigh Interests. Yet the *Investors Chronicle* went on to recommend the shares in the company as a buy. The real lesson is that information is a very rich commodity that can appear in a wide range of forms from a computer database to something in someone's head. Any study of management information systems that fails to recognize this richness may limit their effectiveness, even before anyone goes 'to his grave'.

Information as interest

People often love to talk and exchange information. One of the vivid memories I have of my early childhood in a small Cornish community was of people talking. My mother, her two sisters, one of her brothers and my grandparents; all squeezed into the little kitchen of a terraced house and discussing everything from who had had what baby to what was right or wrong with the new Labour government.

Exchange of information for reasons of interest and entertainment takes place in most societies, including those within businesses and organizations. Indeed, in organizations where I have worked, knowing where people informally congregated and conversed seemed to be one of the most important pieces of information a manager could have. Often the kind of information acquired in such situations gives power in the way described above, but other times it is less specific and less threatening. Listening to people talk, finding out their interests and their attitudes can lead to an understanding that facilitates relationships and working together. It is not hard to see that such information can be relevant to management and business, and that it cannot always be dismissed as gossip and time wasting.

However, it is hard to imagine information like this being processed by the computer system along with the monthly payroll. We shall therefore need some way of deciding what consideration should be given to such information in a book about information systems in business; and if so, how it can be related to the other forms of information we have discussed.

Information as intuition

The story goes of an Englishman who went to live permanently in the Gaelic-speaking Western Isles of Scotland. Wishing to fit in socially, he taught himself Gaelic from a book. One day two local people observed him going past. 'Ah', said one, 'there goes the Englishman who speaks the Gaelic'. 'Aye', said the other, 'he speaks it, but he doesn't know it'. When I was told this story by a Gaelic speaker myself, I recalled how the great jazz trumpeter Louis Armstrong once remarked that if you had to ask what jazz was, you would never know the answer.

Both of these examples from different cultures illustrate a kind of information which appears to crop up in business too, but is often the subject of controversy. Characters like Harry Seaton of BSW Windows seem particularly good at dealing with the kind of information that has to do with a 'feel' for a market or 'knowing what makes people tick'. Where such people rise to the head of big organizations they are often thought to have charisma or even genius.

But there are other less macho examples of intuitive information. Sympathetic listeners, confessors and counsellors often seem to 'understand' in a way that can't be defined in a logical, formal way. This sort of information comes into business when we consider questions of product design and people's tastes, or in the application of sympathetic and supportive leadership. BSW Windows often had the job of designing replacement windows for older buildings. The new designs changed some of the materials and manufacturing methods of the originals, but still managed to keep in spirit with them. It is unlikely that information which defined this spirit could be formalized. In practice, the sales representative and the client came to an agreement after holding discussions and looking at examples of possible designs.

Whilst I think most people recognize this view of information, there is often controversy about its value, its role in any information system, or even the fact of its existence. The contrast between the quotations from Edie Brickell and Lord Kelvin at the beginning of this book highlight the main issue. From Lord Kelvin we learn of the danger of accepting the existence of things which cannot be defined and detected through observation and measurement. Like the emperor's new clothes in Hans Anderson, they can be a complete confidence trick. But we also know that the word 'nothing' can hide powerful human forces. It may not be possible to computerize this kind of information, but its real business effects can be dramatic. Much of BSW Windows success came from Harry's feel for the market, personal contacts and infectious enthusiasm; some of its downfall came from when he got it wrong.

I think this selection of views of information justifies my earlier assertion that information is a rich subject. This richness implies however that we shall need some way of deciding which views may be relevant to information systems in business. The next section will propose such a way.

2.3   INFORMATION, SYSTEMS AND MANAGEMENT

Section 2.2 has left us with a selection of possible answers to the question 'what is information?'. As Fig 2.2 shows, these different views of information often overlap and can be related to each other. If we were to stop at this point in our exploration of the question, we should be left with a complex range of possible answers with little guidance as to how we should choose between them. Our attempt to answer the question would then look suspiciously like a soft stereotype learning exercise.

One way to progress further would be to select one of the views as being the best answer for a book concerned with information in a business context. I think this way is unlikely to work. In looking at the different views we have seen that all of them can be relevant to a business context. The important point is however that they are not all relevant all of the time.

An alternative way forward could therefore be to recognize that we need a criterion or yardstick that will enable us to recognize when a particular answer to our question is acceptable and when not. This would result in there being many answers to the question 'what is information?', but all of these answers would share a common property. This method of defining things is one I used in my previous book, Harry (1990),

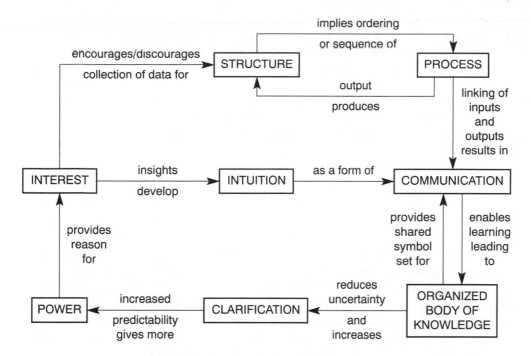

Fig 2.2 Some Possible Relationships between Different Types of Information
This diagram does not pretent to cover all possible views of information nor to exclusively define their interrelationship, but it should open up the concept of the *richness* of information.

and is one I will explain in detail in Chapter 3. For the moment we can note that it is a way of avoiding both the open-ended vagary of the soft stereotype learning and the simplistic simple answers of the hard stereotype teaching.

The criterion that I shall use to assess answers to the question 'what is information?' is relevance to *management*. This book is concerned with information systems *in* business. Deciding what information is will therefore come from looking at its role and function in businesses and organizations. When we do this in Chapter 3 we shall see that an information system is an essential component of a management system. Answers to the question 'what is information?' can therefore come from understanding the concept of a *system* and the particular relationship between management and information systems.

The results of this approach may sometimes give a different view of both information and information systems from that you might find in books bearing titles containing the words 'management information system'. The rich view of information we opened up in the previous section includes such factors as power, interest and intuition as well as structure, process and communication. The last three views look similar to those found in most books on management information systems that regard an information system as being not too far away from a computer system. Information like that in Fig 2.1 is just what we would expect to be on a computer system in a modern business. It is harder to imagine information as power, interest or intuition being machine based. By their very nature they seem strongly human, so why bother about them in a book which concentrates on management information systems?

The answer to this last question brings us back to just that common criterion of *management* and the rich nature of the information it uses. If we are going to study information and information systems in business rather than 'some information in business' or 'computerizable information systems in business', we need some way of looking at information as *whole*. To do this we need a *model* that will enable us to understand how all the different forms of information play their roles and interact as part of the whole business or organization, whether or not they are processed by a computer or stored on a database.

Even from a computer-biased view of information systems there are beginning to be good reasons for taking this wider view. As information technology has advanced, forms of information that were once thought not to be relevant to computer systems are now being machine processed. Within the last decade, for example, a personnel database has gone from being one which only stores information about people in the form of words and numbers. Now a picture of the person can also be included. Current advances in video disk technology mean we can add moving pictures and sound to the information that can be stored. Quite subtle information about people's character and behaviour can now be captured, stored and transmitted by such technology. So perhaps information as power, interest and intuition is not as separate from the computerized information system as we might have thought.

Whatever the advances in technology however, information in a management context will involve a mix of human and machine systems. Having a model that covers and relates both kinds will not only give us the whole view, but will make sure that we identify important issues of the connexion between them. Designing a successful interaction between human activity systems and computer systems will be essential if the whole is not to fail.

Box 2.2

LOOKING BEYOND THE TORNADO . . . OPTIONS FOR A 21ST CENTURY BOMBER

(*Financial Times* 28/6/96: all italics are mine)

In the run-up to the Gulf war General Colin Powell, then the top US military commander, graphically described what the allies intended to do to Iraq's forces in Kuwait. 'First we're going to cut them off', he said, 'and then we're going to kill them'.

His stinging phrase summarizes western military strategy. Modern doctrine says a commander's first job is to disrupt an enemy's ability to fight: *by destroying their radar, cutting their communications* and sealing off supply routes. Only then does the army move in for the kill. The UK will push that strategy a step further next month, when the Ministry of Defence begins a study into how to use the air force in the 21st century . . .

But for the next generation of strike aircraft, more radical options are being considered. The most likely is a two-man bomber . . . another is to have an unmanned bomber which is controlled by pilots from safe air space . . . . Another alternative would be to have a large adapted transport aircraft carrying bulk cruise missiles . . . .

COMMENT

Chilling stuff! As someone who can remember being bombed by military aircraft I don't quote this extract without feeling; but it does give a particularly dramatic illustration of the essential role of information as *communication, clarification* and *power*. The purpose of the bomber is to remove power from the enemy by destruction of information as communication, and thereby as clarification and power.

Note also that all the 'hardware' in the world, whether it's bombers or computers, is impotent without the essential role of information as a link to the wider military or business system of which it is part. The pilots may be in the bomber or back somewhere in 'safe air space', but they still need to be *connected* with the plane, even if they aren't sitting in it. The concept of *connexion* as more than 'bums on seats' is an important one which we shall explore in Chapter 3, and *information* is an essential component of this process.

You may feel that references to warfare don't have much to do with information systems in business until we look at the origins of many common management terms. Words like *operations, logistics, tactics* or *strategy* have military origins. Thus *strategy* comes from an ancient Greek word meaning an army general, and *tactics* from a word meaning army officer or lieutenant. Long after the military origins of these words have been forgotten, a military view of management still survives. Thus 'top executives' are portrayed as fulfilling the strategic or generals' role, whilst their 'middle management' are assumed to act as day-to-day tacticians controlling operations.

Using the same word in very different areas of management in this way can be dangerous. Words bring their own pre-set values with them. Thus 'fried steak' and 'partly burnt dead cow flesh' are two ways of referring to the same thing, but they imply rather different views of diet management. The danger of using management words and concepts with a particular origin, like a military one, is that they push us towards a particular view or style of management. This then leads us to assume that the information system must be designed to support that particular view. In this book we shall look behind the particular labels that are used in information systems and business in order to see what very different organizations have in common, and where differences matter.

FURTHER STUDY

Consider the simple triangular diagram of Fig 2.3 which you have probably seen in some form in many books on management. Versions of this misleading diagram have been appearing in management texts for many years. It implies many untruths, but the one that is relevant to the systems view of information presented in this book is the view that each 'level' of management is solely involved with its own separate 'level' of information. I think that this implication can be very dangerous when we design information systems. It pushes the systems designer and the management user of the designed information system towards a *particular selection* of information, rather than a freedom to use any selection which may be relevant to their role as a manager. So consider your view of the following questions:

1 Do senior executives or top managers in an organization known to you spend their time exclusively considering *strategy*? If not, what else do they legitimately do as managers?

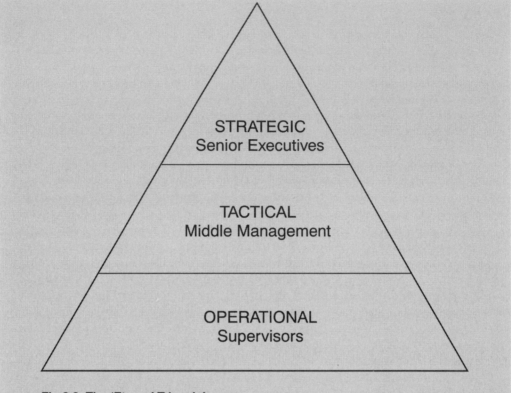

Fig 2.3 The 'Eternal Triangle'

2 Is the information used by lower levels of the management of your chosen organization exclusively valuable to tactical management or operations?

My answers to these questions are to be found in Harry (1995):

1 Most people in organizations fulfil a complex role in terms of *strategy*, *tactics* and *operations*. So that senior people in organizations are often involved in day-to-day operations.

2 Operational information is an essential component of strategic planning.

Hence the roles of managers and the form of their information needs is much more complex than the simple divisions of the 'Eternal Triangle'. In Chapter 6 of this book we shall develop this view further.

SEMINAR AGENDAS AND PROJECT/DISSERTATION TOPICS

Consider the following:

1 Take an edited collection of readings like Galliers (1987) and compare the views of information presented by a wide range of authors. Are we near having some widely accepted view of what information is? Are there identifiable schools of thought? Is there such a subject as 'informatics'?

2 In Section 2.1 I frequently referred to the linguistic source of the meaning of words like *method* or *science.* Does all information depend on language? Is, say, 'Je suis un homme' the same information as 'I am a man'? Is the concept of information as a *what* that is manifested equivalently in various *hows*, like languages, real or useful?

3 Investigate the uses of the term *information* by computer hardware manufacturers in their sales literature. Do they equate the term *information system* with a computer system?

4 In the last section of Chapter 1, I emphasized that the concepts in this book are as relevant to bringing up a family or being a student as they are to running a commercial organization. Take some of the possible answers to 'what is information?' in Section 2.2 and consider how they might apply to a football club, play group or students union.

5 Look at a textbook that may be recommended for one of your courses in the human aspects of management, and which apparently has nothing to do with information systems. The closer it comes to the context of the soft stereotype of Chapter 1 the better. Then consider information in the human systems context. Try out an exercise like that in Pegler et al. (1986) which invites you to explore the telephone directory of your organization or the location of people's offices to discover who is who. How might the results of such an exercise be seen in terms of the answers proposed in Section 2.2?

6 Refer to **4** if you don't like **5**.

7 Where do staff meet in your organization?

8 Consult Janis & Mann (1977). Does information reduce risk?

9 Consider a successful attempt to bridge human and computer use of information like Microsoft Windows. Compare this with the role of information in communicating a popular product to the customer in the fast-food retailing industry. Is there any connexion between the use of the word *menu* in these different applications?

REFERENCES /BIBLIOGRAPHY

Adams, D. (1979). *The Hitch Hiker's Guide to the Galaxy*. Pan Books.

Flew, A. (1983). *A Dictionary of Philosophy*. Pan Books.

Galliers, R. (1987). *Information Analysis: Selected Readings*. Addison-Wesley.

Janis, I. & Mann, L. (1977). *Decision Making: A Psychological Analysis of Conflict, Choice, and Commitment*. The Free Press.

Lacey, A.R. (1986). *A Dictionary of Philosophy*. Routledge.

Urmson, J.O. (1991). *The Concise Encyclopaedia of Western Philosophy and Philosophers*. Routledge.

'She didn't say yes, she didn't say no' – Britain hesitates over European Monetary Union

What happened

In the early 1960s it was the British Labour Party who were uncertain about Europe. The then Conservative Party leader Harold Macmillan mocked this uncertainty at a Conservative Party conference. He quoted an old music hall song, 'she didn't say yes, she didn't say no; she didn't say stop, she didn't say go'. His audience loved it. Macmillan was fond of portraying himself as the old English country gentleman who could remember things like the music hall, whilst Labour were trying to project themselves as the progressive party. Yet here was the old country gentleman showing that he was the real progressive.

By 1996 the positions seemed to be reversed. The Conservative Party, which took Britain into the European Community, was undecided about European Monetary Union (EMU), the next major stage of European integration, and were being chided by the Labour Party for their uncertainty.

Britain's back-peddling on EMU had begun with the events of 'Black Wednesday', 16 September 1992, when Britain left the European Exchange Rate Mechanism (ERM). The ERM was instigated as one of the major parts of a wider creation known as the European Monetary System (EMS). Although the details of how this system was intended to work are quite complicated, what it was designed to achieve was very simple: the vision of all the countries of the European Union having one currency. Such a currency would mean that trade between member states would be as simple as trade within them. No longer would there be uncertainty about selling or buying prices of goods between countries, brought about by changes in their relative values. One unit of currency would be used from Athens to Dublin.

The EMS was set up to bring about this vision and it included two particular ideas. The first was the idea of creating a currency unit, initially called the 'ecu', whose value was automatically linked to that of individual currencies within Europe. The second was the ERM, which was designed to reduce instability, and finally bring about a fixed relationship between individual currencies. The ultimate result of a successful implementation of these ideas would therefore be a fixed relationship between individual currencies and a fixed relationship between the ecu and all these individual currencies. At this point all states would be effectively using the same currency in all but name. Thus if my pound is always, and always will be, worth ten of your francs and three of his marks, then we are all effectively using the same currency in all but name. Substitute the word 'ecu' for say one mark, a third of a pound and three and a third francs, and we have a common currency.

A central problem in implementing this ideal was the ERM, since this represented the first step to bringing the values of currencies closer to fixed relationship in their value to each other. In practice the value of currencies fluctuates for many reasons. The most important comes from the fact that currencies can be bought and sold. For most people the obvious example of this is when they go to another country and want to convert their own currency into the one used in the country where they are going. Thus a French tourist converts francs into pounds when visiting the United Kingdom. We would call this process 'buying' pounds and 'selling' francs. The conversion of currencies in this way effectively makes them products or commodities which can be bought and sold. As with other commodities, buying and selling results in their value rising or falling according to how much they are being bought or sold at.

However, the real market in the buying and selling of currencies is much more than what comes from tourists visiting eachother's countries. International transactions resulting from the import and export of goods all involve currency transactions. When one country sells goods to another it gains some of its currency, whilst the buying country loses some of its own. The currencies of successful exporters therefore become rarer and more highly valued, whilst those of heavy importers become worth less.

To counteract these trends countries can take short-term measures on investment. They can increase or decrease the value of their currencies in the interest that they pay to investors. Thus if I can get 5% for money invested in Germany but 10% for money invested in the United Kingdom, I might be attracted to selling my German marks and buying United Kingdom pounds. On top of these commercial factors there are psychological ones too. If I think a major revolution is about to engulf a nation and send it into chaos and bankruptcy, I might sell its currency regardless of interest rates or anything else.

The effects of all these factors are brought into the international currency markets. Since currencies can be regarded as a commodity like anything else, these markets have been set up to trade currencies. Such markets not only buy and sell on the basis of what a thing is worth now. They also speculate by buying what is now cheap, but may be worth much more in the future.

The ERM required that member countries took whatever measures were required to keep their currencies' values in the international currency markets within certain ranges of value to each other. Thus if currency dealers who had money in the form of United Kingdom pounds felt that the pound was going to be worth less, they might sell pounds and buy some other currency. This would usually result in a decrease in the value of the pound relative to other currencies. If the United Kingdom was in the ERM with an aim of limiting changes of value in the pound relative to other currencies, its government would have to take measures to counteract the fall in value of the pound. It might do this by raising its interest rates or buying in pounds, using its stocks of other currencies.

This second method will only work if you have enough of other currencies or if other countries will lend you some of their currency to use in this way.

On 'Black Wednesday', 16 September 1992, all these complexities came into play. Given that the United Kingdom was in the ERM, with a duty to keep its currency within range of certain values relative to others, any change of value which drove the pound outside this range had to be counteracted by raising interest rates or borrowing money from other countries to buy up pounds and try to maintain their value.

At first the United Kingdom government announced that they had loans amounting to billions of pounds worth of other currencies to be used for this purpose. Currency dealers however did not believe that this would be enough to prevent continual selling, and therefore a permanent lowering in the value of the pound within the ERM. The more the pound was sold, the lower its value became. The lower its value became, the more dealers felt encouraged to sell and the press said that 'millions of pounds were changing hands'. The pressure on the pound was such that eventually the British Chancellor of the Exchequer, who was at the top of the financial hierarchy within the United Kingdom, and therefore responsible for the role of the pound in the ERM, withdrew the United Kingdom from the ERM.

There is still debate about whether Black Monday was a liberation or a disaster. There were newspaper reports that the British Chancellor of the Exchequer, Norman Lamont, was singing in his bath with joy. Similarly, I remember being at a small hotel in the north of England, training young managers on a computer course. They felt quite cheerful. Their company made most of its money from exporting aerospace products. A 'cheaper' pound meant that their company's products were more competitive in international markets. For them, Black Monday was a very bright day. Others saw it differently. The very fact that currency dealers could attack the value of the currency of an individual nation was a good reason for unifying national currencies into a stronger whole.

But Britain was just one country within an expanding European Union. A new Single European Market formed in 1993 and was supported by Britain, which allowed free trade between European states without border or customs controls. In this context, the commercial necessity for traders to swap between over a dozen currencies with fluctuating currency values looked like nonsense. At the Inter-Governmental conference at Maastricht in 1992, the majority of countries who had succeeded in staying within the ERM pressed for completion of EMU. The so-called 'Maastricht Treaty' defined procedures for the formation of a single European currency starting in 1999, with Britain retaining the right to opt out of the single currency at such time as it was formed.

The Maastricht Treaty defined a set of criteria, known as the 'Maastricht criteria'. These were designed to ensure that a new European currency, now called the 'Euro', would not take on a disproportionate amount of the debts of individual member countries. This had to be avoided if the Euro itself were not to be the victim of currency speculation caused by lack of confidence in its sustainable value against other world currencies.

As I write this in late 1996, the chances of different countries within the European Union meeting the Maastricht criteria seem varied. There is some concern, from the Germans in particular, that the criteria might be fudged to allow countries to join the single currency even when their economies did not strictly conform to them. However the debate continues, one thing seems certain: EMU will be on the European agenda for some time to come.

The words and phrases

The account of EMU contains words and phrases that may be found in a range of literature from a tabloid newspaper to an academic document. If words are meant to communicate meaning, we would expect them to be used in a way that fitted in with some commonly agreed meaning like that found in a good dictionary. However, a word can have more than one meaning in the dictionary, and when we use words they often carry our own emotional, ethical and other meanings with them as well.

In this section I would like to consider a selection of these words and phrases to open up some of the questions that would need answering if we were to give some idea of what a *systems* view of a situation might look like.

We can begin with the key word *system* itself. It occurred as a major term in the case since the various events were all ultimately concerned with the European Monetary *System*. The particular part of this system we were concerned with was the Exchange Rate *Mechanism*. We often use the word system to mean a way of doing something, so system and mechanism look to have similar meanings. We can go further and say that when we talk about a system we don't mean just any way of doing something. How often have you heard someone say 'what you need is a system' when they are criticizing disorder or chaos and suggesting an ordered or systematic approach? We might therefore expect a system to be associated with dynamics (doing something) and order.

However, our case and its title referred to the events which led to 'leaving' something which was 'European' and talked of 'membership'. Words like these extend the meaning of the word system to imply that it is made up of parts like 'members' who play a role in the dynamics such as the Exchange Rate Mechanism.

Mixed in with the words and phrases which focus on the idea of a system as a practical way of doing things are some more philosophical ideas. For the EMS these would be what former Prime Minister Harold Wilson called the 'theology' of Europe. The real everyday practical problems of the United Kingdom came ultimately from a system set up to serve the ideal of European Monetary Union. We made a distinction between what the system was aiming to achieve and how it was hoped to achieve it. Behind the system was a 'vision' and 'ideas', and the system itself was seen as 'implementation of these ideas'. If we confine the term *system* to mean a way of doing something it leaves us with the question of what it is we are trying to do. Is that also part of the system or is it something else?

Another problem that comes along with the idea of a system as being a way of doing something is that in practice it seldom if ever seems to work out. It was not part of the plan for the ERM that countries should leave it, but then, when did anything go exactly according to plan? Our description of the events contains words like 'uncertainty', 'problem' and 'complexities'. In practice, ways of doing things get upset or even terminated by outside events like the actions of currency dealers. Ought we then to think of a system as a collection of different ways of doing things with the choice of chopping and changing according to different circumstances? If so, who decides? Some of the people in our case 'felt quite cheerful' at the apparent failure of the 'mechanism'. Can a system be identified as separate from the effects of 'psychological' factors? Whose system was it anyway?

The issues raised

Discussing some of the words and phrases used in the mini-case suggests two things about possible meanings for the term system. First, using the word system to mean an ordered way of doing something is not necessarily wrong, but it is incomplete. Second, however we may extend the meaning of the term *system* that meaning has to be closely associated with some other concepts if it is to be understood. Our issues are then:

Issue 1. How do we define the term system?
Issue 2. What are the related concepts?

Our first issue is therefore that of the *process of definition* itself. Is it worth trying to define the term system when it seems to be used to cover such a wide variety of concepts? Might it be worth regarding the term as a family of concepts or to make distinctions between different types of system?

Whatever approach we make to sorting out the concepts associated with the term system, we have already seen that it will include such wide-ranging areas as dynamics, order, membership, relationship, ideas and beliefs, psychology, complexity, uncertainty and decision. Given the introductory nature of our discussion, this list is likely to be added to if we look more deeply. Definition will therefore bring with it the issue of the *selection and ordering of concepts*.

The related issues of definition, selection and ordering are in danger of becoming strongly theoretical however if we overlook the context in which we want to resolve them. Our reason for sorting out the term *system* and related concepts is to put them to use in the field of information systems in business. We shall therefore also need to decide whether the issues raised by the term system can be separated from deciding what we mean by information business. If they cannot, then we need some common approach to link them.

LEARNING OBJECTIVES CHAPTER 3

1 To identify and understand the range of concepts which may be associated with the term system.

2 To establish a framework of these concepts which can be used as a context for understanding the role and nature of information systems applied to business.

3 To characterize systems behaviour in the context of this framework.

4 To introduce elementary understanding of selected non-verbal techniques used to describe systems for subsequent use and development.

CHAPTER 3

Systems Concepts

3.1 SYSTEMS LANGUAGE AND DESCRIPTIONS

3.1.1 The definition of a system

Why use definitions?

Defining what we mean by the term system would appear to be essential in a book called *Information Systems in Business*, and one in which the term will be used hundreds of times. In fact I am not going to actually define the term at all. There are three reasons for this:

1. There is no *universally accepted definition* of the term system.
2. The concept of a single definition can often imply something that is *alien to a systems approach* and systems thinking.
3. I believe that starting with a ready-made or acquired definition of a concept can sometimes be *bad educational practice*, and indeed is so in this particular case.

Let us look at each of these points in more detail.

Definitions of the term 'system'

The word *system* is used widely in everyday speech as well as in a broad range of subjects such as physics, engineering, biology, economics and sociology. A good reference for selected readings over this range are the editions of Beishon and Peters (1972), (1976), and (1981).

Given this subject range, we will concentrate on attempts to define *system* in the areas of management and business. Thus a well established source such as Schoderbeck et al. (1985), now in its third edition, proposes a definition which they think is 'extensive enough to allow for wide applicability, and at the same time intensive enough to include all the elements necessary for the detection and identification of a system':

> *A set of objects together with relationships between the objects and their attributes related to each other and to their environment so as to form a whole.*

However, if we look back to Beishon and Peters (1972) p. 12, we find the same definition described as 'widely quoted' but criticized as failing to recognize the 'subjective aspect' of systems. These authors then go on to define a system as:

> *An assembly of parts where:*
> 1. *The parts or components are connected together in an organized way*
> 2. *The parts or components are affected by being in the system and are changed by leaving it*
> 3. *The assembly does something*
> 4. *The assembly has been identified by a person as being of special interest.*

Part 4 of this definition attempts to cover the main reason why the authors of the second of these definitions were unhappy about the first: the issue of the 'subjective aspect'. Beishon and Peters are emphasizing the point that *what* a system is seen to be depends on *whose* view we are taking and *why* they are interested.

We shall be considering the effects of this issue in much more detail both later in this chapter and throughout the book. In the fields of management, organizations and business, where human beings and their 'subjective' aspects are always present, any attempt to say what we mean by a management, organizational or business system must take account of them.

Alternatives to specific definitions

We therefore find that the term system is used in a very wide range of subjects, and that what is seen as a system can vary according to who is using the term. In these circumstances I think the chances of success for a very specific definition of the term are very limited.

Apart from this practical reason why we are unlikely to find a single acceptable definition, there is another reason why we might be against it in principle. Perhaps the success of systems thinking in being so widely applied has come from its flexibility and avoidance of a definition strait-jacket. The fact that a physicist, an engineer, a biologist, an economist and a sociologist can all use the term system is one of the strengths that comes from diversity. Indeed, maybe *diversity is part of systems thinking itself*. If this is the case, then we would wish to actively avoid a single definition as being 'alien', as we said above.

If we take this position however, we need to provide an alternative to providing a specific definition. I think the best alternative is to use what I called 'confining' in Harry (1990) when considering the term *management*. Since I wrote that book, I have heard this alternative approach better described as 'extensive definition'. Whatever word we use, the alternative is to consider the *common properties* that a range or family of uses would share, rather than define the term itself.

Thus for the remainder of this chapter we will look in more detail at the shared range of properties that characterize the different uses of the term system in the fields of management, organization and business. We shall find that when we do this, the meanings of the terms *information* and *information system* can then be understood in this context.

Before we do this however, it remains for me to justify the assertion that starting with a ready made or acquired definition of a concept can sometimes be *bad educational practice*, and why I believe it to be so in our case.

Definitions and the learning process

Although we shall be considering a range of theoretical material in this book and will emphasize the role of *concepts,* our ultimate goals are concerned with information systems *in business*, i.e. practically applied. When we consider the practical application of information system concepts, we shall find that the process of application has two important characteristics:

1 Definitions need to follow our understanding and experience, not precede them. Definitions play the role of concisely summing up the results of our experience and helping us form a model of our understanding. Thus if a statistician defines 'arithmetic mean' as $\Sigma x_i / n$, anyone with even limited experience of statistics would find it trivial to understand: but to someone with no mathematical experience it would be mysterious gobbledy-gook. (Indeed, I think that this is a common reason for mathematicians not getting their message across. They will insist on beginning with definitions for reasons of 'purity'.)

2 When we come to the practical activity of defining particular information systems and their properties, we shall find that we have to go through a discovery, learning or heuristic process before we can form a definition. We shall find that much of the actual 'problem' is not what *follows* having formed a definition, but what precedes it. This will be an important part of systems development in Chapter 7.

All of the preceding arguments of this section therefore lead us to consider the *common properties* that a large range of uses of the term *system* would share, and we cover these in the following section.

3.1.2 Components

The concept

We began this chapter by discussing a particular monetary system; but is the British £1 coin, or any other coin, a *system*? The answer to this question is likely to depend on who you ask. An economist or an accountant would probably see a single coin as just one tiny part or piece of what they would see as the system. The system for them would probably be seen as the financial workings of a whole company or even the whole world economy.

To a metallurgist a £1 coin might look very different. He could show that the coin is made up of metals with different sized atomic nuclei, arranged in particular geometrical structures. Around these nuclei it is possible to portray a swirling 'cloud' of electrons, repelling each other but attracted by the nuclei. The particular way these parts behave and interact gives the whole coin certain properties. The ease with which the electron cloud can flow means that the coin can conduct heat and electricity. The way the nuclei are ordered in a structure means that the coin is more likely to bend than snap when we distort it. Hence something which to an economist is just a single, almost insignificant part of the world economy is quite a complex *system* to the metallurgist.

The clue to the different views is the use of phrases like 'part of' and 'made up of'. If we consider something that someone calls a system we shall find that it is seen as containing at least two, and usually many more, parts or *components*.

Our simple £1 coin can take us further. When news reports talked of 'millions of £s changing hands' in the lead up to Black Wednesday, we do not imagine that earnest bankers were running around London with large sacks of £1 coins on their backs. Money in fact changed hands simply because buyer and seller agreed that it should. The transfer of the money was regarded as having happened once the agreement was recorded as figures in a bank account. There never was any *physical* or *concrete* transfer of money, but the money exchanged was very real nevertheless.

We can take the concept of a system as being made up of components a stage further and recognize that the components of a system may be *concrete* or *abstract*. Concrete components have a physical existence, like the £1 coin, and can be detected by at least one of our senses. Abstract components are mental concepts and are not physically detectable.

◆ **STQ 3.1**

Is it possible to see one of the cupboards produced by Carry-Out Cupboards as anything other than a system of concrete components?

This leaves us with one other important issue which we need to understand about components. What if we were asked whether a £1 coin was a lot of money? While we were considering the amount of money involved in the Black Wednesday affair, we might have been tempted to say that £1 was very little indeed. Yet we could also consider that on that same day £1 could have saved someone's eyesight or even their life in poorer parts of the world. From that viewpoint, £1 is hardly 'very little indeed'.

We therefore need to say something more about the components of a system beyond describing them as concrete or abstract. It also requires us to consider their *hard* and *soft* properties. A property which can be defined, measured, or assessed in some way that does not depend on someone's personal sense of value is called *hard*. If we have to count how many £1 coins there are in a purse, to measure their diameters or to weigh them, we know that the answers we get can be checked to see if they are correct. If two people count or measure the same thing and their results are not the same, they would agree that both of the answers couldn't be right. They would not consider the number of coins or their measurable properties as just a matter of opinion.

Soft properties are different. If one person thinks a certain sum of money is a large amount and another person thinks it small, there is no agreed objective test to prove one of them right and the other wrong. Questions which depend on personal *values, opinions, tastes* or *ethics* cannot be resolved by counting, measurement or some kind of proof. They depend on who you are and what you think important in life. Such values are often described as making up your *weltanschauung* (velt-an-show-ung) or *world view*. We shall have more to say about this later in this chapter and again in Chapter 8.

Some writers talk about *fuzzy* properties. This term needs to be treated with caution. We need to distinguish between two different meanings sometimes given to the word.

The first meaning can be illustrated by continuing our monetary example. If we were asked to say how much money we had in a bank account or what we expected to have left in the account in a weeks time, the answers to these questions could be fuzzy in the sense that we could not be certain about them. We might say that we thought we had about £500 in our account and that by next week it might be down to zero. In each case there is *uncertainty* about the answer to a question. However, this uncertainty can in principle be resolved by counting the money at present in the account, then waiting for a week and counting again. The questions are both about *hard* properties of the bank account. The amount of money in a bank account is not determined by personal values, opinions, tastes or ethics. Even if we cannot get agreement over the amount of money, this disagreement will come from disputes about the bank records or the correctness of the calculations, not from the possibility of legitimate differences of opinion about what we mean by '£500' or 'counting up'. The kind of fuzziness that comes from uncertainty about hard properties we call *hard uncertainty*.

A second use of the term fuzzy coincides with the meaning of *soft* which we considered above. Where something is an issue of legitimate dispute coming from differences of personal values, opinions, tastes or ethics, it is fuzzy in the sense of having several possible answers; some of which may differ more than others.

In this book we will avoid using the term fuzzy just because there is this ambiguity about it. However we will come across it in Chapter 4 when we mention *fuzzy logic*. This is a term that does have a clear meaning but is used mainly outside the subjects covered in this book.

◆ **STQ 3.2**
What hard and soft properties might a customer of Carry-Out Cupboards see in one of their products?

The practical implications of the concept

So far we have discussed the concept of a system having components and the properties of components, but why should this be important for *information* systems? The full answers to these questions will come when we consider the application of systems theory in the remaining chapters of this book. For the moment, we can establish the following important points:

a The distinction between *concrete* and *abstract* components is important because *information* and *data* are themselves abstract concepts. The amount in a bank account, a customer name or any other piece of business information is *not* a concrete thing. However, the medium on which it is recorded or by which it is transmitted *is*. Thus the amount in the bank account is the same figure whether recorded on a printed statement or recorded magnetically on a computer disk. This distinction between the *abstract* concept of information, and the *concrete* component of the system that records it, is important because it separates our understanding of *what* an information system does and *how* it does it. When we look at the design and use of *databases* in Chapter 5 or information systems development in Chapter 7, we shall find that this distinction of the concrete and the abstract has practical implications. As we first saw in Chapter 1, we shall frequently refer to this *whats* and *hows* distinction in these and other systems contexts.

b The distinction between *hard* and *soft* properties of components and systems is important because it enables us in turn to distinguish different *kinds* of information. We shall explore these differences in more detail in section 3.2.4, but for the moment we can show two reasons why it is important from a *practical* viewpoint:

i. Since hard properties like a bank balance can be defined and assessed, it makes it easier to design routine, computerizable procedures to calculate and process them. Dealing with soft properties cannot be left to machines because the weltanschauung of the people involved has to be taken account of. The soft properties of information systems require us to look carefully at the ways in which the *information* system should interact with the wider *management* system of which it is a component.

ii. The different nature of the problems which come from hard and soft properties of systems can mean that different *methods* are needed to deal with them when developing information systems. We shall study this in detail in Chapter 7.

3.1.3 Connexion

The concept

It is not sufficient to identify a system as a collection of components. We could, for example, describe a microcomputer system as consisting of a central processing unit, disk storage, a screen, keyboard, etc., as in Fig 3.1. For it to work as a system however, these components need to be connected. We do this for a microcomputer system by making *physical* connexions with cables between *concrete* components, but *abstract* systems components cannot be connected in this way. We would not imagine that when the British £ left the ERM on Black Wednesday that some mooring cable which stretched across the English Channel was disconnected to allow Britain and its money to float freely in the Atlantic.

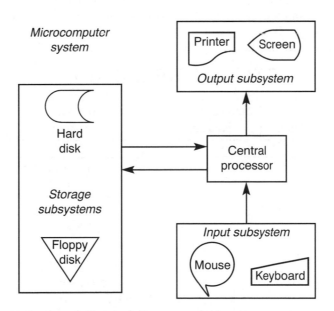

Fig 3.1 A Typical Microcomputer System
This shows the *hardware*, but could only be seen as a *component* of an information system. Where is the software, and where are the human beings who decide what it must do and make it do what is needed?.

Connexion is therefore an essential property of a system, but it may be a *logical* or *conceptual* connexion which will be physically manifested in the way components relate and interact with each other, rather than through concrete physical links.

◆ **STQ 3.3**

Are all of the connexions between the concrete components of a cupboard physical?

The practical implications of the concept

The particular importance of this concept for information systems comes from the implications of abstract components being *logically* or *conceptually* connected. As we saw in the previous section, information and data are themselves abstract concepts that may be physically manifested in different ways. If we are designing or implementing an information system we need to decide or know how information and data can be, or are, connected together. Thus in a business like Carry-Out Cupboards there will be a connexion between the number of various products in stock and the entries in the stock record as in Fig 3.2. The stock record itself will consist of data which is *logically* connected because it makes up information about the particular stock item, and *physically* connected by being printed on the same document.

It is important to notice in the last example that what should be in the stock record has to be decided first before we can decide how to record the details in terms of medium and layout. In Chapter 5, where we study *data modelling*, we shall look in detail at defining the *logical* connexions between data and information components of systems, as the necessary prelude to deciding how they should be *physically* recorded.

STOCK RECORD

PART NO.	DESCRIPTION	UNIT DESCRIPTION
DN 3480	CALABRIA 35	PACK

REORDER LEVEL	MINIMUM LEVEL	ORDER QUANTITY
50	10	50

LEAD TIME	STANDARD PRICE	IN STOCK
4	205.00	47

ALLOCATED	FREE	ON ORDER
10	37	50

Fig 3.2 A Printout of a Stock Record
As with Fig 2.1, *how* this information is presented needs to be distinguishes from *what it shows*.

In explaining the importance of understanding the nature of connexion as a systems property, we have started to imply two other closely related concepts. In referring to how components are related and interact, we are beginning to introduce the related concepts of *structure and hierarchy* and *interaction*.

Box 3.1

EUROTENS

'Eurotens' is a policy document which the European Union issued in 1995 to propose policies on the exploitation of advanced telecommunications networks as 'an essential component of the Information Society' (*sic*). The document recognizes that telephone systems are no longer simple carriers of voice communication: they can be deliverers of images and text, as well as sound.

The European Union's interest in the integration of all EU countries into the Information Society requires the connexion of not only national telecommunications systems, but also cable and satellite networks. Eurotens sees it as crucial that these services and applications are able to work together if Europe's Information Society is to become a reality.

The document then covers four key areas:

- Creating the right regulatory and legal framework
- Identifying networks, basic services, applications and their content
- Assessing the impact on citizens, their societies and cultures
- Promoting awareness of the Information Society.

COMMENT

The specific details in Eurotens may soon be outdated, since both Europe and information technology are changing very fast. But the issues raised in the document are unlikely to go away, either within Europe or in the world as a whole. The important systems concepts behind these issues are:

a   Physical or *concrete* connexions may be the most obvious ones when we first look at any particular system, but they are not always the most important. Thus 'awareness of the Information Society' requires that the people of the European Union are not merely connected by telephone wires, but by an understanding and a belief in the concepts of Eurotens. The idea that systems can be created merely by making physical connexions is as false for a small office local area network as it is for a continent of many nations. Chapters 7 and 8 develop the role of human and social connexion in systems development.

b   Human and social connexion are only possible where there is *communication* and some *shared* view of what is being communicated. Chapter 4 develops these and other concepts of communication systems.

FURTHER STUDY

Pursue the developments that followed Eurotens by exploring the European Union web site europa.eu.int, or in a library. Can we separate *information* connexion from other forms of connexion?

3.1.4 Structure and hierarchy

The concept

We used the example of microcomputer systems components to illustrate the need for connexion as a systems property. We can now take this example further and note that the way in which components are connected will also be significant. Thus, components of a microcomputer system not only have to be connected: the way in which they are connected will affect what kind of overall system we get. For a working system, the keyboard has to be connected to the central processor, not directly to the screen or the disk drives, for example.

Whilst for the microcomputer there is only one way of connecting the components that will make the whole work in any useful way as a system, this is not true of all systems. In many cases alternative ways of connecting components all lead to working systems, but systems with different overall properties. In our Black Monday case, the form of Britain's and other component countrys' logical connexions within the European Monetary System could have been different but still leave a whole system that might have been politically acceptable. Before Black Monday, the exchange rate for the £ could have been adjusted whilst still keeping Britain within the exchange rate mechanism or the ERM. Even when the £ changed from floating within limits to complete flexibility, and Britain was no longer 'in' the ERM, the EMS itself continued only slightly changed. It is therefore possible to see a whole range of different forms of European monetary systems, but their overall nature will depend on the particular way the components are connected as well as which components are involved.

Does the same point apply to physical connexions? If we consider Fig 3.2, the individual entries like 'Lead Time 4' or 'In Stock 47' could be rearranged in many ways on the sheet and it would appear to make no difference to the overall information given by the stock record. However, if we rearranged the previous components to read 'Lead Time 47' and 'In Stock 4' the overall information given by the stock record would be very different.

What is important for both abstract and physical connexions, therefore, is that certain details of the *logical form* of the connexion between components cannot be altered without giving the connected whole such very different properties that it ceases to be the same system. As with our microcomputer system example, the basic logic of some connexions must remain unchanged if the system itself is to continue to exist. The EMS too would have ceased to exist if all of the currencies had followed the British example. With our stock record we could rearrange some groups of components without significant effect but, again, the form of certain logical connexions could not be changed without significantly altering the properties of the whole.

The logical form of connexion between the components of a system that remains unchanged during its life we call its *structure.* There is one particular form of structure that is found in some form in all systems. This we call the systems *hierarchy.* Figure 3.3 shows the concepts and language used to describe systems hierarchy. A system may consist of two or more *subsystems* and a subsystem will consist of two or more *elements.* Thus elements are *components* of subsystems and subsystems are *components* of systems. We have shown only three levels in the hierarchy in Fig 3.3. In practice we may have simple systems with no subsystems which just consist of elements as their components. We can also have systems with many hierarchical layers with subsystems of subsystems.

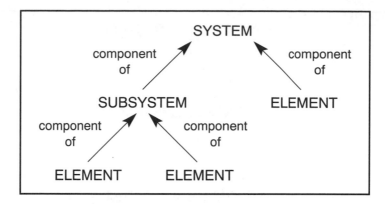

Fig 3.3 Describing Systems and their Components
Just as a system may have subsystems as its components, so a subsystem may be regarded as a system with subsystems as components of itself. A system hierarchy may therefore have many more than the three levels shown.

We can now see that our hierarchical view of a £1 coin will vary greatly according to our systems interest. To the metallurgist it can be seen as a system with nuclear and electronic subsystems whose components are elementary atomic particles. To the financier it may be seen as the smallest element in the British monetary system, which itself is but a subsystem of the international monetary system.

Generally, an element will be the lowest-level hierarchical component that is of interest, and the system the highest.

◆ **STQ 3.4**
How might this principle apply to perceptions of a cupboard to a sales manager and a production manager at Carry-Out Cupboards?

The practical implications of the concept

The two connected concepts of structure and hierarchy lead to a whole range of related practical implications for the understanding, design and implementation of business and organizational information systems. Some of these practical implications will become clearer as we consider the concepts of *holism, emergent property* and *control* later in this chapter. These in turn form the basis of the practical information systems development material of Chapters 5 to 8. However, there are two important practical implications we can cover immediately:

1 Understanding the hierarchical structure of management systems will be the key to our understanding the role of information systems as a component of management systems. Figure 3.4 summarizes this relationship, which we will develop further throughout this chapter and on through the book.

2 Understanding the role of *data* as a component of *information* will be the key to constructing the information from its data components and understanding the role of data processing as a component of information systems. This will be particularly important when we consider data and databases in Chapter 5.

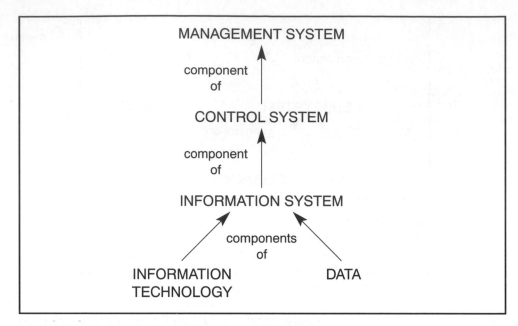

Fig 3.4 The Components of a Management System
Seen as a *system*, management is viewed in terms of *what* its components are, not *how*
any particular management organization may be arranged.

At first, the use of the term 'understanding' may not sound like a *practical* implication.
However, we need to recall that deciding *what* a system should be in terms of its *logical
form* is the essential prelude to detailing *how* it should be implemented. A whole range
of practical topics such as information systems development or database management
require understanding and decision concerning the logical system as part of the implementation process. In our microcomputer example, we cannot go about the practical
business of getting the system into operation if we don't understand what form of
connexion has to be made between what components.

3.1.5 Process and interaction

The concepts

A connected structure on its own does not make a system. When we connect our microcomputer components correctly another vital property has to be present for us to
describe it as a system. The components have to *interact* so that the system *does something*.

   In the case of the microcomputer, the movement of keys on the keyboard must be
converted into electronic signals which are sent to the central processor. This component
will process these signals and convert them into other signals which go to the screen and
are used to determine what images an electron beam produces on it. In this simple
description, each of the components carries out a *process* which takes *inputs* and transforms them into something different as an *output*. The interaction of components within
the system takes the form of one component's output being another component's input.

   The term *process* therefore describes the *dynamic* properties of the system, both of its
individual components and the overall system itself. An important aspect of the con-

cept of process is that any process *transforms* inputs into outputs. This may seem a trivial point at first, but we should look at it more closely. The concept of transformation means that any output is not something separate from the input, but rather the input *emerging in a different form.*

If we consider a system which carries out a physical process using concrete components like in the case of Carry-Out Cupboards, the concept of a transformation process is fairly easy to understand. Inputs such as bonded chipboard, cupboard fittings and packaging are transformed by the assembly and packing process into complete kits.

◆ **STQ 3.5**
What transformation processes might be carried out by a system such as the EMS?

Abstract transformation processes aren't just relevant to large institutional systems like the EMS. The simple stock record of Fig 3.2 contains an example of recording an important conceptual change in state. The items 'Free 37' and 'Allocated 10' refer to how many of the stock items have been allocated to a particular retail outlet, and which are free for future use. Once a particular batch of cupboards is allocated in this way, the transformation from one state to the other involves no physical change in the cupboards themselves.

We see that just as the system, its components, their connexion and structure may be concrete or abstract, so what they do, their transformation processes, may also be concrete or abstract.

The practical implications of the concept

We have established another important property of a system: its components have to interact so that the system does something. We shall see that for an information system this means processing input data, or previously processed information, to produce output information which we need to manage our organization or business.

The transformation processes carried out by an information system may involve a wide range of operations such as recording, communicating, calculating, updating, sorting or merging. They may also be done in many different physical ways.

Thus our stock record in Fig 3.2 shows the amount of a particular item in stock. This amount can be calculated by subtracting any stock which has gone out since we last updated the record, and adding any new deliveries. The output of this data processing is placed in the stock record. Notice that I have just described *what* the process of updating the stock record involves, i.e. the *abstract* or *logical* process. If we consider *how* it could be done, we then identify the *concrete* or *physical* ways in which the process could be carried out. We might update the stock record by manual calculation and record the result on a paper sheet looking like Fig 3.2. We might computerize the process, so that the calculation is done electronically and the results recorded on a computer disk. In this form of the process the stock record would normally be shown on a computer screen.

We shall therefore find that we need to distinguish clearly between *what* an information system process does, and *how* it is or can be done. The practical reason for this is that, as with our simple stock record, one particular logical process may be carried out in several alternative physical ways. When we come to study information systems development in Chapter 7, we shall find that making this distinction enables us to improve existing systems and develop new ones by separating what is essential from what is a matter of choice.

3.1.6 Holism, emergent properties and behaviour

The concepts

'A mother holding her child is a group of two human bodies, a human body is a collection of cells, cells are entirely made up of molecules, molecules are arrangements of atoms; so a mother holding her child is just an atomic arrangement.' Whilst such a statement might be a good way of starting a discussion and/or spoiling a social occasion with an argument, few people that I know would find such a statement acceptable or satisfactory.

The problem is not that the statement is untrue, but that it is *incomplete*. When we see a mother holding her child we do not see atoms: atoms cannot be seen anyway. But the fact that we do not talk of mother and child in terms of the atoms does not mean that the image of the mother and child is an illusion. The mother and child may feel a strong emotional relationship, but the fact that molecules do not have emotional relationships does not make these emotions a fiction. The child will be growing day by day through the reproduction of its cells, but the fact that atoms or molecules do not reproduce themselves does not mean that the child will weigh the same in two years time.

What we find in our mother and child example is something that occurs across the whole range of our experience. We find that we can understand, interpret and talk about *wholes* in a way that does not necessarily work with their individual *parts*. When we consider collections of atoms and molecules making up cells, the whole cell has properties like reproductive ability that the atoms and molecules do not. Similarly, if we bring together a whole collection of cells in the form of a human being, then we can identify properties like colour or emotion that just don't make sense when applied to an individual atom or cell respectively.

The concept that a *whole is more than the sum of its parts* is called *holism*. The properties that make sense in terms of the whole but not in terms of individual parts we call *emergent properties*.

We can now see that we were already implying these concepts previously when we made statements like 'the components have to *interact* so that the system *does something*' or 'their *overall nature* will depend on the particular way the components are connected as well as which components are involved'. When we did this we implied that a system itself is a holist concept. The need to see a whole, which we call a system, implies that the whole has emergent properties which motivate us to consider it more than just a collection of components.

Thus a wide range of different properties that we find emerging from the workings of the ERM, like international cooperation and rivalry, exchange rate panic or currency dealing, are properties of the whole. If we wish to deal with these properties, either in an attempt to promote closer European monetary union or to prevent it, we need to regard the whole as a system. Thus it is only at the level of different national currency systems interacting as components of a greater system that concepts like cooperation and rivalry, exchange rate panic or currency dealing have any meaning.

The twin concepts of holism and emergent property enable us to understand the concept of systems hierarchy (Fig 3.3) in more depth. If it is the need to recognize emergent properties that leads us to see a collection of components as a greater whole called a system, so within the system we might wish to identify groups of components that exhibit emergent properties.

In our mother and child example we can see that certain *levels* of *aggregation* of components show properties not shown by the components themselves. Thus cells reproduce but their component molecules do not. Or again, a single human being has emotions but the cells making up the human being do not.

Choosing to see a system as a hierarchy, and also the particular hierarchy that we choose to see, reflects our view of what emergent properties we think important and therefore what levels of aggregation we wish to distinguish.

So far we have not mentioned our third concept, *behaviour.* We first noted that a system *does something* and we then link this with *emergent properties* of the whole, like say 'cooperation' or 'dealing' in the Black Monday example. What we can now note is that some emergent properties like these are explicitly *dynamic* and involve a *change in state* of the system over time. Thus 'dealing' is seen as a 'property' which 'emerges' from a system like the EMS when the state of various dealers who are components of the ERM changes over time as a result of their interaction.

Normally the term *behaviour* is confined to such clearly dynamic emergent properties of a system, but we can note that *all* emergent properties are dynamic in some sense. An emergent property like colour may seem static, but it only comes about because a coloured object reflects light. In this book we will avoid being over-correct and use the term *behaviour* for overtly dynamic emergent properties.

Before we move on to the practical implications of holism and our development of hierarchy, it is worth saying something of how both terms are used in everyday life. Sometimes they are used with the same meaning as the systems use, but not always.

Thus holism is sometimes used to describe a view of human health that takes in the whole person. According to this use of the word, health involves the mental, psychological, spiritual and social aspects of a person's life as well as their physical well-being. Physical well-being on its own would not be regarded as 'holist'. From a systems view we would see it differently. Physical well-being is a property of the whole body, which only has meaning in the context of all the bodily components coming together to exhibit it. We can therefore say that it is a holist property in the systems sense because it is an *emergent property,* and emergent properties are a holist concept.

I also think I should be fair and warn you that I am presenting some degree of personal bias in my view of holism. As we shall see in Chapter 8, when we come to consider *soft systems methodology,* even many systems practitioners seem to imply that for a view to be holist it *must* take account of psychological, social and other human aspects. Whilst I think that human aspects are virtually always relevant to *management* systems, this is because I think management is a human activity, *not* because the concept of holism logically demands it.

A similar caution is needed with the term *hierarchy.* In everyday life this is often associated with ideas of class, authority and control. Thus a colonel is seen as further 'up' the army hierarchy than a private soldier, and it is implied from this that the colonel is the 'boss' who controls the private by giving orders which he expects to be obeyed. Our systems view of hierarchy is different from this since we see it in terms of levels of aggregation associated with emergent properties. We would see the whole regiment of the colonel with his soldiers as 'higher' in the systems hierarchy than either the individual soldiers or the colonel which are its components. In this view both colonel and privates are elements at the lowest level of the hierarchy. We shall be relating *control* to hierarchy, but since our concept of *hierarchy* differs from the popular use, so will our concept of *control*.

Finally, it is worth noting that other views of hierarchy are used in the field of information systems. We shall cover these under the subject of object-orientation in Chapter 8.

◆ **STQ 3.6**

How might the ecu currency unit be seen in terms of emergent property and hierarchy?

The practical implications of the concepts

The concepts of holism and emergent property will recur frequently in this book as we seek to understand the role and application of information systems in businesses and organizations, but there are three major practical implications that come from the concepts:

1 We explained above that understanding the hierarchical structure of a management system (Fig 3.4) is necessary if we are to decide *what* form any information system should take before deciding *how* it should be developed. If we now recognize that it is our view of the emergent properties that defines the systems hierarchy, then identifying the required emergent properties of a system will be the necessary first step to developing it. Most of the practical systems development methods of Chapter 7 are based on this conceptual view.

2 The concept of holism in relation to the hierarchical view of Fig 3.4 implies that a *management* system will have other components beyond the *control* system shown. As we saw above, there will almost inevitably be a human component which will bring *soft issues* with it to the whole management system. When we develop an information system, it will be just one component that has to go with others to make up the management system's desired emergent properties. We shall therefore need practical ways of coordinating information systems development with clarification and management of soft systems issues. Chapter 8 will cover these practical ways under the subject of *Soft Systems Methodology*.

3 *Information* itself is an *emergent property*. When discussing structure and hierarchy we established that certain details of the logical form of the connexion between components cannot be altered without giving the connected whole very different properties. We saw that this could refer to a whole system or a component like a stock record. We can now see that the 'properties' referred to are the emergent properties of the whole in question. We can now add the concept of emergent property to our previous identification of data as a component of information, and the construction of information from its data components. In this context, information is the emergent property which comes from processing data so that it is transformed into a structured *whole* we call *information*. Chapters 4 and 5 will cover the properties of information and data in this relationship.

3.1.7 Environment, boundary and identity

The concepts

We have now got as far as seeing a system as a whole, with its internal structure and processes, and its overall emergent properties. This enables us to talk of 'a' system or 'the' system in a way that implies that we can:

      a. Identify a particular system as something *separate* from other things.
      b. State what *is*, and what *is not*, a component or a property of a system.

Identifying a system by making statements about what it *is*, involves using the concepts of structure, process and emergent property which we have already developed. Making statements about what a system *is not*, requires the two further concepts of *boundary* and *environment*.

    We can illustrate these two concepts by referring to our Black Monday mini-case. We could have identified whether or not a country's monetary system was a component of the European Monetary System by seeing whether it was logically connected by legal agreement and whether it participated in the processes of the Exchange Rate Mechanism. When the UK left the system we talked of it being 'outside' the mechanism. Yet for a country to 'leave' and to be 'outside' has nothing to do with physical movement or crossing some geographical border. Instead, we find ourselves using physical, concrete words to describe conceptual or logical changes. So the term *systems boundary* refers to our conceptual dividing line between that set of conditions which defines membership of a system and those which do not. Perhaps we come near to this in everyday life when we describe bad behaviour as being 'beyond the limit' or 'outside' the law.

    Once we have the concept of an identifiable system separated from what is not the system by a conceptual boundary, we now need to consider what may be 'outside' that system. When we do this we can distinguish two different types of thing. Some things, like the Japanese or the US economies and monetary systems, are not members of the European Monetary System, but we do not see them as being totally disconnected and irrelevant. Other things are not only outside the European Monetary System, but are completely irrelevant to it. Thus most of the universe with its distant galaxies falls into this category.

    Those things which are outside the system but have relevance to it and interact with it, we call components of the system's *environment*. We also conceive this environment *as a whole* as having more effect on the system than the system does on that environment. Thus, whatever the strengths of the Japanese, US or other national economies individually, the whole world economy has much more effect on the European Monetary System than the other way around. We could put this concept in another way, and say that a system has little control over its environment, but an environment can have a major disturbing effect on a system.

◆ **STQ 3.7**

    Are we defining the term environment here to mean something different from its use in the context of conservation and 'green' issues?

The practical implications of the concepts

The practical implications of the concepts of boundary and environment can be understood in terms of Fig 3.4:

a We need an *information system* because it is an essential component of a *control system*, which is in turn an essential component of a *management system*. As we shall see in Section 3.2, this need for a control system arises from the fact that all management systems have an environment which is a source of disturbances. These disturbances cannot be fully predicted or prevented, but they have to be allowed for and responded to if management is to achieve its goals. It is the control system which enables the management system to do this, and an information system is an essential component of any control system. Developing and maintaining an information system which supports the goals of a business or organizational system therefore needs a clear identification of that system's environment and its disturbances.

b Even where a need to identify a business or organizational system's environment has been recognized, the system's boundary must be correctly defined. If the concept of a business or organizational system's boundary fails to include all its components, then we miss the opportunity of minimizing uncertainty and maximizing control. As we shall see in the rest of this chapter and in the next, information systems reduce uncertainty and support control. If, however, the concept of the boundary is set so that components of the environment are wrongly seen as components of the system, then we wastefully attempt to control the uncontrollable.

Common examples of failing to understand **b** are those which require recognizing the role of human components both inside and outside the system. Frequently quite elaborate *technical* expertise is used to develop, implement and operate information systems, whilst the *human* component is either ignored or wrongly treated as if it were no different. Again, Chapter 7 will look at these issues in depth.

3.1.8 Conceptualism

Conceptualism

Throughout this section we have established a set of properties which would be possessed by anything we would call a *system*, and we have called these *concepts*. If we take a *conceptualist* view of systems and their properties, then *what* a system is seen to be, and *what* properties it is considered to have, depends on *whose view* or *concept* of the system we are taking.

We can find examples of this around us in everyday life. My house has an electrical system, a water system, a computer system and a telephone system. All these are concrete and fairly easily identified, but there are important systems that are not so obvious. Ours is an old house with a complex biological system of spiders, summer flies, woodworm, small mites, the cat, and occasional mice. There is also the human activity system of myself, my wife and our children and friends when they visit. It would hardly make sense to talk of 'the' system in this context without knowing whose viewpoint we were taking. So that when a man turned up last week and said he had come to 'check the system', we needed to know that he was a telephone engineer before we knew what system he was talking about.

With systems which have more soft and abstract components in their make-up than the telephone system, the issue of *whose* system becomes stronger. I guess most telephone engineers would agree what 'the' system was in our house, but if we considered my business system it would be more complex. The fact that my wife and I use the computer system, the car, etc., both professionally and privately, means that defining their role in my business system for tax purposes is much more complex than identifying what constitutes our simple telephone system.

Since most businesses and organizations can be seen as systems with significant soft and abstract components, any attempt to understand the relationships of Fig 3.4 as a prelude to information systems development and implementation must recognize that a system is a *concept*.

The practical implications of conceptualism

Having established that any approach to developing and using systems which claims to be practical must take account of the essential principle of *conceptualism*, it is very important not to interpret this principle as some kind of woolly relativism. Conceptualism does not claim that all systems are 'equally valid' or that 'there are no right answers'. Instead, it emphasizes that terms like 'valid' or 'right' imply a standard or yardstick against which they can be measured. We have seen that conceptualism means that what a system is seen to be, and what properties it is considered to have, depends on whose view or concept of the system we are taking. Therefore any practical attempt to develop and implement a 'valid' or the 'right' system must include some means of *systems specification* or *definition* as part of its methodology.

One common type of information systems development problem will illustrate this principle. Case histories of practical problems in organizations and businesses associated with the supposed failure of *computer* systems are numerous. I expect that there will be one in the news when you are reading this. What so often is blamed on the computer in fact turns out to be a failure of the *management* system to have a clear idea or agreement as to what the computerized information system should achieve. The common reason for subsequent failure is that *hard, technical* approaches are then applied to computerize existing ignorance and disagreement.

Thus, a project named TAURUS, which was the first attempt aimed to computerize share dealings on the London Stock Exchange, was abandoned in 1993. Does anyone, I wonder, really believe that this is because we do not possess the knowledge of computer hardware and the software programming ability to create such a system? I am quite sure that all the tasks which such a system would have to carry out are versions of ones which have already been successfully computerized. The problem with TAURUS was of trying to satisfy the complex and conflicting needs of stockbrokers, banks, investment funds, the British government and many others with legitimate and often powerful interests in what the eventual system should deliver. These problems have little to do with computers per se, and very much to do with the conceptual relationships between the various systems shown in Fig 3.4. TAURUS wasn't a computer systems problem, but it was an information and management systems problem. Compare it with Box 7.1 in Chapter 7.

As we progress through this book to Chapters 5–8, we shall look at the implications of applying systems principles to the practical tasks of information systems development. When we do so, we shall find that the essential importance of deciding *whose* and therefore *what* system we are concerned with, is never far away in any practical application.

3.2 MANAGEMENT, INFORMATION AND CONTROL SYSTEMS

3.2.1 Management and decision-making

The management, control and information relationship

The role of management and its *hierarchical* relationship to control and information is summarized in Fig 3.4. We will now look in detail at this relationship by establishing a meaning for the three terms *management, control* and *information*. When we do this we shall aim at a *systems* view, using the concepts and language introduced in the previous section.

The definition of management

We shall approach the issues of *whether* and *how* we should attempt to define the term *management* in much the same way as we did for the term *system*. I think we can find from even a brief investigation that the term *management* is used in different ways both in academic literature and everyday life, and as we found with the term system, there is no universally accepted definition. Rather than attempt to produce one definition therefore, we will use the alternative approach of extensive definition where we consider the *common properties* that a range or family of meanings can share.

Our use of the term management will be like our use of the term system in another way: we shall use *management* to describe a *concept* not a particular way or *style* of doing something. Hence our now familiar distinction of *what* something is from *how* it is manifested or practised.

Having settled the way in which we will use the term management, I think that the extensive common ground found in many views is that which I suggested in Harry (1990). There I said that a range of different management styles, from the very authoritarian to the very egalitarian, shared a common characteristic: they saw management as *an activity aimed at achieving something desirable*.

This view of management implies some important concepts:

    a. There is something we wish to achieve which can be expressed as one or more *goals*.
    b. We have a *meliorist belief:* that is, we believe our choice of actions may have some effect on whether we achieve our goals.
    c. We have a *choice of actions*.
    d. We have a *decision-making* ability that enables us to make a choice.

Goals

When we described goals as something we wished to achieve, we were doing so in the context of a *systems* view of management. This means that our view of goals should be consistent with our view of systems. In particular we recognized that systems can have:

    a. Abstract as well as concrete components
    b. Soft as well as hard properties.

The fact that systems can have *concrete* components means that the goals of such a system may also involve concrete, physical achievements. Thus in cases like Carry-Out Cupboards or the East Farthing Drainage Authority, processes like the assembly and packing of kits or the pumping of water are physical actions using concrete components like machinery. Not surprisingly, much of what the management of these organizations seeks to achieve is also concrete in the form of kits for sale or drained water. However, just as a system can have *abstract components*, so it may have *abstract goals*.

◆ STQ 3.8

Can you think of some for the European Monetary System?

There is no automatic link between whether the systems components are concrete or abstract and whether its goals are concrete or abstract however. The East Farthing Drainage Authority may have an abstract goal like 'a good public service image' and the European Monetary System may aim to build itself a brand new office block in Brussels.

The possibility of *soft* and *hard* properties of systems means that goals too may be hard or soft. Thus a particular exchange rate in the Exchange Rate Mechanism is something that can be measured, and is therefore a hard goal; but 'a good public service image' for the East Farthing Drainage Authority is a soft goal: it only means something in relation to a particular weltanschauung or set of values.

Finally, we saw above that all systems do *something*, i.e. they are *dynamic* and carry out *processes*. If we consider organization or business systems which are being *managed*, they are likely to have a range of concrete, abstract, hard and soft goals. Given such a mixture of goals, how does management choose between them? Thus the East Farthing Drainage Authority has goals relating to accessing and clearing drainage channels, but it also has goals relating to tree and wildlife conservation. Which does management try to achieve when they appear to conflict?

We shall study this issue further later in this chapter, when we look at the concept of *control systems hierarchy* and develop a general control model. This theoretical basis will then be used in detail in Chapter 6, where we look at organizations and businesses as systems. For the moment it is worth noting that just as a system can have a hierarchical structure, so the goals of an organization or business seen as a system can be placed in this hierarchical structure. The overall, high-level *emergent property* that comes from this goal structure hierarchy we will call the *central purpose* of the organization or business system.

Meliorism

We said that meliorism is the belief that our actions can have some effect on our success in achieving our goals. An alternative to this belief could be that our efforts are irrelevant to success. The inevitable result of this latter view would seem to be 'why bother to manage?' In this book however, we take the view that actions can have some effect on outcomes, and that attempts to manage are worthwhile.

The question of whether we believe in meliorism only becomes an issue *after* we have identified our goals. If we don't want anything or we don't know what we want, then concern about whether we can do something about it is irrelevant. This may sound like a purely theoretical point, but it has practical implications for both the way that we manage and the *kind of information* we need to do it.

If we refer back to our discussion of the term *fuzzy* in the previous section, we can see that not knowing or being *fuzzy* about our goals may be due to unresolved *soft issues* or *hard uncertainty*. As an example of soft issues, the East Farthing Drainage Authority may face conflicts between ecological and commercial farming interests over a proposed new drainage scheme which mean that its goals for the scheme are unclear. The kind of information needed to resolve the soft issues involved in this example will be about such soft components as human values and perceptions as well as hard facts of law or the technicalities of drainage engineering. It is unlikely that much of the information relating to the soft issues will be found on a computer database. Hard uncertainty could arise over a specifically technical problem like the width of a drainage channel needed to guarantee a certain volume of water flow. Past statistics on rainfall and volumes of water pumped might be needed to resolve this uncertainty by enabling engineers to do calculations. Information of this kind and methods of calculation are just the sort of thing we *would* expect to be computerized.

Finally, we should note that meliorism only implies that our actions *can* have some effect. Given that any system has an environment over which it has little control, so a management system may well be disturbed and frustrated in a way that prevents it achieving what it desires. In our Black Monday mini-case, the world currency speculation environment of the European Monetary System frustrated very active management by the British to prevent the devaluation of the £.

Choice of actions and decision-making

If we know what we are trying to do and we think it reasonable to assume our actions can have some effect, then the next question is what choice of actions we make. This implies both an idea of what the choice might be and the ability to decide.

Two related major subjects called *decision theory* and *operations research* cover the methods we might use to make decisions about our choice of actions. An enormous range of books has been written on these subjects in the last four decades: I would suggest Ackoff (1962), Ackoff & Sasieni (1968).

Given the breadth of decision theory and operations research as subjects, covering choice of actions and decision-making could fill a whole book. I will concentrate briefly on the three essential stages of decision-making, as in Fishburn (1967) or Ackoff & Sasieni (1968), which are relevant to our information systems interest:

1. Problem formulation
2. Model construction
3. Deriving solutions from models

The classic decision theory view of problem formulation is that choices of actions can be linked to possible outcomes as in Fig 3.5. The nature of this link may vary according to our degree of certainty in our knowledge and understanding of the problem:

1 *Certainty:* where each choice of action is linked with only one particular outcome. Thus in a simple stock control situation like that in Fig 3.2 we know there is a certain link between the amount of stock we decide to issue and the amount that will be left.

Outcomes

	O_1	O_2	• • •	O_j	• • •	O_n
C_1	V_{11}	V_{12}	• • •	V_{1j}	• • •	V_{1n}
C_2	V_{21}	V_{22}	• • •	V_{2j}	• • •	V_{2n}
• • •	• • •	• • •		•		•
C_i	V_{i1}	V_{i2}	• • •	V_{ij}	• • •	V_{in}
• • •	• • •	• • •		•		•
C_m	V_{m1}	V_{m2}	• • •	V_{mj}	• • •	V_{mn}

Choice of actions

Key C = choice of action
O = outcome
V = value of outcome

Fig 3.5 A Decision Theory View of Problem Formulation
Subscripted variables, or letters with other letters or numbers tucked into their bottom right-hand corners, are merely a way to indicate rows and columns in a matrix.

2 *Risk:* where each choice of action may result in one of several identified possible outcomes. Thus in the Black Wednesday mini-case, a decision by the Bank of England to spend £2 billion intervening in the currency market might have maintained the value of the £ within the Exchange Rate Mechanism or not. Whatever the *probabilities* associated with either outcome, neither of them was *certain.*

3 *Uncertainty:* where the possible outcomes resulting from each choice of action are not necessarily known, and in any case we cannot assign probabilities to them. Thus the wider implications of the Black Wednesday decisions for the whole process of European integration, enlargement of the European Community, world trade, etc., cannot be neatly listed as a series of possible outcomes whose probability can be estimated.

These three types of problem represent places on a spectrum. The less risky a problem becomes, the more we move to certainty; the more risky it becomes, the more we move towards complete uncertainty. Each kind of problem however has different information requirements if we are to follow the next two stages of decision-making involving *model construction* and *deriving solutions.* We shall study models later in this chapter, and the relationship between information and uncertainty more deeply in Chapter 4. For the moment, we can note that after formulating the problem, we need information on:

a. *The relationship between the choices of action and the possible outcomes.* This information we use to provide our *model* of the problem.

b. *A means of evaluating the outcome.* Decision-making requires more than just knowing what choice of action produces what outcome. We have to have information about the value of the outcome to the decision-maker if we are to assess its desirability or otherwise.

c. *A strategy or policy for choice.* To finally *decide* on our choice, we have to have information about how we choose between different valued outcomes.

We will now see what form these three information needs take for problems formulated under conditions of certainty, risk and uncertainty.

Decision-making under conditions of certainty

In problems where there is *certainty* in the link between choice of action and outcome, the relationships are described as *deterministic. Models* of such problems often take the form of mathematical formulae, logical procedures or even just a look-up table that enable us to determine the outcome that follows a choice of action. Thus in a simple stock control example like Fig 3.2, we model the relationship between amount issued and amount remaining as a simple formula:

Amount remaining = initial stock – amount issued

However, although the method of calculating stock levels is simple arithmetic, it tells us nothing about whether high or low stock levels are to be preferred. We need a *means of evaluating the outcome.* Until we have this knowledge, we cannot decide when it is best to reorder stock, or what level of stockholding is preferred. The information we need next is how we relate a bare figure like a quantity of stock to a measure of desirability or undesirability. In our stockholding example this measure is likely to be cost, but the general decision theory term for measures of desirability and undesirability are called *utility* and *disutility* respectively.

It is important to realize that utility is not a measure in the objective sense that quantity or cost is a measure. The quantity '47' or the cost '£205.00' on the stock record of Fig 3.2 are all measurements in accepted units whose values can be confirmed by agreed testing methods. They are in fact *hard* measures in the systemic sense. Utility, on the other hand, is a general term for a measure of desirability whose actual units of measurement depend on whose concept of desirability we are referring to. Thus in our stock control example, whether we are attempting to minimize stock levels, minimize the proportion of time we are out of stock, or minimize the overall cost of the stock-holding operation, depends on who we are and what we see as the best policy. In this case we are dealing with a *soft* issue in the systemic sense, when we choose a measure of desirability or *utility.*

Not surprisingly therefore, measures of utility can vary according to whose they are and where they are used. Note that this *soft uncertainty* does not make the concept of utility unreal. Two products in a shop or two meals in a restaurant may be the same price, but you and I might have different views about which we preferred. When we consider the commercial effects of our choices, we can see that soft aspects of systems can still have very hard effects. We shall say more about the utility of outcomes later in this section, and in Chapter 4 when we consider the subject of *risk.*

Once we have the utilities of the various outcomes we need a *strategy or policy for choice.* For deterministic problems this is normally a trivial question: we wish to maximize utility or minimize disutility. However this may not be as obvious in practice as it may seem. If we decide that our measure of disutility is stockholding costs, then minimizing stockholding costs looks like making the obvious decision of choosing the course of action that the model says will lead to the least cost outcome. However this may not be so obvious if we have a real-life business like Carry-Out Cupboards which stocks hundreds of items. In that situation literally millions of different combinations of stock levels for the different products could result in the same overall cost. Unless we are able to keep the stock levels of every product exactly at its ideal minimum or optimum level, we are left with choosing between millions of supposedly 'equal cost' *sub-optimum* solutions. What we are discovering in this situation is that individual measures of utility are seldom additive. To put this last statement in a form we are familiar with: *the whole is more than the sum of the parts;* i.e. utility at any level of a systems hierarchy is a *holist* concept.

Decision theory can only solve part of our management problem therefore. It tells us how to build a model of the decision-making problem. This model shows us what *information* we need to make decisions by choosing between *evaluated* outcomes using a decision *strategy.* But our systems view of management also tells us that we need to clarify what components of the systems hierarchy can deliver these different kinds of information. Clarifying our concept of *control* later in this chapter will be our first step towards this, and Chapter 6 will place this concept in an organizational and business context.

Decision-making under conditions of risk

We saw that problems with an element of *risk* are those where a choice of action can have two or more possible outcomes. For these types of problem we again need information on the *relationship between the choices of action and the possible outcomes* in order to model the problem, a means of *evaluating the outcomes,* and a *strategy* for choice. Since there is no longer a single determined connexion between choice of action and outcome however, we need one additional form of information for decision-making under conditions of risk. This information will enable us to indicate how likely the various outcomes will be once we have chosen a course of action. We do this by describing the links between choice of action and outcome in terms of *probabilities,* and such links are called *stochastic.*

Probability is normally expressed as a numerical value between 0 and 1. If a particular outcome has a probability of 0, it will never happen; if it has a probability of 1 it is certain to happen. The fractional values between 0 and 1 then represent increasing levels of certainty. Thus a probability of 0.5 means that an outcome has an equal chance of happening or not. In everyday life we call this level of certainty 'fifty-fifty', meaning it has a fifty per cent chance of happening. Indeed, probabilities are often popularly expressed as percentages between 0–100% rather than as fractions between 0 and 1. However, the fractional scale makes calculations easier and is more mathematically 'respectable', so we will use it.

This is not a book about probability and statistics, but it is worth noting certain basic points about probability as a concept, in addition to understanding how probability is numerically expressed. Our justification for this in a book about information systems in business is that *information* about probability plays an important part in management and decision-making, and modern computer-based information systems, particularly in the form of databases, now make the provision of such information much more possible than it was in the recent past.

We can therefore consider three views of the concept of probability:

1. *A priori* or *rational*
2. *Empirical*
3. *Subjective.*

A priori or *rational* views of probability are appropriate where we understand the link between a choice and its possible outcomes, so that we are able to model the *process* that connects them. Thus if we toss a coin, we not only know that it has two faces that can give us a head or a tail as outcomes, we also know that it is symmetrical and evenly balanced. This knowledge enables us to understand how it will spin regularly as it falls and make the outcomes of head or tail equally likely. The probabilities of 0.5 for the outcomes can be reasoned ('rational') in advance ('a priori') because we understand the process which connects them to our choice of action.

Empirical views are appropriate where we do not understand the process that connects choice of action and outcome, but we do have *past experience* of the results of our choices. In these situations the process which connects *input* choices to the outcomes which are its *output* is a *black box*. (The term *black box* is generally used in systems thinking to describe a process that we do not understand, but one where we can observe which inputs produce which outputs.) Thus, like the the East Farthing Drainage Authority, I do not come anywhere near understanding the complex weather machine which operates in the part of Britain where I live. What I do know from past experience, however, is that if they were to schedule outdoor excavation activities for next February 11th in my area, there is a 0.4 probability of being delayed by snow. My figure of 0.4 is based on past years' data for February 11th showing significant snow occurring 40% of the time. Note that empirical probability uses the past *proportion* that an outcome has occurred as an indicator of its future probability.

Subjective views are appropriate where we neither understand the process linking choice of action to its possible outcomes, nor do we have any past experience enabling us to form an empirical estimate. In such a situation any statement of probability is a statement of *belief* or *opinion*. Before Black Wednesday, assessing the probability of whether the £ would remain in the Exchange Rate Mechanism could only have been done on a subjective basis. The workings of international currency speculation were too complex to fully understand and there was no previous experience of the same 'black box' process from which we could get data.

If we consider the views of probability most likely to be useful for management, then *empirical* and *subjective* views are the best candidates. Simple processes like coin tossing, dice rolling or the collecting of coloured balls from urns are popular in mathematical texts concerned mainly with *a priori* probabilities, but organizational or business problems are usually more complex. In particular, the presence of human beings and their behaviour brings in *soft issues* which reduce the potential for clear *a priori* rationality.

The need for and use of empirical and subjective views of probability has important practical implications for the role and design of information systems. We will consider these further later in this chapter and in Chapter 4. For the moment let us see the role of probability in decision-making under conditions of risk.

Figure 3.6 illustrates a simple decision problem for the the East Farthing Drainage Authority. As the case in Appendix 2 shows, the government has encouraged them to bid for additional private work where they might use their specialist equipment and skills. Just recently an opportunity has come up where they could earn an estimated £100 000 profit if they landed a particular contract. Their chance of success however depends on whether they are prepared spend £10 000 on a detailed promotion of their bid.

Figure 3.6 summarizes this situation in terms of the general model of Fig 3.5. The choices of action are to promote their bid or not. The possible outcomes are to gain the contract or not. The values of each outcome, given the choice of action, are shown in the table. (For example, if they promote and then gain the contract, it's worth £100 000 less the £10 000 promotion cost = £90 000...etc.)

However the table in Fig 3.6 does not contain all the information needed by the East Farthing Drainage Authority to make their decision. They need to know what differences there are in the chances of them gaining the contract according to whether they spend the £10 000 on promotion. Figure 3.7 shows some subjective probabilities estimated by those responsible for the decision. Essentially they believe that they have a fifty-fifty chance of getting the contract with promotion but only one in ten if they don't promote. With this information it is possible to calculate an *expected value* for each choice that averages out the values of the outcomes against the probability that they will occur.

		Outcome	
		Gain contract	Lose contract
Choice of action	Promote bid	+ £90 000	− £10 000
	Do not promote bid	+ £100 000	£0

Fig 3.6 The East Farthing Drainage Authority Contract Bid: Value of Outcomes
The possible choices, the outcomes, and the figures for the values of the outcomes, have been kept simple for learning purposes. The important point of principle is that both choices and outcomes are mutually exclusive, i.e. distinct; and mutually exhaustive, i.e. cover all possibilities.

	Gain contract	Lose contract
Promote bid	$p = 0.5$	$p = 0.5$
Do not promote bid	$p = 0.1$	$p = 0.9$

Fig 3.7 The East Farthing Drainage Authority Contract Bid: Probability of Outcomes
What probability values are intended to show, and how they are determined, depend on what view is taken of the concept of probability. *See* section 3.2.1.

Thus choosing to promote averages out as:

> Half a chance of £90 000 gain + half a chance of losing £10 000
> = (0.5 × £90 000) + (0.5 × –£10 000)
> = £45 000 – £5000
> = £40 000 expected value.

whereas choosing not to promote works out as:

> One in ten chance of £100 000 + nine out of ten chance of £nil
> = (0.1 × £100 000) + (0.9 × £0)
> = £10 000 expected value.

If the the East Farthing Drainage Authority were to take straight monetary value as their measure of utility, then they'd go for the promotion choice. But what if they felt the subjective probabilities were just too woolly? One answer is to abandon any attempt to pretend they can be estimated. If this position is taken, then the problem becomes one of decision-making under conditions of uncertainty, which we consider next.

Decision-making under conditions of uncertainty

Conditions of uncertainty are those where the possible outcomes resulting from each choice of action are not necessarily known, and in any case we cannot assign probabilities to them.

Where all the possible outcomes are not known we can still model the problem in terms of Fig 3.5 by listing the outcomes we do know and then adding a final general outcome that stands for all the remaining possibilities. Thus in Fig 3.6 the East Farthing Drainage Authority could consider that there might be some compromise or delay over the awarding of the contract, rather than a straight outcome of gaining or losing it. In this case they would add a third outcome called 'other' or something similar. Such a level of uncertainty usually makes a formal approach like the model of Fig 3.5 of only limited value. A better approach would normally be to investigate the problem in more depth to reduce the uncertainties. If the uncertainties were soft in origin, then an approach like the *soft systems methodology* of Chapter 7 would be more appropriate.

The model of Fig 3.5 is still useful when we know the outcomes but lack any confidence about assigning probabilities. This would be the case in Fig 3.6 if we felt the probabilities of Fig 3.7 not very useful. In such cases we again need information on the *relationship between the choices of action and the possible outcomes* in order to *model* the problem and a means of *evaluating the outcomes*, but we need a new view of strategy for choice. There are several different strategies of choice possible for conditions of uncertainty, see Luce & Raiffa (1957). We will consider the example of the maximin strategy as an illustration.

A *maximin strategy* is one where our aim is to choose the decision which has the *maximum* utility *minimum* outcome. In less formal terms, we could describe this as the choice of action whose worst outcome is least bad. Consider Fig 3.6. If the East Farthing Drainage Authority chooses to promote, it could end up, at worst, losing £10 000. If it did not promote, the worst would be losing the contract but losing no money either. If the strategy is to choose the action with *maximum* minimum outcome, then not promoting is the choice to make.

It is worth noting that this strategy gave a different result from assigning probabilities to outcomes in an attempt to maximize expected utility. There is no way *before* the outcome of its decision that the East Farthing Drainage Authority can know which method is best. Even after the outcome, there is no guarantee that the next decision they face will be similar. What this simple example illustrates is that decision-making requires *different* kinds of information for the *different* needs of problem formulation, model construction and the derivation of solutions from them. We now need some way of understanding how these different forms of information relate to the different kinds of functional components we find in an organization or business when we view it as a *system*. Chapter 6 will be entirely devoted to looking at organizations and businesses as systems in this way. Meanwhile, as Fig 3.4 shows, it is the concept of a control system that enables us to make the link between *management* and *information*.

We shall study the concept of a control system next, but we will return to decision-making in Chapter 4 after we have built up our understanding of information in the context of management.

3.2.2 The classical control systems model

Control as a concept

The term *control* represents a central concept in this book. We will begin in this section by explaining a generally accepted basic view of the concept. In subsequent sections I would like to develop a more complex view of my own for use in an organization or business information systems context. Although this is an individual view *overall*, I will show that each of its components are either closely related or identical to other established views.

Throughout this book it will be *essential* to recognize that the term *control* refers to a *concept* and *not a particular way of doing things or a management style*. In popular use, the word control, and the related concept of hierarchy, are used to imply a rather rigid, authoritarian approach to management. In this simplistic, stereotyped use of the word, 'management' is seen as 'the boss' which exerts 'control' by 'giving orders' which employees have to 'obey'. I think that this stereotype is dangerous for two reasons. First it fails to recognize the rich choice of ways in which control may be exerted, including ones with little trace of the stereotype. Second, an assumption that 'orders' or 'obedience' are *always* wrong seems as bigoted as the stereotype which such an assumption wishes to condemn.

Figure 3.4 has led us to anticipate that the concept of control is the link between the concepts of information and management through a systems hierarchy. In this hierarchical structure, an information system can be seen as a subsystem of a control system, and a control system as a subsystem of a management system. To understand control as a component of management and as a concept rather than a management style, consider the Ecology Group in the East Farthing Drainage Authority case.

The Ecology Group has no one in its membership called a *manager*. It is a voluntary, egalitarian group whose hierarchy in the everyday sense is limited to having the usual elected secretary and treasurer you find in most societies. Anybody who tried to be 'boss' would soon be told where to go.

Despite the differences between the Ecology Group and a commercial business organization like Carry-Out Cupboards, I think it is possible to assert that the Ecology Group is very effectively managed, and that its members have a very clear concept of what management involves.

If 'management is an activity aimed at achieving something desirable', as we stated above, then the group is certainly very actively managed. They have clear ideas of what things they think are 'desirable' for the ecology of the East Farthing and they act positively in trying to 'achieve' them. They show themselves as meliorists by the fact that they thought it was worth getting together, forming the group, turning up to meetings, producing their magazine, campaigning, and all the other activities which were aimed at 'achieving something desirable'.

The whole of this successful attempt at management by the Ecology Group can be seen as a complex system with various components like a human subsystem, a financial subsystem, etc.

However, at the centre of this management system are those activities directly concerned with trying to make sure that the group achieves its ecological aims. These activities would include:

> *a.* Identifying which areas of ecological interest which the group wishes to influence.
> *b.* Agreeing what the group is trying to achieve in these areas.
> *c.* Identifying potential disturbances and threats to their areas of interest.
> *d.* Making sure they get to know about what is happening in their areas of interest.
> *e.* Communicating what is happening to all the members.
> *f.* Checking what is actually happening against the view the group has about what should happen.
> *g.* Having decided and agreed what should be done in the way of lobbying, meetings, etc., putting these decisions into effect.

These components at the centre of the group's management activities make up an identifiable subsystem which we shall see as an example of a control system. It is also worth noting that many of the components are concerned with the *communication* of *information*. So we would rightly expect to find some form of information system as a further subsystem of the control system.

We will now identify and explain the components of a control system. The particular model I shall use is that of *closed-loop* control with *negative feedback* which I will call the classical model. There are other forms of control model, but this form is widely found in management, as well as in subject areas ranging from engineering to biology. (The terms *closed-loop* and *negative feedback* will be explained at the end of this section.)

Figure 3.8 shows the essential components of the classical model, and Fig 3.9 shows how this might be interpreted in terms of the specific example of stock control. This example can be linked in turn to Fig 3.2 and the control of stock at Carry-Out Cupboards.

Transformation process

The first component of any control system must be something that needs controlling, which will be some form of *transformation process*. In our stock example this will be the process of receiving stock, responding to orders and safely retaining unsold stock ready for when it is needed. We might call this the 'stockholding process' as in Fig 3.9.

As we saw in section 3.1.5, we are only aware of a process if we can detect some change or *transformation* that it carries out. *Inputs* have to be transformed into detectably different *outputs*. Stockholding as a process will transform an existing set of stock conditions to a new one as a result of its actions in receiving and issuing stock. In particular, as in Fig 3.2 these conditions would include the amount in stock, allocated and on order.

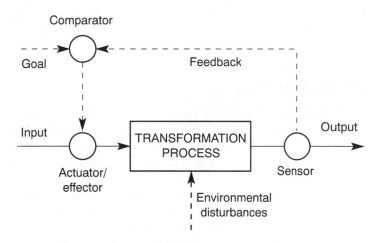

Fig 3.8 The Classical Control Model
This title ought not to imply that this is the only form of a control model. Two features should be noted. First, the model assumes *feedback*, rather than *feedforward*, control. Second, the feedback is assumed to have a *negative* rather than a *positive* effect on the way that the actuator is instructed.

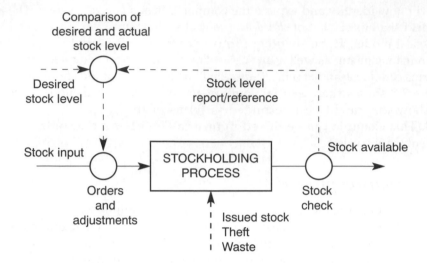

Fig 3.9 Stock Control
The stockholding process is disturbed by customer demand, theft, loss and depreciation. Inputs to the process are adjusted to turn the stock available towards the goal of a desired stock level.

Goals

We have already explored the concept of goals in detail in the previous section. It is important to note that according to Fig 3.8, goals are not actually a *component* of the classical model. Instead they are seen as something that comes from the outside and are used by it. *Where* goals come from, we will explore in the next section. For the moment we note that the goals of stockholding might include maintaining stock levels within a desired range.

Environmental disturbances

We saw that real-life systems have an *environment* that disturbs them and on which they can have only limited effect. In fact, *the existence of environmental disturbances is the only reason we need control at all.* If our stockholding process could be set running in the confidence that nothing would ever happen to disturb it, we could set it up and leave it to run itself.

In practice no such conditions exist. Real-life systems always have environments which disturb their processes and we need control to try and bring them back towards our goals. The stockholding process will be disturbed by such environmental factors as customer orders, theft and damage. Any attempt to predict or affect these will never be completely successful. In practice we cannot tell customers what they must buy and when they must buy it. Despite security and care, thefts and damage can happen. A real system has to live in such a world and cope with it. Hence the need for control.

It is important to note that the model distinguishes inputs from the environment like customer orders which are outside our control, and inputs like orders on suppliers which are in our control because we initiate them.

Sensor

So far we see the model in terms of a process which is being disturbed by the environment and we want to keep turning the output of the process back towards our goals. For a stockholding process we want the stock available to be within certain desired levels. This view assumes however that we know what amount of stock is actually available. We need some way of checking this information. In practice this will be done by someone looking, counting and recording the figure. It might be done using a bar code reader or simply by making a mental note. The important point is that there has to be some form of *sensor* which records the output from the process.

Feedback

Recording the output from a process is a waste of time if we do nothing with it. Our motive for having some form of sensor is that the information which it gathers can be used to help make the process achieve its goals. If the sensor in our stockholding example finds that the stock available is below the reorder level, that information needs to be *communicated* to the person or department responsible for deciding when to reorder stock. Communicating sensed information for such a purpose is called *feedback*. In practice this could be anything from one person telling another to the formal passage of a document.

Comparator

In our stockholding example we see feedback as communicating information about the stock available output from the process we wish to control 'to the person or department responsible for deciding when to reorder stock'. Their job is then to *compare* the value of the output from the process, which is amount of stock available, with the goal of maintaining stock levels within a desired range. The word 'compare' is used to explain why this component is called the *comparator*.

It is also worth noting that the comparator works by *processing information*. This is an important point which is the beginning to our understanding of the relationship between management, control and information outlined in Fig 3.4. We will develop this further later in this section. Meanwhile, in the stockholding example, comparison is carried out using information about the output of the process and information about the control systems goals. The *output* from this information processing is a decision about whether to reorder stock, and if so, how much.

Actuator/effector

The comparator delivers information on what must be done to turn back the process output towards where we would like it to be, as expressed by our goals. This information is translated into action by the *actuator* or *effector* which initiates or adjusts inputs to the process in a way which it anticipates will have the desired corrective effect. Thus for our stockholding example, the actuator would consist of the reordering function which organizes the delivery of replenishment stock.

Other forms of control system

I called the control model we have just described, the *classical control model*. This is a term of my own which I've used for convenience. We noted however that it would strictly be called *closed-loop control with negative feedback*.

It is called *closed-loop* control because information gathered by the sensor is fed back to the comparator which in turn passes information on to the actuator. The information flow path from sensor to actuator can be seen as a *closed loop*.

Another form of control is *open-loop* or *feedforward* control. This occurs where the actuator controls the inputs to the process but does not monitor the outputs or subsequent state of the process through sensing and feedback. Such control is only likely to result in the outputs we desire if either:

    a. There are no significant subsequent environmental disturbances to the process, or
    b. We can predict the disturbances accurately and allow for them.

Condition *a* is not likely to be relevant to any but the simplest mechanical system. As we saw in section 3.1.7, management systems have environments which disturb them. Condition *b* is only likely to apply where the workings of both the process and its environment are fully understood and therefore predictable. Again, real-life management systems are unlikely to be in such a context, particularly given the presence of *human* activity systems with their accompanying *soft uncertainty*.

Negative feedback is so called because the feedback loop works to *reverse* the effect of any environmental disturbance. Thus when customer demand reduces stock levels below the desired range, the effect of the feedback loop is to push them up again through replenishing stock. Generally, negative feedback control has the effect of keeping process outputs fluctuating about the level as in Fig 3.10.

Another form of feedback, known as *positive feedback*, has the effect of making the process *follow* the direction of the environmental disturbance. An example of this

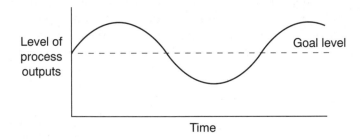

Fig 3.10 The Behaviour of Process Outputs from the Classical Control Model

The wave-like swing of the outputs in the diagram is intended to illustrate the principle of oscillation about a desired, or *goal*, level. Each real-life example of the model will have its own pattern. The important point is that negative feedback should result in the outputs being continually returned towards the goal.

might be the effect of investment on the profits of a firm. Greater profits can lead to greater investment in the firm, which leads to greater profits, and so on. Similarly, low profits could lead to less investment which would lead to less profits. What we notice from both these examples of positive feedback is that it has a *destabilizing* effect on a process and is therefore normally *undesirable*. This contrasts with the popular use of the term 'positive feedback' as something 'nice'. Since positive feedback is undesirable, we would not seek to have it in a management control system.

◆ **STQ 3.9**

What was a very dramatic example of positive feedback on Black Monday?

The information systems component of the classical control system

Our study of the classical control model shows the first of several links in the hierarchical structure of Fig 3.4, in which an information system can be seen as a subsystem of a control system, and a control system as a subsystem of a management system. If we now consider the classical control model of Fig 3.8 in terms of *information*, we find three types of information are used by the model:

1 Information about *environmental disturbances.* For our stockholding example this would include information about customer orders, theft or damage.

2 Information about the *state of the process* being controlled, in the form of its *outputs*. For our stockholding example this would include information about amounts in stock, allocated and on order.

3 Information about the *goals* which the process being controlled should attempt to achieve. For our stockholding example this would include information about desired stock levels reflected by the values of the reorder level and the reorder quantity.

We also noted that information has to be recorded by the sensor, processed by the comparator, and communicated along a path through feedback from the sensor to the actuator. All of the activities by components of the control system which are concerned with information can be seen as making up a *subsystem* within the control system itself. Figure 3.11 shows what this *subsystem* does in the context of the classical control model. Since it is exclusively concerned with *processing information*, it seems sensible to call it an *information system*. The question then comes: is it the *information system* referred to in the title of this book and used by management to control an organization or business?

The answer to this question becomes clearer if we consider the role of information about goals as shown in Fig 3.11. This shows that our explanation of the classical control model so far tells us nothing about where the information about goals comes from. Figure 3.11 therefore shows us partly what an information system does, but a complete view of an information system must also explain *goal-setting*. We will consider this next.

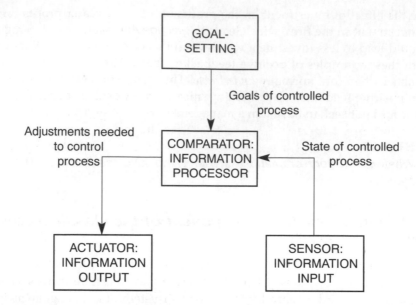

Fig 3.11 The Role of the Information System as a Component of the Control System

The main processes carried out by the information system in the context of Fig 3.4.

3.2.3 Control systems hierarchy

The role of goal-setting

When we considered the nature of goals in section 3.2.1 we used the Monetary Union mini-case to illustrate many of the points. There was one important point which went by unmentioned, yet it was at the centre of the dramatic events of that day. After spending over a billion pounds supporting the currency, the British government *changed their mind* and gave up trying to maintain the £ within the Exchange Rate Mechanism. In changing their mind, they were *changing their goals*.

In practice, changing goals isn't confined to dramatic situations like Black Wednesday. Nor is goal-changing necessarily a sign of 'failure' as it might have been seen in the Black Wednesday case. If in hot weather I try to keep cool and in cold weather I try to keep warm, I think few of us would see this change of goal as 'failure' or 'inconsistency'. So with the management of organizations and businesses: goals have to be changed to reflect changes in the environment. Changes in the economy, the market or in legislation can all mean that goals have to be modified.

Even if the environment does not significantly change, there may still be good reasons for changing goals. There were some opinions at the time of Black Wednesday that it was not the goal of ERM membership that needed changing, but just the exchange rate within it. We could imagine that although the market for a particular Carry-Out Cupboards product had not changed, the original sales target goals may have been badly estimated.

◆ **STQ 3.10**
How are goals set for the East Farthing Drainage Authority?

Goal-setting may therefore range from minor modifications to goals to complete changes in direction. What all practical goal-setting has in common is that it takes account of how well the the control system performed with a particular set of goals. In the light of this experience, the goals may be then left unchanged, modified, or completely altered. Just as classical control modifies the inputs to a process to keep it moving towards its goals, so goal-setting modifies the actual form of the goals to keep them relevant to the wider aims of management.

Box 3.2

FAMINE OF DIGITS

(Financial Times 6/8/96)

Telephone numbers sounded like old friends in the days when detectives at country house murders would say: 'Operator, get me Fambridge 2323'. But country exchanges have long since been swallowed up in a blizzard of digits.

Digits proliferated as automatic exchanges and computers drove down costs, creating an explosion of demand for more telephones, more services and now for mobile phones.

As a result the UK is running out of telephone numbers. To remedy all this, all UK numbers were changed on 'Phone Day' in 1995 by the addition of an extra digit. Little more than a year later, Oftel, the telecommunications regulator, is proposing another complete set of number changes. . . Customers, who will be required to change their lists, databases and stationery a second time, may justifiably ask why. . .

COMMENT

Are we really still surprised by the effects of environmental disturbances on a control system? It is 2500 years since Heraclites said that no man steps in the same river twice. Yet here is another industry-political-media skirmish over the issue of *goal-setting*.

The General Control Model of Fig 3.14 shows that goal-setting involves several levels of control. *Normative goal-setting* involves values or principles: this might be relevant if changing telephone codes raised a moral issue. *Reflective goal-setting* involves choosing a method: yet the method of using dialling codes will not be changed. *Automatic goal-setting* is occurring however, since the *goals/standards*, in the form of particular numerical codes, are to be changed.

Two control issues are therefore raised by the case. The first is one of processing the results of *feedback* to modify goals appropriately: how far should changes in goals reflect the views of the users? The second issue is one of the *costs of control*: does the frequency of changing goals optimize costs for all of those involved, not just one particular group?

Then comes *forecasting* – the supposed 'IT revolution'. This supposed revolution has not always implemented the practical implications of its message. Perhaps there is an industrial revolution analogy. The relationship between the power of industrial production and methods of transport could be being replayed in a different form.

Petrol/diesel-driven road transport reduced the importance of steam-driven railways which had reduced the importance of horse-pulled canal barges. It's hard to imagine that our copper wires or satellites will be as important in fifty years as now.

FURTHER STUDY

Compare the control systems issues raised here, with stock control goal-setting at Carry-Out Cupboards. Aren't managers frequently dealing with the 'revolutionary' or the 'unexpected'? Perhaps the problems associated with these higher levels of control in management should always be part of the normal control system. Consider how an organization familiar to you last dealt with dramatic changes in its environment? Was the management system equipped for surprise?

We can therefore regard goal-setting as itself a control system, with similar components to that of the classical control model. Where the classical model sought to control a process by modifying its inputs through an actuator in the light of feedback on the process performance, so goal-setting control modifies the *goal inputs* to the classical control model in the light of its performance.

Figure 3.12 summarizes in a simple way this concept of goal-setting being an additional control system acting 'in addition' to the classical control model. These two forms of control can be seen as two components or subsystems of a greater whole. The control of the classical model is *goal-seeking* or *first-order control*, which takes its goals from a *higher-order, goal-setting control*.

This concept of *orders* or *levels* of control can be extended. We said above that 'goal-setting modifies the actual form of the goals to keep them relevant to the wider aims of management'. If we consider this statement, we can see that it implies that there are higher-level standards or 'aims' that enable us to decide which goals to choose. Thus decisions about such goals as exchange rates or stock levels have to be made against higher aims like maintaining Britain's solvency or the profitability of Carry-Out Cupboards. We can conceive that goal-setting itself has to have goals, and that above goal-setting will be another control system which sets the goals for goal-setting. Presumably we could then conceive a control system that sets the goals for the control system that sets the goals for goal-setting: and so on *ad infinitum!*

How therefore can we avoid a model of control which does not result in an endless hierarchy of orders of control? In the next section of this chapter I aim to present my own view of this in the form of a general control model (GCM). But as I noted at the beginning of the previous section, although this is an individual view *overall*, each of its components are either closely related or identical to other views. Two additional views are particularly worth considering to show how the reasoning behind the GCM fits into a wider picture:

1. Distinguishing *automatic* and *reflective* goal-changing, Schoderbeck et al. (1985).
2. The concepts of *operational, strategic* and *normative* levels of management. Ben-Eli (1988), used by author in Espejo & Harnden (1989).

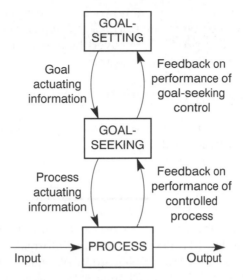

Fig 3.12 Control Systems Hierarchy
A goal-seeking system itself can be seen as a process. The goals for this process have therefore to come from somewhere. The concept of *goal-setting* implies a *hierarchy* of control systems in which each level of the hierarchy sets the goals of the subsystem process below it. The use of the word 'below' should not be seen as a judgement of the *value* of each level of the hierarchy in management terms.

Automatic and reflective goal-changing

We have already identified the concept of *goal-setting* as a *higher-order* component of a control system which is concerned with modifying or completely changing its goals. Reference to other well established views, as in Schoderbeck et al. (1985), shows that what we have called goal-setting may take two different forms. We have implied this in our previous discussion, but now we need to make it explicit. Schoderbeck et al. (1985) present the distinction between:

- *Second-order* or *automatic* goal-changing
- *Third-order* or *reflective* goal-changing

Second-order or *automatic* goal-changing control is possible where:

a. All the potential set of alternative environmental conditions has been identified.

b. The *method* of linking *courses of action* and *outcomes* is defined.

c. The system can *store information.*

Comparing conditions *a* and *b* with section 3.2.1 shows that automatic goal-changing is only going to be possible where all the components of our *decision model* have been defined in such a way that selecting a goal can be done by calculation or some other formal procedure or *method*.

An example of automatic goal-changing would be setting the reorder level for stock control as in Fig 3.2. As we saw in the Carry-Out Cupboards case, the reorder level is set so that the stockholding process can cover the maximum expected demand over the lead time. Thus for a weekly demand figure:

Reorder level = maximum weekly demand × lead time in weeks

If there is any change in the maximum demand or the lead time, the new reorder level goal can be automatically recalculated.

However, to know that a change has taken place in either of the values used in the calculation, the second-order goal-changing system has to *store information*. How else could a change in demand or delivery lead time be noticed if we did not keep sales figures or records of supplier performance? Here we can see something very important about the role of the information system as a component of the control system which goes further than Fig 3.11. Besides *processing* information in support of a control system, an information system must also store it. We shall look at this aspect in great detail later in the book, particularly in Chapter 5, but for the moment we can note it as building on our understanding of the relationship between management, control and information as in Fig 3.4.

◆ STQ 3.11

How can it be possible to know the maximum weekly demand for the formula above?

Third-order or *reflective* goal-changing involves more than the automatic application of a preset method or formula. Besides the ability to set goals using a *method* and *stored* information, third-order control requires the control system to *learn*, so that it can *choose* the appropriate method where the set of environmental conditions changes. Thus second-order control can adjust a reorder level for a stockholding process using a method and stored information, but what if the method itself becomes irrelevant? If Carry-Out Cupboards found there was no longer a market for a product and its weekly demand fell to zero, the reorder level formula above would be useless, even though it can produce a nonsense theoretical reorder level of zero. Similarly, if a country decided to leave the European Monetary System, any method of determining the value of its currency within the Exchange Rate Mechanism would become irrelevant.

Third-order or reflective goal-changing control will be possible where:

a There is a means of identifying, distinguishing, choosing and defining different methods or procedures, which we may call a *methodology*. This will be used to deliver to second-order control the appropriate method to be used, given the environmental conditions, including any change of method.

b Access is available to any *policies* on *soft issues* and higher aims required by the third-order control methodology to decide between methods of goal-setting.

We can develop the stockholding example to illustrate these two conditions. We saw above that second-order, automatic goal-changing control is only possible within the set of environmental conditions where we can apply the reorder level calculation method and only have to accommodate changes in demand or lead time. Where the sales of a product fall to zero or a new product is introduced, environmental conditions require a different method of dealing with stock levels. How do we decide when to discontinue stocking a particular item? Do we drop the price and have a sale to get rid of the remaining stock? How do we decide on the initial stock level and ordering for a new item? A wide range of answers is possible to these and other questions we might ask. What third-order control needs is an understanding of the choices of method available to cope with these problems and a set of principles to help choose between them. We shall call the subject which studies method in this way *methodology*, and note also that the existence of methodology implies that our experience of choosing and applying methods leads to a *learning process*.

Methodology on its own is not enough to enable a choice of method to be made however. Different methods carry their own assumptions about *values* or *soft issues*: behind any method there is an implied *weltanschauung* or *world view*. Thus the reorder level method of stock control assumes that we do not want to run out of stock and dissatisfy the customer and the reorder quantity will be set to minimize stockholding costs. A decision to discontinue a stock item carries with it certain assumptions about how important we think it is to continue to satisfy a minority demand. Choosing a method therefore also requires *policies* on *soft issues* and higher aims for a methodology to be applied.

The concepts of second- and third-order control therefore help us to enrich our view of control and the different forms of information it uses. Our model is still incomplete however. We are left with a need to include the role of information on weltanschauung or world view in our model of a control system and to say more about the concept of learning.

Operational, strategic and normative levels of management

Before we look at these three levels of management, I would like to check what we are *not* talking about. The picture of levels of management with 'strategic' at the top of some hierarchical pyramid, 'tactical' at a middle level, and 'operational' at the bottom, is a standard cliché to be found in some form in many books on management: e.g. Gorry & Scott Morton (1971) quoted in Davis & Olson (1984). Such a view, often with an accompanying pyramidical diagram, paints a picture of 'top management' thinking great strategic thoughts, whilst the lowest level just does what it is told and carries out 'operations'. Going along with this stereotype is likely to be some assertion that the different levels of management use different kinds of information and information systems.

In real organizations and businesses it seldom works like that. So-called top management often spends much of its time engrossed in the fire-fighting of day-to-day operational crises, and middle management plot and scheme in a way that has major effects on strategy. As to the information used by management, much strategic information flows between 'operational' staff in the company's restaurant, and a lot of tactical information is exchanged between 'top executives' in the washroom.

What the traditional, pyramid cliché gets wrong is not its recognition of the existence of strategy, tactics and operations. Rather it confuses the *whats* and *hows* of the three levels. Whilst there are levels of management, the 'management' referred to is *what* is done, not necessarily *who* does it or *how* it is done. If we concentrate on the conceptual whats of management, we do not have to get trapped into an artificial view of individual managers falling exclusively into particular categories and only being concerned with certain separate and disconnected forms of information system. We shall cover this concept in detail in Chapter 6, but for the moment we note that 'levels of management' refers to the processes of management, not a particular organizational structure, set of people, or method of doing things.

If we can build up a conceptual, *systems* view of what is involved at different levels of management, we can use this as a means of building on our view of what is done by different levels of control, since we see control as a component of management as in Fig 3.4.

For an example of such a modern systems view, I have chosen Ben-Eli (1988). He puts forward the concept of levels of management shown in Fig 3.13. Of these levels he says the pertinent point is that approaching problems that are related to each such level requires a '*different conceptual orientation*' and '*information aggregated at different levels of detail*'. In terms of the systems view presented in this chapter, two words from this quotation are significant: they are the words *conceptual* and *aggregated*.

The use of the word *conceptual* shows that he is focussing, like us, on the whats of management rather than the *hows*. The use of the word *aggregated* makes a clear link with our concepts of *hierarchy* and *emergent property*. As we said in section 3.1.7: 'our systems view of hierarchy is different from this (the traditional view) since we see it in terms of levels of aggregation associated with emergent properties'.

What management does at any level according to Ben-Eli, and the information it uses, can therefore be seen by us in terms of the *emergent properties* associated with the

Fig 3.13 Levels of Mangement/Planning according to Ben-Eli (1988)
This is my interpretation of the original diagram in the reference quoted.
Espejo & Harnden (1989) should also be referred to.

various levels of control which management exerts. We can therefore consider how his hierarchical view of management might enrich our model of control. Ben-Eli's levels of management are:

- Normative
- Strategic
- Operational.

Normative levels of management are concerned with forming policy and deciding how an organization should react to decisions on change and adaptability in the face of environmental disturbances. These activities imply the concept of an 'institutional mission' which is reflected in policies and commitment. The case used by Ben-Eli was a medical centre. When questions about the purpose of the centre were asked, it was first thought that the answers to the questions were obvious and had little practical management value. In fact, more detailed investigation showed big differences in views. Until these differences were resolved, 'practical' management of programme priorities and resource allocation was difficult and limited.

Strategic levels of management are concerned with integrating and coordinating the many activities of an organization so that the behaviour of the whole is optimized and its *overall* direction is consistent with policies formed at the normative level.

Operational levels of management then implement activities according to plans which have been coordinated at the strategic level.

Given these views of what the different levels do, what differences do we see between them in terms of *'different conceptual orientation'* and *'information aggregated at different levels of detail'*?

A *norm* is a standard or a criterion against which something is judged. We can therefore see why Ben-Eli describes the highest level of management which decides purpose and policy as normative. In the Monetary Union mini-case, decisions about exchange rates could only be made *after* decisions about the wider issues of Britain's attitude to European integration and membership of the Exchange Rate Mechanism.

However, the Black Wednesday example takes us further in understanding the difference between normative decisions and those which follow them. Whether Britain should become more closely integrated with Europe is not just a technical question of finance and economics. It raises strong emotional and other *soft* issues. Besides the disputes about facts and figures or ways of doing things, there are differences of *weltanschauung* or *world view*. These latter differences have to be resolved before any decision on purpose, policy or norms.

Once norms have been decided, it is possible to determine a *strategy* whose goal is to make sure that the overall direction is consistent with policies formed at the normative level. Thus if it is decided that Britain should participate in European integration, then operating outside the Exchange Rate Mechanism would be seen as the best method available at a particular point in time and under particular conditions. At some future time, with a *changed environment*, rejoining the Exchange Rate Mechanism or negotiating a new arrangement might be more appropriate. Thus strategy involves *choosing the appropriate method of operation*, given the environmental conditions, which is in line with our policy or purpose.

Once the method of operation has been chosen, then *operational* management is concerned to see that it is correctly carried out. Whilst in the Exchange Rate Mechanism, the British government was required to adjust interest rates and purchase sterling in a way that maintained the £ within certain exchange rates. When the £ was withdrawn from the Exchange Rate Mechanism, the method of operation was less interventionist and interest rates could be lowered. Thus operational management is mainly concerned with hard, technical decisions which involve logic and numbers.

The need for fourth-order control

If we now consider what Ben-Eli's three levels of management do in terms of *control*, we can see close links with the classical model and the concepts of second- and third-order control which we have discussed so far.

Operational management is concerned with using a particular method to achieve goals which have been set for it. Thus if a decision has been made to maintain a currency at certain values by adjusting interest rates, then interest rates are raised in response to excessive falls in value, and lowered in response to excessive rises. In this example the value of the currency can be seen as a goal and adjusting interest rates as an actuator adjusting the *inputs* to the exchange rate *process*. Hence operational management is principally concerned with *first-order control*.

Strategic management has to choose what method or mix of methods should be operated and appropriate goals for them. Thus decisions had to be made about whether to maintain the £ in the Exchange Rate Mechanism, and if so, what mechanisms should be used to support it. When this no longer looked like the best way to operate, then decisions had to be made about when to withdraw and what new goals and ways of operating were appropriate. Hence strategic management is concerned with similar processes to those of automatic and reflective goal-setting which we saw making up *second-* and *third-order control*.

It would not be difficult thus far to closely relate our exploration of levels of control and Ben-Eli's concept of levels of management. A further element comes into our discussion however when we consider the normative level. As we saw above, normative management processes require the resolution of *weltanschauung* or *world views*. As we also saw when discussing second- and third-order control, our model was incomplete because we were 'left with a need to include the role of information on weltanschauung or world view'.

Our exploration of management and control therefore leaves us with the recognition that the highest process in the control hierarchy will be concerned with deciding purpose and policy in the context of a stance on weltanschauung or world view. I shall call the process that does this *fourth-order control*. In the next section we will see how all our discussion on control can be brought together as a general model.

3.2.4 GCM: the General Control Model

Introduction to the General Control Model (GCM)

Figure 3.14 shows my model of a control system in the context of management as summarized by Fig 3.4. Although the *whole* of the GCM in Fig 3.14 is a personal view, I think that all of its features and components come directly from the widely used systems thinking and concepts discussed so far in this chapter. Since it is intended to cater for the issues we have raised about the nature of management and its relationship with information and control, I will explain its overall structure and then look at the details of some of its components.

The model in Fig 3.14 shows:

- The *control system* itself
- The control system's *environment*.

The *control system* consists of three components:

1 The *process* which is being controlled. This is the component which represents the same concept as that we have referred to throughout this chapter, as exemplified by the stockholding process, Exchange Rate Mechanism and other examples. The process transforms *inputs* into *outputs* and is *disturbed* by the environment.

2 *Goal-seeking control* which aims to control the process so that its outputs conform to the goals of the whole system. Again this component is the same concept that we encountered in the classical control model. Goal-seeking control uses a *sensor* to *assess the process outputs; feedback* of this assessment is used by the *comparator* to determine the deviation from the system's *goals*, and to determine what changes to the *inputs* to the process need to be made by the *actuator* to bring the process back on course.

3 *Goal-setting control* which sets the goals for goal-seeking control and modifies them in the light of *feedback* on the goal-seeking control system's performance. This overall concept is one we have already discussed, and would be represented by our previous examples of changing currency exchange rates or stockholding reorder levels. What is new about the GCM in Fig 3.14 however is that the goal-setting control is itself seen as a subsystem consisting of the three components *second-*, *third-* and *fourth-order* control. These additions to the classical model have been made to accommodate the other issues raised when we considered the concepts of *automatic* and *reflective goal-changing*, and *levels of management*. Since these aspects of the GCM are new, we will look at them individually below.

The control system's *environment* consists of four components:

1. The *source* of *inputs* to the process which is being controlled.
2. The *destination* for *outputs* from the process which is being controlled.
3. The *source* of *disturbances* to the process which is being controlled.
4. The *source* of the *weltanschauung* or world view being used by the control system.

The first three components are those we already know from the classical control model. The fourth component takes account of the need to identify how the *soft* issues relating to control are to be resolved. These range from specific issues such as *utility* or *subjective probability* raised in our discussion of decision theory in section 3.2.1, to a more general issues *policy* which we introduced in section 3.2.3. The position taken on soft issues depends on the *weltanschauung* or *world view* which is assumed, and this in turn depends on *whose* concept of the system we are taking as our model.

The General Control Model of Fig 3.14 is therefore a development of the classical control model which takes into account the need to detail the processes of goal-setting

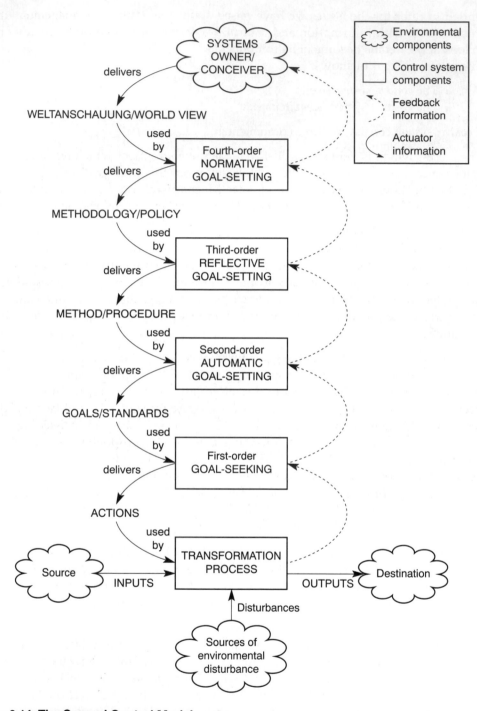

Fig 3.14 The General Control Model
This diagram epitomizes the approach I have taken to interpreting the role of information systems in business. As section 3.2.4 shows however, the General Control Model derives from a range of working views of control. The essential point is that the model is *conceptual*. It shows *what* goes on, rather than the *physical* implications of *how* things are done, *who* does them, or *where* they are done. Real-life applications are likely to be a mixture of the conceptual processes shown.

by identifying three additional levels of control, and the need to link this with the weltanschauung of the conceiver or owner of the system. Since these are further developments of the classical control model, we will look at them in more detail in the rest of this section. Before we do so however, there is one feature of the General Control Model which is relevant to all the levels shown.

Each level of control can be seen as carrying out similar processes in relation to the processes at levels immediately above and below it. This relationship is summarized in Fig 3.15. Generally, the process at level L uses feedback from level L – 1 and output from level L + 1, to set the input to level L – 1. All of these inputs and outputs are flows of *information,* which are processed and sometimes stored. Thus as we saw in section 3.2.2, defining the control model also defines the role of the *information system* as a component of the control system.

Goal-setting: second-order control

This lowest level of goal-setting represents the technical or hard component of the process of goal-setting. It compares feedback on the performance of the goal-seeking control system with the results of using the method set by third-level control to set the goals for goal-seeking control. The words hard and method are used here to show that second-order control processes work through the application of decision models, formulae or other formal procedures to produce hard goals that are used by first-order control. Given the defined, formal nature of these methods, second-order control can be seen as *automatic* goal-setting.

Our previous example of the stockholding example of section 3.2.3 can be used to illustrate the hard, automatic nature of this, the lowest level of goal-setting. In that, we saw that the goal of maintaining stocks within certain levels could be implemented by a reorder level calculated according to the formula:

Reorder level = maximum weekly demand × lead time in weeks

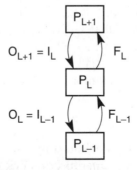

Process $_L$ uses Output $_{L+1}$ and Feedback $_{L-1}$ to set Output $_L$ = Input $_{L-1}$

Fig 3.15 A Generalized Model of the Relationship between Levels in a Control Hierarchy
The output from the level above is also the input to the level below.

In terms of Fig 3.15, the second-order (L = 2) control process P_2 uses feedback F_1 data from the first-order control process P_1, in the form of weekly demand figures for the stock item in question, and records of supplier performance on lead times for delivery. By application of the formula it then delivers as an output O_2 the goal of a reorder level for the first-order goal-seeking process.

Note also that the assessments of weekly demand and lead time are *stochastic* in the sense that we explained in section 3.2.1. This means that individual figures from the data for each instance of demand and delivery have to be stored in order that their probabilistic estimate can be calculated. As we saw for the classical control model in section 3.2.3, 'a second-order goal-changing system has to store *information*'.

This level of goal-setting or changing can be seen as automatic since once we have the data on delivery lead times and demand, the calculation of the reorder level is pre-determined by the formula. In other examples of second-order control the method of setting the goal may not be a ready-made formula, but the goal-setting is still automatic in the sense that the *method* for doing it is fixed. In the Exchange Rate Mechanism example we would not expect there to be a formula connecting exchange rates with interest rates or money spent on supporting the currency, but any country which wished to continue within the mechanism had only certain decisions and actions open to it. Thus when an exchange rate reached its lowest allowed value within the mecha-nism, intervention buying and/or raising interest rates were as necessary to the Exchange Rate Mechanism system as reordering was to our stockholding example.

Our stockholding example brings up an important practical point about second-order control and its implications for the information system. The example we used is typical of many real-life examples of this level of control. In them we find that the data needed for automatic goal-setting is *already being processed by the information system, but being ignored*. Thus every time a replenishment order is made for stock and subse-quently delivered, some part of the information system is recording the details in terms of product, quantities, dates, etc. Similarly, every time stock is issued, the details are recorded. Thus first-order control is *already* capturing the data needed by second-order control, and all that is required in addition is that the data be stored and processed using the automatic goal-setting formula. Yet I see many organizations with computerized so-called 'stock control' systems where goals like reorder levels are inserted manually, and any attempt at statistical analysis of past data requires a spe-cial exercise. Not surprisingly, when there are hundreds of different items in stock this exercise is often skipped and 'guesstimates' used to produce reorder levels. Hence tight controls are kept on costs by strict monitoring of stock issued and delivered, but slovenly cost control is then applied to the operation of the first-order stock control system itself.

However, the success of first-order control depends on the use of an appropriate method for setting its goals. In our stockholding example, any recalculation of the reorder level will be irrelevant if this method of stock control itself is irrelevant. As discussed in the Carry-Out Cupboards case, other stock control methods like periodic reordering may be more appropriate in some situations. A complete control system therefore needs a third-order control level which produces the appropriate method for second-order control.

Goal-setting: third-order control

In terms of Fig 3.15, third order control is the process which uses the feedback on the performance of the second-order goal-setting process to modify or produce a new *method* for second-order goal-setting.

Modification of existing methods or the production of new ones requires an input from fourth-order control. This input has to provide third-order control with a method or a policy for choosing between methods themselves. In our stockholding example, this might be a choice between a reorder level or a periodic reorder method of stock control. In the Black Wednesday example it might be to stay within the Exchange Rate Mechanism or adopt a floating £.

We call a method that enables us to distinguish, assess and choose between methods a *methodology* (*see* Chapter 7). If however our method of choosing between individual methods is less formal in its approach, we might use a broader term like *policy*. In our stockholding example the term methodology is probably appropriate because we can define quite specifically how the two systems of stock control work and even produce formulae to calculate such critical factors as the costs of operating the various systems. For the choices to be made in the Black Wednesday case it was more a question of having a broad policy of trying to remain in the Exchange Rate Mechanism if the costs of supporting the £ did not become excessive.

What differentiates third-order from second-order control is the presence of *soft* issues in the third-order process. When third-order control selects a method, defines a decision model or specifies a formula, judgements have to be made about soft issues such as *utility* or *subjective probability*.

Thus a decision to apply a formula to calculate a reorder level in the stockholding example can only come after we have first made a decision on the soft issue of whether running out of stock is an acceptable policy. This is because the reorder level formula is designed to ensure that stocks are replenished before we run out. If we were in a market where the demand for our product was such that we thought that customers were willing to wait, we might decide not to keep stocks at all. Suppliers of luxury goods often operate such a policy. Choice of stock control formulae also requires decisions on the utility of various costs such as those associated with stock-outs and customer dissatisfaction.

Similarly, a decision to take action on interest rates and currency buying in order to keep the £ at a certain level within the Exchange Rate Mechanism can only follow a soft decision that staying in the ERM is a desirable policy.

The presence of soft issues in the third-order control process should not be automatically confused with uncertainty in general. In section 3.2.1 we made a distinction between *hard* and *soft uncertainty*. In the Exchange Rate Mechanism example there is not a clear formula to connect interest rates and the exchange rate, but the connexion is a hard one. Both interest rates and exchange rates are variables that can be *measured* with *objective values*. The costs of stockouts are not measurable in the same way. A dissatisfied customer who cannot buy a product off the shelf and goes elsewhere is a cost which depends on the *weltanschauung* or *world view* of the person assessing it.

The presence of soft issues and the need to make judgements as part of the third-order control process makes it reflective rather than automatic. The feedback from second-order control's use of any method chosen by third-order control results in *experience* and *learning*. This learning can take various forms but all of them imply an ability to *record* and *store* both the method used, the data used by the method and the outcomes that resulted from the use of the method and the particular data.

Notice that whilst third-order control shares the need to be able to store information with second-order control, there is a difference in what is actually stored. Second-order control merely stores data like delivery lead times or demand for stock. Third-order control records *models* of the methods which may be chosen by the reflective goal-setting process for use by second-order control. Thus stock control formulae, decision models like those of section 3.2.1 or minutes of meetings which established government policies on Exchange Rate Mechanism membership are all examples of what third-order control must record. In practice *how* they are stored may be very different indeed, but *what* is being stored is conceptually equivalent.

Here again we see that the distinction of whats and hows means that a *systems* view of information can look very different from a conventional organizational view. This distinction is not just a theoretical nicety. Failure to recognize, for example, that committee minutes can be part of the information used by third-order control can mean that no *feedback loop* is established to ensure that *learning* takes place. How often do organizations use lower orders of control to ensure that every penny of expenditure is accounted for, while policy disasters costing the earth sail blissfully on without feedback, analysis and learning?

If however third-order control is successfully operating, this in turn means that the methodology or policies used by third-order control can be built on and developed by fourth-order control, as we shall discuss next.

Goal-setting: fourth-order control

Fourth-order control determines both the range of methods and the principles for choosing between them. We use the terms *methodology* and *policy* to describe this output from fourth- to third-order control. Thus in our stockholding example, fourth-order control would decide the policy on how far stockouts were acceptable and what types of reordering procedures might be operated. In the Black Wednesday case, deciding on the desirability of Exchange Rate Mechanism membership, and the methods that might be used to maintain it, were fourth-order decisions.

However, words like 'policy', 'acceptable' or 'desirability' imply soft issues. Deciding just what is, and is not, an issue, as well as deciding where we stand on the issue itself, are questions whose answers depend on our *weltanschauung* or *world view*. At Carry-Out Cupboards, the desirability of having the range of cupboard kits in stock and available to the customer comes from a weltanschauung which sees the company as popular, easily accessible and cheap. Britain's attempt to remain in the Exchange Rate Mechanism implies a weltanschauung which believes in closer European ties rather than insular independence.

Another form of soft information which fourth-order control must deliver, as its contribution to goal-setting through third-order control, is information which defines the values used in building the decision models selected by the third-order control process. The decision theory explained in section 3.2.1 requires information which evaluates outcomes and defines decision strategies. It may also require subjective estimates of probability. All of these components of a decision model depend on the weltanschauung or world view of the decision-maker and the feedback from the use of methods by third-order control.

Fourth-order control is essentially concerned therefore with the translation of values into practice. Values differ between individuals, and an individual's values may change over time and in different circumstances. To complete our understanding of the whole control model therefore, we need to identify whose values the control system seeks to implement. We call this person or group of persons the *systems owner/conceiver*. For reasons which we will explain next we take the owner/conceiver to be a component of the control systems environment, not of the control system itself.

Systems owner/conceiver

We established in section 3.1.8 that what a system is seen to be, and what properties it is considered to have, depend on whose view or concept of the system we are taking. To call such a person or group the systems *conceiver* is therefore natural enough, since what the system is seen to be is their *concept*. But why the term *owner?*

The answer to this question comes from the fact that we are considering a *control* system which is acting as a component of *management*. If we look at the role of the descending levels of control, we see a sequence of control functions which take a set of values which express a *weltanschauung* or *world view* and ultimately *implement* them in the process which is being controlled. In a management context, whose values would we expect these to be? The answer is that person or group in the wider management system who have power to influence the control system, but over whom the control system itself has only limited influence.

Conventional organizational views of management would take this group to be 'high-level management' or the directors of the company. More paranoid views might invent some 'ruling class' or hidden conspiracy. A *systems* view would recognize that the weltanschauung taken on by the control system is an *emergent property* resulting from the views of a range of environmental components coming together. This range is likely to include both formal and informal social coalitions and structures whose rich variety will give *some* support for organizational, paranoid, Freudian, and just about any other view that provides some insight into the different weltanschauungen that might be implemented in real organizations or businesses. Even systems with the most severe dictatorial management like Hitler's Germany or the Stalinist Soviet Union did not perfectly reflect the weltanschauung of a single systems owner. As the control system was implemented other values infiltrated the system.

The *systems owner/conceiver* of Fig 3.14 is therefore seen as a component in the environment of the control system which itself is likely to be a subsystem of the greater whole of the organizational or business system.

Hard and soft information in the general control model

Our analysis of the General Control Model of Fig 3.14 and the form of its processes in Fig 3.15, shows that both *hard* and *soft* information flows and is processed by any management control system. The model of Fig 3.14 also shows the *relationship* between hard and soft information in a control system. If we look at the information flows and their environmental sources, we can see two sources for them:

1. Information from the systems owner/conceiver about the weltanschauung or world view to be used by the control system.
2. Information about disturbances to the controlled process from the system's environment.

The effect of these two information flows works in opposite directions.

As we saw above, the control system attempts to implement the weltanschauung of the systems owner/conceiver from the choice of policy at the fourth-order level through to the actions carried out by the actuator at first-order control level. Thus the soft input from source 1 above results in the cascade of policy, method, goals and actions.

However, *hard* information comes from source 2 above about disturbances to the process which is being controlled. This results in a succession of feedback paths from first- to fourth-order control levels whose effect is to modify goals, method and policy in the light of experience.

The General Control Model shows a management control system as something which is dynamic and *adaptive.* At the higher levels of method and policy we can see this overall process of modification in the light of experience as one of *learning.* It is important to note that this learning process is not confined to objective, technical, exterior learning associated with hard information and 'facts'. There is also an implication from the presence and role of soft information in the model that subjective, personal, *interior* learning can take place. The model does not require us to ignore the role of personal or self management as part of the whole management process.

Specialist components of information systems

The General Control Model also enables us to relate kinds of supposedly separate or different forms of commercial, and usually computerized, information system such as:

- Decision support systems
- Executive information systems
- Expert systems

Decision support systems (DSS) are designed to *support* the decision-making processes of management. The word *support* is emphasized because DSS do not replace management decision-making, but are intended to help the decision-making process itself. The most common way in which they do this is to automate the type of decision model we discussed in section 3.2.1, so that managers can test the potential results of setting particular values to their choices as actuators in the control process. DSS do this by *automating* the decision model by the use of computer software.

One sophisticated example of this might be the use of a computerized model which was designed to reflect the effects of the various decisions on interest rates and the amount of supportive intervention buying of the £, on the value of the British currency on Black Wednesday. Another much simpler example might be a manager at Carry-Out Cupboards using a computerization of the reorder level formula on a spreadsheet to work out whether a particular reduction of lead time was worth a particular increase of price by a supplier.

What all DSS have in common, however simple or sophisticated, is that they enable management to try out the 'what if' of decision-making through the convenience of an automated model. In terms of our General Control Model of Fig 3.14, this represents the use of computerized support for goal-setting second-order control.

Executive Information Systems (EIS) are usually described, e.g. Davis & Olson (1984), as being principally concerned with providing a wide variety of summarized data that will enable management to strategically plan. This strategic planning checks and ensures that the various functions of the organization are properly coordinated, and that the organization is going in the right direction in terms of markets and opportunities. Typical information to be summarized might relate to competitor performance, the legal context, the economic environment or market preferences. Generally EIS are designed to process data which summarizes the performance of the *whole* organization in relation to its *environment*. In order to carry out this function, such a system usually takes the form of a set of software that can access the database of the organization to obtain the data it needs to summarize.

At first sight, such a description of EIS enables us to place it clearly in the General Control Model as supporting the fourth-order level of control. In terms of the model, EIS provides feedback on the performance of the whole in relation to its environment and enables any changes of policy to be made. A danger comes, however, when many well established and respectable books on management information systems picture EIS in the stereotypical context of the non-systemic organizational hierarchy we were critical of in section 3.2.3. The danger of this approach is that the logical *what* of an organizational activity becomes identified with a particular *who* or *how*. Thus Davis & Olson (1984) see EIS as the concern of 'top management' or 'chief executive officer plus staff'. This may be true of many organizations but it is not a necessary characteristic when we view an organization as a *system*.

Automatically linking the conceptual *what* of strategic policy formulation with a particular *who* or *how* can dangerously suggest that small organizations or businesses do not need or do not have a fourth-order-level control function. Such a view is not only false from an academic systems viewpoint: it can also lead to poor practical management. In a small business like MX Marketing of Appendix 3, a busy man like Ben Lister with limited clerical support might particularly benefit from access to software and a database that could summarize competitor performance, the legal context, the economic environment or market preferences. The fact that it might not be economic for him to own it is a separate issue of the *how* not the *what*. Once he recognizes that MX Marketing has a need for fourth-order control just like any other managed organization, he might consider access to agency information databases and computer systems bureaux. Automatically associating EIS with the 'top management' of large organizations could mean that an important information systems opportunity was lost to MX Marketing.

Expert systems can be placed in the context of the General Control Model once we recall the role of *learning* in higher-order control. So far we have implied in all our descriptions of the development of *methodology* at fourth level, and our definition of method at third-order level, that this development and definition is done by the *human* components of the system. Expert systems are attempts to model the human ability to use reasoning and acquire knowledge. Thus in our stockholding example we saw the identification of the different methods of stock control and the choice of method to be a human activity. Expert systems software would seek to gather information from the user about how the different methods worked and the rules or reasoning used when choices were made. The so-called *knowledge base* of the expert system stores both rules to represent human reasoning and *semantic nets* which represent how the different components of this knowledge can be classified and interrelated. (We shall say more about classification of information in Chapter 4.)

The systemic view of management presented in the General Control Model is therefore intended to represent the *logical* or *conceptual* relationship between management, control and information to be found in *any* organization or business which claims to be *managed*. The particular *ways* or *hows* may vary, but our aim is to recognize underlying common systems structures.

Cybernetics and control

The General Control Model has shown the details of the relationship between management, control and information. It has also distinguished the different kinds of information and their role in the control system's hierarchy. In Chapter 4 we shall look more closely at some of the properties of information itself, and in Chapter 6 we shall look further to see how organizations and businesses can be regarded as systems, using the concepts of the General Control Model.

If our view of information systems in organizations and business is to be based on the principles of this model, it is finally worth noting the kind of model that it is in terms of management and systems thinking. I think that reference to a range of very different works on the subject of management and systems such as Beer (1985), Espejo & Harnden (1989), Flood & Jackson (1991) or Schoderbeck et al. (1990) would describe our model as essentially *cybernetic.*

The word cybernetic comes from the Greek for a governor or steersman. The term cybernetic therefore seems very appropriate for our view of management as one based on *meliorist belief* and functioning through *control*. The Greek vision of the steersman who believes it to be worthwhile trying to steer the ship towards a desired harbour in the face of disturbing winds and currents, chimes in quite well with our view of management. What we do not take on board with this analogy, however, is the assumption that the ship must be propelled by slave oarsmen under the steersman's whip. As frequently repeated above, we take control as a concept not a particular management style. Control does not automatically equate with coercion.

Box 3.3

LIES, DAMNED LIES AND EMU STATISTICS

(*Financial Times* 9/10/96: all italics are mine)

Are EU states engaging in creative accounting to qualify for a single currency?

Europe's statisticians do not usually like the limelight. . . As one says: 'It is absolutely not statisticians who are manipulating the figures. We have a *proper* system to check that this does not happen. What politicians do, though, is their affair'. . . But their problem is that this *system for measuring* deficits is complex – *even before the politics*. For the essential difficulty is that the way government finances are structured is evolving *much more quickly than the statistical systems that measure them*. . .

The French budget, for example, is to be boosted by a one-off, anomalous FFr37.5bn (£4.6bn) payment. . .

The Italians have used L12,000bn (£5bn) of ambiguous 'treasury operations'. . .

The Belgians have also used one-off, short-term items. . .

COMMENT

The important systems lesson from this article does not depend on who are the good guys and who are the bad guys. Instead, it shows that any control system is an implementation of a set of values or *weltanschauung*.

The problem for the statisticians seems to be that they believe in 'proper' systems of control which should not be affected by 'politics'; while the politicians appear to think that the 'system of measuring' should be serving the ideal of EMU, and not the reverse.

Reference to the General Control Model of Fig 3.14 shows what is going on behind the rhetoric. European Monetary Union is a *policy* which has come from *normative* goal-setting intended to reflect a *weltanschauung* which believes in the merits of European integration. There have been other policies which have intended to do the same, such as the Common Agricultural Policy or the Single European Market.

The *reflective* goal-setting process has chosen a *method* by which the policy may be implemented. In this case that includes a 'proper system' of measurement and calculation for a particular relationship between budget deficits and gross national product (GNP). Using this method, *automatic* goal-setting merely has to calculate the *goal* level of budget deficit.

However, the goal-setting process does not end there. *Feedback* from the *goal-seeking* process shows how successfully goals may have been implemented. Failure to achieve goals may be merely due to poor management. In this case this might reflect an inability of the government finance system in a particular country to do its job. But even the most well-intentioned finance minister may be limited in what he may achieve in practice. Failure to meet goals can sometimes be a comment on the appropriateness of those goals.

In the case of EMU, the reflective goal-setting process requires a major European decision-making conference, like the one held at Maastricht which defined the method for determining EMU membership criteria. If, meanwhile, 'the way government finances are structured is evolving much more quickly than the statistical systems that measure them', the goal-setting processes are responding fast enough to feedback.

FURTHER STUDY

Section 3.3 looks further into the concept of the *behaviour* of control systems in response to environmental disturbances.

You may feel however that it is not the EMU control system which is wrong, but the willingness of the European Union to see that member states conform to its goals without 'creative accounting'. This raises a further concept which is covered in section 3.3.6: that of *requisite variety*. Is it even possible for a large, complex and cumbersome device like an international conference to control the ingenuity of individual states? Try studying the Bosnian conflict or other attempts of the United Nations to keep the peace.

3.3 INFORMATION AND CONTROL SYSTEMS BEHAVIOUR

3.3.1 Emergent properties and control systems behaviour

In section 3.1.6 we saw that a system as a *whole* will have overall properties called *emergent properties*. One particular *emergent property* shared by all systems is that of 'doing something', which we called *behaviour*.

Behaviour itself can then be seen as being made up of component *transformation processes* which change the *state* of the whole system in terms of the values of its component properties. Thus the overall or whole behaviour of a monetary system like the EMS is an emergent property resulting from individual processes of buying, selling and exchange of currency. The effects of these processes, or the overall *behaviour* of the monetary system, is seen in terms of changes in the amounts of different currencies held by various banks and dealers, or the level of the exchange rate for particular currencies.

Since we are concerned with *management* systems, then the behaviour we are particularly interested in is that which is linked to their component *control* and *information* subsystems, and the processes they seek to control. Section 3.1.6 emphasized that emergent properties should not be exclusively associated with dynamic emergent properties of a system. When considering the behaviour of control systems in a management context however, we are concentrating on dynamic properties. This is because the General Control Model of Fig 3.14 is principally a dynamic model which concentrates on the interaction of processes at different levels.

Given this dynamic emphasis, we will consider how the following factors affect the behaviour of systems in terms of the General Control Model and explain their use of information:

1. Control frequency
2. The role of transaction and master files
3. Lags in the control loop
4. The effects of control hierarchy
5. Forecasting and buffers
6. Trade-off and optimization

In subsequent sections we will look at these in detail.

3.3.2 Control frequency

The costs of control

There is an old country saying that 'the best fertilizer is the farmer's boot'. The meaning being that those fields where the farmer walks and takes the trouble to check are the fields which will do best in growing crops. As a principle of management control, whether in farming or any other business, very frequent checking seems like a good thing. But is it? In this section we will consider how often the 'boot' of management control should tread on a particular 'field' of a process we wish to control. How often it does, is a measure of control frequency.

When we use the term *control frequency* we refer to how often in a particular time interval the *sensor* of a control system checks the value of the *outputs* from the *transformation process*. This value is then *fed back* and used by the *comparator* to instruct the actuator what modifications have to be made to the *inputs* to the transformation process. As we saw in Fig 3.11, this sequence of activities represents the contribution which the information system makes as a component of the control system.

'Very frequent checking' is therefore a colloquial way of describing a high control frequency. If we go close to the limit of checking all the time, then the control frequency is near its highest value and can be considered as continuous. To understand whether or not high frequency or even continuous control is always desirable, we can return to our stockholding and Exchange Rate Mechanism examples.

Exchange rates for currencies can go up and down many times in a day and still end up with little overall change. Government finance ministers do not necessarily need to know their currency's changing exchange rates every second of every day. Nor do they need to continuously intervene in the markets by buying and selling every time an exchange rate changes by one tenth of a percentage point. Indeed, if a minister did behave in this way, he would probably cause more panic and instability than if he had just left things alone.

Similarly, in a stockholding example like Carry-Out Cupboards, we might consider that a retail outlet manager had suffered a mental breakdown if he set the staff on continuously counting and recounting the number of cupboards kits in stock.

Both the stockholding and Exchange Rate Mechanism examples show that in practical applications of control systems, the operation of the information systems component itself brings costs. High-frequency control may bring good crop yields to our farmer and his boot, but much of the profit from these yields can be absorbed by the time and money spent travelling around the farm on inspection visits. Similarly, stock checking cuts down the costs of stock-outs, theft or wastage; but stock checking itself costs money.

◆ **STQ 3.12**
How often do you check your bank balance?

Optimizing total control costs

Figure 3.16 summarizes the costs which have to be considered when deciding on control frequency. The horizontal scale represents how frequently output from the transformation process is sensed, fed back and used to determine the adjustments made to the inputs by the actuator. The extreme left of the scale represents a frequency of zero, i.e. *never* checking. Moving to the right along the scale represents increasing frequency to the point that the checking is virtually continuous.

The cost effects of frequency are measured by the vertical scale. By 'cost' we mean in the broadest hard and soft senses of the word. Hence soft costs of aggravation and inconvenience would be included as well as hard costs like money or time.

If we now consider the effect of control frequency on the total costs associated with running a control system, we can see that this total cost is a combination of two components:

1 The *cost of checking*, which is made up of costs associated directly with operating the control system itself. In a stockholding example these would be the costs of counting, calculating and recording stock levels, as well as keeping track of stock issued, reordered and delivered.

2 The *cost of error*, which is made up of the costs associated with any failure to perfectly achieve the control system's goals. In a stockholding example these would include the costs of being out of stock, like lost sales and customer ill will; and the costs of being overstocked, such as obsolescence, extra storage or tied-up capital.

The *cost of checking* will be greater the more frequently we check, since every check made requires further counting, calculating, etc. as above. The *cost of error* works in the opposite way. The less frequently we check, the more likely it is that stocks will run out because they have not been reordered, or stock levels will become too high because no check has been made of falling demand.

If we look at the *total* costs we can see that they tend to be higher at very high and very low control frequencies. This is because at low frequencies the cost of error becomes large, and at high frequencies the cost of checking becomes large. Between these extremes we can see that there is a range of frequency corresponding to lowest overall cost in operating a control system.

In theory, the total cost relationship of Fig 3.16 has a single minimum or *optimum* (from the Latin word for best) value. In practice, the presence of both soft costs and hard uncertainty means that it would be impossible to calculate the control frequency corresponding to minimum cost as an exact value with complete confidence. It *is* possible however to take the principles illustrated by Fig 3.16 as a guide to what *kind* of information is needed if we are to attempt to estimate a good choice of control frequency.

The role of the information system in control frequency

Besides helping to show what kind of information is needed to decide on control frequency, the analysis of Fig 3.16 tells us something about the role of the information

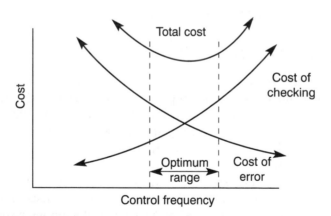

Fig 3.16 Optimizing Control Frequency
The particular shapes of the curves will vary in individual real-life examples, but the principle behind the general form will always apply where the Cost of Checking rises with control frequency and the Cost of Error falls. In these situations the Total Cost curve will be concave upwards with a minimum corresponding to an optimum control frequency. I have indicated a range containing the optimum, rather than the optimum itself, to imply that in real life *exact* estimation of optimum control frequency is unlikely.

system itself. If we look back to our analysis of the classical control model in section 3.2.2, we can see that the feedback path from sensor through to actuator shows one of the major roles of the information system as a component of the control system as in Fig 3.11. When we compare this with the activities associated with the *cost of checking*, they are all activities of the *information system* as a *component* of the control system.

Practical decisions about control frequency based on costs must therefore take account of a total cost which includes the *cost of checking.* Since all of this latter cost arises from the operation of the information system, understanding the role of the information system, and the kind of information it uses, is a major element in designing control systems for management.

One important example of assessing the cost of this role is the issue of *real-time* versus *batch processing*, which is so often found in exam questions for computer studies students. To understand this issue we should first check on the meaning of the term *real-time processing*, since it is often used incorrectly. The term real-time processing should refer to situations where any change in the state of a system which is being controlled is immediately reflected in the *information stored* about the state of that system. In a stockholding example this would mean that any addition or withdrawal of stock would be immediately sensed, fed back, etc., by the information system so that the amount of stock held would always be up to date.

Real-time processing implies that the control frequency is very high. Every time that there is a stock movement for example, the information system will immediately process the information about additions or withdrawals. As we saw above, such a high control frequency is likely to be expensive in terms of the *cost of checking* in Fig 3.16. For a manual system it implies that the people involved have to be always available to collect and process data. For an automated system using a computer, both the people and the equipment involved have to be continually on call and ready to respond. Since this often means that computers have to be continually connected on-line, the term *on-line* is sometimes wrongly used to mean the same as real time.

Batch processing is different. Batch processing systems record and then *store* information gathered by the sensor. This stored information accumulated over a period makes up a batch which is used by the comparator at the end of the period to decide the information which is passed on to the actuator for modifying the inputs to the process which is being controlled. In a stockholding example this would correspond to keeping records of stock issued and received from suppliers, and then updating a stock record such as that in Fig 3.2. This might be done at the end of every day or only once a week. The longer the period between updates of the stock record, the lower the control frequency.

Batch processing can lower the *cost of checking*, since the information system does not have to incur the cost of comparison and actuation of the reaction to every disturbance from the environment the moment it occurs. Instead, the accummulated record of disturbances can be processed at a time *chosen at the convenience of the information system.* Thus batch processing in a stock control system would be able to choose when updating the stock record was done, and so give the opportunity for using much more modest and economic clerical or computer facilities which did not requires the system to be continually ready and on-line for processing.

Batch processing and real-time information systems

If the cost of checking was the only cost to be considered when deciding the frequency of control, then it would be hard to see any role for real-time information systems. However our study of Fig 3.16 tells us that the cost of error also has to be considered.

When we look at some kinds of real-life control systems, the cost of error associated with low control frequencies is not acceptable. Most forms of *booking* system are good examples of this. Imagine telephoning an airline to see if there were any seats left on a particular flight and being told 'well there were a couple available the last time we checked so it *might* be OK'! It would be equally inconvenient for the airline to advise you not to book with them just in case the seats had been taken up. Airline booking systems therefore need to ensure that what is recorded accurately reflects the state of the system being controlled. As we saw above, this means they need real-time processing.

Even systems which do not need every update of their state to be immediately recorded in real time, still have limits on how out of date the record can be before the cost of error makes total control costs too high. It may not be necessary to update stock records every time there is a stock movement, but failure to update records over long periods could mean that wastage, theft and other costly happenings could be taking place without being detected. Generally, the longer such things go on unchecked, the worse their effect, so there will always be some economical limit to the time between processing batches of update information.

The period between batch processing may also be governed by the fact that a particular process which is being controlled is a component of a wider control system. Thus a stockholding system may check all the stock movements which have taken place in a day's trading, and update the stock records at the end of each day so that any replenishment orders can be placed on a daily basis. Here the stock control system is a component of a wider logistics and supply system. The retail outlets of Carry-Out Cupboards are in this position. Another example might be a payroll system. This would save all the time sheets for its employees for a week and then use them to calculate total hours worked, overtime, etc., for the wages payment at the end of each week. The wider context of personnel relations and employment law mean that a weekly batching period for the payroll control system is imposed on it by its environment.

Whether the information system which supports a control system is real-time or batch processing, our study of the workings of the information system reveals an important principle about the way in which information systems *capture, store* and *process* information, which we will consider next.

3.3.3 The role of transaction and master files

The previous section has expanded our understanding of the role of the information system as a component of the control system. It has also enabled us to look more closely at the different ways in which an information system may work in such a role. In particular, we began to look in more detail at the way in which information systems *capture, store* and *process* information in real-time and batch processing systems.

Both ways of making an information system work as a component of a control system aim to do the same thing. Data which is captured by the sensor has to be fed back and processed by the comparator, to enable appropriate information to be passed to the actuator. For the comparator to do its work of instructing the actuator, it has to know about the *state* of the system which is being controlled. Thus the aim of stock control, for example, is to maintain stock levels within the range set by the systems goals. This is done by issuing the appropriate information about what stock may be released in response to demand and when replenishment stock should be ordered from suppliers.

The essential component of any such procedure therefore is having a record of the state of the system. The difference between real-time and batch processing lies in whether that record is continually up to date or whether it is updated on a periodic basis. This difference arises in turn from whether *capturing* data and *processing* the *record* of the state of the system takes place together or not. Thus in stock control, is data captured about stock movement used immediately to update the stock record, or is the data recorded for use at the end of the day?

Both ways of processing differ therefore in the way they coordinate the treatment of:

> *a.* Data captured by the sensor about *changes* to the state of the system being controlled.
> *b.* Information on the *state* of the system used by the comparator for comparison with goals and instructions to the actuator.

In real-time processing the data captured is used immediately to update information about the state of the system. In batch processing however the captured data is stored and then used at a later time to update information on the state of the system. This separation means that batch processing systems record data and information on two types of file:

> *a. Transaction* files
> *b. Master* files.

Transaction files record data captured by the sensor about *changes* to the state of the system over the batch processing period. *Master* files record information about the *state* of the system at any one point in time. Thus a record of the amounts of stock issued in response to orders during the day, and quantities delivered from suppliers' would be a transaction file. A record which showed how much was in stock, on order, etc., as in Fig 3.2, would be recorded on a master file. (Note that what is shown in Fig 3.2 is therefore incomplete, since it does not include an indication of when this record was last updated.)

How batch processing uses these two types of file is shown in Fig 3.17. It is worth clarifying two important points that have practical implications for our treatment of *records, files* and *databases* in Chapter 5.

First, you will find that many books on data processing attempt to make the distinction between transaction and master files essentially *relative*. Thus transaction files may be described as containing 'temporary' or 'short term' information, while master files contain information which is 'permanent' or 'long term'. Such descriptions are confusing and disguise a distinction *in principle* between the two types of file and their roles. Transactions take place over a period of time and are *dynamic:* they reflect changes. A master file reflects the state or condition of the system at a point in time. The *behaviour* of the system is represented or *modelled* by the information system processing the two kinds of file as in Fig 3.17.

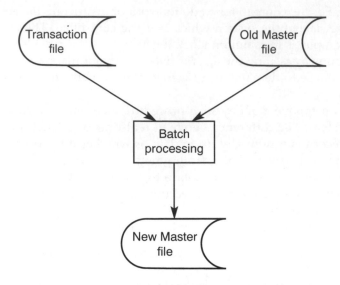

Fig 3.17 The Standard Model of Batch Processing
Like Fig 3.1, some version of the diagram is found in most books on computer-based information systems. The old standard symbols for a file are an
example of the carry-over of old technology which we discussed in Chapter
2. The shape of the symbol is chosen to pictorially represent a stack of
disks or a drum. We no longer automatically link an information system concept with its physical manifestation in this way, as we shall explore further in
Chapter 5.

Second, it is important to realize that, as so often in this book, we need to distinguish between the conceptual, logical *whats* and the concrete *hows* of the system.
Although transaction and master file information can be logically distinguished, a particular physical record may contain both kinds of information. Thus a monthly
statement of an account for Carry-Out Cupboards from a supplier, like Fig 3.18, might
include a list of deliveries during the month in question as well as a statement of any
payment and the amount owing at the end of the month. The details of deliveries and
payment represent transaction data, while the final statement of the amount owing is
master file information. The first shows changes over a period of time, the second
shows the state of the system at a particular point in time.

Any attempt to refer to transaction files and master files in terms of *how* information
is actually recorded can confuse *what* the information is and what it is being used for.
Such a view stems from the days when the term *file* referred to a particular reel of
magnetic tape on which the information was recorded. Thus the data on a transaction
file (i.e. one tape) was fed into the computer to process the master file (i.e. another
tape). Modern systems do not work like this. As we shall see in Chapter 5, a *file* in a
modern database management system is purely a *concept* used to explain the logic of
data processing and does not necessarily exist as a separate physical thing, like a tape,
which we can identify.

SAXUN OFFICE SUPPLIES

21 Saxun Way
Viking Trading Estate
North Coates
Barsetshire
BA99 9ZW

Telephone: (0176) 992992

Fax: (0176) 993993

VAT Reg. 478 8748 44

Carry-Out Cupboards
Cowford Business Park
Kirton
South Riding
SR77 7DQ

Account No. C2256

Page 1 of 1

28.05.96

STATEMENT

DATE	TYPE	REFERENCE	STATUS	DEBIT	CREDIT	BALANCE
05.02.96	Invoice	1820	Paid	15.43		
11.02.96	Invoice	1832		68.24		
22.03.96	Invoice	1864		94.16		
28.03.96	Cr.Note	1866			10.00	
06.04.96	Invoice	1872		23.23		
27.05.96	Invoice	1892		48.29		
27.05.96	Receipt	Cheque	Alloc.		16.24	

THREE MONTHS & OVER	TWO MONTHS	ONE MONTH	CURRENT MONTH	TOTAL DUE	223.13
67.43	84.25	23.16	48.29		

Payment due 28 days from date of invoice.
Payments received after the end of month are not shown on statement.

Fig 3.18 A Typical Customer Account Statement
Note that much of what appears on this document, and how it appears, is not determined by the information system's designer but by the commercial environment. The implications of this for systems designers are considered further in Chapter 7, when we distinguish *derivative* and *innovative* methods for information systems development.

In case any of this section seems rather theoretical and new, consider some very conventional financial accounting concepts that have been used for centuries: the *balance sheet* and the *profit and loss* account. A balance sheet records the *state* of the company at a *particular point in time* (e.g. 'as at the 31st December 1995'). The profit and loss account records the *transactions* for a company over a *period* (e.g. 'for October–December 1995'). Long before computers therefore, the logical concept of a list of transactions being used to update a record of the state of the system has been well established. Note also that this process has been developed to ensure financial *control*.

3.3.4 Lags in the control system loop

In section 3.2.2 we showed how the classical control system of Fig 3.8 contained a loop. This loop is formed by the interaction of the outputs from the transformation process with its inputs through the information path from sensor to actuator. The concept of a *lag* in such a loop is a recognition that it takes time for the transformation process to change inputs into outputs, and for the information system to process information through the sequence from sensor to actuator. Thus in a stock control system it takes time to accept deliveries, move stock on to shelves and into bins, take stock out of storage and deliver to the customer, record stock levels, compare it with the desired range of stock levels, and implement any reordering procedure.

The effect of any lag in the control system loop is to *delay* the effects of any control action. The *outputs* from the processes being controlled are always the result of trying to make the state of the system correspond to what was thought desirable at an earlier time by the comparator. This was decided on the basis of feedback resulting from what the sensor picked up even earlier still. In everyday terms we could describe the effect of lags on control systems as meaning we are always trying to sort out yesterday's problems. In the analysis we made of the Carry-Out Cupboard's reordering procedure, there were lags in the system due to the time taken from deciding replacement stock was needed to receiving its delivery. These lags meant that deliveries received by both the retail outlets and the central assembly and packing facility were those which were relevant to some *previous* state of the stockholding process. In the time taken for the reordering and delivery loop to function however, customer demand had changed, and different reorder quantities were appropriate.

Generally, the effect of a lag in a control system loop is to introduce instability into the behaviour of the system. This takes the form of increasing the *fluctuations* of the outputs from the system in its attempt to achieve its goals. The greater the lag from sensing the output from a process to modifying the input, the greater the time for the environment of the system to change, and the greater those changes may be. This in turn increases the potential deviation of the system from its goals and the need for greater changes to the inputs by the actuator.

A particular example of the effects of lags in the control system loop can be seen in the Carry-Out Cupboards example of Fig A1.6 (Appendix 1), but we can see many examples of this principle in a whole range of our lives. Most processes that we seek to control, not just in business, *take time*. Inputs are not immediately transformed into outputs. It takes time to make products, educate and train people, build schools, hospitals, roads, power stations and factories, grow food and trees. In most transformation processes there is a *lag* between input and output.

There is also a further contribution to the lag from the information system which closes the loop between sensor and actuator. It takes time to assess the market for products and to develop and design them. Our buildings have to be authorized, sited, planned and financed. In my lifetime it has taken decades for the political system to respond to the disappearance of natural woodland and plan for new broad-leaved forrests in my country. Meanwhile, the conifer forests which are now sneered at by some conservationists are the output from a control loop which began in World War I, when it was realized that Britain imported over 90% of her timber.

Thus a control system loop in real life has built-in lags which are often measured in years, but when we look at this lag we find that it is made up of two components:

    a. The time required for the transformation process.
    b. The time required to operate the data capture and information processing from sensor to actuator.

Component *a* is often something which is fixed by technical or natural restrictions: there tend to be limits on the rate at which buildings can be built, people can be educated, or trees grown. Indeed it is impossible to make some transformation processes take less time: you can't change a child into an adult overnight.

Component *b* however represents the contribution of the information system to the control loop. It is potential improvements in this component that interest us as students of information systems. In the next section we shall consider how certain principles can be incorporated into the design of information systems which can reduce the effects of lags in the control system loop in two ways:

    1. *Reduction* of the lag itself by reducing the time lag along the information systems path from sensor to actuator.
    2. *Anticipation* of the effects of the lag in the control system loop.

For *reduction* of the lag we will consider how the structure, and in particular *hierarchy*, can affect the time taken for an information system to work. We will then see how *forecasting* and *buffering* can help with *anticipating* the effects of lags.

Box 3.4

CASUALTIES OF THE INFLATION WAR

(*Financial Times* 24/9/96: all italics are mine)

. . . The old economies of scale which gave larger companies an advantage and allowed them a degree of discretion in setting prices are being *undermined by computer technologies* that allow smaller companies to target specific market niches. You can see the effects in almost every industry: banking, insurance, telecommunications, clothing, entertainment, appliances, transport.

    Entry barriers are falling, *product cycles are shortening*, large companies are scrambling to maintain market share. This revolutionary change has made all producers more reluctant to raise prices even in the face of rising costs, and more aggressive about holding costs down.

A second feature of the economy of the 1990s is that the *'knowledge' content of goods and services continues to climb as a percentage of total cost*. . . more value is added through design, styling, manufacturing-engineering, process-engineering, advertising, marketing, servicing, selling, consulting and advising. . .

. . . prospective workers are unable to respond to the tightening demand because they lack education and skills, or they have the wrong skills, or they do not know what skills are required. . .

COMMENT

These extracts are just a small part of a main *Financial Times* article by Robert Reich, the US Secretary for Labor. In the article as a whole, his main concern is with unemployment. But it is important to notice how he is using information systems concepts to explain what is happening in a major economic area. I have used italics above to highlight two important examples of these:

1 The ' "knowledge" content of goods. . . ' quote is an illustration of how the *abstract* components of a system may be as much, or more, important than the *concrete* components of any system. Robert Reich's article highlights how the value of 'knowledge' can be a greater component of production systems costs than 'materials'. Any idea that abstract components are less real because they cannot be seen or touched is negated by the examples in the article.

2 The *loop* in any control system includes the path concerned with the *communication* and *processing* of information, as in Fig 3.11. The *lag* in this loop is therefore reduced if 'computer technologies' increase the speed and efficiency of this process, including 'product cycle . . . shortening'. Robert Reich's article shows how these systems concepts are played out as the awful problem of poverty and unemployment. More efficient information systems used by organizations are able to respond to environmental disturbances much more quickly than the mental information systems of individual human beings, who need 'better or different skills' to give themselves value in the employment system.

The article therefore shows that the effects of information systems make them of much wider significance than just pieces of information technology looked after by computer specialists. Information systems now intrude into just about every part of human life at the end of the twentieth century; whether for good or ill.

FURTHER STUDY

I suspect that political theories will be coming back into fashion by the time that you read this book. During the 1980s, the political theorizing that so dominated the late 1960s and the 1970s seemed to be less important than accommodating to the practical effects of developments in information technology. There was much talk of the 'information age' or the 'silicon chip revolution'. Now the results of these changes are becoming clearer, information systems issues are likely to become increasingly politicized. Attempts to censor the Internet are an early example of this.

Start with the recent history of a society like Singapore which has wide-ranging and well developed social and commercial information systems, as in Cash et al. What gains and losses does such a high state of information systems development bring with it? Are the gains and losses which you identify inevitable?

3.3.5 Reducing the effects of lags

The effects of sequence and hierarchy

Our investigation of the effects of control frequency and lags in a control system did not always make a clear distinction between controlling the *behaviour* of a *whole* system, and controlling an output from a particular *process* carried out by a *component* of a system. This was because the principles that we established about the effects of control frequency and lags can be applied both to the individual outputs of *component* processes and to the connected multiple outputs of a *system*. We can understand this shared effect of frequency and lags when we see that the outputs from the various individual processes carried out by individual subsystems become an emergent property which we call systems behaviour when they are connected.

The concept of systems structure involves two ways of connecting systems components: horizontally and vertically. *Horizontally* and *vertically* refer to the systems hierarchy. A horizontal connexion, in terms of systems behaviour, would be between two processes at the same level of the systems hierarchy. A vertical connexion would be between two transformation processes at the same levels of the hierarchy in terms of the General Control Model.

Figure 3.19 shows how there might be horizontal connexion between processes in a situation like that of Carry-Out Cupboards where a retail outlet, a warehouse or a factory acts as both customer and supplier according to whether we consider their inputs or their outputs. Figure 3.19 is a more generalized version of Fig A1.4.

Our study of control systems hierarchy led to the General Control Model of Fig 3.14. In this model, overall control exerted by management can be seen as being made up of a series of individual instances of the classical control model, each with its process and control loop linked vertically. This looks rather like Fig 3.19 rotated through 90 degrees.

The effects of both types of connexion on behaviour can be understood together if we note that the essential point is that processes are linked in *sequence*. Thus the output from one process becomes the input to the next and so on, either between processes at the same level of the hierarchy, or between processes at adjacent levels. Each has a *loop,* whether it is the closed loop of classical control or the demand/supply loop between adjacent horizontal processes. Each loop has the potential for a lag, and the behaviour of the whole system will be an emergent property resulting from the interaction of the individual levels of the control system or adjacent processes acting as components of this whole. Thus the effect of a lag in any individual process or

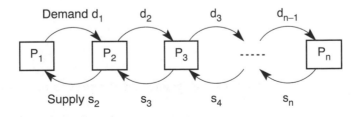

Fig 3.19 Interacting Processes in Sequence
In real life *every* cycle of supply and demand will involve a *lag*.

level of control will interact with the effects of lags in other levels or processes to have an overall effect on the behaviour of the whole system.

The example of stockholding for Carry-Out Cupboards in Fig A1.4 shows how lags in interacting processes in sequence can lead to instability as shown in Figs A1.5 and A1.6. A simple step disturbance in the input at one end of the sequence led to increasingly complex disturbances as fed through each process with its lag. What we have in Fig 3.19 is a generalization of this kind of interaction, where a series of processes in a system interact with one another. What can be demonstrated mathematically, but we already have a hint of in Fig A1.4, is that every addition to the sequence of a process results in a further directional movement in the effects of the disturbance. Thus Fig 3.20 is a generalization of Fig A1.6 in the same way that Fig 3.19 is a generalization of Fig A1.4.

The essential lesson from the principles behind Figs 3.19 and 3.20 is that every addition of a process to the interacting chain increases the potential instability of the system both in terms of it severity, shown by the 'size' of the fluctuations, and its complexity, shown by their 'pattern' of peaks and troughs.

The significance of this general analysis of systems behaviour for the development and implementation of *information systems* comes from looking at how information flows through the sequence of processes. What we see is that information output from one process becomes the information input for the next. Hence the further two processes are separated along a sequence, or up and down a control hierarchy, the greater the destabilizing effect of this method of transmitting information. The answer to this problem is to *reduce the overall sum of the lags* by giving decision-making and communication access to information through a *common database*. When information systems are designed so that all the processes in a chain or all levels of a control hierarchy have direct access to information, cutting out all intermediate transmission reduces the cumulative lag effects of Fig 3.20.

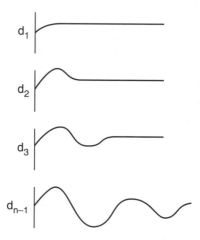

Fig 3.20 The Responses of a Sequence of Processes to an Initial Disturbance

As we move from process p_n to process p_{n+1}, the change from disturbance d_n to disturbance d_{n+1}, involves an extra movement in direction of the disturbance.

Forecasting and buffers

Even if the effects of both individual lags and the way they are accumulated can be reduced, they can never be totally eliminated. As we saw above, processes in the real world take time. An additional way to improve systems behaviour is therefore to design systems to be able to cope with the effects of lags as well as reduce the lags themselves. Two ways of doing this are the use of *forecasting* and *buffers*.

Forecasting enables us to *anticipate* what outputs will be needed from a process in the future so that inputs can be set in a form now that will result in the desired output at the end of the lag time. We order stock, start constructing buildings or plant trees now in anticipation of what we will require in terms of types and quantities by the time delivery takes place, the building is complete or the trees have matured.

The essential lesson from this approach for *information systems* is that a major component of most forecasting is the analysis of trends and other movements shown by records of data we have made in the past. Past sales figures for a product, population and economic trends, or demand for timber would be the type of data for the examples we have given. All of this data is likely to be already being recorded for other purposes like keeping accounts, monitoring sales performance, etc., so all that remains is that the information system should contain a subsystem which is designed to pick up and analyse the data for forecasting purposes. Again, a modern *database* makes this much more possible than in the past because, as we shall see in Chapter 5, modern database remove many of the old restrictions of having data compartmentalized and hard to integrate.

◆ **STQ 3.13**
What other components might there be in forecasting?

Buffering is what we do when we hold stock. If we wish to satisfy a demand under conditions where we cannot exactly coordinate it with supply, then stocks are essential. In most business situations this condition applies. We cannot determine when customers should come to us and what they should buy. They are part of the *environment* and their disturbances to the system cannot be controlled. So even if good forecasting tells us that we are going to sell 10 of a particular product in a month, we don't know when the individual items will be required. The only way to deal with this if we want to be able to immediately satisfy demand is to hold the items in anticipation, i.e. in stock.

Many business books give the impression that stock is somehow a 'bad thing' to be avoided. This is too simplistic. While stocks play the essential buffering role which enables the coordination of different patterns of supply and demand we have just shown, holding stocks also costs money. It costs money to have storage space, heat and ventilate, keep secure and all the other things necessary when holding stock. What is important therefore is that we don't hold more stock than we need. Hence our aim is not no stock but keeping stocks at an optimum level. Figure 3.21 illustrates the principle. With stock levels very high we incur high stockholding costs. With very low levels we increase the chances of stock-outs and the costs associated with lost sales, bad commercial image, delayed production, etc. The overall relationship between the total cost of the stockholding operation and the stock level shows a potential minimum which balances these costs.

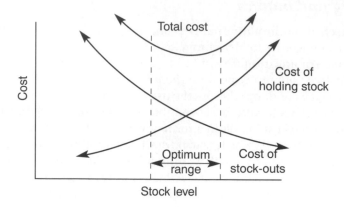

Fig 3.21 Optiumum Stock Level
Holding stock is not automatically undesirable, as some of the poorer advocates of financial accountancy might imply. Stocks have an important role to play as buffers between different patterns of input and output. The aim should be to *optimize* stock levels, not eliminate them. The interpretation of this diagram follows that of Fig 3.16.

Box 3.5

TRADE TOO TEMPTING FOR THE TRUSTS

(*Investors Chronicle* 2/8/96: all italics are mine)

Churning – *buying and selling stock too frequently* – pushes up a fund's *dealing costs* and damages its capital growth. Despite this, our research indicates some managers are trading too often.

A reader recently wrote to us complaining that the manager of his investment trust was churning his portfolio. Why, asked the reader, in indignation, had the manager invested the starting sum, sold most of those holdings again, and then bought new ones – all within the first year?

It's a good question. High turnover like this undoubtedly pushes up costs. . . Trusts typically pay 0.2 per cent dealing commission, 0.5 per cent stamp duty. . . plus a buy–sell spread ranging from 0.5 per cent. . . to 3 per cent. . . Taken together, annual dealing costs for a high turnover trust can amount to 1 per cent or more of the portfolio's value.

More important than the effect on costs, however, is the reason why a trust has a high turnover – and the likely effect on its *performance*. Analyst Philip Middleton of Merrill Lynch believes 'these high-income trusts are looking a bit racy. If turnover is above 30 per cent, the most obvious explanation is that the manager is *trading in and out to collect dividends*'...

COMMENT

A fund manager who seeks to maximize the return from money invested in stocks can rarely leave the money in any one investment for a long period of time. Changes in the fortunes of companies mean that the returns from investments rise and fall. The essence of good fund management is therefore to sell stocks whose return is likely to fall and to buy those whose return is likely to rise. Buying and selling stocks costs money however. Transactions attract stamp duty, dealing and other costs, as the extract shows.

The essential decision that fund managers face in such situations is *when* and *how much* of any stock to buy or sell. But they have to decide in a way that balances the costs of a transaction against the benefit of finding a stock with a better return.

What we have here is yet another example of the principles of Fig 3.22. The 'controllable variable' in this case is the frequency with which the fund manager decides to turn over stocks through buying and selling: so-called 'churning'. The cost that increases with churning is 'Cost A' of Fig 3.22. This represents stamp duty, dealing, and other costs. The cost that decreases with churning, 'Cost B', is that associated with staying too long in investments whose returns are declining. Figure 3.22 suggests that there is an optimum or appropriate level of churning that balances these two kinds of cost. The *Investors Chronicle* article implies that some fund managers have not got this right. Too high a level of churning is leading to a disproportionate amount of Cost A.

FURTHER STUDY

The original *Investors Chronicle* article includes a fairly familiar photograph of a room packed with computer screens, and young dealers speaking into more than one telephone at a time. This element of visual interest has been trawled out of a photo database by the desktop publishing software of the journalist concerned, but is it a cliché? What information do dealers in investments have to have on their computer screens? What software do they use? Is the world of buying and selling investments that different from buying and selling any other commodity?

Try exploring the Web with www.FT.com as a starting point.

Trade-off and optimization

Figure 3.21 is in fact just one example of a standard control principle which is shown in Fig 3.22. When we study control systems we find that this principle comes up in many forms. We have already seen it in Fig 3.16. It shows that often when trying to design a control system, we find that a variable whose value we can set as part of our controlling actions has a double effect. Its effect on one set of costs is to increase them as the variable increases, while its effect on another set of costs is to decrease them as the variable increases. The total effect on costs of the choice of value for the variable implies that there is a lowest cost or optimum.

Since knowing the particular form of these relationships in any control situation depends on *information,* the information system has a role in optimizing the behaviour or performance of the control system as well as the transmission and storage roles we have considered so far.

Not surprisingly, versions of Fig 3.22 will crop up elsewhere in this book. Its universality has led to it being called the 'rubber stamp of operational research', after the subject which first widely emphasized it .

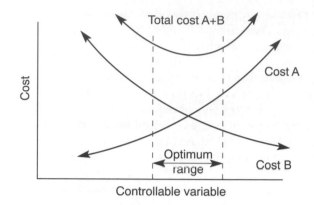

Fig 3.22 'The Rubber Stamp of Operational Research'
Figures 3.16 and 3.21 are just two examples of the concept of optimizing control systems. In these and further examples in this book, the basic format consists of a variable under our control which has opposite effects on two costs associated with the control system. The first cost increases as the variable is increased, while the second cost decreases. In all cases, the total cost has a concave upward shape that implies a minimum.

Box 3.6

A LETTER FROM THE DUKE OF WELLINGTON TO THE BRITISH GOVERNMENT IN WHITEHALL, LONDON, AUGUST 1812

Gentlemen,

Whilst marching from Portugal to a position which commands the approach to Madrid and the French forces, my officers have been diligently complying with your requests, which have been sent by H.M. Ship from London to Lisbon and thence by dispatch rider to our headquarters. We have enumerated our saddles, bridles, tents, tent poles, and all manner of sundry items for which His Majesty's Government holds me accountable. I have dispatched reports on the character, wit, and spleen of every officer. Each item and every farthing has been accounted for, with two regrettable exceptions, for which I beg your indulgence.

Unfortunately the sum of one shilling and ninepence remains unaccounted for in one battalion's petty cash and there has been a hideous confusion as to the number of jars of raspberry jam issued to one cavalry regiment during a sandstorm in Western Spain. This reprehensible carelessness may be related to the pressure of circumstances, since we are at war with France, a fact which may come as a bit of a surprise to you gentlemen in Whitehall.

This brings me to my present purpose, which is to request elucidation of my instructions from His Majesty's Government, so that I may better understand why I am dragging an army over these barren plains. I construe that perforce it must be one of two alternative duties, as given below. I shall pursue either one with my best ability, but I cannot do both:

1. To train an army of uniformed British clerks in Spain for the benefit of the accountants and copy-boys in London, or, perchance

2. To see to it that the forces of Napoleon are driven out of Spain.

Your most obedient servant,
  Wellington

COMMENT

Ancient History? Not if we consider some of the changes which have taken place in the management of British public services in recent times. The demands for accountability have increased the burden of formal reporting procedures. Similar examples can be found wherever top-level management is trying to control costs by demanding more information. But gathering information about costs itself involves costs. In Wellington's time these costs came from ships sailing to Lisbon from London and riders crossing mountains. Today, nurses may spend time filling in forms rather than attending to patients, teachers may be collecting data rather than teaching pupils, while police write about arrests rather than making them. We cannot manage without information, but the costs of control must be balanced against their benefits.

Incidentally, the Duke was a good holist. He recognized that information, useful or otherwise, is as much to do with the *hard* counting of tent poles as the *soft* assessment of officers' spleen.

FURTHER STUDY

Try to identify an organizational example which illustrates each end of the spectrum of balancing the costs of information against their value. Select one organization which loses the 'war', the market or whatever, through lack of information; and another organization where an obsession for information detracts it from its management goals. Look at Fig 3.22 and the *Leigh Interests* of Box 2.1, p. 24. Interpret and compare the systems concepts you find relevant.

3.3.6 Requisite variety and Ashby's Law

All of the explanation of the control concept so far has concentrated on examples of controlling a particular process such as stock levels or financial expenditure. We have considered how some simple action like reordering of stock or authorization of spending can be used to control the process concerned. The examples have been simple because the main aim was to understand the various components that make up a control system.

In practice, management is involved in controlling much more than a single process and has to deal with a much greater *variety* of systems behaviour than a particular form of stock movement or way of spending money. Thus besides stock being supplied, stored and subsequently sold, a stock control manager can expect to deal with theft, damage, returns from customer, returns to manufacturer, obsolescence, changes in demand and price, changes in legislation regarding storage conditions, and many other aggravations that make the job much more *complex*. If all the manager can do in response to this is to decide whether or not to reorder, it is very unlikely that he will be able to control the stockholding system. What is happening in this example is that the system which the manager seeks to control has a wide *variety* of ways in which it can behave, while the manager has only one simple way of responding.

Ashby (1963) recognized the importance of matching the variety of actions available to the controller, to the variety exhibited by the system he is trying to control. *Ashby's Law of Requisite Variety* states:

Only variety can destroy variety

– there must be the same amount of variety in the control process as in the system being controlled.

In our example above, the stock control manager will need to be able to operate security checks on personal access, choose handling procedures, inspect quality, and do many other things if he is to stand any chance of controlling the variety of things that can happen in the system.

However, matching variety is not just a question of *increasing* the variety available to the controller. We can also *decrease* the variety in the system we seek to control. One way we can do this is to *reduce uncertainty*. If we reduce our uncertainty about the behaviour of the system, we reduce the range of possible contingencies we have to allow for. The more we know about customer taste, the easier it is to focus on the products they are likely to buy, instead of wasting time on a whole range of unsellable products. The more we know about how thieves can get into the warehouse, the easier it is to focus on the important security measures, instead of wasting time on a whole range of unlikely possibilities.

If we seek to decrease the variety in the system we seek to control through the reduction of uncertainty, we recognize another important principle:

Information extinguishes variety

We shall say more about this in Chapter 4 when we discuss the concept of *entropy*. As far as Chapter 3 and Sections 3 and 4 of Appendix 1 are concerned, we can now see that many of the methods we have discussed so far for controlling systems behaviour use the concept of information as a destroyer of variety.

One final caution. Note that the term *variety* is being used here in a specific technical sense. We are not using it in its popular, everyday sense. In that context, variety is often a desirable quality. Few of us, I suspect, would want to further destroy the variety of animal species on the earth. But if we wanted to protect it, we would need to gain more information about potential threats. In gaining this information we reduce our uncertainty and therefore reduce the variety of the 'threat system' which we seek to control as conservationists.

3.4 INTRODUCTION TO SYSTEMS MODELLING AND DIAGRAMMING

3.4.1 Types of models

We have already seen in our development of systems language that where a term has both a systemic and an everyday meaning we need to check any distinction between them. The term *model* however is a term which means much the same in everyday life as it does in systems language. The major difference is that the systemic use of the term covers a wider range.

A model is a way of representing something. The thing represented may exist in real life or it may be a concept in the mind of the person making the model. Models can be created using different approaches:

a We can make a physical representation of something by using the same properties for the model as those possessed by what is being modelled. Usually the only difference between the model and the thing being modelled is a change of scale. Such models look like the thing they represent but are just a different size. These are the sort of models that planners or engineers often use to represent a new shopping centre or a new aircraft. They are often called *iconic* models, from the Greek word *eikon*, meaning an image.

b We can represent the properties of the original thing being modelled by substituting different ones to represent them in the model. Thus one property, like temperature in real life, can be represented in a model by another property like length in the mercury column of a thermometer or colour shades on a weather map. Such models are called *analogue* models.

c We can represent the properties of the original thing by using symbols in the model. This is what a mathematician does when describing the behaviour of something using algebra and equations. Such models are called *symbolic*. The most important example of symbolic models as far as information systems are concerned, are those we create when we produce diagrams to represent some properties of a system.

◆ **STQ 3.14**
Are so-called icons, which are used by graphical user interfaces, iconic models? What sort of model is used by computer software that represents the disk storage on the screen by a picture of a filing cabinet or the erase function by a waste paper basket?

Given that diagrams are a form of model, it is worth considering why models, including diagrams, are used. We have already used over twenty diagrams in this book so far, and it, like just about any other book you may find with the word 'system' in its title, contains many more. In the next sections we will see why diagrams always seem to go with systems and how they are used. This should prepare us, as the learning objectives of this chapter set out, for this frequent use of diagrams through this book.

3.4.2 Why models and diagrams are used

Models

We will begin by generally considering why models, including diagrams, are used. We shall then go on to consider specific reasons for using diagrams in the context of information systems development.

Understanding the use of models becomes clearer if we note that they are a substitute or 'stand-in' for the 'real thing'. We would wish to use a substitute in this way when any of the following apply:

a It is cheaper to create a model for discussion or experiment than it is to create the real thing. Producing an architect's model of a new building is cheaper than building it in real life. Producing a diagram of how a system might work is easier than producing the whole system.

b It is easier to experiment with and modify a model than it is to do the same in real life. It is easier to rearrange the components of an architect's model than rebuild the building. It is easier to modify a diagram than to install a new system.

c Mistakes made when experimenting with a model are less disastrous than ones made in real life. Finding that the plastic scale model or the screen image of a car will not fit into the garage is less disastrous than scraping your car against the brickwork as you drive it in. Calculating (= symbolic model) that a particular file will not fit into a given computer memory space is less disastrous than the reorganization of a public records system with questions in parliament and a fall of government. (A completely fictitious example, but it could have happened by the time you read this book.)

d Building a model helps you understand the thing being modelled. The architect's plan help us to see that you don't need to go up any stairs to get into the dining room. A systems diagram shows the order of processes that have to be carried out to update a customer's account.

e Models can be used for communication, education and training. When the architect's client wants to know what the building will look like, or the builder needs to know what he is supposed to be building, the model, in the form of the design plans, show the answers. When the programmer wants to produce the system specified by the systems designer, diagrams will almost certainly be used as part of the specification.

Systems diagrams

Given that diagrams as a particular form of model have already been frequently used in this book, we can list how the broad reasons for using models translate into the need for systems diagrams:

a *Complexity and Holism.* If the whole is more than the sum of the parts, then a description of a system and its components, one at a time in serial fashion, is not an effective way to present the qualities of the whole. A diagram can make use of all of the flat surface of a paper page or a three-dimensional screen projection to give an overall picture.

b *Definition:* If diagrams are more effective at representing the whole form of a particular system and its qualities, then they can equally effectively define existing and proposed systems, relationships, structures and processes.

c *Discovery:* It is hard to represent what you do not understand. Having to discover enough about a system to draw a diagram not only requires heuristic (= discovery) activities, but also implies comparison with knowledge or ideal models that we already have. Ideals imply paradigms, and comparison can imply the analysis and comparison.

d *Recording:* For a diagram to represent what has been defined or discovered about a system, it must also be a record. Systems may have both abstract and concrete components, but a diagram can record both. It can use the principles of symbolic representation to model both abstract and concrete properties of the system.

e *Communication:* As we shall see in Chapter 4, the communication of information requires a *shared symbol set*. Agreed conventions for the use of symbols to represent systems components can mean that diagrams act as a language for communicating information about systems.

f *Education:* One particular form of communication is involved when we attempt to implement and maintain systems. As we shall see in Chapter 7, systems development itself is a systemic process with a human aspects role. Diagrams as definers and communicators of information about systems can support this role.

g *Control:* Attempting to implement a system and maintain its goals is a form of *control*. Diagrams can act as a particular medium for the recording and transmission of information as part of the control loop considered in detail in Section 3.2.

h *Learning:* If diagrams have a control role in systems development, then at higher-order levels of control they can act as tools for learning.

Systems development

We have now referred to *systems development* several times when explaining the use of systems diagrams. Systems development is concerned with the whole process of deciding the need for an *information system*, specifying what it must do, designing how it must do it, and implementing the design.

This process will require the eventual *definition* of the system to be implemented, after *discovery* of the problems of the existing system and improvements to it have been *recorded,* so that it can be *communicated* to the potential users. They are thus *educated* into *controlling* its implementation and subsequently *learning* from their experience.

All of the words in italics indicate the potential role of systems diagrams in systems development which we will cover in more depth in Chapter 7. To prepare us for more detailed use of diagrams through the book and into Chapter 7 however it would be useful to have a simple way of making sense of the many diagrams that can be used. We shall do this in the next section.

3.4.3 Types of diagrams

Even the briefest look at books on systems will show that diagrams are widely used for the reasons we have just given. What is also soon seen if we look closer is that the range of diagrams appears to be very wide, both in what they show and how they show it.

Although attempts have been regularly made by the advocates of particular systems methods or the authors of some books to establish standards, there is no sign of any widely accepted convention for diagramming. Hence any attempt to discuss systems diagrams in detail is in danger of becoming a mere listing of all the different conventions and styles.

There is however one simple but effective way to make some sense of the bewildering range. If we remember that all systems diagrams seek to present one or more properties of a system, then the range of approaches to diagramming is likely to reflect the range of systems properties. The most important of these are likely to be what the system consists of and what the system does, i.e. *structure* and *process*.

Structure

Figures 3.3 and 3.21 represent the two main ways of showing *structure*: that is, they represent fixed relationships between the various components of a system. The positions of the components do not represent any particular sequence of events in time or logic. There is no reason why any one particular subsystem should be in any particular place on the page, or the shapes of the blobs in Fig 3.23 should be of any particular kind. What matters in a diagram showing structure is that we can see the relationships between components rather than worrying about how the individual components are represented.

The diagrams show structure by using one of two basic ways of showing relationships: by linear linkages or by encircling containment. The first method is sometimes called the *digraph convention*, and is illustrated by Fig 3.3. The second method is called the *Venn convention*, and is illustrated by Fig 3.23.

Process

The essential point about any process is that it transforms some input to a different form that we call an output. However the input to a process will have come from some source; either another component in the system or in its environment. Similarly the output will need a destination either in the system or in its environment. For diagrams showing process we therefore need some way of showing:

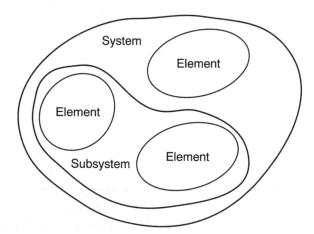

Fig 3.23 Systems Hierarchy
The shapes of 'blobs' in diagrams based on the Venn convention are not significant.

a. Individual processes

b. The flow of inputs and outputs

c. The sequence in which processes are carried out

d. Sources and destinations outside the system

Processes, sources and destinations are usually indicated by some convention of shapes or *blobs* (e.g. Fig 3.14), and the usual way to show flows is by means of arrows. Sequence is then expressed by the logical connexion of processes, sources and destinations through the arrows.

Note also that sequence can be shown by an accepted convention of relative position on the page. Thus in European convention, sequence begins at the top left-hand corner and proceeds rightwards and downwards to the bottom right; but there is no reason as far as I can see why we shouldn't go right–left or bottom up: the main thing is that the convention is understood.

Unstructured or free diagramming

Our analysis of the basic principles and reasons behind diagramming has left out one important example that we shall take up again in Chapter 7. If our need for a diagram is mainly *heuristic* a convention can be dangerous in that it focusses our attention on one particular aspect. Thus attempting to diagram processes means that the system is seen primarily as something dynamic, with structure coming in later. If our heuristic aims mean that we want to keep our minds open to record anything about a situation which may be of interest, a way of diagramming which does not have a predetermined emphasis might be useful.

As we shall see in Chapter 8, such a diagram is the *rich picture* (Fig 8.4). Its aim is to provide a *holist*, open way of recording any situation as we meet it. The lack of strict rules about what sort of symbols, words, or any other way of recording that can be used is deliberate. It is an attempt to prevent us prematurely excluding things just because they can't be neatly pigeon-holed, or only selecting certain kinds of evidence. With a rich picture we can record anything that is of interest and sort out later what sort of themes, topics or issues the picture tells us about.

KEY WORDS

Abstract	Data	Iconic model	Process
Actuator	Dynamic	Identity	Sensor
Analogue model	Effector	Information	Soft
Behaviour	Element	Input	Soft uncertainty
Boundary	Emergent property	Interaction	Structure
Buffer	Environment	Lag	Subsystem
Comparator	Feedback	Master file	Symbolic model
Complexity	Goal	Meliorism	System
Components	Goal-seeking	Model	Transaction file
Concept	Goal-setting	Optimization	Transformation process
Conceptualism	Hard	Output	Uncertainty
Concrete	Hard uncertainty		
Connexion	Hierarchy		
Control	Holism		

SEMINAR AGENDAS, EXAM QUESTIONS AND PROJECT/DISSERTATION SUBJECTS

1 Why do we seek to have definitions for terms in practical subjects? Is defining things useful? Consider the form and role of definition (if any) in engineering, medicine or the law. Talk to fellow students who study these subjects.

2 What were the sources of the systems movement? Why has it become so strong in the last three decades? Take a reader like Beishon & Peters (1972), (1976), or (1981); as a starting point.

3 Discuss the words *holism*, *uncertainty* and *decision* in relation to the three quotations at the start of this book from Lord Kelvin, Edie Brickell and the Duke of Wellington.

4 In answer to STQ 3.10 I said, 'Many of the soft issues connected with goals have often been decided for official organizations by the government and can be less of an issue for them'. A good dissertation topic area? Very broad; you could consider whether soft issues do get resolved or, if so, how.

5 The General Control Model of Fig 3.14 is my creation albeit from various sources quoted. A critical analysis of its features in relation to an organization you know could be a useful exercise. How would you modify it?

6 Investigate the stock reduction/elimination system known as 'Just in Time' or JIT. Does it contradict the concept of buffering set out in Section 3.3?

7 Study the workings of an example of commercial stock control software. Does it really control stock in terms of both goal-seeking and goal-setting, or does it merely use input information to update stock records?

8 How does an organization that you are familiar with actually make forecasts. What are the relative roles of 'guesswork' or 'feel' to formal use of mathematical forecasting methods? Why does it work the way it does? Is it working in the best way?

9 Take the 'rubber stamp' of Fig 3.22 and see if you can find examples in quality control, financial control or controlling the government of a country by the choice of timing for elections.

FEEDBACK ON SELF-TESTING QUESTIONS

◆ STQ 3.1

If we are thinking about the physical cupboard itself, probably not. However, what constitutes a cupboard can be very different for different people in the organization. Thus to someone planning production a cupboard is essentially a job which requires the bringing together of components like production capacity, time and human skill, all of which are abstract. Just as £1 could be the name of something concrete or abstract depending on whose view we were taking.

The importance of deciding whether we are talking of something in concrete or abstract terms will be explained further when we consider entities in the context of data modelling in Chapter 5.

◆ STQ 3.2

Hard properties of a cupboard would be things like its physical dimensions, its weight or its price. Soft properties could be its attractiveness to the customer, whether it was big or small in terms of their perception of its use, or whether they thought the price was cheap.

◆ STQ 3.3

I don't think so. A door for example can be considered as a component of a cupboard from the moment a designer decides to make it so. A logical connexion has been made well before the cupboard is assembled.

◆ STQ 3.4

To a sales manager a cupboard is probably seen as an element in the sales system, since nothing less than an individual cupboard is of much interest. To a production manager a cupboard is seen as a component of the production system, but is also seen as being made up of components which are the parts and subassemblies making up the cupboard.

◆ STQ 3.5

For a system such as the EMS, the transformation processes carried out by the ERM may be mainly concerned with transforming abstract components such as money. As we saw above when discussing abstract components, our awareness of this transformation process is likely to come from the information we record about conceptual changes in the logical state of the system or its components, rather than any observed physical mechanism. With Carry-Out Cupboards we may watch a physical assembly process, but when two dealers exchange currencies they agree to a change in their debtor–creditor states. With an abstract transformation process such as this no physical money changes hands and the two dealers don't suddenly look any different, but this certainly does not mean that the process is 'unreal' or not 'practical'.

◆ STQ 3.6

If we see the ecu as something formed by the coming together of component national currencies, then it represents an aggregation and is at a higher hierarchical level of the monetary system. Its value and overall nature could be then seen as an emergent property.

◆ STQ 3.7

Not necessarily. Where we are concerned with a biological or ecological system the two terms may coincide. If we consider an animal or species as a system, the atmosphere they breath, the plants or other animals they eat, etc., are all part of their systems environment.

◆ STQ 3.8

An abstract goal of the European Monetary System would be a single currency; for the Exchange Rate Mechanism it could be exchange rate stability.

◆ STQ 3.9

The more people sold the pound the lower its value became. The lower its value, the more dealers were alarmed into selling. A good example of the destructive nature of positive feedback.

◆ STQ 3.10

As with many official, government founded bodies the ultimate goals are defined by an act of parliament. Thus the statutory duty to drain or to take account of environmental concerns are in various Drainage Acts. The translation of these high-level goals into detailed operational goals will be done by management. We learn two things from this:

1. *Our control model needs to distinguish different levels of goal-setting.*
2. *Many of the soft issues connected with goals have often been decided for official organizations by the government and can be less of an issue for them.*

◆ STQ 3.11

The short answer is that we can't. Perhaps a better phrase would be the maximum likely demand. 'Likely' could then be defined as something that would not be exceeded more than one week in say ten. A stochastic analysis of past data could then be used to determine this demand level. There is a vital role here for forecasting: see section 3.3.5.

◆ STQ 3.12

Yes, this was meant to be a deliberately odd question, but it does relate to the issues we are raising here and in the next section. I think your answer will be that you tend to look at it more often when there is a lot of paying in and paying out going on? The cost of not being up to date is likely to be higher when you are using the account a lot. The potential effects of such costs push the balance of cost towards justifying the extra nuisance cost of more frequent checking.

◆ STQ 3.13

No good holist would expect forecasting to be purely a hard, quantitative procedure. Anticipating future trends in sales of goods which depend on social fashion, ethical perceptions and other soft questions of weltanschauung or world view requires an input from the higher levels of the General Control Model of Fig 3.14, not just monitoring past sales statistics.

◆ STQ 3.14

The sort of model used by computer software that represents the disk storage on the screen by a picture of a filing cabinet or the erase function by a waste paper basket, are not always iconic models. They are indeed sometimes pictures of what they represent and therefore iconic, but quite often they are symbolic models which do not 'picture' the thing represented.

REFERENCES/BIBLIOGRAPHY

Ackoff, R.L. (1962). *Scientific Method: Optimizing Applied Research Decisions.* Wiley.

Ackoff, R.L. (1971). Towards a System of Systems Concepts. *Management Science.* 17 (11).

Ackoff, R.L. & Sasieni, M.W. (1968). *Fundamentals of Operations Research.* Wiley.

Beer, S. (1985). *Diagnosing the System.* Wiley.

Beishon, R.J. & Peters, G. (Eds). (1972), (1976), 2nd edn. (1981), 3rd edn. *Systems Behaviour.* Harper & Row.

Ben-Eli, M.U. (1988). Cybernetic Tools for Management: Their Usefulness and Limitations, in Sadovsky, V. & Umpleby, S. (Eds). *Science of Goal Formulation.* Hemisphere Publishing.

Davis, G.B. & Olson, M.H. (1984). *Management Information Systems.* McGraw-Hill.

Espejo, R. & Harnden, R. (1989). *The Viable Systems Model.* Wiley.

Fishburn, P. (1964). *Decision and Value Theory.* Wiley.

Flood, R.L. & Jackson, M.C. (1991). *Creative Problem Solving.* Wiley.

Harry, M.J.S. (1990). *Information and Management Systems.* Pitman.

Luce, R.D. & Raiffa, H. (1957). *Games and Decisions.* Wiley.

Schoderbeck, P.P., Schoderbeck, C.G. & Kefalas, A.G. (1990). *Management Systems.* Business Publications.

You can't generalize, or can you?: 'Lies, damned lies and statistics'

What happened

'What is a game?' is a question that the philosopher Wittgenstein (1953) once used as the basis of a very erudite discussion about the 'common features of knowledge'.

None of the management of Carry-Out Cupboards would have been concerned with anything as academic as that; but games and meanings of words came up several times during an important meeting on one particular Monday morning. The meeting had been called by the Marketing Department to discuss the results of a customer survey which had been carried out as part of a review of the company's product range. The results of the survey were being presented by Ray Lister of Bycall Associates, the public relations firm for Carry-Out Cupboards who had carried it out. Since any decision to make major changes to products could affect production methods, those present also included people from the Production Department led by Ian Hunter.

The venue was a plush but formal conference room. As people arrived they shuffled around the large table choosing where to sit and making rather artificial smalltalk to break down the formal atmosphere. When Ian Hunter arrived he asked Ross Carter from Marketing whether he had seen 'the game' that weekend. There was then some confusion in the conversation because, although Ross and Ian shared a strong interest in football, they did not share the same commitment to a particular team. Ross's team were playing to prevent themselves being relegated from the Premier League, while Ian's team were playing for promotion into it. For Ross, 'the game' was the one in which his team lost and were now on their way down. For Ian, 'the game' was the one in which his team won and were now on their way up. For Anne Dickens, the Head of Marketing, 'the game' was the teasing that went on between Ross and Ian, which she recognized as a cover for the continuing friction in relations between Marketing and Production. Marketing sometimes got irritated with Production's apparent inflexibility when they wanted to change or modify products in response to customer demands, while Production felt that Marketing confused being inflexible with having to be practical. Ross and Ian tended to be the particular personalities who perpetuated this bad feeling with their sparring at meetings. Anne recognized the football exchange as part of this destructive tendency and put an end to it by getting the meeting started.

She began by introducing Ray Lister from Bycall and then asking him to talk them through the survey. Ray began by explaining that the survey was just one of a series designed to find out what sort of product the customer would want in the next five years. The aim of these surveys was to establish customer wants in terms of general characteristics and families of products, rather than looking for detailed decisions on designs or styling. This first survey had looked at customer perceptions of health and ethics. Ray explained that the original idea for the survey came from observing what had happened in the food industry through the 1980s. During that period, customers had become increasingly interested in what food contained as well as how it tasted. Concern for 'healthy eating' meant that they wanted to know about such details as fat, fibre or sugar content. Similarly there had been an increasing interest in how food was produced for ethical reasons. Customers were concerned with how farm animals were treated, or for vegetable products they wanted to know if they came from countries where labour was exploited or the environment damaged to produce them. So far such concerns had not significantly entered into peoples thinking about the way they furnished their houses, but was it going to? Ray explained that that was what this survey set to find out.

Ray then reminded the meeting that the present product range of Carry-Out Cupboards was almost entirely made out of wood and plastics. He asked how long would it be before some pressure group started a campaign against Carry-Out Cupboards because wood meant chopping down trees and plastics meant using non-renewable fossil fuels. At this point Ian groaned and said that 'the whole conservation thing' was a dying trend left over from the 1980s. All a survey like this did was to encourage people to consider things they otherwise would not have worried about. He thought that what usually passed as public thinking was misleading anyway, it was usually media generalization based on selective evidence.

Ross asked whether Ian was therefore saying that any attempt to survey public attitudes was a waste of time. Ian pointed out that it was a matter of interpretation; as Mark Twain had said, 'there are lies, damned lies and statistics'. Surveys showed that people with big feet are better at mathematics than people with small feet: that was because babies have small feet and aren't much good at maths: so they bias the figures. The discussion then ran away with itself as various people tried to tell their favourite story about misleading statistics; such as the high correlation between how much money clergymen had to spend and the profits made by breweries, or between the incidence of venereal disease and the amount of railway travel in any particular country.

Anne stopped all this diversion and got the meeting back on course. It went without saying that the Bycall team included qualified statisticians who didn't need lessons in such obvious and elementary points. Although she did not say so to the meeting, she knew that Ian knew that too. His attempt to rubbish the survey was more to do with interdepartmental politics than what he really believed.

Ray then went on to look at the figures for the responses to the questions in the survey. He admitted that many of the results were disappointing, for two reasons. First, there were high levels of 'don't knows' to many of the questions. Second, there was often little difference between the proportion of respondents agreeing or disagreeing with the propositions put to them in the survey questions. Thus one series of questions aimed to find out how important customers felt that it was to know where the materials used in products came from. Most of the answers to these questions came out evenly balanced. For every customer who felt strongly about an issue there was one who didn't seem to care.

The survey also showed great confusion over the meaning of words used in arguments about conservation and other ethical issues. Quite a high proportion, for example, considered that wood was not a renewable resource. When asked the same question about metals, the majority in one age group actually said they didn't know. Ray developed this theme of confusion by showing that the survey indicated some confusion about the meaning of 'renewable' and 'recyclable'. He concluded that the survey could have been better designed if they'd picked this up before.

At that point in the analysis Ian surprised everyone by being very constructive. He reminded the meeting that the success of the company derived from its concept of building a family of products based on a common set of designs and materials that could be permutated to form a range. Provided any changes in materials could be applied to a whole class of Carry-Out Cupboards products, they would not make great problems for the Production Department. Generally, changes to any part of the range could be accommodated provided they were applied in a systematic way and not to random selections.

By this time the meeting had reached some kind of agreement on one point at least, and Anne thought it a good idea to break for coffee while everyone was in a constructive mood. She felt that the score in the game so far was 1–1.

A management and control systems view

In Chapter 3 we developed the General Control Model of Fig 3.14 as a way of making sense of the different forms of information and their roles in management. If we apply this model and use our understanding of systems concepts to consider what happened in the mini-case, we can discover another major concept that will help us identify further issues about the nature and role of information in the context of control. If we begin by considering what happened at the marketing meeting in terms of the General Control Model of Fig 3.14, we can then go on to see what this concept is and the issues it raises.

As recounted in the case, the aim of the meeting was to explore the results of a market survey of customer attitudes. The survey was one of several which were being carried out with the aim of finding out what sort of product the customer would want in the next five years. The survey was focussing on general characteristics for products like being ethically acceptable or ecologically conscious, rather than setting details of design or styling. In terms of *control systems hierarchy* we would describe this as trying to set *high-level goals*. Thus if the survey was successful, it would help Carry-Out Cupboards decide whether they should switch entirely to renewable materials and whether they should start to be fussy about where these came from. Only once these decisions had been made would Carry-Out Cupboards then consider which particular materials and sources they ought to choose.

In terms of the General Control Model the survey was therefore mainly concerned with *fourth-order* or *normative* goal-setting. The eventual output delivered by this process would be a *policy* enabling Carry-Out Cupboards to set lower-order goals like the material content of their product or sources of supply.

We can also note that this goal-setting was looking to the future and trying to anticipate or *forecast* potential *environmental disturbances* in the form of changing customer attitudes. Such anticipation was necessary because it would take time to decide on new materials, review sources of supply, develop new cupboard designs and modify production processes. There was, as in all real-life control systems, a lag in the control loops.

This interpretation of the case in control systems terms can be further developed if we note that what links all of the activities of the General Control Model's components is information *flow*. These flows represent the inputs and outputs of components of the information system which itself is a subsystem of the whole control system. If the activities of the marketing meeting are interpreted in control systems terms, it is not surprising to find examples of these flows present. Thus the survey was an attempt to gain information on *environmental disturbances,* while the ultimate aim of the meeting was to deliver information on *policy*. When Ian Hunter was explaining the implications for Production of potential changes, he was providing *feedback* information.

Understanding that a system is a *concept* however tells us that we can see the activities of the meeting in terms of other systems. We could see many of the events described in terms of a *human activity system*. Opening conversation and smalltalk to relax the atmosphere, the political sparring between Ian and Ross, or people's attempts to get a laugh by telling the best false statistical correlation story; these all required information flow to make the human activity system work.

The goals of the human activity system were not always the same as those of Carry-Out Cupboards seen as an organizational system. As we also saw in Chapter 3 any control system is just a subsystem of the wider *management* system. Anne's eventual success at controlling the meeting and its members as well as acting as marketing professional is a good example of this. Here again however information flow was required: if only to tell Ian to shut up!

Thus when we look at what went on at the meeting we see that *information flow* is an essential component of the management system and the control systems which are components of it.

The issues raised

The need for an important additional concept with the issues that it raises can be established by asking whether information *flow* is a sufficient way to describe the way the information system links together the components of management and control systems. We can answer this question by looking further at what went on at the marketing meeting.

To carry out the survey it was necessary that information in the form of questions had to flow to those interviewed and more information in the form of answers had to flow back. This had happened and the survey was completed, but its success had been limited because respondents had not always *understood* words like 'renewable resource'. Even when the results of the survey did seem to be reliable, they were not always very useful in the sense of being *informative*. Questions with a high proportion of 'don't know' replies didn't help Carry-Out Cupboards much in deciding their policies on the issues. Finally, both Ian and Ross knew what a game was, without consulting Wittgenstein, but they were at cross-purposes because they were referring to different ones. An example like this shows that the need for correct *interpretation* is closely connected to the need for understanding. Bycall Associates recognized this when they avoided asking customers whether they preferred 'green' furniture; thereby risking confusion of furniture colour and ecological consciousness.

There is therefore an additional important concept which is highlighted by both the official business of the marketing meeting and the informal behaviour of its members. This is the concept of *communication*. It is not sufficient that information should flow for a management or control system to work: the results of the flow should mean that both the *sender* and *receiver* have the same understanding of the *message*. If we are to build on the systems concepts of Chapter 3 to have a greater understanding of what information is and what its role in business is, we need to settle two issues:

Issue 1. What is communication?

Issue 2. What is needed to ensure that it is successful?

LEARNING OBJECTIVES CHAPTER 4

1 To specify a model of a *communication system* in the context of *management* and *control* systems.

2 To understand the implications for the concept of *information* which come from identifying the role of the components of a communication system.

3 To translate these implications into an understanding of concepts and language used to describe *stochastic* and *complex* information.

CHAPTER 4
•••••••••••••••••••

Information Concepts

4.1   COMMUNICATION

Figure 4.1 shows a model of a communication system. Since we shall use this to understand a range of different examples, I shall refer to it as the General Communication System Model. We will begin by looking at the overall form of the model and then at its components. After each of these subsections I will include a subsection on the practical implications of the concept, using the same approach we made in Chapter 3 to the concept of a system.

The General Communication System Model

An important feature of the model that should be noticed from the beginning is that it is a model of a *system*. We can therefore expect that it will have all those *systemic properties* that we introduced in Chapter 3.

◆ **STQ 4.1**
Use the subsection headings of Section 3.1 as a check list to confirm that the General Communication System Model conforms to this last statement. I suggest you keep referring back to this STQ as we explore the model and its components, and then consider the feedback.

Although I shall present the model in a way designed to support the objectives of this chapter and the book generally, the form of the model and the names of its components are very similar to those you will find in standard books on information systems, e.g. Davis & Olson (1984), p.83. Thus the General Communication System Model is not as individual to this book as the General Control Model.

Like the General Control Model, the General Communication System Model derives originally from hard engineering systems applications. Names like *channel* or *encoder* referred to technical equipment. But as we used control to represent a *concept* rather than a particular physical application or management style, so we shall take communication as a concept that can be applied more widely than physical systems like telephone or radio networks. As with other systems, we focus first on the General Communication System Model as a *what* rather than a particular *how*.

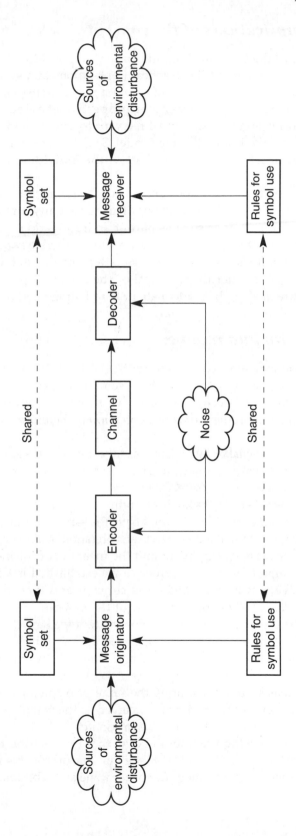

Fig 4.1 The General Communication System Model

As with the classical control model of Fig 3.8, this represents a version of a widely held view. The annotation of the diagram might be improved by showing that a shared symbol set could also be described as a 'closely approximated' symbol set.

The practical implications of the concept

Once we recognize that the General Communication System Model is a model of a *system*, then all we have said about the practical implications of a systemic approach in Section 3.1 apply to it. The implications of components, connexion, structure, hierarchy, process, interaction, holism, emergent property, behaviour, environment, identity, boundary, and conceptualism are all relevant to understanding the implications of the General Communication System Model. STQ 4.1 is designed to encourage critical thought about this, but we will also look at the individual concepts as they come up.

At this point however, the most important practical implication of the concept is one that it shares with other business systems. This is that any attempt to develop and implement a communication system as part of an information system must take account of its holist nature. It will have both abstract and concrete components, and it will involve hard and soft issues. Consequently attempts to establish or improve communication that ignore either the technical or the human aspects of the system and their interaction are likely to be inadequate or to fail altogether.

Message originator and receiver

The first point that you may have considered for STQ 4.1 is that communication is an *emergent property*. Putting aside trite jokes about schizophrenia, it takes at least two people for communication to occur: we don't see someone communicating with themself. The minimum requirement of communication is therefore an originator and a receiver.

I have chosen the word *originator* rather than 'sender' because we are concerned with *whose* message it is rather than who sends it. This emphasis on the original source of a message is one essential if it is to be correctly *interpreted* and *understood*. I put those last two words in italics to refer back to the analysis of the issues raised by the mini-case. As with Ian and Ross, even if the word 'game' does have the same meaning for two people, knowing who is using it is essential for a correct interpretation of a message.

This link between the message originator and the meaning of the message is a particular instance of an important systems principle we established in Chapter 3. There we recognized that every system is someone's concept and that the nature of the system reflects the *weltanschauung* or *world view* of the system's owner or conceiver. For information in the context of an information system we saw that this principle governed what data was collected, processed, stored and output; how it was assembled into a whole structure to form information; and what role this information played in the wider control and management system. Here we see the concept of a message as part of a communications system illustrating the same principle. Just as the model of any system reflects the views of its owner or conceiver, so the meaning of the information in a message will reflect the intentions of its originator.

We decided, when discussing the issues above, that information flow alone was insufficient for communication. We can now see one reason for this is that, besides receiving the flow, we need to know about its source if we are to be able to interpret it.

The practical implications of the concept

A simple but effective example of this can be found in the stock record example of Fig 3.2. Practical information systems in business still include paper records like this as an essential component, despite claims that computers would lead to 'the paperless office'. If we consider *any* piece of paper which circulates in a real business, the message that it actually transmits, as opposed to what the words logically say, depends on who sent the memo, invoice, or the record of stock; and their reasons for doing so.

In practical terms it is not sufficient to receive an information flow requesting 'the balance of the account', 'what have we sold', or anything else. Understanding through interpretation only comes from knowing who the originator is, and how they fit into the wider business system in terms of their function or role.

When we consider the roles of all who are involved in the workings of an information system and the implications for systems development in Chapter 7, we shall find that identifying the roles of originators and receivers is as important as understanding procedures. Many systems development methods have important first stages that record and analyse such flows and roles in the existing information system as a prelude to specifying improvement. We shall also see that good systems methodology generally recognizes that we need understanding of the soft issues behind what people seek, or do not seek, to communicate about their needs from a system and their role in it.

Shared symbol set and rules for use

The implication of needing to know the originator of a message was that without this information, the receiver would not be able to *interpret* its meaning. Understanding the *weltanschauung* of the originator, for example, enables the receiver to resolve the *soft* issues behind the use of words, language, and symbols. Thus if two people use the word 'game', the receiver of the message can only be clear about which game is referred to once they know who originated the message.

This analysis of the use of the word game in the mini-case still contains an assumption. We said that 'both Ian and Ross knew what a game was, without consulting Wittgenstein'. There is an implied sneer in this remark which is misleading. The view that everybody knows what words mean, and that only impractical people like academic philosophers argue about them, is not supported by what we find from practical evidence. In the mini-case, Anne was not perverting the meaning of the word game when she used it in a different sense from Ian and Ross to describe their behaviour. That was just an example of how words can legitimately mean different things to different people at different times, or in different contexts. It is not only necessary to know who is sending a message if you are a receiver: you also need to have some common ground of understanding with the person who is originating the message.

This 'common ground' is represented in the General Communication System Model by two components:

1. *A shared set of symbols*
2. *Shared rules for symbol use*

Thus for communication using language, a *shared set of symbols* implies that people have to use the same alphabet and words. The *shared rules for symbol use* imply in turn that they agree on such things as spelling, pronunciation, or which direction the writing flows on the page.

◆ **STQ 4.2**

Interpret the other important means of communicating information about systems that we considered in addition to language in Chapter 3.

The practical implications of the concepts

In the field of computer-based information systems we are surrounded with practical examples of the importance of these concepts. For communication to take place between the components of an individual computer system, or between computers themselves, there has to be a *shared symbol set* like the ASCII standard. Since digital computer systems only communicate on the basis of sending binary signals, there has to be an agreed way of linking specific patterns of binary digits, i.e. numbers, with specific letters or characters. The ASCII tables you find in the appendices of computer and printer manuals list these specific linkages, so that the letter 'a' is represented by the hexadecimal number 61.

In terms of wider applications covered by language, you are only able to read this page because we share the symbol sets and rules for use of the Latin alphabet and the English language. This is not quite the same as the ASCII shared symbol set because there is no such thing as a standard. Legitimate differences exist in the forms of English spoken throughout the world. When we want to remove the potential this gives for poor communication and misunderstanding we have to adopt a formally agreed standard. As we saw in Chapter 3 and developed in STQ 4.2, diagrams provide one means of overcoming ambiguity when seeking to communicate information about systems themselves. In Chapter 8 we shall find that other tools may be used for this purpose. Thus communicating clearly what a process does in a system may require us to adopt an exclusive set of defined words and ways of using them called *structured English*. Such a tool is designed to ensure that the *originator*, in the form of the systems developer, successfully communicates a definition of what a process should do to the *receiver*, in the form of the systems builder or computer programmer.

Encoder, channel and decoder

If we consider examples of communication we find that the component processes called *encoding* and *decoding* connected by a common *channel* in the General Communication System Model are required for two related reasons:

1. The originator and receiver have different ways of describing or recording information.
2. It is not possible for the information to flow in the form that both the originator or receiver describe or record it.

An example of these reasons is why the computer programmer has other roles beyond that described above of being the receiver of instructions on what a program must achieve. The role of programmer came from the need for encoding and decoding: indeed, we actually call what a programmer ultimately produces 'code'. Computer code is essentially a set of instructions in a digital form a computer can understand, recorded in an electronic medium it can read. Human beings however issue instructions in the aural medium of speech or the visual medium of writing, and record them on the medium of paper or brain memory.

Until recently this example would illustrate both reasons 1 and 2 above. Thus if humans recorded on paper and computers did so electronically, then reason 1 applied. If humans sent out speech in the form of sound waves and computers could only receive electronic signals, then reason 2 applied. The advent of such devices as document readers and the understanding of words by computers have weakened reason 2 and thereby removed some of the old roles for computer programmers. Humans can communicate with computers directly with printed documents or by typing instructions in simple English that computers can understand. So-called *high-level* computer languages can be understood by both computers and humans.

Note however that this does not represent a removal of the need to encode and decode. Instead what has happened is that the removal of reason 2 above comes from a change in the nature of the *channel* between originator and receiver. In early computer systems the needs of the computer tended to dominate. The emphasis was on encoding the message in a *logical form* and on a *physical medium* that the computer could deal with. As computers became complex and adaptable, the form of the channel more reflected the human need. Behind these advances however, the computer uses the same principles and media that it did nearly a half-century ago. What has happened is that the computer now offers decoding that adapts to the human-preferred channels rather than the human choosing the encoding that adapts to the computer's preferred channel.

The practical implications of the concepts

I think that the most important implication of these concepts for information systems in business comes when we consider the communication that has to take place between the human and equipment components of a computerized information system. In this situation the sequence of encoder-channel-decoder represents a major connexion between sources of *hard* and *soft problems* and *issues*. The computer system is a mechanical device that operates according to set rules of logic and predetermined standards. The *human activity system* which has to interact with this computer system so that they both act as components of the wider information system, works on the basis of taste, judgement, beliefs and other factors depending on the *weltanschauung* or *world view* of those involved.

We saw in Chapter 3 that information can be seen as an emergent property resulting from the bringing together of data components. The nature of any information in terms of what it tells us and what we can do with it will therefore depend on how data is brought together to form it. Chapter 5 will give examples of how the choice of method used to build individual data components into information depend on both the logical view or model (the *whats*) of the information, and the physical medium (the *hows*) used to record it. For the communication of information therefore, the logical model implies a shared symbol set and rules for originator and receiver, and the medium implies a channel.

Chapter 6 will show that once we see a business or organization as a system, new technological development can be used to provide a common channel for communication for very different originators and receivers. This does not always represent a 'solution' or a 'facilitation', but rather the need to sometimes deal with contemporary information systems in a different way from the old ones.

Chapter 8 will define the subject of systems development methodology in a way that covers the issue of communication between both hard and soft components when we aim to create a new or improved working information system in business.

◆ **STQ 4.3**

Both encoding and decoding represent the processes that happen at the interface or boundary between the technical and human subsystem components of information systems. What types of support are now available to the user for this process?

Sources of environmental disturbance and noise

We have already established that the occurrence of the word *system* in the title 'General Communication System Model' means that all those properties of a system which we covered in Chapter 3 would be exhibited by a communications system. We also asserted in Chapter 3 that no real-life system, like a business system, could be a *closed* system. All real-life systems have an environment which disturbs them and over which they have only limited influence or control.

These properties and principles are shown to apply to communication systems when we consider:

    a. The effect of *environmental disturbances* on the message originator and receiver.

    b. The phenomenon of *noise*.

Environmental disturbance of the message originator and receiver means that in practice neither of these components is a fixed entity whose position or behaviour never changes. Where the originator or receiver is human this means that such factors as tiredness, dishonesty or inconsistency can be present in the message *before* encoding or can be placed into its interpretation *after* decoding. It also means that although the General Communication System Model talks of 'shared' symbol sets or rules for use, in practice we might better add the phrase 'a close approximation to'.

◆ **STQ 4.4**

What would you see as examples of environmental disturbances to communication in the mini-case?

The term *noise* is used to refer specifically to the environmental disturbances which affect the encoding-channel-decoding sequence in the General Communication System Model. In the original technical applications of communications, these effects would literally be the noise we hear when atmospheric electrical effects result in interference on a radio channel. The term was then extended to cover the effects of interference generally, whether or not they resulted in actual aural noise. If you have ever used a computer to communicate over a bad telephone line using a modem, you will be familiar with noise taking the form of odd characters appearing in the middle of messages. If we consider the extension of the concept to cover the range of communication that takes place in information systems in business, we can also see that noise comes into the disturbance of the encoder-channel-decoder sequence of human communication in the form of such factors as tiredness, dishonesty or inconsistency we have already mentioned.

The practical implications of the concepts

The most important *practical* implications of these concepts come from one essential *conceptual* principle which applies if we see all communications systems as open systems disturbed by an environment. This principle is that *all* information will be *fuzzy* in the sense that it will contain an element of *uncertainty*. This uncertainty will come in two different forms that we have already introduced in section 3.2.1:

1. *Hard uncertainty*, which means that information is *stochastic* in nature.
2. *Soft issues*, which means that information may be interpreted differently according to the *weltanschauung* or *world view* of the person viewing it.

This principle, that all information is ultimately fuzzy, is so important that we will use the rest of this chapter to explore it further. Meanwhile there is one major set of practical implications of the effects of environmental disturbance and noise on the encoder-channel-decoder sequence when we consider them in the context of computerized information systems in business. These implications relate to *security*.

We have already seen that the encoder-channel-decoder sequence is most frequently represented in such business applications by the need to communicate between the human and computer components of the information system. A common example would be where written information has to be *transcribed* from a paper medium where it is recorded in the form of visual letters and symbols into an electronic medium where it is represented as, say, ASCII convention digital signals. There are many other examples involving transcription of speech, visual images, magnetic media, mouse movements, etc.; but the important point is that where the encoder-channel-decoder sequence involves a change of medium or *transcription* of information, noise introduces a classic opportunity for the introduction of error. Look at the way practical systems work and you will find that a whole range of practical techniques such as check digits and validation procedures have been developed to reduce the possibility of error; but generally, where there is transcription error checking procedures are essential. Books with a strong practical data processing view of information systems like Laudon & Laudon (1991) or Weber (1988) give details of these.

A further important practical implication of the inevitability of error creeping into the communication of information is to the development of information systems as we shall consider it in Chapter 7. Although systems development is concerned in its early stages with specifying what an information system *should* do, no systems design is practically complete unless it also then includes provision for accommodating what to do when errors occur.

Lags in the system

One final important concept that applies to communication systems as it does to other systems is that of *lags in the transformation process*. We already saw in section 3.3.4 that this was important in control systems. Once we recall however that a major example of a communication system in this context is the *feedback loop*, then the implications of lags in a system which we covered before will have their equivalents here.

The main implication we will focus on here is one which links up with the consideration of the stochastic nature of information which we introduced above, and adds to the study of it that we will make in the next section. The transformation process of encoding the message, transmitting along a channel, and decoding it, will *always take time* in a real-life communication system. There will be a *lag* between the originator's and the receiver's perception of the message. This means that, even if noise does not distort the message in any way, the information that it seeks to transmit may be in error.

We can see examples of this if we return to the role of communication in the feedback loop of a control system. Here the communication system is acting as a subsystem of the control system.

> ◆ **STQ 4.5**
>
> *Is the feedback path of information in the General Control Model always a form of the General Communication System Model?*

In a stock control example like that illustrated by Fig 3.2, the sensor may correctly pick up the figure for the amount in stock and there may not be any noise error introduced by the figure being copied incorrectly or misunderstood when spoken. However, by the time that a comparator, like a stock control clerk working with a software package, has acted as receiver and used the figure to decide on stock allocation, further stock movement could have made the figure out of date.

When we consider the stochastic nature of information in the next section therefore we should remember that this phenomenon does not come exclusively from avoidable errors. 'Total quality' of information will always be a myth in real information systems.

4.2   CONCEPTS FOR FUZZY INFORMATION

The fuzzy nature of all information

At the end of the last section we established the principle that all information will be fuzzy because all systems, including communication systems, have environments which disturb them and introduce an element of uncertainty into:

> *a.* What the information is.
> *b.* What interpretation and meaning should be given to the information.

Uncertainty about what the information is mainly results from noise disturbing the encoder-channel-decoder sequence and takes the form of *hard uncertainty*. In terms of the ideas we introduced in Chapter 3, such information is *stochastic* in nature.

Uncertainty about what the information means or how it should be interpreted comes mainly from environmental disturbances to the originators–receivers and the degree to which their symbol sets and usage rules approximate to each other. Here the uncertainty comes from *soft issues* and differences of *weltanschauung* or *world view*.

In this section we will look more closely at how hard uncertainty, in the form of stochastic information, can be described and dealt with. Our main approach to soft issues will be in Chapter 8, but we will look at two subjects which affect our view of soft issues in later sections of this chapter. These are the effects of attempts to observe and measure all types of information, and questions of generalization and classification.

Box 4.1

THE CLIMATE IS CHANGING: AS USUAL

1996 saw the publication of five years' research carried out by some 2000 scientists working for the Inter-Governmental Panel on Climatological Change (IPCC). The essential conclusions of the research were:

  a The world's climate is changing due to global warming.
  b. Greenhouse gases resulting from human activity are a significant contributing factor to the change.

These conclusions merely confirmed the IPCC's previous 1990 predictions and reinforced existing strong beliefs. Thus in 1994, the Stitching Greenpeace Council of Amsterdam published *The Climate Time Bomb*, an extensive catalogue of news reports covering upsets and disasters in agriculture, insurance, international finance, ecology, human health, energy resources, and many other areas; all resulting from the effects of climate change. In similar disaster mood, Sir John Houghton of the Royal Commission on Environmental Pollution warned that flooding in Bangladesh and Southern China could lead to mass migration and wars over water supplies.

Yet the world has been both warmer and colder than it is now. Thus in a warm period about a thousand years ago, Leif Ericson got to Canada via Viking settlements in Greenland which were subsequently wiped out by increasingly cold winters in the 13th and 14th centuries. This cooling trend was itself reversed by the mid-18th century, well before industrialization or the exploitation of fossil fuels.

So what's new about climate change?

COMMENT

My aim in asking this last question is not to belittle concern about a possible global climate disaster. It is important, however, to look very carefully at the different kinds of information which are frequently muddled together when people debate areas of deep concern.

The first distinction that has to be made is between the hard and soft aspects of information. Thus there is no objective standard that tells us which areas of the world should have priority when it comes to flood defence. Nor is it absolutely clear how much available money should be spent on trying to minimize global warming, rather than to, say, cure diseases. Any statement about the costs of a choice of action and value of the outcomes (*see* section 3.2.1) implies a particular *weltanchauung* or world view.

Even if we agree on our values and remove the wide variety of soft uncertainties in the problem, there remain the issues of hard uncertainty covered in Sections 4.2–4.4. Thus the concept of 'warming' itself is not obvious: how many cold winters does it take to disprove global warming? The analysis of statistical data will show us that any model of the climate's behaviour will be stochastic. There is no certain way of forecasting the future, and any decision based on climate statistics involves risk.

FURTHER STUDY

Choose an organization like the East Farthing Drainage Authority whose water management, flood defence and environmental activities are all closely affected by the climate. You may find it useful to consult the web pages of the Environment Agency (via web address www.open.gov.uk) to explore actual examples. Refer to all the levels of control shown in the General Control Model of Fig 3.14. What kinds of information must the organization capture, process and store in order to control its activities?

Describing stochastic information

In section 3.2.1 we established that describing stochastic information involved talking in terms of *probability*. Although we saw that there were different types of probabilities in terms of how their values were arrived at, the value of a probability was an expression of how likely it was that something would happen or would be the case.

If we apply the concept of probability to the stochastic nature of hard information it means that any piece of information is an expression of something we think is probably the case, and which in principle could be assessed or measured to find out if it was. Thus we believe the amount in stock in Fig 3.2 is 47 packs. But what if it isn't? Or what if it isn't quite or is nearly the case? To understand the answers to questions like these we first need to distinguish:

        a. Continuous variables
        b. Integer variables.

Continuous are those whose values can vary over a range without any gaps or breaks. Thus the volume of fuel that a petrol station might have in stock could be any value within the capacity range of the storage tanks. It would not have to be an exact number of gallons or cubic metres.

Integer or *discrete* variables are those whose values are confined to whole numbers. Thus the number of hinges or packing cases held by Carry-Out Cupboards would be a whole number: a stock record that said there were 3.475 hinges in stock would be nonsense.

A special case of integer variables are *zero-one* variables. These are integer variables that can only take the values 0 or 1 as their name implies. In situations where we are concerned simply with whether something is a fact or not, true or false: making 0 stand for false and 1 stand for true is a convention known as *Boolean* variables.

◆ **STQ 4.6**

If customers of Carry-Out Cupboards were asked how important they thought it was to know the origin of the materials that the cupboards were made of, what kind of variable would the survey be dealing with?

When we come to describe hard stochastic information in terms of the probability that it is correct, the particular way we do so depends on the form of variable used to express such information.

For integer variables, including zero-one variables, all we do is assign a probability to each possible value of the variable to show how probable it is. Thus we might use past figures on customer demand to estimate the empirical probability of different demand levels (an integer variable) in any particular month as in Fig 4.2. We might also use similar past data to estimate the probability that a reported stock figure would change or not (Boolean variable) due to customer demand between stock checks, as in Fig 4.3.

For continuous variables it is a little more complex. Thus if quality control at Carry-Out Cupboards were checking on the small variation in the length of a cupboard door cut from board during manufacture they would expect some variation about the official dimension laid down in the design. Here there is no reason for it to be an exact number of millimetres, it might be anything in a range. The way we can describe this is in terms of *probability density* as in Fig 4.4. What probability density shows is the continuous change in the probability of a variable having any value over the possible range. The changes in probability, like the changes in measurement, do not go in steps like in Figs 4.2 and 4.3. The maths of this theory is quite difficult if you don't know calculus, but the idea is simple enough. The higher the *probability density* curve in any range of measurement, as in Fig 4.4, the more likely that range of measurements will occur.

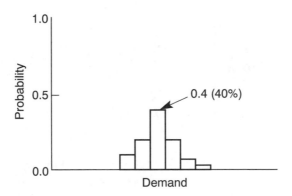

Fig 4.2 The Empirical Probability of Different Demand Levels (1)
Shows how probable different levels of demand are, based on past data.
The particular demand levels are a textbook example, but the fact that they sum up to a value of p = 1 is an essential part of probability theory.

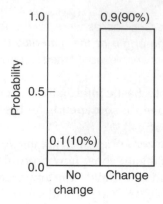

Fig 4.3 The Empirical Probability of Different Demand Levels (2)
Compared with Fig 4.2, this example shows a probability distribution based
on the concept of a *Boolean* variable: change/no change or yes/no, rather
than a range of values for a variable.

What all the common theory behind Figs 4.2 to 4.4 does show is that real-life information has to be thought of in terms of how probable it is of being correct, rather than of being correct, full stop. For this reason we strictly ought to describe all values for variables in terms of estimates or averages, yet we don't. Why is this? To understand the answer to that question we need to recognize a further concept from probability theory.

Figure 4.5 shows information about the same example as Fig 4.2 but with different data. Here the data shows both a narrower range of possible values and one particular value with a very high probability. The overall shape of the distribution is narrower

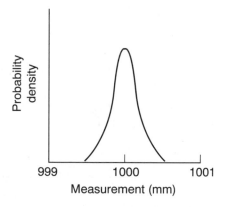

Fig 4.4 A Probability Distribution for a Continuous Variable
The changing level of probability for different values of the measurement is
shown by the *probability density* curve. Ranges of measurement corresponding to high levels on the curve are more likely than those where it is
lower.

and more peaked. Both of these features work together in showing more certainty in the information given by Fig 4.5 than Fig 4.2 about the demand for the product. Generally, the taller and narrower a probability distribution like Figs 4.2 or 4.5, the more certainty it provides. Conversely, the wider and flatter it is the less certainty it provides. For continuous variables the same principle applies. Thus curve A in Fig 4.6 shows a situation where there is a high probability that the dimensions of a product will be confined to quite a narrow range of variation. This gives us a high level of certainty as to what the dimensions of the product might be in practice. Curve B,

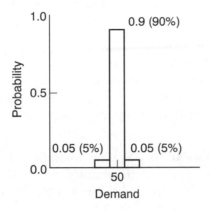

Fig 4.5 The Empirical Probability of Different Demand Levels (3)
This distribution of demand levels has less *dispersion* than Fig 4.2, and enables more certainty in estimating possible levels of demand.

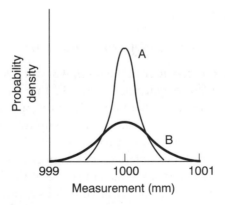

Fig 4.6 Two Possible Probability Distributions for a Continuous Variable
Both distributions have the same average value, but distribution A is less dispersed than distribution B. As with the comparison of Figs 4.5 and 4.2, the less dispersed distribution A enables more certainty in estimating demand levels than distribution B.

however, is wider and flatter, with the implication that a much wider range of values for the measurement is possible and we can therefore be less certain what sort of value a particular measurement might take.

Stochastic variables therefore need some additional way of description beyond estimates of their likely value or average size. We need also to take account of the degree of variation that can occur about that estimated level or average. In mathematics these are called *measures of dispersion,* and the most common one which would be used for the kind of data we have described is the *variance.* Generally, the greater the variance, the greater the level of uncertainty associated with stochastic information.

So returning to our earlier question, why don't we always talk in terms of estimates and averages? Why do we treat much information as if it were correct? The answer is a combination of two factors:

1 The size of the variance in much data can be limited by appropriate use of *control.* Thus an engineer at Carry-Out Cupboards can keep the dimensions of a cupboard so close to the nominal that you or I as customers wouldn't notice the difference. Even where the engineer fails, the quality control is unlikely to let the cupboard pass inspection.

2 Even where the variance in data is large enough to be noticed, the *costs* of the uncertainty it causes may not be important. I'm sure Carry-Out Cupboards don't mind too much if they only have 1345 pairs of a particular hinge rather than the 1346 they estimated.

What both of these factors imply is that it is the balance of the *cost of control* and the *cost of error* associated with uncertainty that matters, not the uncertainty in itself.

◆ **STQ 4.7**
This last paragraph has just implied a central control systems principle. What is it?

Entropy and the usefulness of information

The lessons we learned from considering Figs 4.2, 4.5 and 4.6 have an implication for the concept of *usefulness* of information. Being told that the demand for a product could be anywhere between 0 and 100 in a particular month and that any one figure was as probable as another is *less informative* than being told, as in Fig 4.5, that it will be a figure between 49 and 51, with a 90% probability of being exactly 50.

Communication theory has taken a version of a concept called *entropy* from physics to express this idea. Entropy can be used as a measure of the fuzziness of information and therefore of its usefulness to us in terms of the level of certainty it brings. Note that here we are not talking about the certainty associated with *one* value of probability but of the *overall* certainty provided by a combination of probabilities in distributions like those in Figs 4.2 to 4.6. We might instinctively feel that Fig 4.5 is more informative and certain than Fig 4.2, or that in Fig 4.6 curve A gives more certainty about measurements than curve B. But how can we express this formally as a measurement? The answer is entropy. When calculated (according to a formula I won't bother you with: see Shannon (1963) for a thorough mathematical background to communications) entropy takes account of the degree of peak and spread in a distribution in such a way that flat uninformative distributions have high entropies and more peaked informative ones have low entropies. Since entropy is strictly a measure of the uselessness of information, its reverse, called *negentropy,* is sometimes used instead. Generally, the more entropy in a system the more fuzzy, decayed and useless it is. The purpose of a good information system is therefore to keep entropy at an optimum level that balances the costs of certainty against the costs of uncertainty and error. (*See* STQ 4.7.)

4.3 THE EFFECTS OF MEASUREMENT AND OBSERVATION ON CERTAINTY

We saw that uncertainty came from various forms of environmental disturbance, including noise, on the components of a communication system. We also noted that the communication system was a vital component of the information system, itself a subsystem of the control system. It therefore seems that ensuring we successfully gather this information through the sensor component of the control system and transmit it using the communication system is essential to the success of information as a component of control as a component of management.

There is another important principle that again limits the degree of certainty we can expect in practice, however carefully we design and operate an information system. This principle can be summarized as:

All observation disturbs what it observes.

I will use two very different examples to illustrate this principle. The first comes from atomic physics, and is known as the *Heisenberg Uncertainty Principle.* Werner Heisenberg set out this principle in 1927 when discussing whether it was possible *in principle* to have exact data about such properties as the movement and position of small atomic particles like electrons. What Heisenberg showed was that the only way you could find out where an electron was and where it was going, was to make it interact with something else. You might try getting it to 'reflect' a small amount of radiation and reveal itself and its movement. After all, the way we see something is because it reflects light which our eyes then pick up and use to deduce its presence as a cat or a computer keyboard.

However there is a difference between cats and keyboards and electrons. Cats and keyboards are big things in atomic terms. They contain billions and billions of electrons. When light hits a cat it doesn't feel a thing, or when it hits the keyboard the keyboard isn't disturbed. For an electron however, a small amount of radiation is a bit like one snooker ball is to another snooker ball. When the radiation bounces off the electron it also knocks the electron off somewhere else. So when the radiation returns from being reflected by the electron, the electron has moved off somewhere else. Our observation can only tell us where it *was,* not where it is now. Now we might try to get over this by using very 'gentle' radiation that wouldn't disturb the electron, but alas the equivalent of 'gentle' radiation is rather like a snooker ball stuffed with feathers because its ability to bounce or reflect accurately is much reduced. So it doesn't disturb the electron much, and the way it gets reflected gives less reliable, fuzzy results.

Thus our example shows that it is *impossible, even in principle,* to devise an experiment to tell us exactly where an electron is and where it is going. Modern physics, in the form of the Heisenberg Uncertainty Principle, recognizes this and always talks about electron movement in *stochastic* terms.

Modern physics may seem a long way from management but in fact a similar principle applies to social observation too. In 1924 some famous experiments were carried out at the Hawthorne plant in the US whose original objective was to adjust such factors as plant lighting with the aim of improving worker performance. After many complex adjustments to the tests it was found impossible to separate the effects of one particular adjustment from other factors. Indeed improving the lighting in one situation had the same effect as not improving it somewhere else. The Hawthorne researchers found it impossible in particular to separate the effects of their presence in the measuring process from the values of the measurements themselves.

In everyday life we are aware of this principle from our own experience. Doing something when you are watched is not the same as doing it privately, and if someone is recording the results of their observation, our behaviour is likely to be even more distorted.

For information systems in business therefore, with the inevitable human component, the concept of certainty of information is limited. Whether the uncertainties matter however depends on the costs associated with them, as we saw above.

4.4 CLASSIFICATION AND HIERARCHY: DEALING WITH COMPLEX INFORMATION

One of the important ways we deal with complexity in information is to place things in classes and categories. Thus in a business like insurance where decisions have to be made about insurance cover for millions of individual people, some way has to be found of estimating an individual's lifespan, their likelihood of having a car accident or their probability of being burgled.

One thing that is not possible in those circumstances is to have vast amounts of detail on each person. What insurance companies do is the same that we do as individuals, they classify their experience so that they can use commonly shared characteristics as a basis for simplifying the processing of large amounts of information. Once you know that a particular person falls into the classes of 'male' and 'aged 54', you can use the results of processing data about previous 54-year-old males to estimate how long you expect the individual to live. This information can then be used to estimate what amount of money you will require as an annual payment from the man to guarantee his estate £10 000 when he dies.

Such information and calculations can be used successfully in business. A whole insurance and pension industry has ended up being the majority owner of British industry on the basis of being able to deal with complexity and uncertainty in information. However, where I think modern popular thinking has become confused is in not distinguishing between typing or classifying information, and stereotyping individuals. Stereotyping does occur, and its results can be the Death Camps, but there is a constructive and positive way in which concepts of classification and hierarchy can be used too. In this section I want to distinguish some elementary points which will add to our concepts of *hierarchy* and which we can take up in Chapter 8.

One simple piece of classification which a life insurance business might make is that women are a group of people who live longer than men. Is this stereotyping? After all, my father has lived longer than my mother, so in one sense it seems to be untrue. There are two important points that help us analyse such questions. The first comes from the systems concept of emergent property. What is called something like 'expected male lifespan' is *not* the property of any man any more than having 2.4 children is the property of any family. Instead 'male lifespan' is the emergent property that comes from the aggregation and processing of component data. Stereotyping occurs when we transfer properties appropriate to one level of the systems hierarchy down to an individual component.

A second potential cause of confusion is failure to recognize two different types of hierarchy. When studying systems we have used a concept of hierarchy based on *levels of aggregation* or being *part of* some greater whole. Another concept we shall come across when we study object-oriented methods in Chapter 8 is a hierarchy that deals with components being a *kind of* a general class. The fact that a component can be seen as a member of a *part of* a hierarchical whole does not imply that it automatically has properties in the way that being a member of a *kind of* does.

Box 4.2

PLAYING FOOTSIE WITH INDICES

(*Investors Chronicle* 16/8/96: all italics are mine)

From the All-Share to the FT-SE 100, UK share indices seem to be quoted just about everywhere. But *which companies are included* and just *what is the use* of all those numbers?

For many people, indices are the only contact they have with the City. The two-minute financial slot at the end of the news is a *brief but familiar snapshot* of what's happened in the City during the day. . .

The FT-SE 100, sometimes called the Footsie, is an index – an average of the share prices of the 100 largest companies quoted on the stock market. . .

In fact, the FT-SE 100 is just one of a range of indices used to *measure* the performance of the stock market. The oldest, the FT Ordinary Share Index, often called the FT 30, was established in 1935 by the *Financial Times*. It reflects the share prices of the largest companies in the UK. . .

So there are now a range of other indexes in use. . .

The most comprehensive index – the FT-SE All-Share Index – is also calculated as a *weighted arithmetic mean*. . .

Indices have also spawned a range of investment products known as tracker funds. These are funds which *aim to match the performance of a particular index* by holding shares that exactly replicate the shares in the index or are meant to be a representative sample of those shares.

COMMENT

These are extracts from an article which appeared in the *Investors Chronicle* as one of a series for 'Absolute Beginners'. If you read the whole of the original, you will find that it covers many different financial indices.

Does it all sound rather advanced for 'absolute beginners'? I don't think it does. Populations in developed countries are ageing. Concern for the use of financial investment as a means of security is increasing. Whether people invest directly or use professional advisors, investors need some way of assessing how well their money is doing. In the complex world of finance, an *index* provides a way of *generalizing* information about the performance of investments.

The original *Investors Chronicle* article also includes a picture of a woman with four quadruplet babies in a basket. The caption reads 'Indices use baskets of shares'. This convenient use of a picture library, with its cheerful caption, fulfils a similar function to an index: it summarizes something complex in a simple, readily digestible form.

Just as modern information technology makes it easy for a journalist to search and select pictures to fit almost any theme, so the storage and calculating power of information technology enables almost unlimited analysis and presentation of simplified quantitative information, like an index. And this is where the danger lies: the user gets a *simple message* from *complex analysis*. In such circumstances there is a strong pressure to accept the index as some kind of objective or authoritative statement.

Reminding ourselves why we produce indices in the first place, gives an information systems view of what they are. Like any output from an information system, an index is a reflection of what data we use as its components and the particular way we assemble them to produce an emergent property called information. Any index therefore reflects how the *normative* assumptions of management about goal-setting are translated into the *method* we choose to set and monitor our goals, as in the General Control Model of Fig 3.14. Thus financial indices are not objective measurements, but views of managing the financial world.

The author of the book which first taught me statistics, Moroney (1951), expresses the extreme version of this view. He describes the widespread use of indices as a 'compulsion neurosis', and that 'only lunatics and public servants' would indulge in the 'academic tomfoolery' of compiling them. He considers that all they do is tell us what we know already: the cost of living is going up or shares are worth less than they were last week. In his book of over 450 pages he devotes a mere six pages to the subject of indices. All six are entirely concerned with showing that the contents and calculation of indices is based on subjective judgement. For example, who decides whether the cost of tobacco or meat should be in a cost of living index, and what weighting they should be given?

In systems terms we would describe indices as *soft*, since they are based on particular value judgements. This does not make them useless, but it does mean that we have to understand where they come from and why we are using them. Moroney was concerned with uncritical calculation and use of indices in the days when calculating machines were operated by someone cranking a handle. How much easier it is to indulge in a 'compulsion neurosis' when widespread computers and database systems make it possible to do complex calculations so much more easily, and then present them with a convincing graphics package.

FURTHER STUDY

If your university or college course includes a study of quantitative methods, statistics, economics or social studies, it is worth finding out more information about the indices quoted in the textbooks you read. In particular, try checking the following points:

1. What are the data components of the index?
2. Who decides that these should be the components?
3. What method is used to calculate the index?
4. Who determines the method of calculation?
5. What procedures are defined for reviewing the data components of the index or its method of calculation?
6. What is the *management* function of the index? Who are the people and processes involved? What are their normative assumptions?

KEY WORDS

Boolean variable	Fuzzy	*Part of* hierarchy
Channel	Integer variable	Probability density
Communication	Interpretation	Receiver
Continuous variable	*Kind of* hierarchy	Shared rules for symbol use
Decoder	Measure of dispersion	Shared symbol set
Discrete variable	Messenger	Uncertainty principle
Encoder	Negentropy	Understanding
Entropy	Noise	Variance
Environmental disturbance	Originator	

SEMINAR AGENDAS, EXAM QUESTIONS AND PROJECT/DISSERTATION TOPICS

1 What other 'shared symbol sets' are common in computer usage? How universally are they shared? What are the political pressures against the adoption of such common standards. Examine international and inter-company rivalry.

2 Are computers enhancing the ability of human beings to communicate? Or are computer-based information systems de-skilling the communication process by their inability to accommodate soft issues?

3 Do computer systems, particularly with their recent ability to present GUIs (*see* STQ 4.3), limit the potential for the computer by indulging a conservative view of the potential application of systems concepts? For example use of so-called icons as encapsulating old thinking, or use of screen colours when the printer can't deal with them anyway?

4 Is statistics an entirely soft subject disguised by hard techniques?

5 Is the success of Microsoft Windows a reflection of the success of Microsoft or Its product?

6 What words do people use when estimating probabilities and certainty? Can mathematical theory deal with these uses, or is there a hard–soft divide here?

FEEDBACK ON SELF-TESTING QUESTIONS

◆ STQ 4.1

The model has components such as the originator, channel, etc. We can also see that some of its components are abstract, like the symbol set and the rules for its use.

Although the diagram doesn't show much concept of a hierarchy, the fact that I had to repeatedly use the grouping encoder-channel-decoder suggests that this could be regarded as a subsystem. In a computer system this grouping might be regarded as the input subsystem, or the output looking from the other direction.

The whole has the emergent property of communication itself, as pointed out in the text, and we can see that it is a concept once we recognize that it can be applied to very different physical situations from human conversation to radio transmission.

◆ STQ 4.2

What I was thinking of here was diagramming. The shared symbol set and rules for use are normally called the diagramming conventions, and we now have electronic as well as traditional paper-based media both as an encoder-decoders and channels for communicating. Communicating by diagrams is now supported by sophisticated software such as CAD and communicating channels such as fax. Note the large increase in the use of visual information in business in recent years. Business information no longer implies just letters and numbers on documents.

◆ STQ 4.3

I intended this question to lead on from the point made in the previous STQ. What I had in mind was the widespread use of graphical user interface (GUI) products such as Microsoft Windows.

◆ STQ 4.4

Given that the originators of the various messages at the meeting were human beings, and that the case says nothing about environmental disturbances from such things as bad office lighting or ringing telephones, I'd say that the major environmental disturbances came from the 'mental luggage' in the form of attitudes, education and emotions brought into the communication system by the behaviour of people like Ian.

My aim in using a soft personal example like this is to emphasize that talking of the environment as being 'outside' the system should not deceive us into making a physical, geographical interpretation of 'outside'. Reference to a good reader which covers the human aspects of information systems such as Galliers (1987) should show that the soft components loaded with human values are always part of the business system environment. Even the most ruthless dictators we find in history have been powerless to overcome this feature of systems.

Another important example occurred outside the meeting. As we saw when discussing the issues connected with the market research, they revealed that respondents had not always understood words like 'renewable resource'. Whatever reasons may have caused this, from poor education to media misinformation, environment disturbance had decreased the close approximation of the symbol set.

◆ STQ 4.5

In terms of the view of systems concepts of Chapter 3 it always is. What appear to be exceptions to this, like when one person records the information as actuator by seeing it, feeds it back by remembering, and makes a personal comparison with their own goals before acting or actuating a change, does conform to the General Communication System Model once we remember that the model is a concept. The implementation of this concept may be carried out by one person. What happens in this case is that one person takes on several roles: one particular how for several whats.

◆ STQ 4.6

It would depend on the question that they were asked, but I would expect it to be some form of integer or discrete variable. If the question asked whether they thought it 'very important', 'important', 'not very important' or 'completely irrelevant', then we see four discrete possible values for a reply. If the survey asked for 'yes' or 'no' (which no good survey would), it would be zero-one. I think it very unlikely that interviewees would be asked to reply on a continuous scale from 0 to 10 that included the possibility of 5.288347.

◆ STQ 4.7

See section 3.5.5 and 'Trade-Off and Optimization'. Here the cost of control increases in terms of the frequency, effort, manpower or money put into it. The cost of error decreases in relation to the same. The optimum cost will be the minimum of the combination of the two.

REFERENCES/BIBLIOGRAPHY

Davis, G.B. & Olson, M.H. (1984). *Management Information Systems*. McGraw-Hill.
Galliers, R. (1987). *Information Analysis: Selected Readings*. Addison-Wesley.
Laudon, C.L. & Laudon, J.P. (1991). *Business Information Systems*. Dryden.
Moroney, M.J. (1951). *Facts from Figures*. Penguin.
Shannon, C.E. (1963). *The Mathematical Theory of Communication*. University of Illinois.
Weber, R. (1988). *EDP Auditing*. McGraw-Hill.
Wittgenstein, L. (1953). *Philosophical Investigations*. Oxford.

Changes at Norris Trainers

What happened

Friday the 13 August turned out to be unluckier for some than for others at Norris Trainers, the big sports equipment retailers.

It was also a bad day for PQ Plastics. They had been suppliers to Norris Trainers for many years, but their recent quality and delivery performance had become so bad that Norris's Chief Purchasing Manager Keith Patel persuaded his directors that the PQ Plastics contract should not be renewed. PQ Plastics were replaced by NM Moulders. This led to changes in the sports shoe range that Norris offered to their customers; but products manufactured by PQ Plastics were replaced, where possible, by the nearest NM Moulders equivalent.

Friday the 13 August was a day of friction between the Finance Section and Computer Services. A young financial graduate trainee called John MacLeod tried to be innovative at a routine computer users meeting by suggesting that the recording of sales figures and amending of stock level records should only need one entry into the computer system. At present, when any item was sold at a retail outlet it was recorded as a sale on the sales file and the stock file was separately amended with a copy of the same figure. Computer Manager Guy Hennessy said he already realized this, but the present system could not accommodate the suggestion in a practical and economic way: it could only be achieved by writing special software. Since this was not the first time that Guy Hennessy had killed off one of John's ideas, John lost his temper and made sarcastic comments about 'dinosaur systems'. For him, it was not a very constructive end to the week.

For someone else in the Finance Section however, it was a lucky day. Jane Isherwood was on leave getting married. She and her husband moved into a new house, and she took on her husband's surname to become Jane Berlin.

For sometime after Friday the 13 August Keith Patel found that changing from PQ Plastics to NM Moulders created a lot of work for the computer and clerical staff updating important computer files. It wasn't just a question of modifying one computer file by replacing the name and details of PQ Plastics with those of NM Moulders. Details of PQ Plastics appeared on three separate files and each of these had to be modified, often with the same details. PQ Plastics appeared on a file used by Purchasing to identify which suppliers could supply what kind of product together with a quality rating of past performance. They also appeared on an accounts file which was used to ensure correct payment for goods supplied. Finally, the stock file had to have the new NM Moulders products added to it. Those products previously supplied by PQ Plastics were left on file until stocks ran out. Since the stock file identified the supplier of each item, a special new file was created to show which NM Moulders products could act as substitutes for the old PQ Plastics ones.

Computer Manager Guy Hennessy did his best to accommodate the changes brought about by Keith Patel's decison on PQ Plastics, but there were problems. Since many of the details of NM Moulders products appeared on more than one file, there were errors and inconsistencies in the records of such items as product code numbers, product descriptions and prices. These errors and inconsistencies were either a result of mistakes made in the original data entry, or failure to update all three files at the same time when changes were made. Guy Hennessy's problems were not helped when John MacLeod pointed out to Keith Patel that this wasn't the only example of how the appearance of items in more than one file caused problems.

Jane Isherwood found that her next salary was paid correctly into her bank account in her new name of Jane Berlin. Unfortunately her change of name was not picked up in time by personnel to appear in the new internal phone book. The phone book was produced every two months by a section of the Personnel Department who printed out names from a personnel records file which was separate from the payroll file. Both files contained personal details like name, age and address; but the personnel records file kept details of employees careers and their qualifications, while the payroll file covered payment and tax. Jane remembered to inform payroll of her new situation because she was anxious to be correctly taxed and paid, but she did not officially inform Personnel until later. In the following two months Jane seemed put out with various irritations arising from having different surnames and different addresses, until both files and the new phone book were updated and consistent with each other.

An information systems view

Like all of the mini-cases, the selection of events described ranges from very public events, like the strategic commercial deal, to individual events like a change in one persons private life; yet each event raises the same issues at its own level of importance.

The big bust-up with PQ Plastics and the marriage of Jane Isherwood were both inputs from the environment of Norris Trainers which disturbed its operations and required changes in the way it would have to manage those operations in the future. As we saw in Chapter 3, an essential component of any management system is the hierarchy of goal-setting and goal-seeking within the control system. Within such a control system, an essential component is the information system whose job is to provide the information that enables the control system to work. We also saw that the information used by any control system may be divided into three types:

1. *Information which sets the goals from the wider system which the process under control must attempt to achieve.*
2. *Information which helps to control the behaviour of the process itself so that it aims at these goals.*
3. *Information which enables the control system to identify, anticipate and allow for the effects of disturbances to the system coming from its environment.*

The changes resulting from the PQ Plastics affair and Jane Isherwood's marriage involved all three types of information.

Information which sets goals had to come from the wider system to those subsystems of Norris's which were concerned with purchasing, accounting and stock control. The information defined the new range of products to be bought, stocked and sold. It gave quantitative details on pricing, costs, desired stock levels and all other details which defined *what* the various processes controlled by the various subsystems were trying to achieve.

When Keith Patel and his clerical staff carried out the various tasks needed to update the computer files, they were implementing the changes in those goals which were recorded on the computerized information system.

When Jane Isherwood got her personal and tax details changed on the payroll file she was modifying the goals of that particular process by redefining *what* name, tax, bank account number, etc.

Information which helps to control the behaviour of processes such as purchasing, accounting and stock control at Norris's continued to be used in controlling processes aimed at the new goals as it had for the old ones. One example was that Purchasing continued to record such details as quantities bought and prices paid to NM Moulders as they had done previously for PQ Plastics when it was a supplier.

Similarly, Payroll continued to collect the necessary information on hours worked or expenses incurred in order to calculate pay and tax for the new Mrs Jane Berlin in the same way as it had for the former Jane Isherwood.

An example of *information which enables the control system to identify, anticipate and allow for the effects of disturbances from its environment* was that recorded on the quality and delivery performance of PQ Plastics. It not only enabled Keith Patel to pick up individual lapses by PQ Plastics: it also gave him a more strategic picture that justified choosing a replacement supplier with anticipated long-term benefits.

Personnel and Payroll both had the means of reacting to disturbances from the environment like changes in personnel employed, names and addresses, hours worked, tax coding, etc.; but the method of gathering the information and updating records was not always reliable, as Jane found out.

The issues raised

Our information systems view of the situation at Norris Trainers included four issues which frequently come up when we consider the role of information as a component of a control system which in turn is a component of the management system:

> *Issue 1. How can information be described, defined, or explained in terms of the data from which it is constructed?*
>
> *Issue 2. How can information be recorded?*
>
> *Issue 3. How can information be manipulated or processed?*
>
> *Issue 4. How can possible answers to these issues 1–4 be coordinated into a successful overall approach to the description, recording and manipulation of information?*

To understand Issue 1, we should recall the systems concepts of *structure* and *emergent property* which were covered in Chapter 3 and then used to help our understanding of the relationship between information and data. We saw that information could be regarded as a property which emerged from the whole when component elements of data were brought together in a particular relationship or structure. If we take this view of information, then one way in which we can consider how it could be described, defined, or explained in terms of the data from which it is constructed would be to consider:

>   *a.* What are the *elements of data* that go to make up the information as a whole?
>   *b.* What is the *structural relationship* between these elements of data?

An example of *a* from the Norris case might come from quoting the phrase 'the quality and delivery performance of PQ Plastics'. When Norris's needed some way of assessing this, they had to decide what goes to make up 'quality' and 'delivery performance'. But 'quality' and 'delivery performance' would need in turn to be defined in terms of how many late deliveries, how many products with faults, which shoes were sent to the wrong place at the wrong time, etc., etc. In other words data, in the form of quantitative figures or qualitative description, had to be assembled together to make a whole like 'the quality and delivery performance of PQ Plastics'.

◆ STQ 5.1

Can you suggest some examples of this issue for Jane Isherwood?

An example of *b* from the Norris case might come from thinking about Jane Isherwood's salary. At the time of writing, she was being paid an annual salary of £19 000. If we look at these figures as data, we have a '1', a '9', and three '0's. We could put these elements together as 120 different combinations:

> £91 000
> £90 100
> £10 900
>   etc.

but I think we can see that the way that they are put together, or the *structure*, can make a very big difference to what the whole combination of data means. £91 000 and £10 900 are made up of the same individual elements of data, but the information that they transmit, in terms of 'Jane Isherwood's salary', is very different.

To understand Issue 2, which considers how information can be recorded, we need to recall the essential distinction between 'whats' and 'hows' that we go on repeating throughout this book. It may be that 'what' information Norris's management need for their stock control will include details made up of data such as product code number, product description and price. Although these details will take on just one particular value for any product at a particular time, 'how' they are recorded may vary considerably. To form a stock record containing such details they could be recorded by typing them on a card to be inserted into a box file, or they could be handwritten on to a paper sheet which goes into a ring binder. In the case of Norris's they were in fact recorded as magnetic fields on computer disks.

Recognizing that the data making up particular information can be recorded on different media is only part of the 'how' issue. There is also the question of how it is actually recorded on the chosen medium itself. Given that we may be using a card index for our records, there is then the question of how the data making up the information is laid out on the card itself. We could arrange items like product code number, product description and price in many ways on the card, and we could use many dif-

ferent formats, typefaces and formats to do so. This may seem like getting down to trivial details which could be easily sorted out by someone interested in designing forms,
but if we consider storage on magnetic media like computer disk we shall see later in
this chapter that the issue is important. Data on disks is not and cannot be recorded in
the same arrangement as it would appear on a screen or a printout. Far from being a
problem, this actually enables computer-based information systems to be released from
the constraints placed on the manipulation and processing of information by the old
paper-based systems. We shall see more about this when we come to Issue 3.

There was one other aspect to the 'how' issue which came up in the Norris case.
The friction between John MacLeod and Guy Hennessy, as well as Keith Patel's problems, stemmed from the fact that the same information was sometimes recorded more
than once on the same medium. In Jane Isherwood's case it was recorded more than
once and on two different media.

Hence Issue 2 can be seen to arise in different ways:

a. What medium (or media) should be used to record the data which makes
   up the information we want to use?
b. What physical arrangement, format or structure should be chosen?
c. What duplication (if any) of recording should occur?

Whatever issues arise concerning the description or storage of data, we are only interested in the data in the first place because the right *elements* of data assembled together
in the right *structure* will provide the information needed to enable us to manage. This
need to select, assemble and generally *process* brings us naturally to Issue 3: how can
information be manipulated or processed? In considering this issue we can consider
both information and data together. Whether we are considering the processing of elements of data like individual numbers or information like a complete personnel record,
the principal questions as to how we manipulate or process are the same.

The replacement of PQ Plastics by NM Moulders as a major supplier meant replacing details of PQ Plastics products with those of NM Moulders on three of the existing
files. This involved various actions. For each of the new NM Moulders products the
computer and clerical staff had to *create* new records. Once the old PQ Plastics range
was finally cleared out, they would have to *drop* the old records. In the meantime they
had to *alter* the format of the existing records by adding new data showing which new
products were the equivalents of the old ones. Once an equivalent product was found,
it would be necessary to *select* its record from the file to find out details of its price,
stock level, etc. As further NM Moulders products were added to the range it would
be necessary to *insert* them in the file and to *delete* old ones. Where prices or stock
levels changed it would be necessary to *update* the file entries.

This description covers just some of the actions which had to be carried out when
processing data at Norris's, but they are good examples of the actions which are
common to any information system, whether computerized or not. I haven't just put
the words that describe these actions in italics to emphasize them: they are in fact a
selection of commands from a widely used standard data definition, manipulation
and control language called SQL. (Smart people pronounce SQL like the word 'sequel'
to show they know something about its ancestors, but people like me seem to get by
calling it 'ess kew ell' without too many problems.)

This consideration of Issue 3 implies that we will need to look in more detail at the principles that enable us to make sense of how information can be manipulated or processed. That leaves us with the Issue 4 which asks how possible answers to Issues 1–3 can be coordinated into a successful overall approach to the description, recording and manipulation of information.

Issue 4 is illustrated by the argument between John MacLeod and Computer Manager Guy Hennessy, where both of them realized that the recording of sales figures and amending of stock level records should need only one entry into the computer system. The issue is also illustrated by Keith Patel's experiences in having to modify three computer files, each involving the same information. What Issue 4 shows is that even when we have decided on how information can be described, defined, recorded, manipulated and processed, we are left with problems that arise if it is stored in more than one place. When this happens we are likely to find:

a. Processing becomes more complicated because we have to repeat the same or similar processes for each record of the same information.
b. This complication of the processing gives extra opportunity for errors or inconsistencies to creep into the recorded information.
c. Recording the same information more than once uses extra storage space.

When considering Issue 3 we saw that a wide range of processes is likely to be carried in practice by information systems. Some of these, like updating data, are likely to occur very frequently. It makes sense therefore to minimize unnecessary duplication or redundancy in recording information. Since this recorded information is made up of individual items of data, we shall need to consider how the recording of data can best be done to minimize the unnecessary duplication of information. Putting this issue in the appropriate technical way, we need to consider how best to manage our *database*.

LEARNING OBJECTIVES CHAPTER 5

1 **To understand how the concepts** *entity*, *attribute* **and** *relationship* **can be used to describe how data can model information.**

2 **To distinguish the main types of data models:** *hierarchical, network, relational, object-oriented* **and** *semantic.*

3 **To identify those parts of the theories of** *relational algebra* **and** *relational calculus* **which help to understand how data can be described and manipulated.**

4 **To understand the principles of managing data to meet the needs of an information system as implemented in the main features of a** *database* **and** *database management system (DBMS).*

CHAPTER 5

Data and Database Concepts

5.1 DATA ANALYSIS AND DATA MODELLING

5.1.1 The elements of data

We have already recalled the concept, which we established in Chapter 3, that information could be regarded as a property which emerged from the whole when component elements of data were brought together in a particular relationship or structure. In this section we will see just what these elements are and how we can describe their relationship.

A starting point for understanding the elements of data in these terms is the review of information we first carried out in Chapter 2. There we found that all the forms of information we considered as relevant to management are *about something.* Management uses information about customers, products, employees, items of equipment and many other things in order to set its goals and attempt to achieve them in the face of disturbances from the environment. Whatever this 'something' is, and which the information is 'about', we term an *entity*. If we consider the example of Carry-Out Cupboards, a cupboard, a customer, a supplier or a supplier's account would all be entities about which we would need information.

> ◆ **STQ 5.2**
>
> *What is the relationship between the concept of an entity introduced here and the concept of an element used to describe the smallest component of a system in Chapter 3?*

Entities may be of different types. A cupboard, for example, is a *concrete* entity: it is something we can see and touch. Figure 5.1 shows the details of some cupboards sold by Carry-Out Cupboards, with various characteristics like surface finish or height. A supplier's account, however, is an *abstract* concept. When we talk about the characteristics of a supplier's account we would be concerned with quantities of items supplied, dates or amounts of money. Entities are not always inanimate things, whether concrete or abstract: we often need to have information about people such as employees. Nor need entities be components of the system of interest: the suppliers of Carry-Out Cupboards may be outside the Carry-Out Cupboards *system*, but they are part of its *environment* about which we need to have information.

Whatever the different types of entities we decide are of interest to us, the reason for our interest is the same. The entities are considered to be relevant because certain information about them is also relevant: we need it to define goals, control behaviour and cope with environmental disturbances to the system. The information we need to have about an entity we call its *attributes*. Thus we need to have information about the attributes of surface finish and height for a cupboard to decide whether it is suitable for a particular market, or we might need to know its surface finish and height in order to check that the customer had received the correct product.

Just as entities may be concrete or abstract, so attributes may also be either or both. The cupboards in Fig 5.1 have concrete attributes like surface finish or height, but they also have abstract attributes like price or stock class.

Having identified the concepts of entity and attribute, we need to make a further distinction. Entities and attributes can be regarded as sets made up of particular *instances* and *values*. Thus Fig 5.1 shows a sample of different individual *instances* of the entity 'Cupboard'. Similarly for a particular cupboard in Fig 5.1 the attribute 'surface finish' may take on a particular *value* like 'Floral' or 'Veneer'.

Entities do not just exist as a collection of instances within a particular system. If they are *components* of a system we would expect them to be connected together either physically or logically, as we saw in Chapter 3. In the Carry-Out Cupboards case we would expect each instance of the entity 'supplier' to be associated with the occurrence of another entity called 'account'. We therefore see a *relationship* between the two entities. The particular form of this relationship we call its *degree*, depending on the number of entities involved. Since it would be unusual in normal practice for a supplier to have more than one account, or still to be a supplier without having an account at all, we describe the relationship as having a *degree* of *one-to-one* (or 1:1), since one supplier goes with one account and vice versa.

Relationships may be to other degrees. Thus the relationship between 'Central Assembly and Packing' and 'Retail Outlet' is *one-to-many* (1:*n*), since one central assembly and packing facility at Carry-Out Cupboards supplies many retail outlets. For the entities 'Cupboard' and 'Part' however, the relationship is *many-to-many* (*m:n*) since a particular cupboard may contain more than one kind of part; and one particular part may go into more than one kind of cupboard.

STYLE	SIZE	SURFACE FINISH	HEIGHT	FITTINGS	PRICE £	SITING	STOCK CLASS
Calabria	3S	Veneer	3480	Triple/A/S	215.00	Lounge	LG
Calabria	3S	Antique	3480	Triple/A/S	205.00	Diner	DN
•	•	•	•	•	•	•	•
•	•	•	•	•	•	•	•
Classic	1S	Fabric	870	Single/S/S	100.00	Diner	DN
•	•	•	•	•	•	•	•
•	•	•	•	•	•	•	•
Country	1H	Floral	870	Single/N/H	90.00	Diner	DN

Fig 5.1 Details of Some Cupboards Sold by Carry-out Cupboards
The whole of this 'C' range (Calabria, Classic, etc.) is shown in Fig 5.14.

Besides having degrees, relationships may be compulsory (sometimes called *mandatory*) or they may be *optional*. Thus the relationship between supplier and account is compulsory because it is not possible to be a supplier without having an account. The relationship between 'employee' and 'retail outlet' would be optional however, because not all the employees of Carry-Out Cupboards work in the retail outlets.

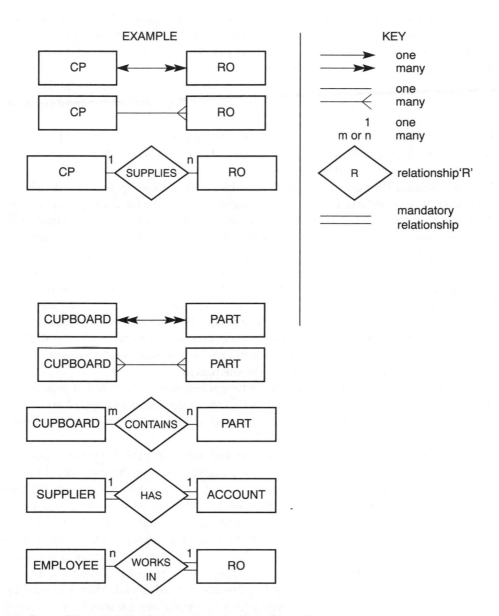

Fig 5.2 Some Diagramming Conventions for Data Modelling
As with other diagramming conventions, it is unlikely that one convention becomes a universal standard. What is important is to recognize the essential that any convention must cover. Here, the bare minimum is a way of representing *entities* and the *relationships* between them.

Like other kinds of systemic relationships, relationships between entities are sometimes better shown using a diagram (*see* Chapter 3). Figure 5.2 shows some common conventions used for diagramming data relationships: whether entity relationships (ER) or entity attribute relationships (EAR).

5.1.2 Data models

We covered the subject of models and modelling in Chapter 3. For the subject of *data modelling*, it will be sufficient to recall that a model is a way of representing and describing a view of something. In this case that 'something' is the whole collection of data we need as the potential components we bring together to form information. We call this 'collection of data' the *database*, and understanding the way a database can be described, defined or manipulated is only possible if we first understand more about the modelling of data itself.

It is also important to note that we described a model as 'a view of something' rather than 'the view' because the way we look at data will depend on who we are and what we want to use it for.

If we consider the concepts of *entity, attribute* and *relationship* that we have just covered, they have been essentially *high-level* and *abstract*. We used them to describe the data in *logical* terms. This kind of analysis and description is about *what* entities have *what* relationship with *what* other entities, and *what* attributes are associated with them. I don't think that I need to go on putting the word 'what' in italics any more to make the point that a *logical* view of data is about 'whats', and that this needs to be distinguished from the *physical* view of *how* the data is recorded, accessed or transmitted. When we described the relationship between supplier and account in the previous section, we said nothing about whether this account was recorded on computer disk, printed out as a document or recorded on a card file. Still less did we get involved in the details of how the data would be physically arranged on the disk, accessed by the software or laid out on the document.

We can therefore make a distinction between *high-level, conceptual* or *logical* models that describe what view a user may have of the data; and *low-level, physical* models that describe how the data is recorded, accessed or transmitted as a result of *implementation* by a computer specialist.

This reference to implementation reveals the need for a third type of model which can make the link between a very abstract, logical view of the data and the way in which it is physically recorded. Our high-level view of the data may show that there is a one-to-many relationship between the entities retail outlet and employee at Carry-Out Cupboards. It may also show a one-to-many relationship between central assembly and packing, and the retail outlets. What this high-level view does not give us, however, is some logical structure or descriptive *schema* to direct us in the ordering and arranging of this data when we come to physically record it. Thus there is nothing in the ER or EAR model of Carry-Out Cupboards that tells us whether we should keep individual *records* of retail outlets with lists of employees on them, or whether we should have separate records for employees with their attributes.

The third type of model which enables us to translate the high-level concepts of the ER or EAR model into a logical description of how the data will be represented, we might call an *implementation* model. We shall consider some examples of these in the following sections, and we will look more closely at some of the terms like *record* and *schema* which we introduced in this section to see how they relate to the different views of data given by the models.

5.1.3 The hierarchical data model

The use of the word *hierarchy* to describe this data model is a good example of the danger we noted in Chapter 3 of a term having different meanings according to where it is used. It may have several meanings in the systems context, as well as in everyday life. In Chapter 3 we discussed two meanings of the term hierarchy, before favouring its use to describe the concept of *levels of aggregation* within a system, rather than the popular everyday meaning associated with the concept of *levels of command*. In Chapter 4 we then distinguished *part of* and *type of* hierarchies.

The term *hierarchical data model* uses the description 'hierarchical' to describe a model as having a *tree structure*. If we consider how a tree is made up, we can see two examples of the same structure. One trunk or base leads to many branches and each one branch leads to many twigs. Below ground, one base sends out many roots and each one root has many smaller ones leading from it.

◆ **STQ 5.3**
   What kind of hierarchy is that?

In our tree example the words 'one...many' occur several times, and this is one of the essentials of the *hierarchical* or *tree* data model. In such a model the entities are all connected in terms of *one-to-one* or *one-to-many*: there are no *many-to-many* relationships. Figure 5.3 shows the essentials. The tree is made up of a hierarchy of elements called *nodes*, with a single topmost node called the *root*. (Yes, it does seem odd that the root is at the top of the tree!) All the nodes except the root have a node above them which is called a *parent*, and each parent may have nodes immediately below it which is called

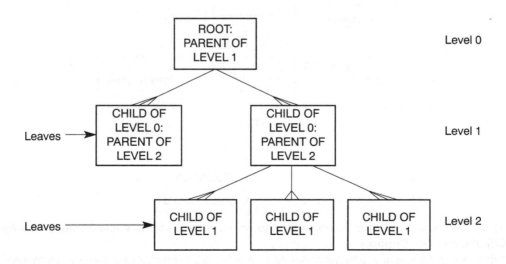

Fig 5.3 The Diagramming and Labelling Conventions for a Hierarchical or Tree Data Model
An important feature of this data model is that a child may have only one parent.

a *child*. (Parents without children are sometimes called *leaves* because they are correspondingly at the very end of branches.) The other important feature of this data model is that *a child may have only one parent*.

These features appear to make this form of data model contradict real life. As we have seen above, many-to-many relationships are frequently found in practice, and child entities may resemble real-life children by having more than one parent. So how does the model cope? We will use Fig 5.4 and Figs 5.5a and 5.5b as examples. They show some of the entity relationships for the central assembly and packing facility (CP) of Carry-Out Cupboards. In this example the entity 'operation' has two parents: 'operator' and 'production facility'. There is also a many-to-many relationship between 'product' and 'production facility'.

The phenomenon of two parents can be represented in two ways: either by the use of *replication* (Fig 5.5a) or by the use of a *pointer* (Fig 5.5b). Replication is essentially solving the problem by separating the model into disjointed components. This can hardly claim to be a *systemic* approach since *connexion* is an important property of any system. The use of pointers is better from a systemic viewpoint because it retains the important quality of connexion, but it does introduce a *soft issue* as to which entity is seen as the *source*, and which the *destination* of this connecting pointer: terms like *source* and *destination* carry a very strong *Weltanschauung* with them.

The use of a pointer would not solve the problem of many-to-many relationships like that between 'product' and 'production facility' in Fig 5.4.; since each production facility would need to be connected to each product and vice versa. A solution to the problem is available if we look again at the many-to-many relationship. It is possible to see the relationship itself as an entity, which may or may not have a corresponding

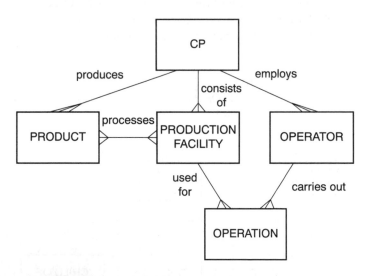

Fig 5.4 Some of the Entity Relationships for the Central Assembly and Packing Facility (CP) of Carry-Out Cupboards

In this example the entity 'operation' has two parents, and there is also a many-to-many relationship between 'product' and 'production facility'. (Appendix 1 explains the function of the CP within Carry-Out Cupboards.)

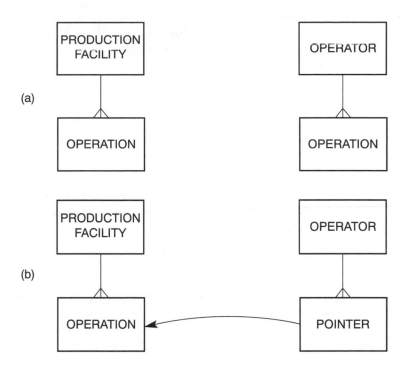

Fig 5.5 Resolving the Phenomenon of Two Parents in a Hierarchical Model

This can be done in two ways: either by the use of *replication* (a) or by the use of a *pointer* (b).

physical equivalent in real life. What connects the various products with the various production facilities is their coming together when any product is processed by a particular production facility. We could call this coming together a *production order* or *job*. We could then use this new concept or logical entity to modify the model as in Fig 5.6, and replace the many-to-many relationship with two one-to-many relationships. This modification still leaves us with a two-parent relationship, but we have already seen how a pointer can deal with this. (It is worth noting that the new conceptual or logical entity *production order* or *job* is also one which would have a physical representation as a document or screen in the physical system of Carry-Out Cupboards. *See* Chapter 6.)

A hierarchical model constructed in the way described so far will show the logical or conceptual relationships between entities. Once these have been defined, an *implementation model* can be used to develop a description of the *database* to be used by the information system. The basis of this implementation model will be a *hierarchical schema*. Such a schema uses the logic of the hierarchical model as its basis and then describes how the data is organized within this structure. Figure 5.7 shows the basic principles and a simple example of this.

The smallest element in the schema is a *field*. This represents the smallest unit of data that can be referenced separately and is used to hold the value of a single *attribute* found in the EAR model. All of the fields referring to a single *entity* are grouped

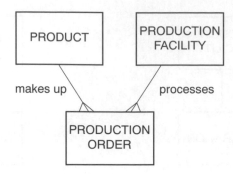

Fig 5.6 Resolving a Many-to-Many Relationship with Two One-to-Many Relationships
Note that this particular example of modification still leaves us with a two-parents relationship. This could be resolved by the use of a pointer as in Fig 5.5b.

together to form a *segment*. One of the fields within a segment, called the *sequence field,* is used for the ordering of segments of a given kind.

Each *segment* therefore consists of *fields* holding the *values* of the *attributes* of one of the *entities* that forms a node in the hierarchical model. The tree structure of the hierarchical model is then reflected by the definition of *logical database records* which consist of named hierarchies of related segments. The whole logical database is made up of these logical database records.

The *implementation* of the *hierarchical data model* is carried out with the use of *data definition* and *data manipulation languages,* which define the features of the schema (Fig 5.8) and enable access to the data stored in the hierarchical database. A major example of such a language is *DL/I,* which is used by IBM's so-called 'Information Management System (IMS)'. This had its origins about 30 years ago. I use the phrase

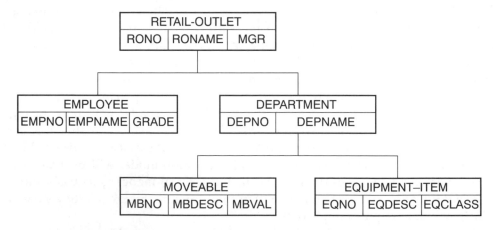

Fig 5.7 A Hierarchical Schema for Part of a Database
Such a schema uses the logic of the hierarchical model as its basis and then describes how the data is organized within this structure.

```
SCHEMA NAME = CARRY-OUT-CUPBOARDS

HIERARCHIES = HIERARCHY1, HIERARCHY2, HIERARCHY3

RECORD
        NAME = RETAIL-OUTLET
        TYPE = ROOT OF HIERARCHY2
        DATA ITEMS=
                RONO        INTEGER
                RONAME      CHARACTER 15
                MGR         CHARACTER 30
        KEY = RONO

RECORD
        NAME = DEPARTMENT
        PARENT = RETAIL-OUTLET
        CHILD NUMBER = 2
        DATA ITEMS =
                DEPNO       INTEGER
                DEPNAME     CHARACTER 25
        KEY = DEPNO
```

Fig 5.8 Hierarchical Data Definition Language
This shows how some of the features of the Schema of Fig 5.7
might be defined using such a language. For more details, try
Elmasri & Navathe (1989).

'so-called' about it here because I think that the whole point of what we have established in Chapter 3 makes a 'Management Information System' much more than software or a computer system. I am not trying to denigrate this application of the model however. I think that Bowers (1988) expresses the practical history very well when he explains that ' hierarchic structures are intrinsically user-oriented: organizations are arranged in hierarchies, filing cabinets are arranged hierarchically; even books are essentially hierarchic. It has long been known that cross-references are difficult to deal with – indeed, it is questionable whether people can maintain adequate mental representations of information plexes other than hierarchies'. The reference to 'plexes' leads into the next model.

5.1.4 The network or plex data model

One of the problems we found with the hierarchical model was that the relationships were ambiguous where a child had more than one parent. The arbitrary choice of parent and the use of a pointer rather put us in the position of a divorce court judge deciding who should have custody of the child and who would be allowed access rights. To pursue that analogy further, as with human parent–child relationships, it is not always obvious in a database which way the allocation should be made. It might be sensible therefore to accept the concept of multiple parents and consider a data model that recognizes this directly. A *network* or *plex* data model does this.

The essential concept behind the network is that of a set. A *set* consists of two entity types between which there is a one-to-many relationship. The entities at either end of this relationship are referred to as the *owner* and the *member* respectively. Since a data model is likely to represent more than just a single relationship between two entities, models are usually created by identifying set types and building them up into a model. The conceptual link which allows this building up is that *entities may belong to more than one set type as owners or members.* Figure 5.9 shows part of the central assembly and packing facility example of Fig 5.4 interpreted in this way.

In describing this model we need to distinguish the set *type* from a particular *instance.* Thus in the example of Fig 5.9, there will be more than one instance of the set type operator-operation. There is more than one operator at the central assembly and packing facility, and each of these might carry out more than one operation: so we would expect many separate instances of an operator carrying out an operation.

The network model still retains the problem of many-to-many relationships we found with the hierarchical model, but this can be resolved in a similar way to before. Figure 5.10 shows the network equivalent of Fig 5.6, where the introduction of the entity production order enabled us to resolve the many-to-many relationship into two one-to-many relationships in terms of a network model.

Like the hierarchical model, the *implementation* of the network model brings with it its own termology. The smallest element is a *data item.* It represents the smallest unit of data that can be referenced separately and is used to hold the value of a single *attribute* found in the EAR model. Unlike the hierarchical model however, the network model

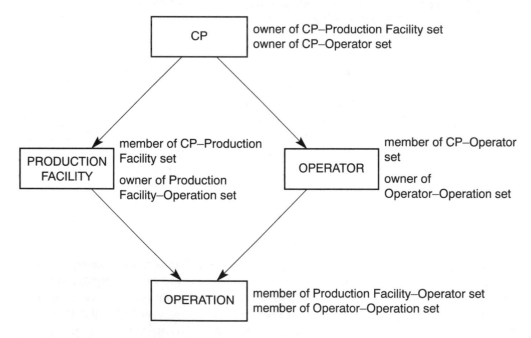

Fig 5.9 Network or Plex Data Model
A network version of the Central Assembly and Packing Facility example of Fig 5.4.

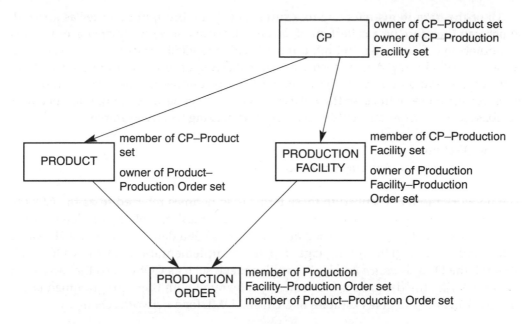

Fig 5.10 Many-to-Many Relations in the Network or Plex Data Model
This is the network equivalent of Fig 5.6, where the introduction of the entity 'Production Order' enabled the resolution of a many-to-many relationship.

allows for multivalues of an attribute. If these are all of the same type, e.g. different values for the attribute 'orderno' for the entity 'production order' in Fig 5.11, then the data items can be grouped together as a *vector*. If the data items are all of different types, e.g. the different types of values for the attributes 'opno' and 'optype' of the same entity then the data items are defined as a *repeating group*.

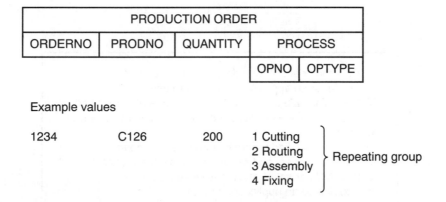

Fig 5.11 A Network Database Schema
Again based on the Central Assembly and Packing Facility example. 'Routing' is the operation which forms the channels in the chipboard sheet material which is used to fit sheets together.

All of the data items referring to a single entity are brought together as a *record*, which can therefore be a collection of *data items*, *vectors* or *repeating groups* in various combinations. A data item within a record which is used for ordering or selecting records is called a *key*. A *set* is then a named collection of records forming a two-level hierarchy, as explained above, with one record type defined as the *owner* and one or more record types defined as the *members*. Figure 5.11 gives an example of a network database schema from our central assembly and packing facility example.

◆ **STQ 5.4**
What kind of hierarchy is referred to here?

The network model described in these terms is sometimes referred to as the CODA-SYL or CODASYL-DBTG model. As with the hierarchical model, the implementation of the network data model is carried out with the use of a data definition (DDL) and a data manipulation (DML) language. For most implementations of the CODASYL MODEL the DML is *hosted* in a high-level language such as COBOL, so that accessing and processing the database is conveniently integrated with other programmed tasks. Figures 5.12 and 5.13 give examples of DDL and DML for a network schema.

```
SET NAME IS OPERATOR–OPERATION
   OWNER IS OPERATOR
      ORDER IS SORTED BY DEFINED KEYS
   MEMBER IS OPERATION
      KEY IS ASCENDING OPNO
```

Fig 5.12 Network Data Definition Language
This example refers to part of Fig 5.9.

```
OPEN: A file or set of records is opened, i.e. made
   available for an application program to use.
MODIFY: The values of specified data items of a specified
   record occurrence are replaced with values in the program
   work area.
DELETE: A specified record occurrence is removed
   from the database, and relationships involving it are deleted.
CLOSE: A file or set of records is closed, i.e. made
   unavailable to an application program.
```

Fig 5.13 Network Data Manipulation Language
These are just a selection of commands. This sample should be compared with Fig 5.22.

5.1.5 The relational model

Although the two models we have looked at so far have been widely and successfully implemented, they both have a potential weakness in relation to one of the issues we raised at the beginning of this chapter: the issue of change in the contents and the use of the database. As in the Norris Trainers case, most databases don't stand still.

The kind of change we saw at Norris Trainers and are considering here isn't just that associated with first-order control like updating stock levels or customer accounts. It also involves higher-order control changes like adding new types of data and requiring new forms of output from new ways of processing the database.

The result of such changes in practice has been that databases tend to become bogged down and cumbersome. The number of logical linkages tends to grow every time a new application is added because fresh ways of querying the database are required from an increasing range of data types. We often find in other applied fields of management or technology that once a particular approach to a problem gets too complex, inflexible and costly to operate, new ways are found to get around the problem. So it was with databases: a new approach based on a *relational* model was proposed by Codd (1970) which overcame the limitations of using hierarchical or network structures. Understanding why an approach based on the *relational* model has an advantage over the others comes from noting a limitation that these previous approaches share. Both of them think in terms of an ultimately *implementable physical structure*, rather than concentrating specifically on the *structure of the data represented*. The relational model concentrates on the *logical* description of the data from the user's viewpoint and is not linked to any one particular *physical* representation. (There are many ways in which a relational database can be *physically* structured.)

The essence of the relational data model is the two-dimensional *flat table* or *flat file*. We can use Fig 5.14 as an example. It shows the selection of the details of cupboards introduced in Fig 5.1. We recall that each of the columns of the table corresponds to an attribute of an entity, in this case, a cupboard. All of the values in a particular row correspond to one particular instance of that entity, and all the instances go together to make up a *whole* concept or an *emergent property*, which in this case is the whole collection of products we call 'cupboards'. In the relational model such wholes are called *relations*, and the table in Fig 5.14 shows the particular *relation* we could call *cupboard*.

A database constructed from relations of this kind is called a *relational database*. Modelling a relational database requires no other device than the flat table itself. As we shall see later in this section, even complex relationships like many-to-many can be represented without resorting to pointers or other complicating devices. The attraction of the relational model is this simplicity and elegance, and I notice that the adage 'great engineering is simple engineering', which I first heard as an early sixties industrial trainee, has been rightly applied by Martin (1976) to the principles behind the relational model.

Given the central role of the relation, we need to understand the terminology which is used to describe its components and characteristics. If we call the whole of a flat table like Fig 5.14 a *relation*, then each of its rows is called a *tuple*. A tuple is described as an *N-tuple* according to the number, *N*, of attribute values represented. The tuples in Fig 5.14 are *8-tuples*. It is important to note that a tuple is an *unordered* row of values rather than a structured record. This flexibility is important because it indicates the potential that a relational database has for presenting data in different ways to accom-

STYLE	SIZE	SURFACE FINISH	HEIGHT	FITTINGS	PRICE £	SITING	STOCK CLASS
Calabria	3S	Veneer	3480	Triple/A/S	215.00	Lounge	LG
Calabria	3S	Antique	3480	Triple/A/S	205.00	Diner	DN
Calabria	2S	Veneer	1740	Double/A/S	185.00	Lounge	LG
Calabria	2S	Antique	1740	Double/A/S	150.00	Diner	DN
Classic	3S	Veneer	3480	Triple/S/S	200.00	Bedroom	BD
Classic	3S	Antique	3480	Triple/S/S	190.00	Lounge	LG
Classic	3S	Fabric	3480	Triple/S/S	180.00	Diner	DN
Classic	2S	Veneer	1740	Double/S/S	135.00	Bedroom	BD
Classic	2S	Antique	1740	Double/S/S	125.00	Lounge	LG
Classic	2S	Fabric	1740	Double/S/S	120.00	Diner	DN
Classic	1S	Fabric	870	Single/S/S	100.00	Diner	DN
Classic	1S	Floral	870	Single/S/S	80.00	Kitchen	KT
Classic	1H	Floral	870	Single/S/H	85.00	Kitchen	KT
Country	2S	Fabric	1740	Double/N/S	100.00	Kitchen	KT
Country	2S	Floral	1740	Double/N/S	100.00	Diner	DN
Country	1S	Fabric	870	Single/N/S	80.00	Kitchen	KT
Country	1S	Floral	870	Single/N/S	80.00	Diner	DN
Country	2H	Fabric	1740	Double/N/H	110.00	Kitchen	KT
Country	2H	Floral	1740	Double/N/H	110.00	Diner	DN
Country	1H	Fabric	870	Single/N/H	90.00	Kitchen	KT
Country	1H	Floral	870	Single/N/H	90.00	Diner	DN

Fig 5.14 The C Range of Carry-Out Cupboards
The background to the principle of exploiting permutations of components to make a complete range of products can be understood in the context of the Carry-Out Cupboards case of Appendix 1.

modate the differing views and differing needs of different users. In our cupboard example a customer might want to think about price and surface finish before considering the model, while a stock clerk might start by looking at the stock class. By not imposing a concept of the 'best' or 'correct' order on the components of the tuple, we make these differing views possible.

A particular column of the relation is called a *domain*. Note that this refers to the *whole* set of attribute values represented, and that we envisage the individual values in each of the tuples as being selected from this whole. A particular tuple can be regarded as a *mapping* between the domains from which the values are drawn.

One or more domains in a relation will be chosen because their individual values enable us to uniquely identify a particular tuple. What is chosen is called the *key* of the relation. We shall say more of this when we look further at the concept of *normalization* in the next section.

The use of conceptual wholes like *relation*, *domain*, etc. is an essential characteristic of the relational model. As we shall see in Section 5.2, to regard the database in terms of sets and wholes enables the application of mathematically based, precise notations for describing relations and for performing operations on them.

The number of components in a relation is described in terms of its *degree*, representing the number of domains; and its *cardinality*, representing the number of tuples.

So does the relational model which we have described above fulfil the objectives we have given it in dealing with problems like '*The number of logical linkages tends to grow every time a new application is added because fresh ways of querying the database are required from an increasing range of data types*'? I think that the answer to this question is a clear 'no'. We know that the relational model gives us an open decision as to which domains we may include in a tuple according to our needs. If we return to our cupboard example of Figs 5.1 and 5.14, we saw that a customer might want price and surface finish but not technical details like stock class, while a stock clerk would just want to identify a particular cupboard and know its stock class. Decisions like these affect what particular form a relation should take in terms of the number and values for these data items in the tuples. Without any consistent way of defining the possible form of the resulting flat tables, we could end up with one of two possible complications to the model which would make it unwieldy or messily complex. One complication comes from trying to see the database as one large flat table, the other comes from trying to see it as several smaller individual ones.

If we try to control the model by viewing all the attributes of all the entities as being in one flat table like Fig 5.14, we don't actually have one relation at all. This point will become clearer if we look more carefully at Fig 5.14. First we can see that it contains several *repeating groups*. Thus, the style 'Calabria' occurs many times because that particular style comes in several sizes and with different surface finishes. We can also see that there are different kinds of relationship or *dependencies* between the domains. Thus, the value for stock class is automatically determined by siting, so this latter domain can be considered as somehow secondary to or dependent on the former.

One single large table therefore tells us about several different things. A particular individual combination of style, model and surface finish indicates the existence of a particular cupboard; whereas siting or price tell us more about a cupboard already on our list. Our use of the phrase 'several different things' indicates that a flat table like Fig 5.14 does not represent just a single relation: parts of the table can be seen as relations in their own right. We shall look at this more rigorously when we come to consider the subject of *normalization* later in this section.

What if we look at the database in terms of several smaller tables, each containing just that selection of domains which are of interest to a particular user? We might just have style, model, surface finish and price for the accounts people; or everything except stock class for salesmen and customers. If we try this approach we introduce a new complication. Once we use more than one table to express our view of the different relations in the database, we will nearly always find that some domains occur in more than one table and introduce the complication of having the same data repeated several times in different parts of the model. This brings with it the potential for inconsistency and unnecessary redundancy.

◆ STQ 5.5

What examples of this can you find in the mini-case?

There are therefore problems and benefits which come whichever way we view the database: as one table or as many. It would be useful to have a set of principles to enable us to come up with a representation which recognized the different relations present in the database while avoiding the complications of duplication and redundancy. Booch (1991) puts this point very succinctly: 'The simplest yet most important goal in database design is the concept that each fact should be stored in exactly one place'. If this simple principle can be implemented it provides a database which:

a. Eliminates redundancy and potential storage requirements.
b. Simplifies the process of updating the database.
c. Makes it easier to prevent inconsistencies within the database.

The process of *normalization,* referred to above, attempts to define a relational database in a way which has these qualities. The next section will look at the principles behind normalization using an illustrative example.

5.1.6 Normalization

Figure 5.14 is a table showing a particular range of cupboards sold by Carry-Out Cupboards. Different details can be selected from this table to express different users views of what it contains, but as we saw in the previous section, the aim of normalization is to produce a model which eliminates redundancy, reduces potential storage requirements, simplifies the process of updating the database and makes it easier to prevent inconsistencies within the database.

The process of normalization exploits the essential property of a relational database that all the component relations can be redefined in terms of flat tables in a way that brings the advantages of eliminating redundancy. To achieve this redefinition, certain features in the original table have to be recognized and dealt with separately in the stages of the normalization process. The stages in this procedure result in the definition of a series of *normal forms* (NF) called *first* (1NF), *second* (2NF) and *third* (3NF) normal forms respectively:

Stage 1. Remove *repeating groups*
Stage 2. Remove *partial dependencies*
Stage 3. Remove *transitive dependencies*

The particular normal form we derive at each stage represents the removal of some *redundancy* from the relational model, and a step towards the aim of redundancy elimination. If we are to understand how the passage from 1NF to 3NF in the normalization process removes redundancy, we need also to understand the difference between *redundancy* and *duplication*. In Fig 5.14, for example, many of the details of the cupboards appeared to be duplicated: but are they redundant? The key to answering this question is the concept of *dependency*. We have to ask whether the particular value for a duplicated data item depends on the value of another.

The difference between redundancy and duplication can be illustrated by returning to Fig 5.14. Does the fact that a cupboard is in the *Classic* style imply that its Surface Finish will automatically be *Fabric* or vice versa? If we consider the frequently occurring value *Fabric* for the attribute *Surface Finish*, we can see that the value of one does not depend on the value of the other. The elimination of all cupboards with a *Fabric* value for *Surface Finish* does not eliminate all *Classic* cupboards in terms of their *Style*. Similarly, there will still be cupboards with *Fabric* for their *Surface Finish* if we eliminate the *Style* called *Classic*. Since the duplication in these examples does not come from any *dependency*, it does not represent something about the *structure of* the relation that needs identifying and separating to remove *redundancy*.

This last point does not apply to the relationship between *Siting* and *Stock Class*: the values of these attributes always go together. If we get rid of all the cupboards whose *Siting* is *Lounge*, we also automatically get rid of those whose *Stock Class* is *LG*. Once we recognize the *structural dependency* of *Stock Class* on *Siting*, then knowing that the siting is, say, *Lounge* automatically also tells us that its *Stock Class* is *LG*.

Given this distinction between *duplication* and *redundancy*, we shall see that they do not have the same significance for the normalization process. Normalization only seeks to eliminate duplication where it is redundant.

We are now ready to consider the stages of the normalization process which are the most important. Other subtleties can come up when we look at particular cases, but our Carry-Out Cupboards relation of Fig 5.14 will illustrate the main concepts.

To establish models in 1NF, 2NF and 3NF respectively we apply the three stages given above to the relation *Cupboard* of Fig 5.14.

Stage 1 requires the removal of *repeating groups*. This is done by separation into different tables, each of which represents a relation with this feature removed. The *Cupboard* relation of Fig 5.14 contains two repeating groups, one of which happens to lie inside (or is '*nested*' in) the other. The repeating groups are separated one at a time, with each separation producing a new relation. The two relations which are then produced contain:

a. The *key* of the original relation, plus any attributes which depend on them.
b. The key of the original relation, plus those attributes which form the *key* of the *repeating group*, together with the attributes of the repeating group.

In the case of the *Cupboard* relation of Fig 5.14, the application of these procedures for each repeating group eventually produces three tables. The first contains *Style* and any (*if there were any*) attributes which are uniquely determined by it: in this case that's zero. The second consists of the remaining attributes, with a key made up of *Style* and *Surface Finish*; but this second table needs splitting again to remove the nested repeating group to allow for repetitions due to the value of *Size*. The result is a second and third table which take on the principle of the 'key of the original relation, plus those attributes which form the key of the repeating group, together with the attributes of the repeating group'. Hence the relation *Application*, with *Style* and *Surface Finish* as the key; and a new version of the *Cupboard* relation with *Style*, *Surface Finish* and *Size* as the key.

Before going on to the next stage of the normalization process, it is worth seeing how the concept of a *key* to a relation can now be developed further. Once we start on the process of breaking down a previous relation into component relations through normalization, we find that one or more keys of a previous relation may appear with new keys to form an overall key to the new relation. Thus in Fig 5.15: the original key *Style* of the *Cupboard* in Fig 5.14 reappeared with *Surface Finish* as the combined key to the *Application* relation. Similarly, *Size* was added to form the key of the new version of *Cupboard*. Such a key of an original table which is passed on down to a component table in the normalization process is called a *foreign key*.

Stage 2 of the normalization process requires the removal of partial dependencies, again by separation into tables representing relations with this feature removed. In *systemic* terms, these can be seen as *components* of the original concept of a relational database. The concept of partial dependency can be understood by looking more closely at the terms *dependency* and *partial* in turn. The dependency referred to is the dependency of the non-key attributes on the value of the key attributes. Thus for the new version of the *Cupboard* relation in Fig 5.15, the values for *Height*, *Fittings* and *Price* will depend on the particular *Style, Size* and *Surface Finish* of the cupboard concerned. But we need to make a distinction between attributes whose value is determined by that of *all* the key attributes, and those whose value is determined by just some of them. In the *Cupboard* relation of Fig 5.15, the value for the attribute *Price* depends on the individual values of all three key attributes: variations in style, size and surface finish can all affect the price. The value of *Height*, however, is only dependent on *Size*: once we know the size of the cupboard we know the height regardless of its particular surface finish or style. Where the value of a non-key attribute depends on anything less than the entire key, we call this dependency *partial*. In our examples from Fig 5.15, the dependency of *Height* on *Size* is such a *partial dependency*.

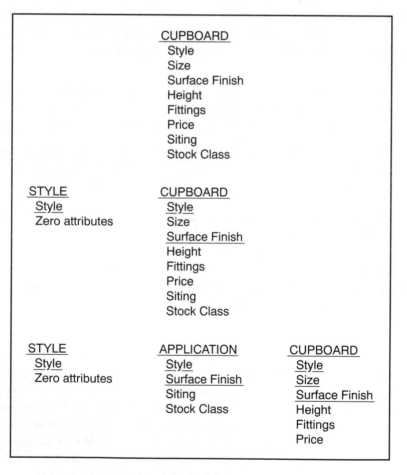

Fig 5.15 Establishing First Normal Form
Removal of repeating groups, e.g. more than one different version of *style* and *surface finish*, or even of one *style, surface finish* and *size*.

◆ STQ 5.6

What form does the dependency of Fittings take in this context?

Any partial dependencies found in a 1NF table are removed by forming them into new separate relations. Thus Fig 5.16 shows the previous *Cupboard* relation of Fig 5.15 split to form two new relations, *Size* and *Model*. The new relation *Size* shows the partial dependency of *Height* on *Size*, while the new relation *Model* covers the partial dependency of *Fittings* on *Style* and *Size*. The removal of any partial dependencies from a 1NF relation then leaves it in 2NF, as in Fig 5.16.

Stage 3 of the normalization process involves the removal of any *transitive dependencies* from the 2NF relations. As in the previous stages, this is done by separation into tables representing relations with this feature removed. Transitive dependency occurs when the value of an attribute does not depend *directly* on the value of the key. Instead, we have a relationship where the value of one attribute depends on that of another, and then the value of this second attribute depends on that of the key. We can see an example of this in the *Application* relation of Fig 5.16. In this relation the value for *Stock Class* depends entirely on that for *Siting*, but *Siting* itself is not a key for the relation: it depends in turn on the key attributes *Style* and *Surface Finish*.

Figure 5.17 shows our original *Cupboard* relation transformed into a series of tables in 3NF, and Fig 5.18 summarizes how these link together. The result of the normalization process is a set of relations which reflect the properties of the *key* and *nothing else*, and thereby achieves our goal that each fact should be stored in exactly one place. This now means that we have a database which eliminates redundancy, reduces potential storage requirements, simplifies the process of updating and makes it easier to prevent inconsistencies arising within the database.

There are more complex issues associated with normalization which we have not covered, including Boyce-Codd Normal Form and the possibility of 4NF and 5NF. For more rigorous, mathematical treatment of normalization, try Stanczyk (1990). For a refreshingly practical and sceptical view of databases and normalization, try Veryard (1984).

STYLE	APPLICATION	MODEL
Style	Style	Style
Zero attributes	Surface Finish	Size
	Siting	Fittings
	Stock Class	
SIZE	CUPBOARD	
Size	Style	
Height	Size	
	Surface Finish	
	Price	

Fig 5.16 Establishing Second Normal Form
Removal of partial dependencies, e.g. *height* does not depend completely on *style*, *size* and *surface finish*.

```
STYLE              APPLICATION        MODEL
  Style              Style              Style
  Zero attributes    Surface Finish     Size
                     Siting             Fittings


SIZE               SITING             CUPBOARD
  Size               Siting             Style
  Height             Stock Class        Size
                                        Surface Finish
                                        Price
```

Fig 5.17 Establishing Third Normal Form
Removal of transitive dependencies, e.g. *stock class* is entirely determined by *siting*.

5.1.7 Semantic models

In the previous sections we have shown some of the development which has taken place in thinking about the principles behind database concepts as well as studying the details of particular models.

In studying hierarchical and network data models we frequently emphasized the important principle of distinguishing between the logical and the physical database, but a link between the *logical* and the *physical* still remained. When we considered, for example, how data could be *accessed* in a structure, we were still thinking in terms of how the database would be implemented.

When we moved on to the relational model, we took a further step in making the distinction between the logical and the physical by concentrating specifically on the structure of the data represented in the database: but why did we do so? The answer was that the elegant principle 'each fact should be stored in exactly one place' brought the advantages of eliminating redundancy, reducing potential storage, simplifying processing and preventing inconsistencies. Thus, even with the strongly logical rather than physical emphasis of the relational model, issues of *implementation* were still present when we discussed it.

To understand why the models we have studied so far still lack something, we must return to the original reason for our interest in them. We decided to study data models in the wider context of *information* and *information systems*. We followed up our assertion in Chapter 3 that information could be regarded as a property which emerged from the whole when component elements of data were brought together in a particular relationship or structure, and we decided that all the forms of information we considered as relevant to management are *about something*. The limitation of the models we have studied so far is that their emphasis tends to be on the *data* structure, rather than the *information* which the *user* is interested in.

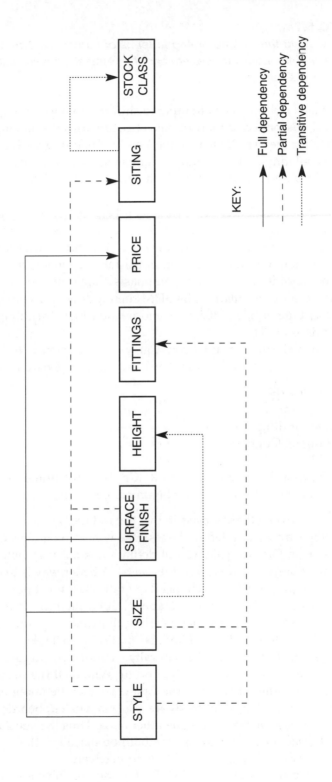

Fig 5.18 The Relationships of Third Normal Form
'The key and nothing but the key'.

◆ **STQ 5.7**

How could this be interpreted in terms of communication between the user and the computer system and the General Communication System Model of Chapter 4?

The *semantic data model* (SDM) attempts to shift the balance of emphasis away from a mainly logical, disconnected view of data structure towards an emphasis on the *meaning* of the data for the user. If we take the Concise Oxford English Dictionary definition of *semantic* as 'relating to the meaning of language', we would rightly expect a *semantic data model* to be based on principles which derive from the user's view of the meaning of the data.

The SDM is defined in terms of *classes* and *attributes*. As in other models above, these *attributes* are characteristics of *entities*; but with the important proviso that the entities correspond to objects in the *real-world*. It is this concentration on real-world objects, rather than logical entities conceived for the convenience of the data model, that gives the SDM its user-meaning emphasis. *Classes* are collections of entities that share the same set of *attributes*. The SDM then follows the conventions of the EAR model in describing entities, attributes and relationships, including possible diagramming conventions of Fig 5.2.

We can take a simple example from Carry-Out Cupboards to illustrate these concepts. Possible classes of products sold by Carry-Out Cupboards might be:

  a. Cupboards
  b. Furniture
  c. Freestanding Cupboards
  d. Hanging Cupboards
  e. Tables
  f. {Cupboard Number CA3SVR, Cupboard Number CL3SVR, Cupboard Number CL2SVR, Cupboard Number CA2SVR}

The difference between the last class in this list and the others illustrates an important principle in the way we can define classes. One way is to define a class by listing all of its members, as in *f* above. This way of definition is not very helpful because it does not answer the question 'why is it in this class?' A better way is to define membership in terms of some property that each member of the class must possess, and which non-members will not, as is done in *a–e* above. Such membership properties will be represented by a set of shared *attributes*. Thus all members of the class 'cupboard' will share the attribute 'door', which will not be applicable to 'table'.

This concept of *class* can then be naturally extended by adding the concept of *subclass*. Figure 5.19 shows how this might occur. Where all the members of a class are also members of some other class, the first class may be taken as a subclass of the second. Thus 'freestanding' cupboards are a subclass of 'cupboards'. It is possible for a class to be a subclass of more than one other class. Thus the subclasses of table called 'square folding' or 'circular folding' can both be placed in the 'folding' category, or individually classed as 'square' or 'folding' respectively.

Another important feature of the SDM is the way in which it regards and represents *relationships*. This goes beyond the definition of basic logical characteristics like the

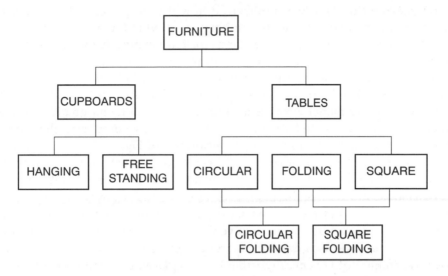

Fig 5.19 The Semantic Data Model
Examples of *classes* and *attributes* in terms of the products of Carry-Out Cupboards.

degree of a relationship or whether it is compulsory or optional. It also goes beyond what we could hope to cover in a non-specialist book like this, but we can at least understand some basic issues.

More developed forms of the SDM would recognize how different kinds of entity may be related through different kinds of relationship. Consider Fig 5.19 again. If we decided to carry out an operation like deleting 'tables' from our database we would automatically get rid of 'circular tables' too; but what about the effect on say, 'suppliers'? These may be represented in an associated class which is divided into subclasses like 'fittings suppliers', 'materials suppliers' and so on. How would the deleting of 'tables' from the database affect 'suppliers' if at all? Should this mean that certain suppliers should be eliminated? Might an irrelevant supplier be left on the database? Generally, how do we ensure that in processing the database we also maintain its consistency and integrity?

To ensure that these goals are achieved, the SDM categorizes relationships and defines what types of maintenance of them is required and allowed. Thompson (1989) looks at this in some detail.

5.1.8 Object-oriented models

We introduced the concepts of hierarchy and classification in Chapter 4, and we indicated there that they form the important basis for an object-oriented approach to systems development which we shall consider in Chapter 7. It therefore makes sense to leave further detailed treatment of the object-oriented view of data and information until then. Meanwhile, I think we have covered enough of object-orientation to understand the important basic principles behind an *object-oriented database*.

◆ **STQ 5.8**
What kind of hierarchy has just been referred to?

When considering the SDM, we emphasized how it represented yet a further move away from thinking about the data to thinking about what the data represented. This can be seen as a process of *abstraction* as far as the hard computer system is concerned. Questions of how data is stored and accessed, which still featured in the hierarchical or plex models, have virtually disappeared from our view of how the data is modelled when we use the SDM. By distinguishing different kinds of entity and relationship types we have a *richer* model which is able to reflect the different qualities of the real life which is being represented. This can be illustrated by comparing the term 'cupboard' as it appears in the relational model examples of Figs 5.15–5.17 with the SDM example of Fig 5.19. The examples of Figs 5.15–5.17 focus much more on kinds of relation than they do on kinds of *cupboard*. This is not the case with the SDM example of Fig 5.19: this looks much more like cupboards as we would regard them in practice.

The SDM still has a drawback. Consider the question of *manipulation* of data. When the models we have described so far involve the creation, deletion or updating of entities there are other processes that follow from them. Thus, if we are creating a new cupboard, we might need to check whether it is a replacement for a previous model or whether some of its components and materials come from existing suppliers. The processes which carry out these checks are governed by the type of entity we are dealing with. Recognizing that a particular entity does or does not belong to particular class will determine which operations are needed. Thus the next stage in the modelling of data is the *integration of defining data modelling with data operations.*

Object-orientation can enable this, and the wider systems development context of Chapter 8 shows how this can be.

Box 5.1

CATTLE DATABASE MAY COST UP TO £5M

(*Financial Times* 12/8/96: all italics are mine)

The creation of an electronic database to monitor the movements of Britain's 11.5m cattle could cost the government between £3m and £5m, according to a report revealed today.

The National Cattle Database working party, an *influential group of farmers and consumer interests*, will call on the government to have all movements of new-born cattle included *on* computer records by the end of November.

The rest of the national herd could be tracked by a nationwide census with the aim of listing all cattle on computer by January 1998. . .

The idea is that the database would offer a single point of access for many details on an animal's history. . .

As an interim measure the government introduced a system of passports for all animals born after July 1– providing a paper trail to follow the cattle around.

But Mr Madders says passports should be phased out as soon as a computer system is developed. The industry will have to introduce a new form of *electronic ear tag* for cattle. . .

Information could be available on demand, with ways of protecting confidentiality.

COMMENT

You may feel that Chapter 5 covers the *hardest* subject area in this book for two reasons.

The first is that the construction of databases is *hard* in the systems sense because it deals with defined, technical procedures. These include the construction of a *data model*, with *relationships* between *entities* and *attributes*, and procedures like *normalization*. Being based on a strict mathematical foundation, these are hard in the systems sense.

You may also think that the procedures involved in producing a data model are hard in the sense of being difficult to do. If so, the National Cattle Database working party seems to agree with you.

The *Financial Times* article comes from a time when millions of people and billions of pounds of money in Europe are influenced by information about the health of cows in Britain. In these circumstances, the construction and use of any database is not a purely technical problem. If you were a British cattle farmer, what attributes would you think important for any database model: a Boolean attribute like 'BSE in herd yes/no'? Or if you were a German consumer: 'British-born calf yes/no'?

I think that the important concern in this case is fear about diseased cattle. The *management* purpose of any cattle database which is part of the supporting information system must include reassurance about *unique physical identification* of animals. This will enable the capture of the *entity* we wish to record and control, and its vital attributes such as *history* or *movement*.

Electronic ear tagging and *data capture* is therefore much more important than the relatively easy problem of creating yet another computerized database system. If it was only a question of knowing 'what-is-what-where', we could register cows on an existing database like the vehicle registration system at Swansea or the UK National Insurance system in Newcastle. We'd just have to pretend that cows were motor cars or human beings. In fact this is not as foolish as it sounds. The principles of *object-orientation* enable us to recognize what characteristics any new system will share with existing systems, and to re-use parts of existing software rather than build entirely from scratch. In the cattle case, however, it is the animal *identification* not the database which is the main problem.

FURTHER STUDY

Explore the concept of object-orientation which is introduced in this chapter and is developed further in Chapter 8. Is the construction of a database which records the *identity, movement* and *ultimate fate* of cattle that much different from the vehicle registration or National Insurance systems which also follow cars or human beings through their lives?

How do we 'ear tag' cars or human beings in the UK? How is it done in other EU countries?

5.2 DATABASE PROCESSING AND MANIPULATION

5.2.1 Database language principles

We introduced the subject of data languages when considering the hierarchical data model. We saw that the implementation of the model required the use of *data definition* and *data manipulation* languages. A *data definition language* (DDL) defines the structural features of the model of the database, while a *data manipulation language* (DML) defines how the data can be accessed and manipulated. We should now add a third type of data language to our list: a *data control language* (DCL) which controls access to the database and helps ensure security.

It is worth noting the order in which we mentioned these three types of language since it reflects something about their relationship to each other in terms of their function. We can explain this by using the analogy of a room plan of a building.

Control of security of a building requires knowledge of the siting of the entrances and how rooms and passageways are connected. We need to know about structure and access before we can control security. So with a database the form of the DCL will depend on the structure and access to the database defined by the DDL and DML respectively.

If we pursue our building room plan analogy further, we come up with an important issue about the relationship between the DDL and the DML. In our building we might say that the structure of the building determines the access. For example, if the bedrooms are upstairs and the living room is downstairs, then this structure for a house defines that access to the bedrooms is achieved by the process of going up the stairs first. By analogy in the database, since the DDL defines the *structure* of the database and the DML deals with *process*, we would expect the form of the DML to depend on the form of the DDL.

However, this conclusion that structure determines process is only one half of the relationship between them. In our building analogy we can see that it could be the other way around. If it is not easy for me to go upstairs because I use a wheelchair or suffer from arthritis, then I might choose a house structured in a way that means I don't have to use the stairs at all, e.g. a single-storey bungalow. In database terms, we might say that rather than seeing the DDL determining the nature of the DML, *data structure* and *data processing* are *complementary systemic properties* affecting each other.

This interrelationship of structure and process enables us to look at data languages in complementary ways. One way is to start directly from a process viewpoint and look at the principles determining the types of operations that can be carried out on a database. Alternatively, we can consider how we might define the relationships behind a database structure and use this to define principles for processing the database.

The way in which either of these approaches can be applied depends on the particular data model we are dealing with. We will mainly focus on the relational data model for the rest of this section because it is a model which has wide-ranging application and support. Semantic and object-oriented models may challenge the ascendancy of the relational model in the future however.

We will therefore consider two theoretical foundations:

1. *Relational algebra* as a way of looking at the principles determining the types of operations that can be carried out on a database.
2. *Relational calculus* as a way of defining the relationships within a database structure and using these to define ways of processing the database.

5.2.2 Relational algebra

Relational algebra begins by recognizing that the relations which make up a relational database are *sets*. It then defines *operators* which can be applied to relations to form other relations:

$$\text{relation}_A, \text{relation}_B \rightarrow \text{set operator} \rightarrow \text{relation}_C$$

There are five standard set operators which are the same as those found elsewhere in set algebra, plus three operators which are specific to relational algebra. We can illustrate what these operators do by referring to Fig 5.14. The standard operators are:

- UNION Brings two relations together into one united relation. For this to be possible, both the original relations must be *union-compatible*. This effectively means that they must have the same attributes ranging over the same domains. Thus Fig 5.14 could be seen as the union of two separate relations: one containing all the 'Country' cupboards and the other containing the rest of the range.

- DIFFERENCE The difference between one relation and another will be a resultant relation which only contains those tuples not present in the second relation. In terms of Fig 5.14, the difference between the relation shown and one containing only 'Country' cupboards would be a new relation with no 'Country' cupboards.

- INTERSECTION The result of applying this operator to two relations is to identify which tuples are present in them both. An intersection of Figs 5.14 and 5.20 would be a relation containing only 'Calabria' cupboards in 'Veneer' and 'Antique'.

- PRODUCT This results in a relation whose attributes represent all the possible combinations of those attributes in the original relations. Figure 5.21 gives a simple example.

- DIVISION This is essentially the reverse of PRODUCT. Thus in Fig 5.21, if we divided the relation 'Style.Surface Finish' by say 'Style', it would result in the original 'Surface Finish' relation.

STYLE	SIZE	SURFACE FINISH	HEIGHT	FITTINGS	PRICE £	SITING	STOCK CLASS
Calabria	3S	Veneer	3480	Triple/A/S	215.00	Lounge	LG
Calabria	3S	Antique	3480	Triple/A/S	205.00	Diner	DN
Calabria	2S	Veneer	1740	Double/A/S	185.00	Lounge	LG
Calabria	2S	Antique	1740	Double/A/S	150.00	Diner	DN
Classic	3S	Floral	3480	Triple/S/S	180.00	Diner	DN
Country	3S	Fabric	1740	Double/N/S	100.00	Kitchen	KT
Country	1H	Floral	870	Single/N/H	90.00	Kitchen	KT

Fig 5.20 A Selection from the C Range
An *intersection* of this selection and the table of Fig 5.14 would be a relation containing only 'Calabria' cupboards in 'Veneer' and 'Antique'.

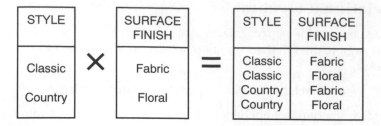

Fig 5.21 An Example of the PRODUCT Operator
Results in a relation whose attributes represent all the possible combinations of those attributes in the original relations.

In addition to these standard operators, the three operators specific to relational algebra are:

- SELECT This applies a predicate, or condition, to a relation to select a subset of its tuples. The general definition would take the form:

$$\sigma_{<condition>} (<\text{relation name}>).$$

An example applied to Fig 5.14 might take the condition 'Style = Calabria' for the relation 'Cupboard', which would result in a list of cupboards in the 'Calabria' style.

- PROJECT Simply extracts a subset of the attributes of a relation. Here the general definition would take the form:

$$\pi_{<attribute\ list>}(<\text{relation name}>).$$

An example applied to Fig 5.14 for the attributes 'Style' and 'Size' of the 'Cupboard' would result in a table consisting of the first two columns of Fig 5.14.

- JOIN Is used to combine two relations on the basis of the value of a shared attribute. The general form is:

$$R \bowtie \text{JOIN CONDITION}> S$$

where R and S are two relations. Thus one relation (R), listing 'Style' and 'Size', could be joined with another relation (S), listing 'Style' and 'Surface Finish', via their common value of 'Style' (which is the JOIN CONDITION), to form a new relation with the attributes 'Style', 'Size' and 'Surface Finish'.

Elmasri & Navathi (1989) do a very thorough job on relational algebra and many other topics in the field of database management.

5.2.3 Relational calculus

We explained above that relational algebra is a way of looking directly at the operations or *processes* that can be carried out on a database; but we saw earlier that defining the *structural* relationships within a database will also imply how a database can be processed, and can be used as a basis for process definition.

Relational calculus uses this latter approach. Our earlier analogy of the room plan of a building showed that defining the *structural* relationship between the components of the building automatically implied what *processes* might be applied to access it. So, although relational calculus is *relational* (concerned with *structure*) rather than *procedural* (concerned with *process*), it can be used to define the processes used in database manipulation.

Relational calculus *itself* is therefore *non-procedural*, even though we know that our interest in it is based on a desire to derive principles for processing databases. We can refer to a commonly used concept in this book: relational algebra is concerned with *how* we retrieve data from the database structure, while relational calculus specifies *what* data in the structure we wish to retrieve.

The formal specification of relational calculus may be alarming for those who find mathematical formulae daunting. Elmasri & Navathi (1989) state that a general expression of the tuple relational calculus is of the form:

$$\{t_1.A_1, t_2.A_2, ..., t_n.A_n| \; COND(t_1, t_2, ..., t_n, t_{n+1}, t_{n+2}, ..., t_{n+m})\}$$

and then go on to define the various components of this heavily subscripted formula, but this perfectly correct mathematical language is not something everyone would want to tackle.

However, the *concepts* behind relational calculus are not that difficult to grasp once we get past the conspiratorial pedantry of the mathematics. Thus in the Carry-Out Cupboards selection of Fig 5.14, we might want to find out what cupboards, if any, of the 'Country' style were available in the 'Fabric' surface finish. We could put this more formally by stating 'retrieve *any tuple* from the cupboard relation, *given that* the values for *style* and *surface finish* are 'Country' and 'Fabric' respectively. So we query the database to find out the values of the *attributes* (hence 'A') of some *tuple* (hence 't') variable *given* (that's what the symbol '|' means) that a certain set of *conditions* (hence COND) applies.

The calculus is therefore essentially built up from the concepts of *tuple variables* and *conditions* (also called *well formed formulae*). Each tuple variable ranges over a particular database relation and can take as its value any individual tuple from that relation. We then use a condition to identify any tuples which fit the criteria we lay down for the query. The essential ingredient of the complex formula above then becomes:

$$\{t| \; COND(T)\}$$

so that:

$$\{t| \; cupboard(t) \text{ and } t.style = \text{'Country' and } t.surface \text{ finish} = \text{'Fabric'}\}$$

defines the tuples in the cupboard relation that meet our conditions.

For most users however, neither the relational algebra nor the relational calculus represents a convenient language for accessing or processing a database. It makes sense, therefore, to develop data manipulation languages which are much easier for the user to use; but at the same time ensuring that these user-friendly DMLs are based on the correct rigour of relational algebra or calculus. In the next section we shall look at some examples of this principle.

5.2.4 Database language applications

We have already established the principle that relational algebra is concerned with *how* we retrieve data from the database structure, while relational calculus specifies *what* data in the structure we wish to retrieve. If we decide to design a *user-friendly* DML, it makes sense to avoid the need for the user to specify *how* the data is to be retrieved from the database. Users are mainly concerned with queries like '*what* accounts are overdue?' or '*what* cupboards are available in a Veneer surface finish?', and provided the DML can get the answers out of the database, users don't want to be bothered with *how* the answers are retrieved.

Given this emphasis on *whats* rather than *hows* it is not surprising that the most popular commercial DMLs are high-level *declarative* languages which require the user to *declare what* result they want from a query. Given the distinction we made between relational algebra and relational calculus in respect to hows and whats, we can also see why several of the most popular declarative DMLs derive their principles from relational calculus. QUEL and SQL are two examples of such languages, although SQL is less closely linked to relational calculus than QUEL. (The degree to which such a language can express any query which can be expressed in relational calculus is called its degree of *relational completeness*.)

QUEL is both a DDL and a DML and is used by the popular INGRES database management system. The original version of INGRES (*IN*teractive *G*raphics and *RE*trieval *S*ystem) was developed at the University of California in the mid-1970s, but the commercial version has been marketed by RTI (Relational Technology Inc.) since 1980. A sample QUEL query like:

```
RETRIEVE (CUPBOARD.SIZE)
WHERE   CUPBOARD.STYLE = 'Country'
AND CUPBOARD.SURFACE FINISH = 'Fabric'
```

shows how closely it corresponds to our relational calculus examples above, while being a high-level language which is easy to understand. There is also an *embedded* form of QUEL, known as EQUEL. 'Embedding' is explained below.

SQL was originally called SEQUEL (*S*tructured *E*nglish *QUE*ry *L*anguage) and was developed by IBM. It is used by several popular database management systems including DB2, ORACLE and INGRES (available as an alternative to QUEL). SQL offers all the three components which make a full database language: a *data definition language* (DDL), *a data manipulation language* (DML) *and a data control language* (DCL). Figure 5.22 gives some examples of commands from each.

The ORACLE language is a popular example of the implementation of SQL in a DBMS. Besides the use of SQL, it provides other enhancements which include:

- SQL*FORMS: a means of creating record input/output formats which bypasses the clumsy procedures of many general-purpose languages.

- SQL*REPORTWRITER: for incorporating various SQL queries into producing a report.

- SQL*MENU: enables the user to produce automated friendly applications through creation of supporting menus.

COMMAND	DESCRIPTION
SQL Data Definition Language	
CREATE TABLE	Creates a table and defines its columns and other properties.
CREATE VIEW	Defines a view of one or more tables or other views.
ALTER TABLE	Adds a column to, or redefines a column in, an existing table.
DROP	Deletes a cluster, table, view, or index from the database.
SQL Data Manipulation Language	
INSERT	Adds new rows to a table or view.
SELECT	Performs a query and selects rows and columns from one or more tables or views.
UPDATE	Changes the value of fields in a table or view.
SQL Data Control Language	
GRANT	Grants access to objects stored in database.
COMMIT	Makes database transactions irreversible.
LOCK TABLE	Locks a table and thus permits shared access to the table by multiple users while simultaneously preserving the table's integrity.
REVOKE	Revokes database privileges or table access privileges from users.

Fig 5.22 A sample of SQL Commands
SQL provides a complete range of commands capable of data definition, manipulation and control. See Perry & Lateer (1989) for full list.

- SQL*CALC: spreadsheet software which can use the data resulting from SQL-based queries of database.
- PRO*C: an example of *embedding* (see below).

These are just *some* examples from *one* particular choice of a DBMS. For more details see, for example, Perry & Lateer (1989).

These examples show that, for most practical applications, data definition and manipulation capabilities of languages like QUEL and SQL need to be enhanced by broader programming capabilities. This need can often be fulfilled by general-purpose languages like PASCAL, C, COBOL or FORTRAN. As our ORACLE example of PRO*C implies, this is because DMLs require other features if they are to be more widely used in developing applications such as more complex calculation procedures, or sophisticated printing and displays. We can express this need by saying that a DML may be *relationally complete* without necessarily being *computationally* complete.

It is common practice therefore to *embed* DMLs in a general-purpose language, called a *host*. Where this is done, the data retrieved by the DML can be processed using the wide range of functions and procedures available from the general-purpose language. When embedding takes place, statements from the embedded language are included in the host language program, but are identified by some distinct prefix character or command so that the preprocessor can distinguish them.

5.3 DATABASE SYSTEMS

5.3.1 Database management versus traditional file processing

So far in this chapter we have developed our understanding of data because we see it as the building material that we can put together to form the *information* we need for management of a business or organization. In this section we will consider how our stock of 'building material' that we call our data*base* can itself be *managed* as a *system* to produce this needed information. Not surprisingly, such a system of controlling our database is called a *database management system* (DBMS).

Why is the distinction between data and information necessary? Even something as authoritative as the United Kingdom Data Protection Act (DPA) of 1984 asserts in one of its opening paragraphs that 'Data is information...'. In fact I think that the reasons why the legislators who drew up the act got so confused is a good example of why we need not only to distinguish between data and information but also to distinguish the traditional *technology-centred file processing view* from a modern *database management approach*. We will continue a little further with the DPA example to consider some of the issues that create the need for both of these distinctions.

The stated purpose of the DPA is to reassure people that *data* held about them on *file* can be openly checked by its subjects as a safeguard against false *record* of the *information* held about them. Now we *would* agree that false data will result in false information, since information is an *emergent* property that results from the coming together of its data *components*. If the nature or value of any one of these components is changed, then it will affect the nature or value of the whole. *Wrong data* on a credit file about what accounts I have paid, or not paid, will give *wrong information* about my credit-worthiness. Thus far, the confusion of data and information by the DPA does not seem to matter, but we need to consider two further questions to see why it does matter:

1. What do the terms *file* and *record* mean, if anything, in the context of contemporary systems practice?
2. If they mean something different, or no longer mean anything, what concepts do we now use to understand the accessing and processing of data to provide the information we need?

We have already given answers to the first question when we considered various data models in previous sections of this chapter. The terms *file* and *record* are still used in some of these contemporary models, but a clear distinction is made between *physical* and *logical* views. A *logical* view of data is about *whats*, and this needs to be distinguished from the *physical* view of *how* the data is recorded, accessed or transmitted.

We saw that in everyday use a *file* is seen as a source of information about a number of people or things, present as a series of *records*. Furthermore, both the records and the file would be seen in *physical* terms. The file might be a box with the records as individual cards inside the box, or the records might be areas of magnetic patterns on a floppy disk. The important point about the physical view is that it sees the *logical connexion* between records in a file, and of data items within a record, as being reflected in their *physical connexion* on the recording medium.

The traditional *technology-centred file processing view* sees the terms record and file completely in these physical terms. It is a classic example of the 'carry over' effect of redundant concepts from an old technology into a new one that we discussed in Chapter 3. The early computer systems of the 1960s took over a physical view of record and file from manual office systems. So just as a box file was filled with individual record cards in sequence, so a magnetic tape had blocks of records following each other in sequence. It was normal practice to use the terms tape and file interchangeably. When I first worked in computers systems in the 1960s a request like 'get me the On-Order file' meant 'get me that tape spool'. The analogy with the old manual systems was not perfect however: the size of records and the size of blocks did not necessarily coincide. It was rather like the individual record cards in a manual filing system not always coinciding with individual records.

The analogy of computer systems with manual systems got further broken down with the increased use of *direct access* disk storage. This happened for two reasons. First, the removal of the need for sequential storage meant that all the components of a record need no longer be adjacent; indeed they were often fragmented and scattered all over the disk. Second, the increasing storage capacity of disks meant that one disk could contain many files. At this stage physically identifiable files consisting of physically identifiable records still remained, but the form of physical connexion had become potentially so much more complex that the analogy with manual systems had almost disappeared. This was rather like parts of different individual records being recorded on the same card in a manual filing system.

As we followed through our study of database models, we found that more recent views of databases saw things less and less in this physical way. Instead, if the terms file and record were used at all, they referred to a *concept*. From this *information* perspective it makes no difference whether the records making up the file of, say, Carry-Out Cupboards products are on a computer or in a friendly old moth-eaten cardboard file. As long as we can end up with details of the style, model and surface finish of some cupboard we are interested in, it will still be the same information. The file and record *medium* has changed, but the contents of the files and records have not.

But if we see information as a property that emerges when data is brought together, we are now considering the second question we asked above as to what concepts we can therefore use to understand the accessing and processing of data once the physical view of files and records has gone. This can be answered by considering what the phrase 'when data is brought together' means in a computer systems context.

To understand this next issue, consider the principle behind two types of coffee vending machines illustrated in Fig 5.23.

The first kind of coffee vending machine has separate columns containing plastic cups already filled with the ingredients. There is one column of cups for every avail-

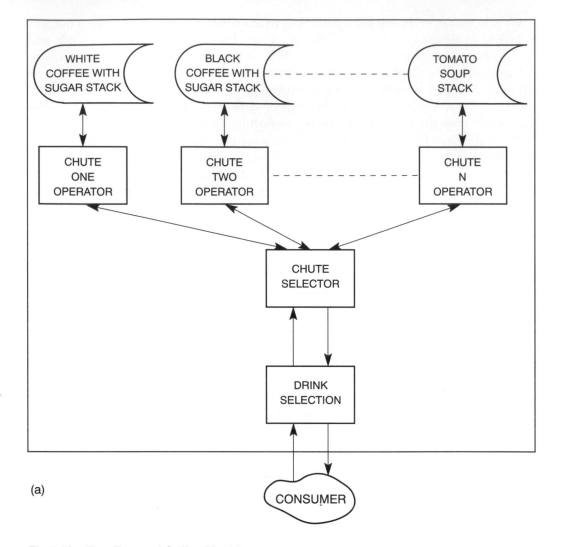

(a)

Fig 5.23 Two Types of Coffee Machine
The first type (a) has drinks ready-mixed in cups and the ability to choose one.

able combination. If you decide that you want white coffee with sugar, the machine gathers a cup from the appropriate column, fills it with lukewarm water, and throws it down the delivery chute.

The second kind of coffee machine does not have ready mixed combinations. Instead, the potential ingredients are kept separate. If you decide that you want white coffee with sugar, what I will call for the moment 'a little green man' (in my experience coffee machines are very sexist) inside the machine pulls the necessary levers to send water, whitener, sweetener, and coffee powder down the various chutes into a previously plummeted plastic cup.

The first thing to notice about these two examples is that the experience of a cup of coffee is an emergent property of either of the coffee machine systems described.

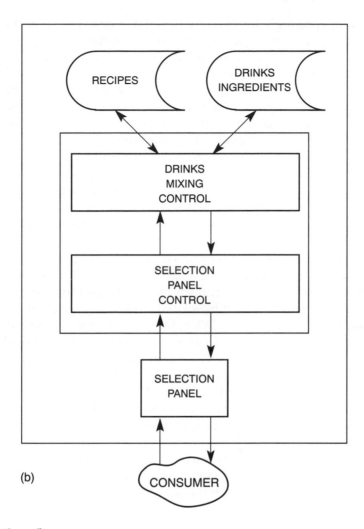

(b)

Fig 5.23 (continued)
The second type (b) has potential ingredients with the ability to select them and make up the desired drink when required.

Consuming the ingredients separately and washing them down with a cup of warm water is not the same as the holist experience of sampling them together as an output of a machine (albeit almost as revolting).

If we put aside the warm water from our previous examples, we find that there is an important conceptual difference between the two systems for producing the emergent property known as 'a cup of sweet white coffee'. In the first kind of machine the mixture is already *physically* there (water apart) waiting to be served on request. The second kind of coffee machine, however, does not contain any cups of coffee. Instead, the second kind of coffee machine contains a *logic* with the *potential* to produce one.

This difference goes an important stage further. Let us suppose that neither of the present machines can produce black coffee with sugar. To meet this new need the first kind of machine will have to *physically* introduce a new column into the machine containing the appropriate ingredients ready mixed in a cup. The second machine will need no such major physical change; instead, the system will merely have to be instructed with a new logic that 'sweet black coffee' means a different combination of pulling the existing physical levers by the 'little green man'.

If we look at the first kind of machine described, we can be clear about what drinks are stored ready for delivery: they are *physically* present in separate columns within the machine. This kind of machine is analogous to the old *technology-centred file processing view* of recording and accessing data. The ready-assembled, physically linked components of white coffee with sugar are the equivalent of the physically linked data item components of a record, labelled ready for access and processing.

With the second kind of machine it is different: the machine does not physically store any drinks at all. Instead, it stores the ingredients plus the *logical* ability to produce the whole range of drinks. Modern *database management systems* work on a similar principle to the second type of coffee machine when accessing a database. Instead of having actual physical records on the recording medium, they use the medium to hold individual data items which can be 'brought together' by the 'little green man' (i.e. the *database software*) in any form that the user requires.

For a modern database managed by a DBMS, what is physically recorded is not records, but individual items of data. When the user asks for a record, the data items making up the record are assembled by the DBMS. This means that neither the computer nor its recording devices actually contain records, any more than our second type of coffee machine contains the various drinks. Instead, a database contains the *potential* to produce any kind of information 'drink', in the form of an assembled record, that can be assembled from the data items by the DBMS.

Figure 5.24 shows the two views of accessing and processing data we have discussed: the technology-centred *file processing* view and *database management*. Having made the case for the database management approach we will now look more closely at the typical components of a complete database system. In doing so, we will consider some of the wider management implications of the use of such a system.

5.3.2 Structure and application of database systems

Figure 5.24(b) shows that a database system has two main components:

1. The database.
2. The database management system.

The *database* consists of two components: *stored data*; and *meta-data*, which defines the characteristics of the stored data.

The range of data which is stored is determined by the needs of the wider information system of which the database system is a component. These needs in turn are determined by the needs of the various management subsystems like the financial subsystem, the personnel, etc., which we shall discuss in detail and give examples of in Chapter 6. For the moment however, we can note some important issues which come from applying a management systems view.

We can begin by recognizing that all the data in a database is there for a purpose: but we need to recognize how different these purposes can be. Each data item is a potential building block for some form of information that management needs to exert

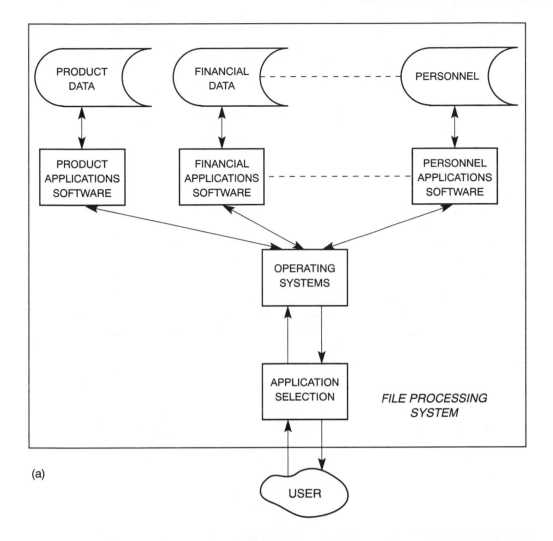

Fig 5.24 (a) Traditional File Processing System
The file processing system uses ready-made files which are designed to fit the appropriate applications software. [(b) *is on page* 192.]

control. As we saw in Chapter 3, the concept control brings with it the concept of *hierarchy*. This means that a particular data item may play very *different roles* according to the *nature of the user*.

Consider, for example, a data item whose value records the sales of a particular cupboard in a particular month by Carry-Out Cupboards. The sales figure could be used at a first-order control level to feedback data on the performance of the retail outlets with a view to controlling stock levels. It could be used at a second-order, goal-setting level as part of an analysis of customer demand aimed at setting future production targets. It might be used at a much more strategic level as part of a study to consider the future of the whole Carry-Out Cupboards product range.

Such needs as those in our example were present long before anyone invented modern database systems, but the important point is that the coming of modern data-

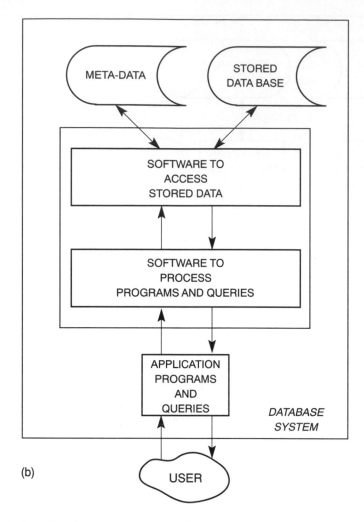

(b)

Fig 5.24 (b) Modern Database Management System
The database management system stores all data as a common resource that can be
accessed, assembled and processed according to the particular application need.

base systems makes them so much easier to fulfil from *one common database*. A *systems*
view of management will recognize the different needs of the different functions and
their interconnexion within management in a way that a departmentalized, organizational view of management will not. The success of a modern database system
therefore depends on it being accompanied by a modern systems view of management. As so often in this book we emphasize that the *information system* is a *component*
of the wider *management system*.

The management systems view that all the data on a database is there for a purpose
linked to one or more management functions has important implications:

1 The principles for *defining* the contents of a database and the process of *constructing*
  it should reflect the needs of the wider management system. This principle implies

that any *method* for development of a database system will include previous stages that analyse the needs of the business or organization concerned. In Chapter 7 we shall say more of this when we study *information systems development methodology*.

2 Control over the *manipulation* and *use* of the database should be set in the context of *user support* rather than computer specialist convenience.

In real life it doesn't easily happen this way. Computer systems personnel, like many others, understandably seek to protect their interests when these are in conflict with the wider management system. But this book is about *information systems in business* and takes the wider view: so I make the point, and we shall develop these issues further in Chapter 7. It is worth noting in the meantime that specialist computer technology follows the history of other specialist technologies in gradually becoming subservient to the wider need that it satisfies.

◆ STQ 5.9

What other 'specialist technologies' would you quote to support this last statement?

Besides the data itself, the other component of the database is the *meta-data*. If we consider a parts database for cupboards, it will contain data about the parts that make up a particular cupboard. The *schema*, as explained above, will define the ordering and arranging of this data in the data model and will enable us to understand the relationship of the parts to one another, and how a cupboard is made up. Just as a database contains data and has a schema, so we can have a further database which describes the database itself and contains the schema as part of its data. Data which describes the database in this way is called *meta-data*.

We have already looked at particular examples of the software used by database management systems. Generally, as in Fig 5.24(b), we classify the software as either *processing software* or *accessing software*.

Processing software can take different forms depending on the sophistication and needs of the user. High-level software taking user-friendly forms has been designed to help casual users query and process the database. In particular, *declarative* (see previous section) or so-called *fourth generation languages* (4GLs) enable the user to do this using English-like statements. Even easier forms of software use graphical interfaces with icons, menus, or some combination of any of these. More specialist users may use host application programs in general-purpose computer languages which have the ability to interface with the accessing software, usually through embedded DML statements, as described above.

Accessing software would normally be the DML itself (*see* Section 5.2 above).

There is one further important aspect of DBMS software which we have not discussed. The user-friendly nature of much of the high-level software means that detailed knowledge of computing is no longer needed to create working computerized information systems which use the database. When we come to studying the subject of *systems development* in Chapter 8, we shall see that *prototyping* using 4GLs or the use of *CASE* tools makes possible much closer links between those who design and build information systems and those who use them.

Box 5.2

CLEAR OBJECTIVES ARE IMPORTANT

(*Financial Times* 4/10/95)

Once the database is established, it can also be a challenge to get the most out of it.

The use of computer databases of information to market products for retail organizations is a tricky and exacting business. . .

According to Glenne Gibson, head of retail services for the UK arm of consulting giant EDS, there are no universal national solutions that can be applied from one country to the next. . .

In the UK in particular, the issue of using information technology – and particularly databases of customer information to do a marketing job – is one of the last jobs that retailers have taken on during their recent efforts to re-invent themselves.

'The better retailers are good now at managing their manufacturing and have stripped a lot of costs out of the whole supply chain,' she says. 'And they have developed good relationships with their key suppliers and are into EDI (electronic data interchange) and the use of electronic catalogues. But where they are weaker is around understanding the customer and relating that to the customer's shopping basket'. . .

She also says that collecting information for the database – through customer loyalty programs or the use of Epos (electronic point-of-sale) terminals – must not interfere with the core activities of the retailer, particularly in retail chains.

HAPPY ANNIVERSARY, JUDY'S COUNTRY GARDEN

(targeted mail shot to a small business partnership, 26/9/96)

Congratulations on our 5 year anniversary together! Your first order with Viking was in October 1991.

Here's your gift from us. . .

COMMENT

The two extracts above refer to very different types of business in terms of their size and function. The first comes from the *Financial Times* and refers to large supermarket chains; the other comes from an office products supplier circular that goes out to a whole range of businesses, both big and small. Both types of businesses are concerned with managing marketing by exploiting gathered and stored customer data.

The *Financial Times* article reviews the opportunities that come from modern information technology like EDI, Epos and various plastic 'loyalty cards'. EDI enables large supermarkets to deal with ordering, supply, stock control and payment from suppliers by connecting computers through telecommunications. The result is a swifter operation of the information system component of the various ordering and payment control systems. Epos and loyalty cards enable both the customer and their purchases to be easily captured as data, and fed into the ordering, supply, stock control systems. In control systems terms this means that goals such as desired product range and stock levels can be more easily monitored to respond to the pattern of environmental disturbances in the form of customer buying behaviour.

This important principle of recognizing that fed-back and stored information from the goal-seeking process can be used for the process of goal-setting is now sometimes called *data mining*. Once we know what sort of customer buys what sort of products, we can respond to their behaviour by determining appropriate goals in terms of what type/quality/cost of product that we offer to them.

The extract from a targeted mail shot to a small business partnership may seem much less spectacular, but it illustrates the same information systems principle. The small business 'Judy's Country Garden' orders some of its office consumables from a firm in Leicester. The firm's computer system automatically checks stored data for the date of a customer's first purchase and adds the anniversary message to the mail order catalogue.

The important systems principle behind all the examples above has *little to do with information technology*. Data mining and similar procedures all exploit the concept that information is an *emergent property* whose particular properties depend on what data is brought together and in what context. In principle, everything done by computer systems in these examples could be done manually, but information technology makes them economically possible.

Since the storage and processing power of computer systems means that data can be combined and analysed in almost limitless different ways, the problem is no longer just one of information technology or database design. The *Financial Times* gets it right: clear objectives are important, and these must be set by *management.*

KEY WORDS

Attribute
Cardinality
CODASYL
Data control language (DCL)
Data definition language (DDL)
Data description language
Data item
Data manipulation language (DML)
Database management system (DBMS)
Degree
Difference
Division
DL/1
Domain
Duplication
Entity

First normal form
IMS
INGRES
Intersection
Join
Mapping
Network
Normalization
Object-oriented model
ORACLE
Parent/child relationship
Partial dependency
Plex
Pointer
Product
Projection
QUEL
Redundancy
Relation

Relational algebra
Relational calculus
Relational database
Relationship
Repeating group
Replication
Schema
Second normal form
Segment
Selection
Semantic model
Sequence field
SQL
Third normal form
Transitive dependency
Tuple
Union
Vector

SEMINAR AGENDAS, EXAM QUESTIONS AND PROJECT/DISSERTATION TOPICS

1 Which microcomputer database packages are you familiar with in popular business use. Are they based on a *relational* model?

2 Investigate the development of a successful database management system in an organization or business that you have access to. Who decided what entities and attributes should be in the model? The developer? The user? Cooperation of both? How was the cooperation organized?

3 Investigate the statements to be found in Appendix 1 of Veryard (1984) which are critical of formal techniques of normalization:

   a. They are not sufficient.
   b. They are rarely applied vigorously.
   c. They are only based on an intuitive connexion between EAR modelling and normalization.
   d. Codd's theory is mathematically questionable.

You may not have the technical ability to analyse them all but see how more informed professionals react to them and try to form an opinion.

4 In a recent survey of the whole of British agriculture as part of a wider EU survey, farmers had to identify attributes of their fields like area and crops grown. Find out about this so-called IACS survey of 1993 and ask the question 'what is the entity *field*?' How did the British Government answer that question?

5 How can a database of visual material be modelled? Consider finger printing or the faces of wanted criminals.

6 Get individual members of your seminar group to investigate their rights under the Data Protection Act. Let everyone try independently to find out their credit rating and report back their experiences. Does the Act protect you?

FEEDBACK ON SELF-TESTING QUESTIONS

◆ STQ 5.1

If we consider her in terms of her being an employee who wanted to be 'correctly paid', then the emergent property of correct payment meant the bringing together of correct, up-to-date personal details like name, bank account number, tax code, etc. In Jane's case, as in any other attempt at a successful whole, one erroneous component destroys everything. 'Minor details' of data can destroy the effectiveness of large information wholes.

◆ STQ 5.2

I think that they are the same concept in that we use both terms to describe the smallest item of interest. A practical difference might be that when we look at an applied database, as we shall later in this chapter, there has to be a common view of the information system for it to work. What constitutes an element of a business seen as a system can be much more diverse, as we saw in Chapter 3.

◆ STQ 5.3

This looks like a levels of command type of hierarchy in the sense that the flow of supporting nutrients and the control of behaviour goes from trunk to branches and from branches to twigs.

◆ STQ 5.4

This looks to me like a 'part of' or aggregation hierarchy because the records at the 'lower level' are members of the 'higher'.

◆ STQ 5.5

The repeated appearance of details about PQ Plastics on three files. Jane's surname appearing at least in two different places.

◆ STQ 5.6

This is also a partial dependency because it is governed by Style and Size regardless of Surface Finish.

◆ STQ 5.7

This has similarities with the shifts experienced in the form of computer languages and the developement of GUIs. The encoding-decoding emphasis is moving away from computer system convenience towards human convenience as computer technology becomes more able to adapt through faster processing and larger storage capacity.

◆ STQ 5.8

Sorry about the unintended pun. It was indeed a 'kind of' hierarchy.

◆ STQ 5.9

The most obvious to me is the motor car. Early owners had to understand how their vehicles worked and what to do when they frequently went wrong. Today you don't even have to know how to change gear if you get yourself an automatic, let alone be familiar with what's under the bonnet.

REFERENCES/BIBLIOGRAPHY

Bowers, D.S. (1993). *From Data to Database*. Van Nostrand Reinhold.
Booch, G. (1991). *Object Oriented Design*. Benjamin/Cummings.
Codd, E.F. (1970). A Relational Model of Data for Large Shared Data Banks. *Commun. ACM* 13 (6).
Elmasri, R. & Navathi, S.B. (1989). *Fundamentals of Database Systems*. Benjamin/Cummings.
Martin, J. (1976). *Principles of Database Management*. Prentice-Hall.
Perry, J.T. & Lateer, J.G. (1989). *Understanding Oracle*. Sybex.
Stanczyk, S. (1990). *Theory and Practice of Relational Databases*. Pitman/UCL Press.
Veryard, R. (1984). *Pragmatic Data Analysis*. Blackwell Scientific.
Thompson, J.P. (1989). *Data with Semantics*. Van Nostrand Reinhold.

A simple commercial transaction

What happened

Some weeks ago I bought some new software for my computer. It wasn't anything very unusual or expensive, and I found that a supplier I have dealt with before had it in stock at a competitive price. Since I live in the country, most specialist things that I buy have to be ordered over the phone and delivered. This is usually a straightforward process of phoning the supplier, quoting an account or credit card number and awaiting delivery. I find that the increase in the range and quantity of delivery services has made living in the countryside and running a business much easier in the last ten years. Occasionally we get a van driver who hasn't heard about maps, but most of them find no problem in whisking around village lanes and up farm tracks to deliver everything from thermal underwear to a piece of computer equipment.

The day after I ordered my software, therefore, I was not surprised when a delivery van turned up my drive, and a driver I recognized from a previous delivery jumped out. She walked briskly round to the back of the van, opened up the doors, handed me a packet, and asked me to print and sign my name. Although I find most of these drivers, except the ones who can't read maps, are very friendly, they are usually in a hurry. I suspect this is connected with the fact that their companies compete on the basis of speed of delivery. I notice, for example, that when I sign the delivery document the time as well as the date of delivery has been entered by the driver.

Although I too am usually friendly, I've learnt to be more assertive on the question of signing before I've had time to check that the correct thing has been delivered. While I was doing this, the driver went back to the cab and brought back a map. She was trying to find someone whose address gave only a house name and our village. Needless to say everyone knows everyone in a village and I was able to direct her. So with a revving of a diesel engine the van was down my drive and off.

A data-based view

The title of the mini-case and its brevity are designed to particularly emphasize simplicity. Given the role of these introductory cases as raisers of issues, you will not be surprised that I now intend to show that what we have described is in fact quite a complex combination of potential data processing procedures hidden behind a simple commercial transaction. We can understand this by considering the implications of two key events.

The first key event took place when I confirmed that I wanted to buy the software and placed my telephone order. Although this simple transaction was recorded by the salesperson on a standard form with customer and product details, it represented data coming into the seller's information system which could do much more than make sure I got the product and the seller got the money.

We should notice first that it wasn't an order for any product, but for that particular software at that particular time in its *market* life, at that particular price, and against a particular promotion background in terms of the way it was advertised and sold. Data like this on the sale of the product had now been captured by an information system which was capturing similar data on other sales and on other products. The system wasn't just finding out about one transaction, it was also potentially building up an understanding of a whole set of *products* and *markets*.

The next thing to note is that it wasn't *anyone* buying the software: it was *me*. The data on the standard form would say something about me, like where I live and my postcode; or that I chose to pay by a credit card with its associated credit limit and implied credit rating. Such data has the potential to tell the supplier something about what sort of *customer* is buying what sort of product. Hence the data recorded for this, as for any sales transaction, isn't just to be used for the *first-order control* of ensuring delivery and payment, it also represents potential *learning* about markets which can be used to set goals.

We can look further by considering what the salesperson did when I enquired and placed the order. When she confirmed that the software was in stock and I placed my order, although nothing *physical* happened to the software, it immediately changed its *conceptual* state in the stock control system. We can understand the distinction between the conceptual and the physical in terms of Fig 3.2 and the description of standard stock control procedures in Appendix 1. Once a stock item is sold it goes from being 'Free Stock' to being 'Allocated', thus reducing the stock level by one unit. If this had resulted in a complete stock-out or a fall below the reorder level, my simple commercial transaction would have acted as an actuating trigger for the reordering mechanism. Whatever the details of how my software supplier's stock control system worked, my order was not only data to be used in the first-order *goal-seeking* control of ensuring appropriate stock levels. As a piece of sales data for a particular stock item, it would also contribute to forecasts and estimates of demand used to set reorder levels as part of the *goal-setting* process of *stock control*.

To the person in the storerooms of the software supplier, my order represented the use of human resources rather than a sale. Together with all the other orders placed that day it was data relating to the amount of moving and packing that had to go on. Data on sales for the store management represented potential information to be used in *personnel management* for planning of such things as the size of workforce needed, and the use of seasonal or temporary labour. It also was needed for decisions on *facilities* such as storage space.

Even as a commercial transaction however, my order may not have been as simple as ensuring I got my software and the supplier got paid. Had I been a fraudster or bad debtor, my transaction would have been one piece of data to have gone into any of the *goal-setting* processes associated with *credit control*.

Once my order had been accepted and the package made ready for delivery, a double copy of the order form was now passed on to the delivery firm. When the order was delivered to me and I printed and signed my name, a second key event took place.

For my delivery driver, as for the store management of the supplier, the data on the order form represented a job. My address implied certain details about mileages and times which affected the incentives and payment of the person making the delivery. Once I signed the double copy of the order form, the copy retained by the delivery driver was the *feedback* needed by the delivery company to help control a number of processes. These included confirmation to the supplier that the delivery firm had fulfilled their contractual obligation, and confirmation to both the driver and those who paid her that she had done the job in a certain time.

There was another copy of the form however. This was the one which *I* retained. As a self-employed person I need to keep my own accounts for tax purposes. The software represented part of the expenses that I incurred carrying out my business. So my copy of the document represented *feedback* on my expenses which I could use as part of my *financial system*. If the Inland Revenue should require confirmation of the expenses involved in my business of writing this book, my copy of the document would be a component of their *control system feedback* too.

The issues raised

The analysis of what happened in the mini-case contains just a selection of details that could be chosen to reinforce two now familiar systems points:

1. The distinction of *whats* and *hows*.
2. The conceptual nature of any system.

In the case, the 'hows' were concerned with straightforward business procedures like phone calls and the processing of documents. To explain the 'whats' which these 'hows' sought to achieve, we referred to such processes as assessing the success of products or understanding customers and markets in terms of *goal-setting* and *goal-seeking control*.

The conceptual nature of any system was shown when we considered these 'whats' in more detail. We found, for example, that what to one person was data about a sale, was data about a warehouse operation or a delivery job to someone else. What you saw the system to be depended on who you were, or to be more correct, what your *role* was in connexion with the system.

In Chapters 3 to 5 we established the basic concepts of systems thinking and used these to understand the role of the information system as a component of the wider management system through the concept of control. In Chapter 5 we explored models of how information could be built up from its component data. In this chapter we once again found the distinction of 'whats' and 'hows' was important in separating the logical and physical views of data. The important concept of a *database*, with its implications of information as an organizational *resource*, was only possible once we made this distinction.

What our simple mini-case is now showing us is that the wealth of concepts we have developed in Chapters 3 to 5 can only be specifically applied to understanding information systems in management once we have clearly resolved two issues:

Issue 1. How can an organization or business be seen as a system?
Issue 2. How can we distinguish the different roles of those involved?

We can see the interconnexion of these two issues if we look back to the General Control Model of Fig 3.14. Here we saw that any attempt to interpret an organization in terms of the model brought with it the concept of a systems owner or perceiver.

As we saw in Chapter 2 however, most of the classic books on management information systems try to marry a conventional, organizational view of the business with a computerized interpretation of information systems. In this chapter we shall consider how the concept of a system can integrate the way an organization or business is viewed and the role of the information system within it. This will then prepare us for Chapter 7, were we shall study how information systems can be defined, developed and implemented to support the management of organizations and businesses.

LEARNING OBJECTIVES CHAPTER 6

1 **To build a generally applicable systemic model of organizations and businesses, based on the concepts and principles of Chapters 3 to 5.**

2 **To interpret both profit-motivated businesses and alternatively motivated organizations in terms of the model.**

3 **To understand the distinction between the conceptual nature of the model and its specific manifestations.**

4 **To use the model as a means of understanding the role of information systems in management.**

CHAPTER 6

Information and Management Systems

6.1 THE ORGANIZATION AS A SYSTEM

Conventional and systems views of organizations

In Chapter 3 we saw how a hierarchical concept of control, as in Fig 3.14, enabled us to make the connexion between information and management. At each of the levels of the control hierarchy, the information system was seen as a subsystem of the control system. We also saw how the hierarchy of control systems led to a relationship between the level of control, the nature of the control exerted, and the type of information used.

In this chapter we shall show how the typical major functions of a business can be understood in *systemic* terms, and hence how a business or organization can be viewed as a management *system*. We shall then see what forms the hierarchy of control systems can take within this *management* system, and the different kinds of practical function the *information* system has to carry out as a component of control. Throughout this chapter I will use the term 'organization' to stand for both commercial businesses like Carry-Out Cupboards and non-commercial organizations like the East Farthing Drainage Authority.

When we take this very broad view of what can constitute an organization, we will be using the now familiar principle that the description of a system as a concept can be very different from its physical or concrete materialization. In particular:

a The *structure* of any particular organization when it is seen as a management *system* does not necessarily have the same named components as those shown on the official organization chart or printed on notices above the doors to its various departments. MX Marketing is an example of this principle. It is a small company of two to three people working from a base of a single office. They are selling products, one of which they designed themselves. Such a small team covers all the functions of a business by each person taking several responsibilities. Just looking at one individual from the team of three: Ben Lister could answer questions like 'Who's the boss', 'Who's the marketing manager', or 'Who was the designer of this product' by saying 'its me'.

b We shall see how the *processes* carried out by different organizations can be interpreted in terms of common systemic principles. Thus when we discuss such diverse organizations as commercial companies, hospitals or official government bodies as systems, we shall see that they share certain common underlying *conceptual* similarities. This does *not* mean however that we regard these organizations as the same. We shall equally acknowledge the assertion that in concrete, physical terms they are very different. We may, for example, describe both the treatment of patients in a hospital and the packing and assembly of products at Carry-Out Cupboards in terms of them both being a *process*. We are not implying, however, that we think that *how* these processes are carried out should be at all similar, or that we would have the same attitude to what is being 'processed'.

In Chapter 2 we already introduced the idea that language can be misleading not only if we do not distinguish whats and hows, but also between the particular hows themselves. This latter point happens to be particularly important when changes in technology take place. Thus just as I am writing this chapter, I hear from newsmedia reports about the new British nuclear submarine fleet with its deadly and sophisticated weapons. Despite this modernity and sophistication, each submarine is described in terms of it *sailing*. When this word is used, no one envisages the captain parading on deck with orders to raise the 'mizzen' or pull up the 'spanker': to quote some old sailing ship terms. Even so, the old fashioned language prevails, and we continue to talk of a submarine 'sailing' not 'fissioning' its way out to sea.

As we saw in Chapter 5, this retention of previous language is not confined to traditional professions like the British Royal Navy. Managers still happily refer to 'files' 'on' their computers even though such files have no more reality than the sails on a nuclear submarine. We warned in Chapter 2 that using the old thinking can be both helpful and dangerous at times of transition. We saw that a computer that presents so-called icons of folders, filing cabinets and a wastepaper basket on top of a worktop can help users interpret the new technology they do not understand in terms of the old that they do. Again in Chapter 5, we warned of the dangers of confusing the logical form of a database with its particular physical implementation.

In the field of information and the management of organizations the retention of old models can be even more inhibiting. Information has emergent properties which mean that advances in the media used for its physical manifestation actually make for qualitative changes in the nature of information itself. Replacing a filing cabinet with storage on disk, like replacing sails by nuclear power, is not just a quicker way of doing the same job: it actually leads to new possibilities for the whole system.

The nuclear power of a submarine not only drives the ship faster than sails. It can also generate power for heating and lighting as well as replenishing its internal atmosphere. This in turn results in a whole system that does completely new things compared with former ships. Nuclear power not only breaks through the surface movement limitations of wind and weather, it also sends the submarine under water or ice caps, and even allows it to sit for days on the sea floor.

Similarly, the advent of large-capacity rapid-access storage of data isn't just a quicker way to do the accounts or to keep up the stock records. As we saw in Chapter 5, a database management system view recognizes that *all* the data is potentially available as a management *resource*. It can be extracted and processed to provide kinds of information that were not possible even a few decades ago.

So the danger is that we have the 'nuclear power' of modern database management systems attached to a 'sailing ship' language for a view of management in organizations. We grow out of thinking in the old terms of file processing into the new view of a database management system, but we still think that, say, 'finance' is the name of a department on a company organization chart, or 'marketing' as the name of a nice new office building set well apart from the factory.

If we are to replace old computer data processing ideas with an information systems view, we need also to replace an organization chart or physical picture of management with a systems view too. Otherwise we shall be fitting nuclear reactors to a wooden sailing ship. Thus if a systemic view is to be presented of information, it is inconsistent to try and marry this to a non-systemic view of organizations.

It is possible to take our analogy further. Some may fear that nuclear power, even when used peacefully, can be potentially dangerous. Likewise large organizational databases can also be regarded with suspicion. Far from being an argument against taking a modern systems view of information and management, this fear makes such a view even more important. If we wish to protect ourselves against a threat, we need to face it and understand it.

General Montgomery, an important British army commander in World War II, always had a photograph of his main German military rival General Rommel to look at when he was planning his strategy. At the very least in self-defence, modern management needs to have a picture of 'the enemy' in the form of understanding modern approaches.

More positively, there is another important reason for seeing beyond a physical system to what is actually going on. Failure to discern the *logical system* behind the *physical system* can greatly reduce the chances of successful systems development, as we shall see in Chapter 7.

The components of a systems view of organization

One way of seeing an organization as a system is one that I first published in Harry (1990), and which I will develop further in this chapter. The important principle behind this view stems from the aim to see an organization as a *system*. If we do this, it then follows that our view will incorporate the systemic properties we introduced in Chapter 3.

One of the important systemic properties we shall use in forming our view of organizations is that a system 'does something', i.e. carries out *processes* and exhibits *emergent properties*. If we then go on to consider systems which are *managed,* the concept of management brings with it the General Control Model of Fig 3.14 and the concept of *purpose*. In Section 3.2 we explored the concept of purpose in building up the model and saw that the purpose of an organization reflected the *weltanschauung* or *world view* of the systems owner or conceiver. We also saw that this was translated down the control hierarchy into information specifying methodology and policy, methods and procedures, goals and standards, and finally information on the actions to be carried out by the transformation process of the system.

If we view a managed organization as a system therefore, we see it as something which tries to carry out *processes* with the *purpose* of producing *emergent properties* which reflect the aims and values of the *systems owner,* in the context of an *environment* which disturbs those processes. Our use of the term *emergent properties* and *processes* reflects the fact that an organization seen as a system will share the property of all other systems in consisting of at least two, and usually many, *components*. These will be both abstract and concrete, as well as hard and soft.

To make sense of the complexity of such a whole, we can first distinguish two major components of an organization when seen as a system, as in Fig 6.1:

1. A *central purpose subsystem* which justifies or explains why the whole organization as a system exists at all.
2. A *central purpose support subsystem* which makes possible and supports the activities of the central purpose subsystem.

Central purposes will differ according to the kind of organization we are considering.

◆ **STQ 6.1**

What would you see as the central purpose of:

a. Carry-Out Cupboards
b. The East Farthing Drainage Authority
c. MX Marketing.

Although central purposes of different organizations may themselves be very different, they all have the common property that without a central purpose, the need for the organization would disappear.

It is also important to note that central purpose is a *holist* concept which may be an *emergent property* consisting of several components. Thus, I was once asked whether an organization might not have more than one central purpose. For example, a firm might make roof racks for cars which it could either fit to customers cars, or sell to customers for them to fit themselves.

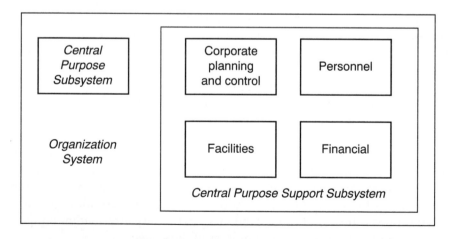

Fig 6.1 A Systems View of an Organization
A first step in identifying the major components distinguishes a *central purpose subsystem*, which justifies or explains why the whole organization as a system exists at all; and a *central purpose support subsystem*, which makes possible and supports the activities of the central purpose subsystem.

◆ **STQ 6.2**

Is the central purpose to sell or to fit roof racks? Or again, a hospital may carry out medical tests and give emegency treatment too. Which is the central purpose?

Box 6.1

SEND ON THE FUNNY GUYS

(Financial Times 12/8/96)

It is too good to last. Second-rank English soccer clubs such as Chelsea, Middlesborough and Newcastle will not field large numbers of the world's best players forever. So it may be worth going to every match you can when the English Premiership's new season starts on Saturday, because the world's best will soon be signing for Italian, Spanish and sometimes German teams again. . . At present the stars are joining English Premiership clubs because these are now the richest in Europe . . . But that won't last. . . The Italians, Spaniards and Germans will learn what their *products* [my italics] are worth . . . their television channels are watched by *most of the population* [my italics again] . . . they are learning from Manchester United that fans will buy anything with the club name on it. . . Cynics might say English managers have signed freakish looking players chiefly to gull child fans into buying replica shirts . . . Football's coming home, but only for a quick visit.

COMMENT

I have quoted only about a tenth of the original article. If you are interested in more detail, you might consult the original *FT* article with its emotive pictures. (I still find football a mystery, but I know enough to realize that Plymouth Argyle will never win the FA Cup.) As organizations, what is the *central purpose* of football teams like Man Utd? Is it revenue? Success? Numbers of fans? The *Financial Times* article seems to recognize that football 'coming home' can have several meanings, not all of them happy ones for those interested in the game itself. Perhaps what has really happened with Man Utd is that they are selling a dream (*concept?*) of which a football match is just part.

FURTHER STUDY

Should the information system of a football club include records of past results, the economics of the local economy, the names and details of media barons, or pictures of the latest star scoring that essential goal? What is *information* in this context? How might the organization be interpreted in terms of the GMOS?

If you have already read ahead to Chapter 8, you might see English football as ripe for a soft systems analysis (SSM).

I would add further to what I have asserted about the central purpose and say that if an organization has no discernible central purpose in this holist sense, why are we viewing the organization as a *whole* in the first place?

The *central purpose support subsystem* makes possible and supports the activities of the central purpose subsystem so that the whole organization will function as a system. It is important to note here that our systems view of hierarchy does not see the word 'support' as implying judgement about the relative importance of the central purpose and central purpose support subsystems. We see the *whole*, which is the *sum* of these two components, as 'the greater', not either component.

Figure 6.1 also shows the four components of the central purpose support subsystem:

1. A *personnel* subsystem which provides the human power and skills which the central purpose requires.
2. A *facilities* subsystem which provides the equipment, machinery, land, buildings and all the other inanimate, concrete components which provide the fixed means to support the central purpose subsystem.
3. A *financial* subsystem which provides the financial operations to support the central purpose subsystem.
4. A *corporate planning and control* subsystem which provides the goals for the organizational system as a *whole*, and attempts to control the *outputs* from the system's components so that the *behaviour* of the whole system meets the organizational goals.

It is important to note that the corporate planning and control subsystem will cover the coordination and decision-making that affect the form of interaction of two or more of the central purpose, personnel, facilities, financial subsystems (Fig 6.2). As we shall see later in this chapter, these subsystems exert *first-* and *second-order control* over their own processes. The higher orders of control of the General Control Model of Fig 3.14, which are concerned with coordinating goal-setting through establishing methodology and policy in relation to the system's *weltanschauung*, is the task of the corporate planning and control subsystem.

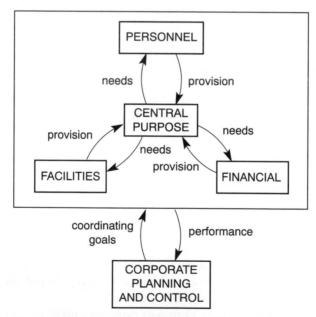

Fig 6.2 The Interaction of the Organizational Systems Components
The Personnel, Facilities and Financial Subsystems support the Central Purpose Subsystem, with the Corporate Planning and Control Subsystem coordinating the whole.

We can consider an example to illustrate this point. Let us examine the decision-making involved if Carry-Out Cupboards were considering buying a new packing machine. The central purpose subsystem would decide what sort of machine was wanted and what operations it had to perform. The facilities subsystem would have the job of acquiring the machine and ensuring it was kept in working order. The financial subsystem would have the job of paying the supplier for it. But the *whole* decision as to which machine to buy, in terms of its technical abilities, reliability and financial costs, requires a decision which coordinates these different goals in the context of the wider organizational system.

Figure 6.2 illustrates the relationships between these subsystems. It shows that the personnel, financial and facilities subsystems have a service or supporting role for the central purpose subsystem. In each case the central purpose subsystem has needs for which it communicates to the appropriate supporting subsystem. Note that the communication of these needs is an *information flow* and that the role of the *information system* will be to ensure that such information is gathered and communicated.

Given that, Fig 6.2 illustrates the role of the corporate planning and control subsystem in coordinating the goal-setting of the individual subsystems in a way which is consistent with those of the organization as a whole. Each of the subsystems will then need its own control hierarchy of second-order goal-setting, and goal-seeking, which we will now consider.

A general model for organizational subsystems

A general systems model of the central purpose and its three supporting subsystems can now be built from the relevant concepts of systems hierarchy and control from the General Control Model. We will call this the General Model for Organizational Subsystems (*see* Fig 6.5).

The first of these concepts are the simple ones of first-order goal-seeking and second-order goal-setting control, as illustrated by Fig 6.3. The *process* which is being controlled in each case will depend on the subsystem we are considering. Thus for the

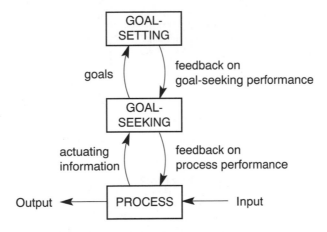

Fig 6.3 Goal-seeking and Goal-setting Control
This repeats the principles of Fig 3.12, but here the flow or input-process-output is shown right to left for subsequent convenience.

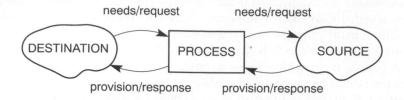

Fig 6.4 Interaction of a Systems Process and its Environment
The process will have needs that its environment can supply as well as itself
acting as a supplier of needs to its environment. Thus a manufacturing
process will have material needs which arise from its aim of meeting a need
for the product manufactured.

central purpose it will be the satisfying of a market, the provision of a service, etc. as
discussed above. For each of the supporting subsystems it will be the provision of the
personnel, facilities or financial needs of the central purpose subsystem.

The next concept we need to introduce is one we have not discussed in any detail so
far, which is the interaction of the various subsystems with the whole system's *environment*. This can be generally illustrated by Fig 6.4. Examples of such interaction
would be the need to pay suppliers by the financial subsystem or to deliver products
to a customer by the central purpose subsystem of a manufacturing organization.

One further point will enable us to understand the General Model for Organizational
Subsystems of Fig 6.5. When we consider the processes of any of our subsystems, we

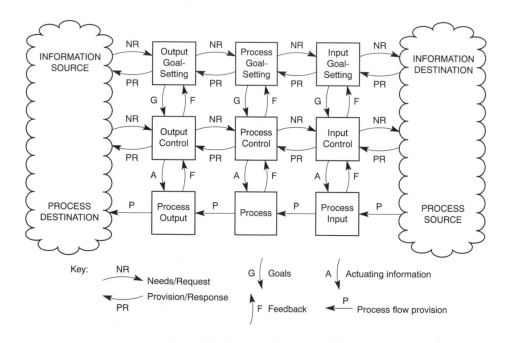

Fig 6.5 A General Model for Organizational Subsystems (GMOS)
This is built on the fundamental concepts of control, as presented in Chapter 3, and the concept of interaction with the environment of Fig 6.4.

will find it useful to distinguish *input* and *output* components from the process itself. The *process* will be what the subsystem does as its main function within the organization, while the *input* and *output* components represent the interaction of the various subsystems with the *environment*. Thus, for example, the facilities subsystem of Carry-Out Cupboards has as its main process the support of the central purpose subsystem by maintaining plant and equipment. But it also has to interact with the environment by receiving new equipment from suppliers or disposing of old equipment.

When we bring these concepts together to form the General Model for Organizational Subsystems of Fig 6.5 we see:

a The *vertical* groupings of the components representing *control systems* with their hierarchies of goal-setting and goal-seeking. Each of these three is an instance of the control model of Fig 6.3, for *input, process* and *output* subsystems respectively.

b The *horizontal* groupings of components representing the *needs/request-provision/response* relationships which track the effect of *environmental disturbances*. These groupings represent an expansion of the model in Fig 6.4, to cover the stages of *input, process* and *output*.

We will now look at how each of the central purpose and supporting subsystems can be interpreted in this systemic model of organizations.

Box 6.2

STRUCTURING COMPANIES FOR MARKETS

(Financial Times 16/8/96)

Since Peter Drucker stated in 1954 that the sole purpose of a company was to create and keep customers, marketeers and many managers have embraced a philosophy loosely called the 'marketing concept'.

The conjecture is that . . . organizations should attempt to ascertain the customer's needs and wants and produce products and services that will satisfy these. . .

Others argue for product orientation . . . that technology can create markets. . .

However, while some have succeeded with these strategies there have also been well-documented failures. . .

COMMENT

I have quoted just a small amount of the article by Pierre Berthon, James M Hulbert and Leyland Pitt in the FT 'Mastering Management' series, but I think that there is enough of the original to reveal some important themes that come from a systems view of management (whether or not the authors intended such a view).

Systems thinking would see marketing as strategic, if the term 'strategic' is seen as a concern with high-level *whats* rather than low-level *hows*. The Central Purpose GMOS of Fig 6.6 shows this view. The article also refers to the marketing *concept*, and systems language would do the same: the 'marketeers' begin with a *high-level* concept about *whats*, which has to be turned into a particular *how* in the form of a *concrete* product. The authors use the example of the Lexus of Toyota, 'where it attempted to establish exactly *what* (my emphasis) the market would require of a luxury saloon car before building it'.

The article then contrasts this with a different view. Is it possible for technology, in the form of a specific product, or *how*, to determine the *whats* or *concept* that the market will accept? Here, the authors use the example of Chrysler, who 'forged ahead with the original minivan concept in spite of market research'.

Does this second view contradict the General Control Model of Fig 3.14, the GMOS of Fig 6.5 on which it is based? Both of these models show the environment influencing the system, and not the other way around. Thus, how could the Chrysler management system dominate its market environment by the use of technology which ignores the apparent *whats* of this market?

The answer is that it didn't. The difference between the Toyota and Chrysler examples comes from how well the respective systems interpreted the *information feedback* from their environments: not that they controlled them. To understand the *FT* article in terms of control systems concepts, we need to refer to *feedback, learning* and *forecasting* as in Chapter 3.

Both Toyota and Chrysler knew that they had to respond to their market environment, but Chrysler went on to recognize that the environment really is uncontrollable. They saw that the way that it might respond to applied 'market research' was neither predictable nor controlled.

FURTHER STUDY

Note that '1954' is being quoted in an article in a leading financial newspaper in 1996.

The article goes back thirty years. Consider the concepts of *lags in the control system, experience* and *learning* as in section 3.2.4. Consider also how the term 'Business Process Re-Engineering', which was very popular in management circles while I was writing the first edition, now sounds embarrassing and out of date.

6.2   THE CENTRAL PURPOSE SUBSYSTEM

The general model of the central purpose subsystem

If we intend to illustrate how the central purpose subsystem of an organization can be interpreted in terms of the General Model for Organizational Subsystems, it will be useful to choose one particular organization as an example. This will be easier for one whose central purpose is marketing and manufacturing, and we will choose Carry-Out Cupboards as our example. We can then use the more subtle example of the East Farthing Drainage Authority to make additional points.

Figure 6.6 shows how the model of Fig 6.5 could be interpreted for Carry-Out Cupboards and many other production or manufacturing based organizations. The components of the subsystem have been given names that commonly correspond to those frequently used to describe practical *functions*. It is vital to remember, once again, that we are referring to *what* goes on in the subsystem, not where it's done or who does it. Furthermore, to avoid confusion, throughout this section we will assume that the term 'system' refers to the whole central purpose subsystem at this level of the hierarchy, and use 'subsystem' to refer to partial aggregations of its components.

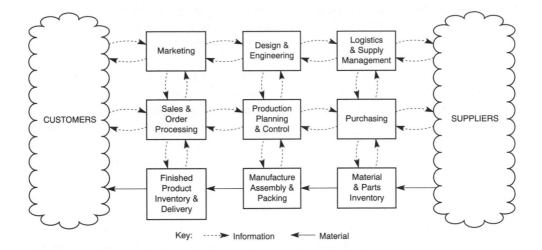

Fig 6.6 An Interpretation of the Central Purpose Subsystem of Carry-Out Cupboards in Terms of the GMOS

It is important to note that the names given to the various processes refer to *what* they do, rather than to names of departments or locations. Thus the Finished Product Inventory and Delivery function is shared by both the CP and the ROs (*see* Appendix 1).

As we established above, an important aspect of Fig 6.5 is the way in which the components can be grouped into subsystems. This may be done either vertically or horizontally in terms of the diagram, but each way represents an important property of the central purpose system which we will now consider.

We will focus on the vertical grouping of components into three subsystems and emphasize the control model relationship. We will look at these three subsystems in turn to get a broad picture of their main components and what they do. We shall also consider how they interact with each other horizontally in terms of the environmental disturbance, needs/request-provision response model of Fig 6.4. In addition to this broad view, a detailed systematic run through the information flows as illustrated by Carry-Out Cupboards is to be found as part of Appendix 1.

The central purpose output control subsystem

The *Output Control Subsystem* is concerned with output from the central purpose system to the environment. For Carry-Out Cupboards this will involve selling products at the retail outlets to the customer.

◆ **STQ 6.3**

Why am I considering the output control subsystem first?

Higher-order control and goal-setting for this subsystem will involve deciding on the type and quantity of products to be sold. This top-level process is carried out by *marketing*. In everyday life the terms marketing and selling are often used to mean the same thing, but for a professional manager this is bad practice because an important distinction can be made between the two terms. Systems thinking also leads us to make a similar distinction to that made by professional management. This can be made clear if we compare marketing with the first-order control and goal-seeking process of *sales and order processing*.

Sales and order processing is concerned with selling products to customers from the existing range. Marketing is concerned with establishing what products we are going to make in the future. To do this it gathers information about unfulfilled existing or future customer needs using market research, and defines what characteristics particular products would have to have to meet them. These characteristics are usually defined as high-level emergent properties, although marketing people would probably not use that systemic term themselves.

In the case of Carry-Out Cupboards, market research might reveal a trend towards more open bright kitchens with a high technology feel to them. This might be linked with a move away from a darker, wood veneer cottage style. Furthermore, this trend might be seen at its strongest among a younger group of society who cannot afford luxury items. The output information from the marketing process would take the form of criteria like 'lots of glass', 'simple geometrical shapes', 'primary colours' or 'economy before elaboration', rather than defining low-level details like how doors are fixed, handle design shapes or colours, or what proportion of the product cost can go on packaging. It is the next process of design and engineering that would take the information from marketing about what sort of product was needed and use it as a high-level specification to create a specific design for a cupboard. Marketing would also assess the potential size of the market in terms of sales, and details of the customer including type and location.

It might be worth referring back to the issues of Chapter 4 at this point; particularly the theme of 'Lies, Damned Lies, and Statistics', as developed in the rest of the chapter. Also, concepts about *decision* in Chapter 3 are relevant.

The results of the decisions by marketing will be a product range aimed at an identified market and will represent goal-setting for sales and order processing. Feedback on control performance for these goals will be the statistical data on sales which will normally be held on some form of product file. This data will be periodically subject to sales analysis and the results used by marketing to decide about modification or additions to the product range. This is how Carry-Out Cupboards might confirm the drift away from 'cottage style' cupboards.

◆ STQ 6.4

What are the equivalent of these processes for the East Farthing Drainage Authority?

Goal-seeking control is carried out by sales and order processing. Customer orders are environmental disturbances to the subsystem because they are inputs outside its control, and the disturbance comes in the form of the orders themselves and their changing demand patterns. The subsystem attempts to influence the environment, however, by carrying out actions like sales promotion or advertising. Note that the particular desired form of these actions, and the original decision to carry them out, is a goal-setting process originating from marketing.

Getting products to customers is carried out by the *finished product inventory and delivery* process. This process takes as its inputs the cupboards from the assembly and packing process, and outputs them by handing them over or delivering them to customers. It is the retail outlets of Carry-Out Cupboards that do this.

◆ **STQ 6.5**

How is this first-order control process carried out by MX Marketing, and who does it?

The control exerted over finished product inventory and delivery by sales and order processing in practice requires the recording of information about both product and customer. We can list some of the typical names for the documents and files used in practice to communicate and store such control information:

a *Product File/Stock Record* (Fig 3.2): Kept by the producer as a list of the products available for sale to potential customers. Gives details of the product identity and qualities by use of code number, description, type or category, dimensions, etc. May also contain information about costs, price, source, reorder quantities or procedures and quantities in stock. Frequently mixes the functions of physical movement and stockholding with financial accounting and sales recording. Carry-Out Cupboards would certainly have one of these, and it would usually be kept as a regularly updated computer printout to enable retail outlets to know what was available.

b *Customer File* (Fig 6.7): Kept by the seller. Gives details of customer identity and location, products bought, credit worthiness and performance, means of contact and market category. Often overlaps and confuses in its actual physical format with the financially precise *customer accounting* functions of the *financial subsystem* that are strictly concerned with recording *who* owes *whom* for *what* supplied *when*. These

```
Customer No: BA 6489              Name:         Barkages Ltd

Delivery        Station Yard      Address:      Barset House
Address:        South Stoke                     High St
                Lifton                          Lifton

Post Code:      NL21 7WB          Post Code:    NL20 67S

Area:           20                Product Groups: A, C, F

Credit Level: 10                  Discount Code:  12.5
```

Fig 6.7 Customer File

Kept by the seller as a means of recording details about a customer as a means of supporting marketing and sales functions. In practice, this usually overlaps customer accounting functions of the financial subsystem. A distinction might be made between information which is *generally* applies to a customer, and information which refers to specific financial transactions.

latter functions would be recorded in the sales ledger. Carry-Out Cupboards would not normally have one of these because most of its sales are *retail*, i.e. direct to the final customer. However, most commercial transactions are done on credit, so one business selling to another would certainly keep some form of this.

c *Invoice* (Fig 6.8): Details what has been supplied, when, and the financial amount owing as the result of a particular delivery. May or may not accompany the products/goods, hence *Delivery/Goods Received Note* goes with goods supplied to confirm/check physical delivery. Again, this is normally associated with commercial sales on credit, but Carry-Out Cupboards would use these for customers who had ordered for delivery on credit.

d *Statement* (Fig 3.18): Reviews and aggregates on a regular time basis (c.f. Chapter 3 and the concept of *batch processing*) the information supplied by a series of invoices. Carry-Out Cupboards would only use this for commercial operations as before, but in everyday business relationships this is a standard document.

e *Remittance Advice:* Confirms the delivery of payment in a similar way to that of the Delivery Note confirming delivery of the goods. Used in connexion with **c** and **d** above.

An important point comes out of our consideration of these typical documents and files. When we look at their contents, some of the data they contain seems more relevant to the *financial subsystem.* According to our systems view, the central purpose output control subsystem is concerned with controlling the delivery of the product or service to the customer; not ensuring payment.

This apparent confusion disappears once we return to our distinctions between systems as concepts and their particular physical implementation, which we introduced in our mini-case. One physical document can play many systemic roles within an organization, just as we saw a person could too in the previous section.

The potential range of roles that conventional documents and procedures like those above can play is a good example of why our conceptual, systems view of organizations is important. If particular *documents* are seen as the 'property' of some particular 'department' or management function, the data they contain is similarly departmentalized. Instead of being part of the organization's database or *information resource,* the data they contain is only exploited to provide the information needs of one of the conceptual subsystems. If this happens, much of their information value to the whole organizational system is lost. If we were developing a new or improved information system, as in Chapter 7, we should need to keep this important point in mind.

◆ **STQ 6.6**

Would a non-commercial organization like the East Farthing Drainage Authority have any equivalent of the above documents?

SAXUN OFFICE SUPPLIES

21 Saxun Way
Viking Trading Estate
North Coates
Barsetshire
BA99 9ZW

Telephone: (0176) 992992
Fax: (0176) 993993
VAT Reg. 478 8748 44

INVOICE

Carry-Out Cupboards
Cowford Business Park
Kirton
South Riding
SR77 7DQ

Date: 11.02.96
Number: 1832
Account No. C2256

Quantity	Description	Product Code	Price	
1	Kayware	I	59.34	59.34

Total Goods	59.34
VAT	8.90
Total	68.24

Fig 6.8 An Invoice

Informs the customer what goods have been sent out and what is charged for them. As with Fig 3.18, much of what appears on this document, and how it appears, is not determined by the information system's designer but by the environment. Thus Customs and Excise have specific rules about what must appear on the invoice of a company which is registered for VAT.

The central purpose process control subsystem

This will control the heart of what the central purpose system actually does. For an organization like Carry-Out Cupboards it is concerned with producing products in response to the output needs identified by the Central Purpose Subsystem Output Control System. Higher-order control and goal-setting is carried out by *design and engineering* using a high-level specification produced by marketing. This specification then acts as a starting point for producing a design which defines which particular product we have come up with to meet the market need.

In our Carry-Out Cupboards example above, marketing came up with concepts like 'lots of glass', 'simple geometrical shapes', 'primary colours' or 'economy before elaboration'. We said that it was the job of design and engineering to translate these concepts into details like how doors are fixed, handle design shapes or colours, and determining the method and style of packaging consistent with the proposed cost for the product.

The output information from design and engineering will also include details of parts and materials, which *logistics and supply management* would use to decide on sources of supply, as we will see below. For Carry-Out Cupboards these details will form a high proportion of the output from *design and engineering*, since the product is mainly assembled from components made elsewhere. For organizations whose central purpose includes more manufacturing processes however, design and engineering would need to define them.

Generally, the design and engineering process is only complete when enough information has been produced to unambiguously define the product and how it should be made. (I once read a good summary of the relationship between marketing and engineering in a student's answer paper. She said 'marketing is the idea: engineering is the fact'. Alas, since it was in a finals paper, I never had a chance to ask her where the quotation came from.) The same statement could be made about the design and engineering of an information system as we will see in Chapters 7 and 8.

The *production planning and control* process will take as goal-setting input the definition of the product design from design and engineering. This will contain all the information needed to make the product. Production planning and control will also take a *needs/request* input from sales and order processing on how many of each product are needed to meet customer orders and when. Both of these information flows will be used to form a production schedule which manufacture and assembly will seek to meet. This production schedule will also produce an output to purchasing of a parts and raw materials schedule to meet the needs of *manufacture and assembly.*

Feedback by production planning and control to design and engineering will give information on the experience of making the product. This experience can result in learning better ways to design and make products in the future. Response on how manufacture and assembly is meeting the production schedule may be used by sales and order processing to in turn respond to customer queries about delivery dates.

Inputs to manufacture and assembly will consist of the raw materials and parts needed to make the product and the outputs will be the products themselves. It should be remembered here that we are only considering the *central purpose* and that interaction with the other subsystems of the organization will involve support from personnel, facilities and finance.

Typical names for the documents and files used in practice to communicate and store control information by the central purpose process control subsystem might include:

a *Production Schedule/Plan* (Fig 6.9): Defines *how much of what product* should be made *when*. The term product here will include parts, quantities of substances or assembly of components.

b *Batch/Job Ticket* (Fig 6.10): Allocates a particular part of the production plan to a particular operator or some component function within the central purpose process control subsystem. Has a mixed systemic role since it may be used to control the physical production process as well as the performance of the people involved and the financial aspects of their payment.

c *Operations Sheet/Card/List* (Fig 6.11): Defines what physical operations must be carried out to produce the product. Of combined interest to both the personnel and engineering supervisory functions in order to see that the job is carried out. Has heavy implications for the operators and their representatives as defining what it will be like to do the job concerned.

d *Engineering Drawing:* Defines *what* the product processing system must produce, and is used in conjunction with the operations sheet which defines *how* it is produced.

e *Clock Cards and Time Sheets:* Record *when* the operators concerned with product processing are functioning. Combines and confuses several different subsystems concerned with product planning and control. The central purpose process control subsystem uses these to monitor production performance. It is also used by the personnel subsystem to check for attendance, absence, sickness, etc. The financial subsystem may use it to calculate wages or other payment and deductions.

PRODUCTION SCHEDULE

Production Facility: Packing   Date: 19.7.96

Time: 1000hrs   Day Number: 256

Prod. code \ Day	256	257	258	259	260	261	262
C127	50			100	100	50	
C156	100	100	50			50	100
C218		50	100	100	50	50	50

Fig 6.9 Production Schedule/Plan
Used to define how much of a product, a part, or assembly should be made, and when. May be expressed in diagrammatic form like a Gantt chart.

```
BATCH/JOB TICKET

Number: 256/12                          Date: 19.7.96

                                    Day Number: 256
```

Quantity	Code	Description	Facility
50	C127	Classic Single/S/S	Packing

Fig 6.10 Batch/Job Ticket

Identifies an operation or set of operations that have to be carried out on a product, or batch of products, as part of the production process. In this example, 50 C127 cupboards have to be packed. Note that this is one of the jobs specified by the production schedule of Fig 6.9.

```
OPERATIONS LIST

Product Group: All S/S Cupboards

Facility: Packing
```

Op. No.	Operation Type	Time
1	Check components complete	1.00
2	Fix wrapping	3.30
3	Assemble container	0.30
4	Pack	0.30
5	Inspection	1.00
6	Seal	0.30
	TOTAL	7.00

Fig 6.11 Operations List

Defines the operations that have to be carried out to complete some particular job. Besides defining the method and facilities used, it may also define the times required. These may be used in helping to plan the production schedule as well as determining the amount of time the operator has to be paid for the job. When used for both of these purposes there is an inherent tension between the interests of the operator, the financial subsystem and production planning and control.

Again we notice how often in conventional physical forms of information systems the whats and hows get very mixed. Any attempt at systems development which aims to be successful for the *whole* organization must take account of this. Ignoring the fact that a particular document has, say, personnel implications as well as financial ones can result in the information system working very differently from what is intended.

The central purpose input control subsystem

In a production-based organization like Carry-Out Cupboards, this subsystem is concerned with ensuring the supply of parts and raw materials needed for manufacturing the product.

As we saw above, the goal-setting higher-order control is carried out by *logistics and supply management* using the output information from design and engineering to decide on sources of supply for materials and parts. This information is used by purchasing together with details on the production schedule from production planning and control to produce an order or procurement schedule on suppliers. It is worth recalling here that the issues faced by purchasing in deciding how much and when to order are an example of classic stock control which we considered in Chapter 3. The performance of suppliers in terms of delivery times and product quality will form the feedback to logistics and supply management which enables poor suppliers to be dropped and new ones investigated. This process of supplier assessment is sometimes called *vendor rating*. Note that it represents second-order feedback on the goal-seeking performance of this control subsystem.

The physical reception of the input from suppliers and subsequently issuing it as output to manufacturing and assembly is done by raw *material and parts inventory*. Although this process may share similar problems associated with stock control with finished product inventory and delivery, it should be noted that the two processes are two different systemic functions.

When it comes to considering some of the typical names for the documents and files used in practice by the central purpose input control subsystem, we would expect to find a similar set to those used by the central purpose output control subsystem, except that now the roles of supplier and customer are reversed.

◆ **STQ 6.7**

We have mainly interpreted the central purpose subsystem in terms of a manufacturing organization like Carry-Out Cupboards. What would be the equivalent of:

a. Design and Engineering (the goal-setting process of the central purpose process control subsystem) for MX Marketing?

b. Suppliers (process source) for the East Farthing Drainage Authority?

Box 6.3

HOW TO KEEP THE CUSTOMER HAPPY

(*Financial Times* 21/8/96: all the italics are mine)

Offer your customers what they want – within limits. For many businesses, the challenge is to embrace enough product variation to satisfy the marketplace while retaining the benefits of the standardized production line.

But getting the balance right is far from easy. The blend of skills required to succeed with 'mass customization', to use the management jargon, may take decades to build up. Hence the strategy is more likely to be adopted by companies which plan on a long timescale. . .

In the case of Trumpf, its main products are sophisticated cutting and punching machines which use lasers rather than conventional tools. The company started moving towards a greater degree of product standardization six years ago. . . Each system within the same family is built to the same basic design to simplify manufacturing and reduce costs while permitting optional variations. . .

According to Leibinger, who joined Trumpf as an apprentice in 1950 and bought out the previous owner in the 1970s, the reduction in costs would not have been possible without a '*master plan' for the design of each new product which brings together engineering, production and marketing specialists.*

COMMENT

The concept of mass customization is an excellent example of how a *systems* view of organizations, like the GMOS of Fig 6.5, can give much better insights than a conventional organization chart.

The first important insight in this case is that engineering, production and marketing are indeed part of the same central purpose subsystem, as in Fig 6.6. Regarding them as separate departments or divisions, on different parts of the company organization chart, can be very misleading. It does not show what they *do* or *process*, their *structural* relationship, how they *interact*, and what *information* they need from the information system. The phrase 'brings together' shows that engineering, production and marketing are seen as components of one system, and 'master plan' indicates common coordination and control within that systemic relationship. The systemic whole focusses on the central purpose of 'keep the customer happy'.

A second important insight follows from this. It is a relationship between the components of the central purpose subsystem and the customer. A systems view sees the market as an environment which disturbs the organization as a system. The organization seeks to adapt and survive in that environment through the *needs/ request/ provision/response* interaction illustrated in Fig 6.5. A systems view of the environment implies that the organization cannot entirely destroy the customer's need for customization, since any system's ability to influence its environment is limited. The system can, however, choose how its goals are implemented. In the case of Trumpf this means 'enough product variation to satisfy the marketplace while retaining the benefits of the standardized production line'.

As in the operation of so many control systems, this balancing act invokes the principles of Fig 3.22. The variable under the organization's control is the degree of standardization. The cost of customer dissatisfaction (Cost A in Fig 3.22) rises with greater standardization. The cost of production to the organization (Cost B) rises with less standardization. Mass customization is one approach to optimizing the balance of these two costs.

Finally, mass customization illustrates another important systems concept which we first met in Section 4.4 when considering *classification* and hierarchy. Products which share common characteristics may be seen as members of a *class*. These characteristics will not only refer to their shape, appearance or other properties once they have been produced. The final shared properties also imply shared methods of production, and it is this sharing that helps to decrease 'Cost B'.

Mass customization is just one more recent approach to designing production and operations to cope with the competing aims of variety and standardization.

Group technology was a name given over thirty rears ago, as in Lockyer, to a system of grouping products with shared production needs into classes. This classification enabled varieties of products, in terms of their market destinations; to be subjected to standardization, in terms of their production procedures.

The Carry-Out Cupboards case of Appendix 1 is based on a real organization which uses a different approach to the competing aims of variety and standardization. Here the production of the components of the final product is very standardized. The variety comes from the different ways in which the components may be assembled into a structure.

FURTHER STUDY

Consider the concept of *requisite variety* in section 3.3.6. In what different ways do organizations cope with the competing aims of variety and standardization? Don't confine your investigation to *concrete* or *physical* products. Take a systemic view and consider *abstract* outputs such as 'services'. How do insurance companies deal with the variety of cars, houses or people when offering what appears to be a standard product?

6.3 THE CENTRAL PURPOSE SUPPORT SUBSYSTEM

The general model of the financial subsystem

The model of an organization as a system in Figs 6.1 and 6.2 identifies three systems which have the role of supporting the needs of the central purpose subsystem: personnel, facilities and financial. This section will cover these systems in more detail by considering them in terms of the General Model for Organizational Subsystems of Fig 6.5.

The aim of this section, as in the previous one, is to show what is going on in information systems terms behind the physical organizational mask. The distinction between the systems view and the conventional organizational view is particularly important in the area of *financial* information systems, so we will alter our usual personnel, facilities, financial sequence and consider this system first. Also, as in the previous section we will assume that the term 'system' refers to the whole of the subsystem when we are looking at its own hierarchy, and use 'subsystem' to refer to partial aggregations of its components.

There are three historical reasons why the distinction between the systems view and the conventional organizational view is hard to establish as a concept when considering the financial subsystem. I find that I am much more sympathetic with the first two of these reasons than with the third.

The first reason for retaining a conventional view of the financial subsystem is *accountability*. The *law*, as a major component in the organizational system's environment, affects the financial subsystem much more than the other subsystems. Schedules in the various Companies Acts actually define what things the financial subsystem must do, and to some degree, how it must do them. A production manager who thinks of a new way of processing a product may be rewarded for being original: an accountant who thinks of a new way of keeping the books may end up in prison! The position is further distorted by the fact that some of the financial information processed is irrelevant to the management and control of the organization. Thus companies in the United Kingdom do not keep Value Added Tax (VAT) recording systems because they help to manage and control their activities: they do it because the Customs and Excise require it. From the systemic viewpoint the company is merely acting as a component of the government revenue collection system when it does this.

A second reason which has a conservative effect on views of the financial subsystem is *commercial practice*. As we saw when considering typical documentation for the input and output subsystems of the central purpose system, most organizations act as both customers and suppliers. The physical form of information used within the organization is also used for two-way communication between them.

◆ STQ 6.8

What role in the General Communication System Model of Chapter 4 is being referred to here?

It would therefore reduce or even eliminate communication if an organization had a totally different internal physical form of information system from that of its customers and suppliers. The most basic example of this is the actual numbers used to represent the sums of money. *Conceptually*, I and many other people could make a good case for us having a number system based on 12 rather than 10, but *practically* it is unlikely that any country, let alone any single organization, could survive going it alone on such a system.

The third reason why a conservative organizational view of the role of financial information has persisted comes from the way that systems were often computerized. Since the financial functions of organizations were usually the first to be computerized, this precedent made the computer system the possession of the finance department. This factor was reinforced by the fact that most early computers required special housing and conditions, and it was therefore easy to regard 'the system' as a separate physical thing.

We discussed in the first section of this chapter why we needed to recognize that this has a much wider application than the particular subsystem with which it is associated. One particular reason why we should look critically at the financial subsystem in this respect is that it helps finally bury the view that an information system is a computerization of historical procedures. We shall also see further in Chapter 7 how it helps with critical appraisal of information systems development methodologies.

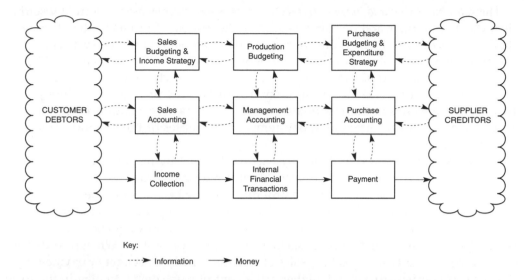

Key:
- - - -> Information   ——> Money

Fig 6.12 An Interpretation of the Financial Subsystem in Terms of the GMOS
The description of the various processes are widely applicable. It is important to note that this subsystem is concerned with the *support* of the Central Purpose Subsystem, Strategic financial processes will be the concern of the Corporate Planning and Control Subsystem.

Figure 6.12 shows the financial subsystem in terms of the General Model for Organizational Subsystems of Fig 6.5. Where the central purpose subsystem was concerned with the flow of material, the financial subsystem is concerned with the flow of money. It should be noted that we use the word money to represent the *abstract concept*, not just one particular *concrete* manifestation. This distinction should now be familiar as it is one we apply to information itself. In the financial context we can illustrate the principle by noting that money can flow in many other ways than as actual coins put into the hand or as notes paid out by a bank. Very often, a transaction is physically carried out by the alteration of data in records.

As with the central purpose subsystem we shall make the bridge with conventional physical procedures by looking at how some of the systemic concepts turn out in practice in the form of documents and files

The financial input control subsystem

Since this is a component of a system which is *supporting* the central purpose, the input of money will be governed by the activities of the central purpose subsystem. So in the case of a marketing and production based organization like Carry-Out Cupboards, the financial subsystem is concerned with control of the input, processing and output of money in relation to the manufacture and selling of a product.

Activity by the environment in the form of the customer buying or returning goods will initiate the need to control input in the form of payment or repayment. Note that this is why the financial flow has been shown in the opposite direction to the central purpose flow. There are other important money inputs like those in the form of loans from banks or money raised from shareholders, but we saw above that these are the concern of the *corporate planning and control* subsystem.

The *sales budgeting and income strategy* process exerts higher-order control by setting financial sales targets and deciding issues like the pricing of products, the offering of discounts or the credit terms allowed to customers. It should not be surprising that this process occupies the equivalent position in Fig 6.12 to that of marketing in Fig 6.6. While marketing considers the type and quality of product that the customer would buy, sales budgeting and income strategy determines the pricing and selling policy that would encourage the customer to buy it. Interactive relationships like this between processes in different subsystems are examples of the general principles shown by Fig 6.2.

Feedback on the success of these goals set by the sales budgeting and income strategy process will come from an analysis of information recorded by *sales accounting*. Sales accounting has the first-order control role over the behaviour of the *income collection* process by recording the sales of products and the receipt of payment for them. As we saw above, sales accounting and the sales and order processing component of the central purpose are usually mixed together in the physical system. When records kept by these components show that the sales of a product are below target or payment by a customer is consistently behind, higher-order control may come into play in the form of price changes for the product or adjustment to the credit rating of the customer.

The close physical interrelationship of sales accounting and the sales and order processing also means that the documents used by both of them overlap. Reference back to the central purpose input and output control subsystems shows some typical examples. Also in practice, our conceptual distinction between the income collection *process* and sales accounting as *control* is hard to determine: usually one department does both. It is possible to illustrate a physical example of the distinction however in the form of debt collectors or bailiffs. Their job is seldom done by accountants or finance clerks.

The financial process control subsystem

This subsystem is concerned with the processing and control of the money flows within the organization in response to the behaviour of the central purpose process control subsystem. For an organization like Carry-Out Cupboards these financial flows will be governed by the activities which take place when the product is assembled and packed. These will include a wide range of costs from work done by personnel, to power consumed by plant, or paperwork used.

Higher-order control takes the form of *production budgeting*, which sets goals for expenditure on these activities of the central purpose subsystem. This process of goal-setting also requires interaction with other subsystems under the coordinating principles laid down by the corporate planning and control subsystem. Thus the amount of time needed by the workforce to assemble a particular product and the materials required will follow from the product design and production procedures determined by design and engineering in the central purpose subsystem. In coordination with this the payrate for the job will result from the operation of the personnel subsystem.

Management accounting will attempt to achieve the goals set by production budgeting by the controlled allocation of expenditure to *internal financial transactions*. The normal business definition of management accounting would cover both these functions just as sales accounting would cover the income collection process in the financial input control subsystem. We need to use this rather artificial term of internal financial transactions, however, to distinguish the actual *process* of financial flow, from the *control* functions exerted by management accounting. An example in practice of this distinction would be the typical payroll department. The job of this department is to make or *process* payment according to the workforce according to preset rules, but not to be concerned with the rules themselves.

The financial output control subsystem

A financial output to suppliers and other components of the environment will result from their inputs to the central purpose subsystem. The financial output control subsystem of Carry-Out Cupboards would, for example, pay for the supply of materials, component parts and packaging. As with the financial input control subsystem, we would exclude corporate planning and control operations like transfer of capital.

The *purchase budgeting and expenditure strategy* process sets the goals which *purchase accounting* seeks to meet. These goals define what money has been allocated for the purchase of materials, advertising, leasing, etc. as discussed above. Purchase accounting would monitor and control the actual *payment* process to ensure that these policies were carried out.

The occurrence of these processes at equivalent positions in the General Model for Organizational Subsystems as logistics and supply management, and purchasing in the central purpose subsystem, leads us to expect close interaction between them. Typical of the mixing of the two conceptual subsystems in one physical manifestation would occur in activities like vendor rating; determination of the best ordering policies against the costs of storage, ordering, and delivery; assessing the benefits of discounts; or deciding the terms of timing and payment to suppliers.

The feedback from purchasing would give information used for the resetting or modification of the above goals. Thus the actual cost performance by suppliers in relation to their quality and delivery might result in vendor rating excluding them as future suppliers, or changes in delivery and storage costs might result in different ordering schedules and quantities.

As with the sales accounting and income collection partnership, the controller and the process controlled are not easily distinguished in practice. Usually a department called 'Purchasing' does both and the documents and records used often have several functions as we saw above. The difference here is that the roles of customer and supplier are reversed.

◆ **STQ 6.9**
What is the financial subsystem in a bank?

The general model of the personnel subsystem

In the previous subsystems we considered it was necessary to define what the *flow* through the subsystem was. In the case of the personnel subsystem (Fig 6.13), is it people? To answer this question we need to go back to two familiar systems principles.

The first is the usual distinction we make between a concept and its concrete manifestation. For people, this often means that we distinguish between the whole person and any one particular *systemic* role they might have. The second is the principle that the *boundary* of a system is determined by the aims and values of the person whose concept it is. So what are considered to be components of a system depend on why we are looking at it.

Complete people are not just 'personnel' components of a particular organizational system. They do many things and have many qualities which involve them in much wider systems than those concerned with their work. Within the boundary of the personnel subsystem we only reveal a particular selection of their qualities which are relevant to that subsystem, not whole human beings. Even if we were just to regard people in this restricted way however, we would still need to be cautious before describing 'people' as the flow through the personnel subsystem. This need for caution comes from our distinction between the roles and people.

An example might illustrate this point. Suppose Jeff Wilson works as a draughtsman for the surveying department of the East Farthing Drainage Authority. The authority decides to install a computer-aided design system which makes manual draughtsmen redundant. However, Jeff is retrained to operate the new system, so although his old job has disappeared he is not made redundant. Would we say that Jeff himself has 'flowed' through the subsystem, when he hasn't even had to change his office? I think we could see that one job or post has been removed from the subsystem and another has come in its place. In that sense there has been both input and output taking place, but Jeff himself has continued to work without a break. In looking at the personnel subsystem therefore, we will be looking at the flow of roles or functions in the organization without necessarily implying any one particular physical flow or that people are *only* what their roles are.

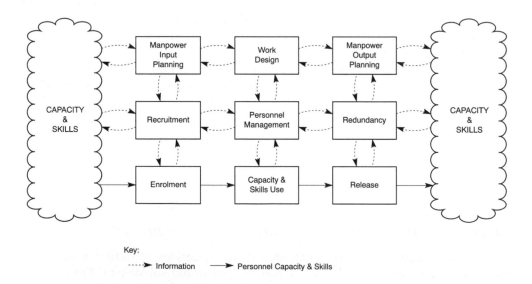

Fig 6.13 An Interpretation of the Personnel Subsystem in Terms of the GMOS
Shows the use of human skills and capacity in support of the Central Purpose Subsystem. The flows controlled are those of the skills and capacity, not the people themselves.

The personnel input control subsystem

The need to recruit skills and roles comes as a result of the activities of the central purpose subsystem. We therefore show the flow of this *supporting* subsystem as in the same direction to the other central purpose support subsystems, i.e. in the revese direction of the product flow which uses it.

The goal-setting process of *manpower input planning* will work in conjunction with the higher-level goal-setting of the other subsystems to determine not only the type of skills, but the number required and the cost and timing of their input to the personnel subsystem. In practice this means that first we need to fully understand the central purpose of the organization itself. For a marketing and production organization like Carry-Out Cupboards this means knowing the kind of product we intend to make and sell, the amount we intend to make, the way we intend to make it, the cost of making it and when we intend making it. This information will, as a result of the activities of the central purpose subsystem, be coordinated with finance and facilities subsystems through corporate planning and control. Once available, it can be used by manpower input planning to decide the skills of the workforce, the number needed, their pay or salary, and when and how long they would be employed for. The process of manpower input planning will also need to work in conjunction with manpower output planning to accommodate the personnel subsystem as a whole to *environmental* disturbances affecting personnel levels, but these are discussed when we cover the output subsystem itself below.

We use the terms *enrolment* and *recruitment* to describe the input process and its first-order control respectively. In practice we will find that the physical form of these components of the subsystem are intermingled. Recruitment will be concerned with controlling the input to the process from the environment by publicity and advertisement, responding to direct applications either in person or otherwise. The environment in this context will consist of all those potential employees whose skills might come to fulfil the roles required. They may not, like Jeff Wilson in the example above, necessarily be physically outside the organization. The enrolment process then has the job of the actual mechanics of signing on, making out contracts, briefing, etc. In practical terms the skills and procedures of interviewing, selection and completing contracts between the organization and its new recruits is usually carried out by the same person or team. So the personnel subsystem is normally similar in this respect to other General Model manifestations of input and output processes and their first-order control.

Higher-order feedback on the results of recruitment's control of the enrolment process, in terms of its success in achieving goals, will determine the need for further adverts, different ways of recruitment and review of how realistic manpower planning goals turned out to be in the light of experience.

The personnel process control subsystem

The use of skills and roles recruited by the input control subsystem is governed by the process activities of the central purpose subsystem which it supports. Thus for Carry-Out Cupboards, who does what job in, say, assembly and packing is determined by what jobs there are to be done, what is involved in doing them and when they have to be done by. Design and engineering will have set these goals for the jobs in terms of their design and production method. Production planning and control will be ensuring that they are done correctly and at the right time.

In this context, *work design* attempts to match the human aspects of work with the goals of design and engineering, while *personnel management* tries to control the human *capacity and skills use* needed to support the implementation of these goals. Work design would look at design and engineering plans to introduce a new process at Carry-Out Cupboards for example, and decide what skills would be needed for the new process and how the workforce should be organized to meet them. Personnel management would have the everyday task of ensuring the workforce kept to the procedures. Their degree of success at this would then be the feedback from the skills-use process which determines what modifications should be made to work design.

The personnel output control subsystem

The central purpose subsystem has to change its behaviour in response to disturbances from the environment. For Carry-Out Cupboards this will mean altering the design of existing products, developing new ones, and adjusting planned sales levels in response to the demands of the market.

The effect of these changes on the supporting personnel subsystem will be a change both in the capacity and skills of personnel needed. There will also be direct disturbances of the personnel subsystem as a whole directly from the environment. Some of the most common reasons for reduction in personnel levels of this type would be people leaving for another job and retirements.

Within the personnel output control subsystem itself, the process for which we use the general term *release* covers any of the particular procedures that result in an intended reduction in the level of personnel employed in a particular role. Most of these procedures are likely to be clerical procedures covering employment contracts, tax and insurance documents, accommodation and equipment. Many of the procedures will be governed by employment law, and will involve coordination with the financial and facilities subsystems. We have also seen that the particular person concerned may immediately then appear as input to the subsystem in some different role.

The need and form of the release process will stem from goals originally set by the *manpower output planning* process. We showed above that manpower input planning was concerned with deciding what capacity and skills were needed by coordination with the central purpose subsystem. In parallel with this, manpower output planning will decide what reductions are needed. In practice therefore, manpower input and output planning are likely to be carried out by one management function within an organization. Indeed, we will often find that organizations do have a department called 'manpower planning' which covers these two processes.

Besides carrying out the goal-setting functions we have described, what is usually called manpower planning also attempts to anticipate and plan for environmental disturbances. The disturbances already considered above were resignations or retirements, and these affected the output from the personnel subsystem. Attempts to accommodate these would come through the actions of the recruitment and enrolment components of the personnel input control subsystem. There are however other disturbances to the personnel subsystem from the environment that will affect these inputs. The availability of personnel may be affected by demographic changes or recruitment competition from other firms. What is often described as manpower planning will use a range of quantitative statistical techniques to model processes like ageing, turnover, or demographic change. Using these models it can set goals which try to anticipate the effects of environmental disturbances. This is an example of the role of forecasting discussed in Chapter 3, and the feedback on the performance of the goal-seeking input and output control subsystems will be important information for use in manpower modelling. Broader policy issues by departments with names like 'manpower planning' are likely to be corporate planning and control subsystem activities, as we shall see below.

◆ STQ 6.10

Is manpower planning for MX Marketing just a question of Ben Lister making sure he has enough administrative and secretarial support?

The general model of the facilities subsystem

The particular version of the General Model for Organizational Subsystems for this subsystem is shown in Fig 6.14. The term *facilities* can stand for a very wide range of buildings, plant and equipment used by the organization. For Carry-Out Cupboards it would include such diverse components of the organizational system as its central packing and assembly factory, the retail outlet buildings, the assembly and packing equipment, the telephones, delivery vans, ventilation system, computers, office desks, etc. Some of the support provided to the central purpose subsystem by the facilities subsystem may seem more direct and specific than others. Thus the assembly and packing equipment or the delivery vans may seem more directly connected with the

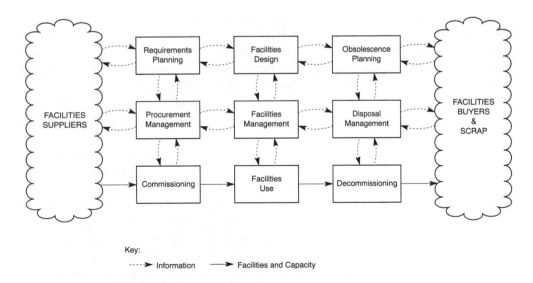

Key:
----▶ Information   ──▶ Facilities and Capacity

Fig 6.14 An Interpretation of the Facilities Subsystem in Terms of the GMOS
Shows the control of the acquisition and disposal of the facilities needed. Even in the simplest organization these can be very varied in nature, value and size.

central purpose than the ventilation system. But once again we remember that all the subsystems are *systemic* components which interact with each other and are coordinated by the corporate planning and control subsystem. For example, if ventilation was removed as a component from the facilities subsystem, the personnel subsystem could not provide its support.

There are two other points which apply to this particular subsystem which need to be clarified before we look at it in detail, which I first raised in Harry (1990). First, formal accountancy rules regard facilities as part of the *assets* of an organization in a way that the skills of personnel, for example, are not. Thus investment in new packing facilities at Carry-Out Cupboards appears in the company balance sheet on the right-hand side under the heading 'assets'. The value of the skills of the workforce which come from investment in training do not appear in the same way. Consider what a major proportion of the assets of MX Marketing lie in the skills of Ben Lister rather than in his small amount of equipment and facilities.

My aim when I originally made this point was not to launch an attack on accountancy, but to demonstrate once again how a *systems* view of an organization will give a different, *holist* perspective from that of particular management functions. It is interesting to note that as I write this in 1996, the phrase 'investment in skills' is on just about every politician's and industrialist's lips.

A second important point about the facilities subsystem is one we touched on earlier in this chapter. The facilities subsystem will only carry out the processes of commissioning, using and decommissioning these assets after financial accountancy decisions on the wider issues of investment have been made by the corporate planning and control subsystem.

The facilities input control subsystem

This has a similar job to do in 'recruiting' the right facilities for the central purpose subsystem as the personnel subsystem has to recruit the right human skills. The higher-order control process of *requirements planning* will set goals in coordination with the needs defined by the design and engineering component of the central purpose subsystem. If the engineering and design function of Carry-Out Cupboards decide to use a new form of packaging procedure, requirements planning will have to identify potential suppliers of any new equipment needed, and decide what equipment to obtain from what source.

As we saw above, the term facilities covers a very wide range of items. Many of the items that come under this heading will involve more than just a simple commercial purchasing process. Items like large production machinery, specialized buildings or chemical engineering plant are often purpose designed and built for the user. In such cases there has to be close technical cooperation between user and the supplier which procurement management will have to facilitate. Activities of this kind also involve coordinated activity between subsystems of the organization. Here again is an important example of why a *systems* view rather than a conventional departmental view is required; and why information should be seen as a resource in modern database terms and not as a series of 'files'. Thus:

- The *design and engineering* component of the central purpose subsystem knows what kind of facilities are required.
- The *facilities* subsystem will have technical knowledge and past data about the availability, reliability and performance of facilities.
- The *logistics and supply management* component may also be able to help with supplier performance.
- The *financial* subsystem will have experience and past data on running costs.
- The *corporate planning and control* subsystem will have the data on the availability of funding, discounting and required rates of return on investment.

Once requirements planning has defined the plant required in terms of its specification, price, supplier, delivery date, etc., *procurement management* will attempt to make sure that the *commissioning* process takes place according to these goals by issuing orders to suppliers and receiving feedback on their performance.

If the new plant is going to require new skills from the user's workforce when it is installed, the supplier may provide the training. In this case the procurement management will be exchanging information with the personnel subsystem. An example of this would be the training often given by computer suppliers or software houses to their customers.

The performance of the supplier in all these areas will form the higher-order feedback which will be used by requirements planning to judge the selection of future suppliers, learn lessons about forming contracts and build on technical experience in producing specifications.

Environmental disturbances will include most of the familiar reasons for the supply of new plant being late, over budget, not up to specification or some combination of all three. Accidents, bankruptcy, strikes and weather are probably the most obvious examples. From the *information* standpoint however it is often an incomplete or ambiguous *specification* that can be at fault because supplier and user do not have a rigorous *information system* to produce it. This issue comes up particularly with the commissioning of computerized information systems from outside contractors. It particularly involves the process of *systems specification* which we will study in the next chapter.

The facilities process control subsystem

The aim of this subsystem is to ensure that facilities are successfully used in support of the central purpose subsystem. This success will be expressed in terms of goals set by *facilities design*. These goals will be as wide ranging as the facilities themselves. They could cover plant and office layouts, operating procedures for anything from a packing machine at Carry-Out Cupboards to the graph plotter in the surveying department of the East Farthing Drainage Authority, maintenance programmes, or planning the delivery of the central heating fuel for the factory.

The goals set by facilities design could be set in terms as wide ranging as the facilities themselves. Examples might include:

a Technical goals, in terms of reliability and quality of performance. Since virtually all facilities require *maintenance* to keep up their performance and prevent failure, goals will include maintenance programmes.

b Financial goals, mainly concerned with making the plant earn its living in terms of the depreciating tied-up capital it represents. Thus deciding on layout, operating procedures and the maintenance programmes will not just be done on technical grounds but also by taking account of the economics of the decisions made. A good example of this might be deciding the frequency of maintenance given to a particular machine illustrated by Fig 6.15. The cost of maintenance means that it would be preferable to have very infrequent maintenance checks. However the costs of failure, in terms of lost production capacity, encourage frequent maintenance. Hence the sum of these two opposing relationships needs to be optimized. Figure 6.15 is therefore yet another example of Fig 3.22.

c Personnel goals relating to the human aspects of facilities design would cover all aspects of operator numbers, skills and the training needed. They would also take into account safety of working practices and industrial relations.

Once goals have been set, they are implemented by *facilities management* controlling the process of *facilities use*. Feedback on the success or otherwise of this control will build up experience for future facilities design.

The facilities output control subsystem

Decommissioning facilities under the control of *disposal management* is carried out according to goals set by a function we could call *obsolescence planning*. At first sight this might seem a relatively crude management system in practice. A machine finally wears out and is not worth repairing, so scrap it. However, in modern organizations the issues involved can be more complex. Environmental concern, rapid technological

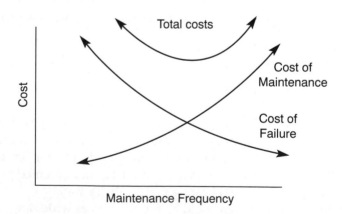

Fig 6.15 Optimizing Maintenance Frequency
Another example of 'The Rubber Stamp of Operational Research' of Fig 3.22.

change and increased social awareness can mean that the environment of the system has a major influence. (Note that we use the term *environment* in both the *systemic* sense and the popular 'green' use of the term.)

The conditions we have just outlined are an example of the importance of *holist* thinking. Failure or obsolescence are *emergent properties* resulting from the coming together of several components. Thus a machine may still work well technically but be too expensive to run compared with more modern equipment or too dangerous or polluting to still be legal. Alternatively it might be perfect in every way except that we no longer had a use for it because of a change in manufacturing processes or the product made.

This holist viewpoint extends to the disposal management of the decommissioning process. Besides controlling *physical* removal of obsolescent plant, through demolition or waste removal, control could be concerned with its sale and financial writing-off and legal negotiations with official bodies. A dramatic example of this might be the decommissioning of a nuclear power plant.

6.4 THE CORPORATE PLANNING AND CONTROL SUBSYSTEM

The role of the corporate planning and control subsystem in the organizational systems hierarchy

The corporate planning and control subsystem has already been frequently mentioned in the previous sections of this chapter. These references occurred when we considered the interaction between any of the four subsystems considered so far. In every case we were concerned with the issue of individual subsystems having to set goals after taking account of at least one other subsystem, or the interests of the whole organization itself. When we did this we were implying a higher level of control than that exerted by the particular subsystem concerned.

The various roles of the corporate planning and control subsystem in acting as a source of higher-order control can be systemically understood by comparing the General Control Model of Fig 3.14 and the General Model for Organizational Subsystems of Fig 6.5.

The central purpose subsystem and its three supporting subsystems were individually interpreted in terms of Fig 6.5. This model saw the four subsystems as exclusively concerned with goal-setting and goal-seeking control of their own inputs, processes and outputs. These four instances of the General Model for Organizational Subsystems were therefore particular examples of the first two orders of control of the General Control Model. Where the *corporate planning and control subsystem* came in was when *methods* or *procedures* of goal-setting were required by two or more subsystems to enable them to coordinate their goal-setting. Reference to Fig 3.14 shows that delivering methods or procedures is the *actuator* or *effector* of *third-order* control, which in turn is done using the *methodology* or *policies* delivered by *fourth-order* control to reflect the *weltanschauung* or *world view* of the systems owner/conceiver.

The corporate planning and control subsystem is therefore the system which completes the control hierarchy which any organization must have to hold together. As we have emphasized many times, this control is a *concept* which can occur in many differing concrete forms. There is no automatic implication of a particular management style, formal or otherwise. The fact that a *weltanschauung* or *world view* is not clearly defined does not mean that it does not exist or cannot have an effect: consider people's subconscious prejudices, for example. The fact that the ways of choosing and delivering methods or policies are not transparent or open does not mean that such processes do not take place: when did you or I have a say in deciding what is socially acceptable behaviour?

As we can see from the last two sentences, the actual operation of the corporate planning and control subsystem is likely to be the most 'political', mysterious or *soft* of the subsystems we have discussed. This has a strong effect not only on the way it operates, but also on how we might attempt to take account of it when trying to develop systems mainly concerned with lower orders of control. We shall see in the next chapter that the *methodology* of *information systems development* has to take account of the higher-order, soft, political *mess* if it is to be managerially realistic.

However, having recognized the often dominant *soft* nature of the corporate planning and control subsystem, we can still explore *what* tasks it does and some typical ways as to *how* the information system can support these tasks.

Processes controlled by the corporate planning and control subsystem

If the role of the corporate planning and control subsystem is to coordinate the goal-setting of the other four subsystems of the organizational system, we can begin by considering how many types of task this can involve. With four subsystems, there are six possible two-way coordinations, four possible three-way coordinations, besides the overall coordination of the four. Thus we could imagine a minimum eleven different ways in which the corporate planning and control subsystem could be delivering policies or norms to coordinate the goal-setting of the other subsystems.

However, this mechanical calculation is an underestimate of the complexity of the corporate planning and control subsystem's role, because there are likely to be many different types of goal-setting involved in any one of these eleven interrelationships. In addition to this, we have not taken account of the rich range of emergent properties which result from the coming together of component relationships.

Despite these reservations, important clarification of the role of the corporate planning and control subsystem in any organization is possible when we consider examples of each component of its elevenfold role as a methodology/policy, method/procedure producer for coordinated goal-setting. This kind of clarification is essential if we are to break through the existing physical system in order to find out *what* information is needed and used by the organization as a *whole*. Without this clarification, any attempt to move to a *database, resource view of the information system* will be frustrated, since much of this information and the procedures used to produce it will be left chained to a particular 'file' or 'department'. The following list some brief examples for each of the eleven cases in the context of a marketing and production organization like Carry-Out Cupboards:

1 *Central purpose–financial subsystems:* coordination of the physical systems mix of receiving materials from suppliers, manufacturing a product and delivery to customers; with payment of suppliers and production workers, and receipt of money from customers.

2 *Central purpose–personnel subsystems:* coordinating the technical and skills objectives of production with the 'people management' aspects of fitting the person to the job, training, sickness, motivation, absence, negotiation, discipline, personnel records, etc.

3 *Central purpose–facilities subsystems:* resolving conflicts over maintenance down-time or standardization versus variety of equipment, coordinating the specification and selection of new equipment. Establishing a system for recording and analysing machine performance information.

4 *Financial–personnel subsystems:* deciding amounts and methods of payment of employees, relationship between supervision of time keeping and payment. Resolving the confusion of logical personnel information with physical financial records and files.

5 *Financial–facilities subsystems:* coordinating procedures for authorization, acquisition and commissioning of equipment with payment for it. Similar coordination for subcontracted or bought-in servicing and supplies. Resolution of conflict where computerized information system equipment seen as 'possession' of financial subsystem.

6 *Personnel–facilities subsystems:* modes of operating equipment, safety, ergonomics. Heating, lighting, noise. Status conflicts over furniture, parking spaces. Morale and conditions decisions over food or welfare facilities.

7 *Central purpose–financial–personnel subsystems:* the jungle of pay and conditions, work study and incentive schemes. Redundancy and recruitment.

8 *Central purpose–financial–facilities subsystems:* conflicts over the cost and timing of maintenance. Allocation of fixed cost overheads.

9 *Central purpose–personnel–facilities subsystems:* matching production objectives with skills, working methods and facilities provision. Training and installation of new physical systems, including computerized information systems. The wider concept of 'manpower planning' mentioned in the previous section.

10 *Financial–personnel–facilities subsystems:* controlling the activities of these three sub-systems so that they remain as coordinated *support* for the central purpose subsystem. Preventing the payroll management overpaying itself, the estates department getting the best parking places and personnel having first choice on holiday dates, etc., etc.

11 *Central purpose–financial–personnel–facilities subsystems:* coordinating and resolving conflicts for all of the above. Setting their goals in terms of high-level policies on issues like return on capital, market share, survival, public image, corporate ethics, minimizing risk, growth in assets.

First consideration of these last examples of high-level goals shows that while some of them are clearly *soft*, like corporate ethics, others, like return on capital, appear to be *hard* and quantitative. However, if we consider how to formulate return on capital, market share, risk or growth, we find them less clear-cut than at first. While they can all be expressed as numbers, the nature of the data collected or the methods used to calculate these numbers can still depend on the policy or motives of those concerned.

It might be worth referring back to what we said about *probability* and *utility* in Chapter 3, and to Chapter 4 and its mini-case, to revise some of the issues involved. A brief consideration of some of these apparently hard goals should then illustrate the principle that high-level goals usually have soft aspects to them.

Whatever their nature however, all of the above examples of the corporate planning and control subsystems activities require *information* in order for them to be carried out. Although this information crosses subsystem boundaries, its physical manifestation is likely to make it the 'possession' of a particular subsystem or one of its components, as we have now seen many times. An analysis based on the systems view of organizations which we have introduced in this chapter will enable us to establish just *what* information *resources* the organization needs and has. But however it is done, such an analysis will have to precede any *technical* information systems development in an organization if we are not merely to computerize or modernize the existing problems and limitations.

In the next chapter therefore, we shall study the subject of information systems development by setting it in the *management* systems context.

KEY WORDS

Batch ticket	Marketing
Behaviour	Material and parts inventory
Central purpose	Needs/request
Central purpose subsystem	Obsolescence planning
Central purpose support subsystem	Operations sheet
Clock card	Output subsystem
Corporate planning and control subsystem	Payment
Customer file	Personnel management
Decommissioning	Personnel subsystem
Design and engineering	Process subsystem
Destination	Product file
Engineering drawing	Production budgeting
Enrolment	Production plan
Expenditure strategy	Production planning and control
Facilities design	Production schedule
Facilities management	Provision/response
Facilities subsystem	Purchase budgeting
Financial subsystem	Recruitment
Finished product inventory and delivery	Remittance advice
Income collection	Role
Income strategy	Sales accounting
Input subsystem	Sales and order processing
Invoice	Sales budgeting
Job ticket	Source
Logistics and supply	Statement
Management accounting	Stock record
Manpower planning	Time sheet

SEMINAR AGENDAS, EXAM QUESTIONS AND PROJECT/DISSERTATION SUBJECTS

1 Does size equate with complexity? Take up the issues raised by the following statement: 'MX Marketing is a complex organization. It owes its existence, not to a range of shareholders like Carry-Out Cupboards, nor to the many people involved in legislation, like the East Farthing Drainage Authority. Instead it is one man, Ben Lister, whose weltanschauung ultimately determines the nature of the company and the way it works. I say 'more complex' because Ben's weltanschauung, like any individual's, is harder to formalize than Acts of Parliament or corporate company procedures.

2 We saw in Section 6.2 that the output information from the marketing process would take the form of criteria like 'lots of glass', 'simple geometrical shapes', 'primary colours' or 'economy before elaboration'. How is it possible for surveys to find out about customers' views on very high-level, abstract concepts like this? Do such surveys really work?

3 We emphasized throughout this chapter that conventional commercial documents like invoices or stock records can fulfil more than one conceptual role and contain information used by more than one subsystem. Obtain a copy of such a document and for every data item on it, try to identify its role in terms of the General Model for Organizational Subsystems of Fig 6.5, by asking the following questions:

   a. What is the information used for?
   b. Who uses it?
   c. Where does it come from?

4 In Section 6.2 we considered how *people* as assets did not appear in a company balance sheet while *things* like equipment and facilities did. Is it possible to assess people as assets? Could accountancy be revolutionized to do this?

5 Investigate what facilities are used by an organization to which you have access. How many different departments control their acquisition and disposal? Is there any concept of facilities as a whole, or a common approach to them?

6 Investigate what policy any organization you know about would have towards the expenditure of £500 on:

   a. Computer equipment.
   b. Office furniture.

Do you find that *a* is controlled in a different way and by different people from *b*? If so, why? Given that we are talking of identical sums of money, should there be any distinction?

7 Attempt to interpret:

   a. A service industry.
   b. An agency.

in terms of the General Model for Organizational Subsystems of Fig 6.5.

8 For a different, and much more widely known, systemic approach to organizations consider the trilogy of Beer (1979), Beer (1981) and Beer (1985); plus a supporting reader Espejo & Harnden (1989). *See* Flood & Jackson (1991) for a critical analysis.

9 For expansion of the issues raised in Section 6.4, consider Stacey (1993).

FEEDBACK ON SELF-TESTING QUESTIONS

◆ STQ 6.1

For a commercial, profit-based, manufacturing organization like Carry-Out Cupboards the central purpose will be to discern a potentially profitable market need and produce the product that meets this need.

For a public service organization like the East Farthing Drainage Authority the central purpose will be to ensure that it fulfils the statutory obligations as laid down by the legislation that set up the authority and gave it its powers.

MX Marketing is more complex. It owes its existence, not to a range of shareholders like Carry-Out Cupboards, nor to the many people involved in legislation, like the East Farthing Drainage Authority. Instead it is one man, Ben Lister, whose weltanschauung ultimately determines the nature of the company and the way it works. I say 'more complex' because Ben's weltanschauung, like any individual's, is harder to formalize than acts of Parliament or corporate company procedures.

◆ STQ 6.2

The way in which a holist view enables us to answer these questions comes once again from the distinction between whats and hows which we said forms the basis of our seeing organizations as systems. What the roof rack producer does is to satisfy a market for roof racks. How he does it can be in various ways, including offering the choice of fitting them. What a hospital does is to provide health care, how it does it can be through a very wide range of curative and preventative medicine.

◆ STQ 6.3

If the central purpose subsystem is indeed central to what the organization as a system seeks to achieve, then it is its output which is the governor of what the system exists for in the eyes of the systems owner/perceiver, so we start with that concept of overall goals.

◆ STQ 6.4

The equivalent of marketing for the East Farthing Drainage Authority is determining what sort of services it will need to supply in the future. These will range from new 'products' like a new set of drainage channels or provision of new forms of environmental protection, to changes in the level of provision of existing 'products' like regular clearing of drainage channels.

The nature of this market is determined at a high conceptual level by the legislation which established the Authority, but detailed identification is carried out by the members of the Drainage Board.

The equivalent of sales and order processing are the legal processes and clerical procedures the Authority has to go through to get access to the land where the works are carried out, and to be able both technically and legally to do the work.

◆ STQ 6.5

Ben and his staff act personally or over the telephone as sales and order processors. The finished product inventory and delivery process is subcontracted but still part of MX Marketing in systems terms, whatever its legal or physical separation.

This example of the role of subcontracting is found quite often in practice. In most cases legal and physical separation does not amount to systemic separation.

◆ STQ 6.6

The short answer is no, because the individual 'products' delivered to customers in the form of development schemes and routine services are not charged to the individual. We can see however that the drainage rate forms a general revenue collection process. In this the list of rate payers is the equivalent of a customer file. The individual records of rates charged and their payment fulfil the role of invoices, statements and remittance advice.

◆ STQ 6.7

The equivalent of design and engineering, the goal-setting process of the central purpose process control subsystem, for MX Marketing can be understood if we first recognize what process the central purpose of MX Marketing carries out.

What Ben Lister essentially does is to match markets for products against potential suppliers. We might say that he 'engineers' this connexion in the sense of 'bringing it about'. MX Marketing is thus an example of a wide class of organization whose central purpose takes some form of agency.

Understanding the equivalent of 'suppliers' or the process source for the East Farthing Drainage Authority is again easier once we recognize the process of its central purpose subsystem. The East Farthing Drainage Authority takes drainage work that needs doing and then carries it out. The source of what has to be processed is the same as the destination to which it is 'delivered' once processed. Thus the East Farthing Drainage Authority is an example of a wide class of organization which provide a service.

◆ STQ 6.8

Communication between customers and suppliers on the basis of shared commercial practice represents an example of a shared symbol set.

◆ STQ 6.9

The source of potential confusion here is to fail to make the conceptual distinction between two different forms of money. The central purpose of a bank is concerned with the process of receiving, lending and investing money which does not belong to it. This is the 'material' which the bank 'processes'. The other form of money is that which belongs to the bank and which it uses to support its operations by doing such things as pay its employees, its electricity bills, etc. This latter form of money is the concern of the financial subsystem.

◆ STQ 6.10

Not entirely. Ben also has to consider his own skills and abilities, and make provision for them. Very often, 'training' for Ben will take the informal form of talking to people in the know, taking friendly advice, or he may occasionally consider going to an exhibition.

REFERENCES/BIBLIOGRAPHY

Beer, S. (1979). *The Heart of the Enterprise*. Wiley.

Beer, S. (1981). *The Brain of the Firm*. Wiley.

Beer, S. (1985). *Diagnosing the System*. Wiley.

Espejo, R. & Harnden, R. (1989). *The Viable Systems Model*. Wiley.

Flood, R.L. & Jackson, M.C. (1991). *Creative Problem Solving*. Wiley.

Harry, M.J.S. (1990). *Information and Management Systems*. Pitman.

Stacey, R.D. (1993). *Strategic Management and Organisational Dynamics*. Pitman.

George Michaelson's first night shift

What happened

George Michaelson was lucky to get a job after he graduated with an honours degree in production engineering in the summer of 1992. At that time British manufacturing industry was under a lot of pressure because of a general economic recession, and defence industries in particular were having a bad time as a result of the 'peace dividend' which followed the East–West detente of the 1980s.

George joined the international company Technoturbines (TT). TT is a consortium of Anglo-French companies that produces jet engines for aircraft and gas turbines for ships and electrical power generation. The original plan for George and the other graduate trainees was that they would receive a two-week induction course at the company's headquarters in southern France and then be individually allocated to posts in one of the companies of the TT consortium according to their intended career specialisms.

In fact nothing like this happened at all. Towards the end of their induction all the graduate trainees were told that an emergency had arisen over the implementation of the new computer-based production planning and control system (known as PROPS). It had been introduced to replace the mixed bag of computer and manually based systems used by the members of the consortium with a unified system that would plan and coordinate production throughout. The problems encountered with the new system (if any) varied according to which part of the consortium you were looking at.

The directors of TT had decided that all the graduate trainees should join trouble-shooting teams that would be sent to any firm in the consortium that was having implementation problems with the new system. The result of this decision was that George and his fellow graduates found themselves sitting in classrooms all day on yet another induction programme, but this time they were mixed in with a wide-ranging group of middle management, computer specialists and representatives of outside computer systems contractors. The idea was to combine specialist systems expertise with management experience. When George asked why new graduates had also been included, he was told it was because they had been 'taught to think'.

This second induction was a very intense three-day course. It covered all the main aspects of PROPS. The new recruits to the trouble-shooting teams were not expected to become experts in PROPS on the basis of these three days, but it was intended that they should understand the system sufficiently to be able to do the trouble-shooting. It was emphasized to the team members that they were not to act as experts or advisors.

Instead, each team would interview users of PROPS and record their problems. These would then be passed back to the systems implementation team for follow-up action.

George was allocated to a team that was sent to the Scottish premises of PST, a small company that specialized in the production of shaped sheet metal components of the engines and turbines. He soon learned that the work done at PST was very skilled. Management and workforce he talked to often repeated that they were not involved in crude 'tin bashing', where some common form of steel sheet was used for the mass production of everyday products like shelving or metal boxes. At PST they formed precision products from sophisticated and expensive raw materials.

The nature of the product and the materials at PST had an important effect on the production procedures. The bending and pressing processes had to result in a product accurately conforming to very tight design dimensions. 'If it isn't shaped right, it won't have the right shape' was the truism that George found was repeated by several of the management and workforce he talked to. After the formation was complete, the heat treatment of the product had to result in the product having very precise qualities in terms of its strength, flexibility, hardness or some other property relevant to its use.

Despite these tough quality standards production at PST had one feature that made life a little easier. It was often possible to avoid scrapping a product that wasn't right first time. Heat treatment could be used to soften the product so that parts of the forming process could be repeated to correct any wrong dimensions. It was also sometimes possible to repeat the heat treatment processes to rescue the resulting product if it did not have the correct properties of strength, flexibility, etc.

These features of PST production processes made it different from many of the other members of the consortium. Most of these other firms made products through processes that involved the *removal* rather than the *shaping* of metal. Where a product is made by the removal of metal there is much less chance of correction once a mistake has been made, and much more chance of it being scrapped. Thus if a hole is drilled too wide or in the wrong position; or if something is cut too short or machined too thin; you can't stick the metal back on. It was these differences between PST and most of the other companies of the TT consortium that led to PST's problems with PROPS: as George found out on the night shift.

When George got to PST he found that he was the only unmarried or unattached member of the trouble-shooting team. Whatever the rights and wrongs of the case, he ended up volunteering to cover talking to the night shift. By chance this turned out to be a lucky break. Most of the night shift had been working on nights for years and they were almost like a separate community from the rest of the workforce. When they realized that George was the one member of what they called 'the investigation team' who was 'willing to give up his social evenings to come and talk to them', they became much more friendly and cooperative.

So by chance it was George who first discovered the real problem of PROPS as far as production operations at PST were concerned. The initial implementation of PROPS was showing that PST seemed to have incorrect levels of stock and partly finished products which didn't fit in with the figures for the amount of work being scheduled.

George interviewed people working on production and in inspection. He found that according to the official procedure, every time a component was formed or heat treated, PROPS required that it was 'logged out' of production and 'logged in' to inspection. This was done by the operator keying into a computer terminal. When it happened, PROPS would adjust its files so that there was one less component allocated to production and one more allocated to inspection. Given the nature of production at PST that we have explained above, many of these jobs came back again after inspection for some form of further heat treatment or forming correction, if they weren't right first time. When this happened, the component should have been logged out of inspection and logged back in to production so that the files were again adjusted.

In practice, the skilled operators and inspectors at PST had been used to cooperating with each other without the formality of logging in and logging out. An operator would form the product and the inspector would then check and explain any corrections needed. The only formal paperwork would be the inspection instructions for correcting the work.

When the new PROPS procedure required the iterations between operation on the product and its inspection to be keyed into the system, many of the operators and inspectors thought it an unnecessary waste of time. The result was that many of the transfers between production and inspection were never keyed in: operators and inspectors kept to the old informal system. This didn't matter when the same thing happened for transfers both ways, but if movements in one direction were not keyed in while movements in the other direction were keyed in, there could be net gains or unrecorded losses in the apparent numbers of components in production or inspection. This error could be aggravated when batches of the same component were split because only some of them passed inspection first time.

George was the first to discover this phenomenon because it was the night shift who were the main source of such errors due to their more informal approach to PROPS. There were many reasons for this, but the main one was that those who originally had the job of installing PROPS and training the users were not too keen on spending a lot of time on the night shift. Once PROPS looked to be going OK on the day shifts, there was a great temptation to assume the system was up and running.

The night shift people that George talked to were quite frank about this and they blamed 'the system'. Several that he talked to felt that they could have designed the procedures a lot better themselves 'with just someone there who knew about computers to help us sort out the technical bits'. Instead of that 'they had someone who came on the day shift and drew lots of diagrams. Then they went off and we heard no more about it until the new system came in'.

George realized that he was getting a strongly partisan view from the night shift, but he was in a dilemma when he reported his findings to the trouble-shooting team. He did not want his report to result in a crude blaming of the night shift workers who had given him their confidence. Although the workers were technically at fault in not keeping to the new PROPS procedures, the source of the trouble was that these procedures took no account of the special situation at PST. PROPS had been developed as a computerized production planning and control system after very careful consultation with the 'most important companies' of the Technoturbines consortium. As we have seen, PST was very different from most of those other companies in terms of the product, the materials, and their effect on the production procedures. The other companies' technology was based on the assumption of a removal rather than the shaping of metal. This meant that for them it was sensible to make a distinction between *production* and *inspection*: for PST it was not.

George was pleased to find that the leader of his trouble-shooting team agreed with him. So a report was put in recommending a modification of the system at PST to take account of their particular needs. George was then quite flattered to find that he was sent to a consortium meeting of all the trouble-shooting groups and the original implementation team to present his report.

When he did his presentation, he found that the contents of his report raised areas of debate which seemed to come up in several of the reports from the other trouble-shooting teams. Although all these other teams did not always come down on the same side as George's team, the three issues did seem to dominate the quite heated debate they raised amongst the systems experts in the implementation team!

The first debate started when George quoted the workers, inspectors and supervisors at PST saying that they could have designed the procedures a lot better themselves 'with just someone there who knew about computers to help us sort out the technical bits'. This led to a long argument about such terms as 'methodology', 'prototyping' and whether 'approaches' should be 'structured'. Although George was not a computer systems man, he recognized all these arguments as just one example of something he had learnt as a production engineer. His understanding came from his training in product design and its practical implications for the production process. This had taught him that there was usually a tension between the informal nature of creativity and the need to organize production so that ideas became realities. When computer systems people tried to design and implement a system they seemed to have the same tension to deal with.

The next big debate came when George made what he thought was the main point of his report. This was that the features of PST production processes made it different from many of the other members of the consortium, and that PROPS needed to be modified to take account of this. Somebody from one of the other trouble-shooting teams at this point muttered 'so what else is new?'. There was then an argument about how far there really were significant differences between the various consortium factories and how far these were only on the surface. People appeared to take sides on this issue purely in terms of self interest. Most of the systems experts in the implementation team seemed anxious to stress the underlying essential similarities between the different production procedures. George assumed that this was because similarities meant it was easier for them to design one system for the whole consortium with the minimum of irritating special cases. Most of the support for recognizing that there were essential differences came from the trouble-shooting teams because they had been focussing on local difficulties. After a lot of argument it was felt that this issue was so big that it would not be resolved at this meeting. Instead, a full report would be presented to the directors of TT for them to decide the next step.

The third debate seemed to come as a mild afterthought following the previously heated exchanges. When the previous argument had died down, a member of the group of systems experts made a very quiet speech that everybody seemed to ignore at first, but then it heated up the argument all over again. George didn't know the person who made the speech, but everyone who knew him referred to him as 'MJ'. MJ said that they had all been obsessed with their systems in terms of what they did, or didn't, do. He said that the whole focus was on *process*. 'Would it not be better', he said, 'to concentrate on *what* information was needed by the various users in the various factories, and start from there?'

George took time to understand what this argument was about until he remembered an amusing lecture he had once had as a student on the interrelationship of design and production methods. In this lecture, the lecturer had pointed out that if your sock was inside your shoe it had implications for which of these you put on first! The desired outcome of a process will determine which choices of method are available. MJ seemed to be saying the same about the design of PROPS: perhaps they had thought too much about the processes and not enough about the desired outcome.

The debate raised by MJ's remark became very high powered, and most of the non-experts present felt left out. In the end it was decided that this meeting was not a place to continue it. George suspected he was witnessing part of something that had been going on between the experts for some time, and that it would continue in the future.

Once the trouble-shooting reports had been presented and the debates were concluded, the job of the trouble-shooting teams was over. The directors of TT and those concerned permanently with PROPS would now need to take up the findings and decide what systems modifications and developments were needed. For George it was frustrating to be only temporarily associated with PROPS and not to see the outcome of his work. In fact he took up a permanent post in production information systems after his training and in later life published a book on the subject.

An information and management systems view

In the previous chapter, Chapter 6, we saw how the systems concepts introduced earlier in this book could enable us to see *organizations* and *businesses* as *systems*. The three main requirements for such a view were:

1. Seeing organizations and businesses in terms of *what* they consist of and *what* they do; as opposed to seeing them in terms of the *how* they happened to be physically manifested and labelled.
2. The identification of a *central purpose subsystem* with *supporting subsystems* coordinated by a *corporate planning and control subsystem*.
3. The use of the *hierarchical control model* to understand the relationships between the components of the business or organization.

When we look at George's experience as a trainee of Technoturbines, there are several examples illustrating that *what* was actually going on in the organization did not fit the organizational labels. One example was that George, as a 'mere trainee', was incorporated into a team with middle management, computer specialists and representatives of outside computer systems contractors. Here we can see that what was actually going on at Technoturbines cut across conventional organizational divisions 'once an emergency had arisen', but its *systemic* function could be easily understood in terms of the *hierarchical control model*.

PROPS was a computer-based production planning and control system designed to *set goals* like production targets and stock levels, and to monitor the *goal-seeking* performance of the system when it attempted to meet these goals. Initial feedback on the poor performance of PROPS suggested that it could be that the implementation was incomplete, that PROPS itself needed modification, or elements of both. Whichever of these reasons we are looking at, they are the concern of a *higher level of control* than *second-order goal-setting*, since it was PROPS itself that was meant to set goals. The design, modification and implementation of PROPS was therefore that part of the *control hierarchy* which *determines the method* by which the goals are set. In Chapter 3 we called this *third-order control*.

The setting up of the trouble-shooting teams was therefore needed to ensure that there was the necessary *feedback* to enable third-order control to design and implement an appropriate *method*. Since third-order control is a *corporate planning and control subsystem* function, it is not surprising that it was a directorship decision to set up the trouble-shooting teams.

There was another important insight to be gained from George's experience in terms of seeing the *organization* as a *system* and applying a *hierarchical* control model view. When the trouble-shooting teams reported back to the consortium meeting, some of the argument was about the method used to develop PROPS and what methods might be used to modify it. This first happened when George quoted the workers, inspectors and supervisors at PST saying that they could have designed the procedures a lot better themselves; and the subsequent argument about such terms as 'methodology', 'prototyping' and whether 'approaches' should be 'structured'. There was also the argument started by MJ that they had thought too much about the processes and not enough about the desired outcome when designing PROPS.

The arguments over deciding the method used to develop PROPS and what methods might be used to modify it represents an example of *controlling the development and use of a method*. This is a level of control next above the third-order control which we saw in Chapter 3 was concerned with *methodology* (in its original sense).

All of the machinations of the PROPS affair, however, confirmed a major aspect of our view of *organizations and businesses as systems*. This was the concept of a *central purpose subsystem* with *supporting subsystems* coordinated by a *corporate planning and control subsystem*. PROPS was vitally important because it was concerned with the *central purpose* of Technoturbines, which was the production of jet engines and gas turbines to meet a market need. Any problem with PROPS had an immediate effect on what Technoturbines was there to do as a system.

Finally, our *organizations and businesses as systems* view of events at Technoturbines brought with it a rich collection of soft issues. These soft issues were mixed with the technical difficulties over PROPS and meant that it was sometimes difficult to know where the problem was. Examples of this confusion included:

- Statements by people at PST who blamed 'the system' and George's dilemma when he reported his findings to the trouble-shooting team.
- Arguments about how far there really were significant differences between the various consortium factories and how far these were only on the surface, with people appearing to take sides on this issue purely in terms of self interest.

The issues raised

Our Business and Organizations as Systems View of Technoturbines raised five issues:

Issue 1.   *What problem features do we have to deal with when attempting to develop an information system?*

Issue 2.   *Should the development of an information system be by an unstructured approach, a structured method, or some combination of both?*

Issue 3. What are the characteristics of the main types of systems development methods and approaches which enable us to make useful distinctions between them?

Issue 4. What are the important issues in systems development methodology? (where 'methodology' is used to mean the study of method).

Issue 5. How can systems development itself be seen as a system? What are its components and how are they related?

Issue 1 is not a new one, and is illustrated by our closing remarks in the previous section. We have frequently stressed the concept that an information system can be seen as a component of a wider management system. Since management inevitably brings with it the *soft issues* characteristic of any *human activity system*, information systems development will take place in a wider context that contains soft issues as well as hard technical problems.

Was the problem that George found on the night shift at PST a *management* problem or a *systems development* problem? Were the night shift the main source of errors because their more informal approach to PROPS stemmed from poor management rather than a poor system? Those who originally had the job of installing PROPS and training the users were not too keen on spending a lot of time on the night shift: maybe if they had, there would not have been a problem. After all, PROPS looked to be going OK on the day shifts, and they were working the same system, in the same factory, with the same product and production procedures: so it was a *management problem*. An alternative view, shared by George, was that good management can make up for a bad system, but it is still a bad system. Strongly active management on the day shift was covering up for a system that was technically inappropriate for the practical situation it was supposed to support: so it was a *systems development* problem.

Issue 1 is therefore one which recognizes that we need to be able to decide the *management* problem and its context before we can choose and *apply a systems development method*.

If we do have a means of resolving Issue 1 and we decide that we have a systems development problem, then Issue 2 brings up the question of how the development of the information system should be carried out. Should we organize our approach in a *structured* way, with a clear-cut plan of what has to be done, when, by whom and using what techniques? Or is a more informal *unstructured* approach appropriate which allows for flexibility and creativity? Or both?

In the Technoturbines case the argument seemed to depend on whether you were one of the night shift people at PST that George talked to, or one of the computer specialists and representatives of outside computer systems contractors. The first group thought that the procedure for developing PROPS would have worked a lot better with a heterogeneous collection of themselves and 'someone who knew about computers to help us sort out the technical bits'. The implication here was that the process would be informal and unstructured. The second group, whom we might stereotype as 'the experts', were present at the consortium meeting. They made several differing technical points, but the assumption behind all of their contributions seemed to be that the development of PROPS should be organized and consistently structured throughout the consortium.

Issue 3 comes up if we have a clear information systems development problem and we decide to choose an approach. We have now to decide what characteristics of the main types of systems development methods are, so that we can make useful distinctions between them and select a suitable one for our needs.

This issue came up at the consortium meeting when MJ said that the whole focus of their view of PROPS was on process. Although much of what was discussed was more technical than George could always understand, he did see that there were different ways you could look at an information system. If you focussed on it as something that processed data to produce the required information, then presumably your systems development method would be one that thought about what processes were needed and what data was needed for processing. George also understood from MJ's criticism that perhaps you ought to start by thinking about the kind of information you wanted first, then to think how the data ought to be structured to produce it, and finally to consider the processes needed to produce it. Whatever the various arguments and their merits, George understood enough to see that your view of *what* an information system was would affect *how* you carried out systems development (i.e. what *method* you used).

Issue 4 arises naturally from Issue 3. Once we can see that there are different methods with their various characteristics, we next consider what criteria we might use to compare and assess them, so that we can make an informed choice of systems development method. We need a *method to study methods* themselves, or a *methodology*. It is interesting to note that George heard a long argument which included such terms as 'methodology', but this was often used to apparently mean the same as method. Part of Issue 4 is therefore to look at the use of the two terms.

Issue 5 is illustrated by the whole of George's experience on the trouble-shooting team. However much the original systems development of PROPS appeared to be a narrow professional activity carried out by computer specialists and representatives of outside computer systems contractors, many other people and things got involved. Expert systems specialists found themselves combined with experienced management and intelligent, but naive, people like George. George, in turn, found himself assessing PROPS with skilled operators and inspectors at PST. Besides this great mix of people, there was the variety of different firms and factories within Technoturbines, and the conflicting views on the analysis of the problems and the methods to be used. In reality therefore, systems development was not just a process but a *system* in its own right whose components and structure also need to be identified and understood.

Our final issue then comes as a result of resolving all the previous ones. If we have clarified the problems of information systems development (Issue 1), used appropriate criteria to select our approach or method according to their qualities (Issues 2–4), and considered who and what is involved (Issue 5); then we come to the issue we shall explore in Chapter 8: what tools are available to support the systems development process?

LEARNING OBJECTIVES CHAPTER 7

1 To understand the role of *systems development* in the wider context of the *management system* of businesses and organizations.

2 To understand the *hard* and *soft* components of systems development *problem*s and the implications for *systems development methodology*.

3 To understand the important features of *systems methods* and the *systems methodology* that enables systems methods to be assessed in terms of their successful application to *systems development*.

4 To understand *systems development* itself in a *management systems* context.

CHAPTER 7
∙∙∙∙∙∙∙∙∙∙∙∙∙∙∙∙∙

Information Systems Development: the Context

7.1   UNDERSTANDING PROBLEMS

The term *problem* can be used in two related but different ways:

1. To imply some rather broad difficulty like a dispute or a doubt, which puts us in a predicament and generally tends to spell trouble: often with emotional overtones.
2. To mean something which is much more clear-cut like a question, a puzzle or a riddle: usually seen in intellectual or technical terms.

We shall look further at the implications of these two usages later in this section, but for the moment let us concentrate on what they have in common.

Both of the usages that we noted for the term *problem* have a common implication that it is something we would like to move on or away from. If it is something vague and broad like a doubt, we would like it to be clarified and cleared up. If it is something quite specific like a puzzle, we would like to know the solution. Either way the implication is that things could be *better* if we could find the right way forward. This general picture of typical problem situations then leads to the questions of what 'find the *right* way forward' and 'better' can mean.

The first of these questions assumes that there is a way to be found. We would not waste our time in a *management* context with problems for which there is no way forward *in principle*. For example, if a doubt or uncertainty is unresolvable because something like *Heisenberg's Uncertainty Principle* (*see* Chapter 4) applies, then it is a waste of time trying to find any 'way forward'. Our view of management, however, is that it is applicable where *meliorism* is an appropriate belief. The 'melior' in meliorism, as we recall from Chapter 3, comes from Latin and means 'better'. So where it is reasonable *in principle* to try and make things better with an attempt to 'find the right way forward', we see management as being relevant.

If we now want to explore the ideas of *better* or *meliorism* we should look closer at the term *right*. As with the word *problem*, we find that it has two different but related meanings:

1 We can use the word *right* to reflect our own *opinions* about something. Thus what is right in the sense of being ethical, fair, just, or socially proper for you, may not be so

for me. Or again, something that is just right in terms of taste or aesthetics for me (like I find that the British climate is right for me) may not be the case for you.

2 We can use the word *right* to mean something that is factually correct in the sense that it can be tested with evidence against agreed standards to determine whether it is accurate or true (like whether Edinburgh is further west than Bristol: which it is).

What therefore follows when we consider the nature of different kinds of *problems* is that they can have *hard* and *soft* properties just as we found when talking about *systems* in Chapter 3. In as far as any problem can be seen 'to imply some rather broad difficulty like a dispute or a doubt, etc.', we would see it as a *soft* problem. If it has qualities which mean it can be seen as a 'clear-cut ... question ... in *intellectual* or *technical* terms', we would see it as a *hard* problem.

Ackoff (1972) calls hard problems *problems* and soft problems *messes*. Figure 7.1 shows what we could consider the main criteria which distinguish hard and soft problems in terms of:

- *Definition*: do we know and *agree* what the problem is? If we do not agree, are there commonly accepted criteria which can be used to resolve the disagreement?
- *Boundary*: does our *definition* of the problem enable us to clarify what the problem *is*, and what it *is not*?
- *Separation*: can we dismiss issues as being *not* part of the problem as a result of drawing this boundary?
- *Responsibility*: does the definition and separation of the problem make it clear who should be involved in its solution and who not?
- *Information*: if we are clear what the problem is and whose responsibility it is, do we now know what information we need for its solution?
- *Description*: do we now know what a solution would, and would not, look like if all the previous criteria have been satisfied?

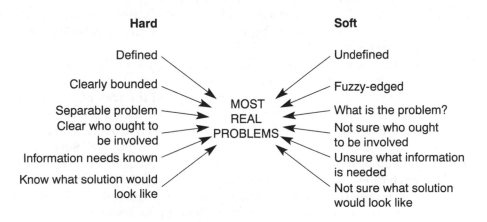

Fig 7.1 Hard Problems and Soft Messes
These should not be seen as mutually exclusive opposites, but rather as extremes of a spectrum that includes most real problems.

If the answer to questions based on all these criteria is yes, then we have a *hard* problem. If any of the answers are *no*, then we could have a situation of *hard uncertainty* or a *soft problem* or a *mess*.

◆ **STQ 7.1**

How would you see the problems and messes in the Technoturbines case in terms of definition, boundary, separation, responsibility, information and description?

Once we have identified that real-life problems can involve both hard and soft issues, and we aim to 'find the right way forward' to a 'better' situation, the next thing we have to consider is *how* we can make this change for the 'better'. This then leads us to consider *approaches, methods* and the study of them both, which can be called *methodology*.

7.2 APPROACHES AND METHODS

The Technoturbines case showed that problems with *information systems* can often be just part of a wider *management system* problem within the *organization or business system*. Part of the problem we may have can be making the distinction between a specific *information systems* problem and a much wider *management systems* problem. Later in this chapter we shall look specifically at methods for dealing with this type of situation, but for the moment we will use the term system in the information systems context, and focus on problems with information systems. We will also introduce the term *systems development* to generally describe the range of activities associated with creating new systems or improving existing ones.

Many different terms are used when describing or discussing the process of systems development. Often the same thing is described by a different term and the same term can mean different things according to who is using them. Since there is no single consistent way of defining these terms, we will begin by trying to clarify some that are commonly used and come up with working definitions. We will also try to keep these definitions close to a mainstream of systems use by referring to other authors.

Approach, method, methodology, technique and *tools* are all terms often used in the context of systems development. We can begin to make a distinction between these if we compare first the terms *approach* and *method*.

The term *approach* seems to be more often used to mean a much less specific way of doing something than a *method*. An approach is likely to involve a set of principles or attitudes for performing a task, but is unlikely to go all the way of defining in any detail how it should be done. Consider how we might describe a 'friendly' approach to establishing a relationship with another person. It is unlikely that we would say, 'first, smile; second, say 'hello'; third, shake them by the hand; fourth,...etc'. Such a mechanical approach would be more likely to have exactly the opposite effect to that intended. It would be much more useful to give more general advice like 'try to put the person at their ease, show a friendly attitude, be prepared to take an interest and listen, etc', and leave some flexibility and spontaneity for the relationship to develop naturally.

This last example is not so removed from systems development as it might first seem. Some of the problems at Technoturbines seemed to arise from too mechanical an approach.

◆ **STQ 7.2**
What were they?

As we shall see when we cover the subjects of *prototyping* and *object-orientation* later in this chapter, an unstructured *approach* based on a set of guiding principles can have advantages over something more *systematic*.

◆ **STQ 7.3**
What's the difference between systemic and systematic?

This last STQ leads us on to saying that a *method* implies something much more *systematic* or *structured* than an approach. We imply this when we use the word *methodical* to describe a systematic way of doing things. The use of the term *structure* in a *systemic* context implies the existence of ordered components. In a method these components will be the steps or stages we proceed through when carrying out the method. Just as defining a system requires us to define its components, so defining a method will require us to define its stages. For the moment we will use the word stages to apply generally to the component steps of a method. As we come to look in more detail in Chapter 7 we shall see that terms like *stages*, *phases* and *tasks* may need to be distinguished.

A method for changing a car wheel would begin 'first, ensure the car is safely anchored; second, just release the tension on the wheel nuts; third, jack up the car; fourth, remove nuts, etc'. Notice that in this case the *order or sequence matters*: it could be very dangerous to regard the safe anchoring and nut removal as informal principles to be brought in at any old time that spontaneity dictated. Just as the structuring of the components in a system affects its emergent properties, so the structuring of the component stages of a method affect its emergent property in terms of the results produced. I always remember the old Victorian cookbook which began a chicken soup recipe with the instructions 'plunge the fowl into boiling water, having first removed the insides and feathers' – it's too bad if you don't read the instructions backwards!

Again, the everyday examples we use are not so remote from systems development as they seem. We shall see in the next section that defining the stages of a method and deciding on their sequence is a major issue which ties in with the broader one of classifying and selecting methods.

We shall use the term *technique* to describe the way in which a *task* is carried out by someone, often with the aid of a *tool*. While we would apply a technique to achieve a particular task, a method could involve organizing a whole series of different tasks. Thus one method might use many tools and techniques, and a particular tool or technique might be used by several different methods. If systems development is a holist procedure, we should not be surprised to find it using tools and techniques from many different areas of management as well as specialist ones.

◆ **STQ 7.4**
How might the last paragraph be summarized as a diagram?

There is a clear comparison here with the use of tools in fields other than systems development. Mechanics, artists and surgeons all use tools, and each may have a different technique with a particular tool. It is also worth noting that the same tool might be used in a different context. Thus a surgeon's knife may be used by an artist to make lino-cuts. We shall find equivalents of this with systems development tools, which may turn up in very different methodologies.

What is sometimes different about information systems developers is that they frequently use logical and abstract tools. These would include the diagramming tools we covered in Chapter 3. Later in this section we shall see how software can be used to support systems development in the form of CASE (*Computer Aided Systems (or Software) Engineering*) tools.

To compare our working definitions of *approaches, methods, tools* and *technique*s with those used by other popular systems authors, see Avison (1988), Flynn (1992) and Olle (1988).

This leaves us with the term *methodology*. In our analysis of the issues in the Technoturbines case we indicated a reservation about the use of the term when referring to the fact that George heard a long argument in which *methodology* was often used to apparently mean the same as *method*. We said that part of Issue 4 was therefore to look at the use of the two terms. I think that this issue has been correctly summarized by Olle et al. (1988) when they say 'It is recognized that the term *methodology* should be used to mean 'a study of method'. However, the common practice over the past decade has been to use 'methodology' in place of 'method' and this text adopts the line of least resistance by following the current practice'. For our purposes this lack of distinction will not always matter and we too have to bow to common practice when quoting or referring to other work. Where there appears to be doubt, the best course is to check whether we are talking about one particular method or the study of two or more. It is worth also mentioning that the term *meta-methodology* is occasionally used to mean methodology in its original sense where the latter term has been downgraded to mean method.

Having raised this caution as to the use of the term *methodology*, in the next section we will look at *information systems methodology* in its original sense of a study of information systems methods.

7.3 METHODOLOGY AND RELATING METHODS TO PROBLEMS

7.3.1 Basic models for methodology

Reference back to the concepts of Chapter 3 will show an important reason why distinguishing method and methodology, as we do in this section, can be important. If a method is a *systematic* way of doing something rather than just a general approach, then in applying a method we are carrying out a *process* in a way that tries to conform to one or more *goals*. As we shall see later in this chapter, depending on the method we are looking at, these goals could take various forms. For example, the goals could take the form of a defined sequence of stages each requiring the production of certain *deliverables* like a flowchart defining what an information system had to do, or a normalized database defining the data that it would use.

By describing *method* in this way we present it in terms of the *control* model of Chapter 3. If we then consider the *hierarchical* aspect of the control model, there will be a *higher-order* control that will occur when we modify or choose a new method in the light of experience. It is a form of higher-order control because any modification or choice of method is *goal-setting*. The *feedback* of our experience of using a particular method can be used as part of a *learning* process which will enable us to design our method, and hence set goals better in the future. In this sense we can see that this higher-order control is the 'study of method' or *methodology* in its original sense.

We can begin our study of method by recalling that *meliorism* lies behind our view of management: we are trying to make things better and we believe our *actions* can have some effect. The actions we are concerned with in this case are those determined by our choice of method. We might summarize such a situation and these assumptions by the simple model of Fig 7.2, which we will call the *meliorist model*.

The present situation, 'where we are now', we call S_0. There will be all sorts of features of the existing situation which could be described, but for the purposes of *methodology* we would confine our description to those aspects of the situation which are relevant to the *problem* in relation to the choice of method. Depending on the nature of the problem, this could be the state of the wider *management system* or confined to the *information system* itself. If S_0 is a *mess* rather than a problem, the boundaries of S_0 may be unclear, and attempting to clarify them could be a methodological issue. We shall say more of this when considering *soft systems methodology*.

S_1 represents 'where we would like to be'. This will be a better state of the wider *management system* or the *information system* which is aimed for. Whether this state is attainable either fully or in part will depend on our practical success, but S_1 must at least be possible *in principle* for a meliorist model to be relevant. We might say that however *probable* S_1 is, it must be *possible*. According to our assumptions about how probable the attainment of S_1 is, so our choice of method may be affected.

To move from S_0 to S_1, as shown by the arrow, we need to take some appropriate set of *actions* for *change* which will be governed by our *method* or *approach*. As we briefly indicated above, the choice of method will be determined by the nature of S_0 and S_1, and as we shall see, the difference between them.

Obvious and simple as this model may appear it can take on a number of complications. We can now use an exploration of these complications as a starting point for our 'study of method' or methodology.

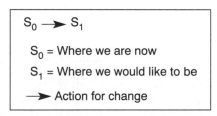

Fig 7.2 The Meliorist Model
The care essentials of any situation where we believe that our actions could
have some effect on their outcomes. 'Meliorism' is explained in Chapter 3.

7.3.2 The effect of motives on choice of method

We have described S_1 as 'where we would like to be'. In the systems context this will mean the kind of system we would like to have, and S_0 will be the one we have now. By looking at the different types of reason that would give us a *motive* to want to move from S_0 to S_1 we shall see that systems development methods can be very different in terms of the stages that make them up and the sequence in which these stages are carried out. The first broad distinction we can make is between:

1. Failure-driven motivation.
2. Aspiration-driven motivation.

Failure-driven motivation can be understood by considering what S_0, the existing system or situation, might be like. Where we have a situation like that at Technoturbines in which something has *failed* or is going badly, then we are *driven* by the existing situation to seek for something better, S_1. Failure-driven motivation starts from the premise that there is an existing system, but it has faults or failures.

When we use the word *failure* it is important to note that it is an *emergent property*. For a failure to occur, two or more *components* have to come together. This may seem an odd statement when we first consider it. After all, many common failures seem to be individual events that just happen. If I'm driving along the road and I suddenly get a puncture, where's the emergent property in that? The answer is quite simple:

Puncture = pneumatic tyre + sharp object

or if we become even more *analytical*:

Puncture = pneumatic tyre + sharp object + contact + sufficient penetration
force + etc.

The serious point to be gained from recognizing failure as an emergent property is an understanding of how it can be removed or avoided. Like any other emergent property it only happens when all the necessary components come together in a particular structural relationship. The removal of a component or an alteration to the structure will result in something different. This 'something different' could be something better like the removal of failure and its replacement with something successful; or it could be an alternative equally as bad or worse.

The *methodological* implication of this view of failure is that *failure-driven motivation* leads to some initial **analysis of the existing system** S_0 that will enable us to understand:

1. The components of the existing situation
2. Their relationship
   and hence:
3. The reasons for the failure or shortcomings of the existing system.

Only when we have carried out this analysis will we be in a position to consider what must be done next, and we will pick this point up later.

Aspiration-driven motivation leads us to start from a different position from that adopted for failure-driven motivation. Instead of considering the system S_0 which we have now, we begin by considering what we would like to have, which is S_1. The most common examples of this occur when there is no existing system S_0 of any relevance.

Just as the first aeroplane was not developed as a result of a detailed analysis of balloons, so we may find that S_1, the system we aspire to, bears little relationship to anything we have at the moment. Aspiration-driven motivation begins, as the term itself makes clear, with our *aspirations*, our hopes or our desires for the new system we wish to develop. The first stage of any method driven by aspiration is to decide just *what* it is we require from the new system. Only when this has been clarified can we go ahead with the detailed systems development.

The *methodological* implication of this view of systems development is that *aspiration-driven motivation* leads to some initial *specification of the desired system* S_1 stage that will include an analysis of:

1. The desired properties of the proposed system
2. Its components and structure
3. Its behaviour and processes.

It is important to notice that this stage may also be called *analysis*. The difference between this use and its use in the failure-driven context is that here analysis refers to S_1 and in the latter case to S_0.

We can now take our methodology a stage further by considering, as promised above, what happens as a result of the analysis of a failure. Let's return to the simple example of the puncture. It may be that when we analyse the existing situation S_0, we find that the removal of the 'sharp object' component and its replacement by a rubber patch will result in a new system S_1 which removes the failure. It could however be that our analysis showed that we got the puncture because we were trying to use the car in unsuitable rough terrain. In this case the desired system S_1 is not a patched-up car tyre but a transfer to horseback or going on foot. Our puncture analogy can go further. It may be that the only reason we got the puncture was because it was sustained as part of a wider car crash. Hardly now worth mending the puncture if the car is a write-off!

A *failure-driven analysis* may therefore lead into the adoption of an *aspiration-driven* method if the analysis stage reveals that 'repairing' S_0 is impossible or irrelevant. This level of failure is almost always due to major *environmental* changes to the system rather than faults in the original design. For there to be any existing system at all, it must have been implemented with some success: major failure must therefore have come as a result of subsequent events. In 1993, the British system of local government taxation known as the Community Charge (S_0) was replaced by the Council Tax (S_1). The fact that councils are having to develop a completely new system rather than modify the old one has nothing to do with how well they designed S_0: it was brought about by environmental change in the form of government legislation.

7.3.3 Derivative and innovative analysis methods

Having considered the different *motivations* for systems development, we can now identify the two different types of method which can result from this consideration. The two types of method can be distinguished by referring to the two different interpretations of the concept of *analysis* which we made in the previous section. These differences affect what kind of initial stages the methods have. In this section we will therefore look at the initial *analysis* stages of the two types of method and leave the remaining stages of systems development for the next section.

Hence, consideration of motivation enables us to distinguish:

1. Derivative methods
2. Innovative methods.

Derivative methods will be relevant to situations where:

- we anticipate that our needs are definable in *hard* terms
- a system S_0 *exists* which is relevant to our needs
- there is a shortfall or *failure* of S_0 in relation to these needs
- it is possible and reasonable to consider the *repair* or *development* of S_0 to meet these needs.

Where such conditions apply, we can see that any new system (S_1) that we develop will have many features of the previous system (S_0), plus other ones which represent modifications or improvements. Hence our new system can be seen as a *derivative* of the old.

Innovative methods will be needed in situations where:

- we anticipate that our needs are definable in *hard* terms
- there is *no system* S_0 existing which is sufficiently relevant to our needs, or S_0 is *irreparable*.

Where these conditions apply, the features of the new system (S_1) will derive directly from a definition of our needs, and any S_0 will have been dismissed as irrelevant. ('Irrelevant' refers here to the *initial analysis stages*: we will find when we get into the development of the system that understanding S_0 is an essential precursor to implementation.)

Figure 7.3 shows how our analysis of *motivation* leads to the choice of a *derivative* or an *innovative* method. We can now go on to see how the form of motivation affects what stages are likely to make up the initial phases of the two different types of method.

We saw in the previous section that *failure-driven motivation* focuses on the analysis of the existing system. Unless this is abandoned as irrelevant for reasons shown in Fig 7.3, it leads us on to the use of a *derivative method*. The subsequent stages following identification of the reasons for the failure or shortcomings of the existing system are likely to be some variant of the following sequence:

1. *Record* the existing *physical* system: i.e. *how* S_0 is implemented.
2. *Define* the *logical* system behind the existing physical system: i.e. *what* S_0 does.
3. *Define* an *improved logical* system to meet defined needs: i.e. *what* S_1 must do.
4. *Define* a new *physical* system based on the improved logical system: i.e. *how* S_1 should be implemented.

In derivative methods, stages 1, 2 and (sometimes) 3 are called *systems analysis* and stages 3 and 4 are called *systems design*. It is also common for these methods to begin with an initial stage called a *feasibility study* which precedes these stages. The purpose of this is to assess whether the systems analysis and design project is worth bothering about; and if so, what resources can be provisionally assigned to it. (I have strong reservation about the assumptions behind this feasibility study stage which I will discuss later.)

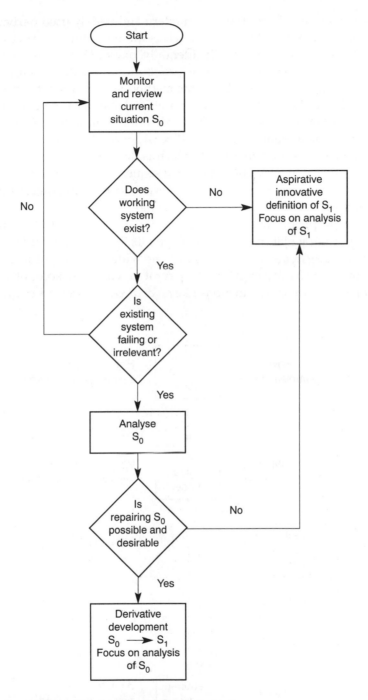

Fig 7.3 Derivative and Innovative Methods
The terms 'derivative' and 'innovative' can have emotional overtones; with the former implying something undesirable, and the
latter presenting a creative image. Here, the terms are used technically, and any judgement of their desirability is based on their
relevance to the existing situation S_0.

We can give a specific illustration of a modern and widely used derivative method by referring to a version of SSADM, which is an acronym of <u>S</u>tructured <u>S</u>ystems <u>A</u>nalysis and <u>D</u>esign <u>M</u>ethodology. (Incidentally, one of Her Majesty's Inspectors of Education once told me that SSADM was pronounced 'sasadom', but I'm not sure if anyone does.) We shall say more about this method later, but for the moment we can note that SSADM has been close to being an official standard in government institutions and with large firms whose systems development activities are required to conform to government requirements (see Box 8.1, page 314). The basis of the analysis stage of this method is shown in Fig 7.4, which is derived from Cutts (1987). Here we can see stages 1 to 3 as the descending vertical sequence, with current system problem and new system requirements inputs. The focus on a current existing system as a starting point clearly makes SSADM a derivative method.

The classic examples of the use of derivative methods are to be found in areas where major environmental change has not been likely to make total failures or irrelevancies of existing systems. These would be the wide range of information systems used mainly in the *financial subsystem* like payroll or company accounts, and conventional *central purpose subsystem* functions like *order processing* or *stock control*. One of the

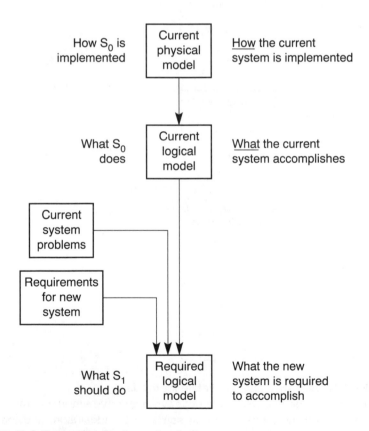

Fig 7.4 Derivative Systems Analysis
Relevant where it is unlikely that it will be necessary to 're-invent the wheel' when developing S_1.

main reasons why such information systems can be seen as *derivative* is because the logical, and even sometimes the physical, nature of many of their processes and outputs is *defined* by *law* or *business practice*.

However, there are situations where an *innovative method* may not only be desirable, but in fact the only way forward. This latter situation is illustrated by a problem faced by one of my students who had been set the task of developing a national dog registration system. He decided on his method *before* looking at the problem, i.e. exactly the *opposite* to what we are advocating here, and chose SSADM. Once he moved into the analysis along the lines of Fig 7.4 he met up with a problem. The conversation went something like this:

> *Student*: Hey Mike, I've been trying to look at the dog registration system using SSADM.
> *Me*: So what's the problem?
> *Student*: You know in the analysis phase it talks about 'the current system'?
> *Me*: Yes?
> *Student*: Well there isn't any 'current system' really, is there? I mean, we don't have dog registration at the moment.
> *Me*: No, we don't.
> *Student*: So how can I use SSADM?
> *Me, musically*: Da-da! You can't...
> *Student*: Oh.
> *Me*:...in its standard form.

Having teased the student a little for ignoring my advice and choosing a method before studying the problem, I was able to point out a very simple remedy. If there is no current system to analyse, we just leave references to it out of Fig 7.4. If we do this we are essentially left with the way innovative methods approach analysis. This involves going directly to determining the 'Requirements for new system' and using these as a high-level specification for the new system, S_1.

Our use of the term high-level here is systemic. We mean high in the sense of defining the boundaries and goals of the system and setting it in the context of the wider management system of which it will be a component. As we shall see in the next section when we list all the stages of systems development, the earlier stages of innovative methods tend to have labels like problem perception, terms of reference and business objectives, strategic requirements planning or simply business analysis, which reflect the wider context of systems strategy.

The result of this approach to analysis is to make methods that use it *top-down* in the *systems hierarchy* sense. We start with the needs of the wider management system and use the analysis of these as a high-level specification for the new system, S_1.

It is worth understanding the reasons for the rise of innovative, top-down methods in recent years. The earliest applications of computerized information systems in the late 1960s and early 1970s were nearly always in the derivative areas we mentioned above like payroll, accounts, etc. It is not surprising therefore that most methods also contained derivative assumptions: indeed, many of the first computerized information systems were essentially computerized versions of the old manual systems.

The big change came in the early 1980s, with the new flexibility brought by the advent of microcomputers. These brought with them more friendly, high-level software like spreadsheets and databases which reduced the emphasis on programming new applications from scratch. After this, dramatic reductions in the cost of large memory and processing capacity made possible even friendlier sophisticated graphical access through so-called WIMP (Window Icon Menu Pointer) user interfaces. The effect of this change was to widen the potential application of computerized information systems to new areas and to make it easier to implement working systems.

Changes like these have had important effects in changing the relative importance of the stages of systems development:

1 A widening of the areas or functions in an organization that may use computer-based information systems has often stimulated a completely fresh look at what the problem is and what the needs are. The move into a computer-based system for the first time in these situations is rather like our earlier analogy of going from balloons to aeroplanes. A derivative method is hardly relevant.

2 Friendlier, easier software has redirected the focus away from programming or systems production problems towards problems of definition of needs and specification of requirements.

The combined effect of points 1 and 2 is that systems development methodology is now seen to raise conceptual as well as technological issues.

7.3.4 The typical stages of systems development

Whatever the differences in assumption and approach between derivative and innovative methods in the initial analysis stages, both types aim to deliver the same result from these stages, albeit in different forms. Analysis should result in a logical specification or definition of *what* the new system S_1 must do. Once we know this, the next stages of systems development will be concerned with *how* it must be done, or design; and finally *doing it*, or production and implementation.

There are many views of what stages, in what sequence, make up the whole systems development process. We will look at three views and make some comparative and critical comments about them:

1. The traditional systems life cycle view
2. The information systems life cycle of Olle et al. (1988)
3. The b-model of software development of Birrell & Ould (1988).

What is important here is to understand some of the issues which the different views raise. Despite the claims of the advocates of different schools of thought, I do not believe there is one exclusively best view, and when we come to look at specific examples of systems development method later in this chapter, we shall find that they are based on very different views of the systems development process.

The traditional systems life cycle view is usually defined in terms of six stages:

1. *Feasibility study*: which looks at the aims and scope of the new system and its anticipated cost benefits in relation to the existing system.
2. *Systems investigation*: a fact-finding investigation and recording of the existing, often manual, procedures.

3. *Systems analysis*: a critical analysis of what the existing system does, as revealed by stage 2, and the derivation of improvements.
4. *Systems design*: the design of output, processes, input and files for the new system defined by stage 3, usually for computerized implementation.
5. *Implementation*: Scheduling the run-in of the new system by direct change-over, stepwise introduction, or parallel running. File conversion and production of documentation.
6. *Review and maintenance*: Monitoring the performance of the new system and repeating the systems analysis and design cycle where the new system has significant faults or omissions.

This is the oldest and most traditional of the three views of systems development that we shall consider. You will still find it referred to in more conservative areas of systems study like the manuals issued by some professional societies for the 'computer' or 'information technology' part of their qualification courses. De Marco (1978) and Yourdon (1978) quoted versions of the cycle as the context of their methods, and this has been kept up by more recent followers, e.g. Page-Jones (1980) or Kendall (1987). So we cannot dismiss this view out of hand; it is worth noting why versions of it still survive.

The first thing that we can note is that the view of analysis follows the derivative sequence we discussed in the previous section. The systems investigation stage corresponds exactly to the activity 'Record the existing physical system', and the systems analysis stage corresponds to the activities 'Define the logical system' and 'Define an improved logical system'. We have already shown that a widely used, contemporary method like SSADM follows this sequence; so this part of the traditional systems life cycle still survives.

A second thing to note is a point we made earlier, that the first stage is called Feasibility study. I promised to be critical of this, so here goes. The feasibility study 'looks at the aims and scope of the new system and its anticipated cost benefits...'. *What new system?* Until we come up with at least an outline specification, what are we 'looking at'? The feasibility study seems to be assessing something which isn't even logically defined until the end of stage 3 of the cycle.

I think we can understand how such an apparent contradiction appears in the cycle if we recall what we saw about the classic examples of the use of derivative methods. In those applications the opportunity for major innovation was limited. It was therefore possible to have an initial outline view of what the new system might entail and to come up with 'anticipated' values.

If we return to a modern derivative method like SSADM, we find that it accommodates the 'What new system?' objection by two modifications to the traditional systems life cycle view. Figure 7.5 shows the six stages of this method. First, we can see that the analysis stage is placed before the feasibility study. As Fig 7.4 shows, this stage of SSADM delivers a logical view of S_1 whose qualities can be provisionally 'anticipated'. Second, the sequence of stages includes the possibility of a two-pass cycle so that a provisional specification for the logical S_1 can then be analysed in greater depth and modified.

This last feature is an example of the important systems methodology concept of *iteration*. The application of most systems methods is a heuristic process, i.e. one of

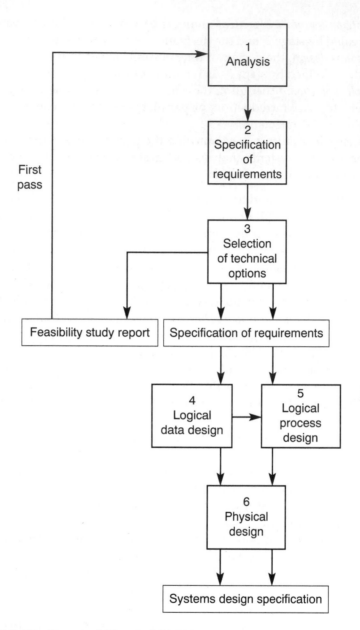

Fig 7.5 The Stages of Classic SSADM
These are the stages of SSADM as practised into the early 1990s. The most recent version, SSADM Version 4, has some modifications: Weaver (1993). The sequence of Feasibility Study, Requirements Analysis, Requirements Specification, and Technical Systems Options still remains as a lead into Logical and Physical Design.

discovery and learning (*see* Chapter 3). This means that the implications of what we did in the early stages often only become apparent in the later stages. If we find at these later stages that we made mistakes or left something out in the earlier ones, then we have to go back and repeat them, i.e. to iterate.

We took the traditional systems life cycle view as an example of derivative methodology. A good representative of innovative methodology is the information systems life cycle of Olle et al. (1988). Their detailed list contains 12 stages:

1. Strategic Study
2. Information Systems Planning
3. Business Analysis
4. Systems Design
5. Construction Design
6. Construction and Workbench Test
7. Installation
8. Test of Installed System
9. Operation
10. Extension and Maintenance
11. Phase Out
12. Post Mortem.

These authors regard stages 2–4, and to a 'lesser extent' 5, as the essential framework for their view. We will look at their view of these stages in more detail before discussing the whole.

Information Systems Planning has the purpose of determining the broad nature of the information requirements of the enterprise and its business objectives. It will also check on any existing information system strategy and investigate what objective it has laid down.

Business Analysis looks at the business to determine which of its activities may be covered by the information systems development process, what these activities involve, and the properties of any existing information system.

Systems Design is the 'prescriptive or definitive activity' which identifies the components of the system to be constructed and describes what they must do.

Construction Design involves how the system, which was designed in the previous stage, is to be constructed.

This view has the important feature that makes it innovative rather than derivative in its approach. It begins not with detailed analysis of the existing information system, but with the organization or business context and the needs of the enterprise. The authors focus, as we have done, on the crucial criterion of how we interpret the term analysis as being the distinguishing feature between modern and traditional views. They say: 'The term "business analysis" is used to refer to this stage in preference to the widely used term "system analysis". The reason for this choice is to emphasize that the business (or enterprise) is the subject of the analysis and not any kind of "system" (extant or proposed)'.

It is interesting to note how the whole sequence of stages as well as this view of analysis reflects a top-down approach to systems development we have already associated with innovative methods. Any method based on this view would be in line with this concept because it works top-down in stages 1–3 by considering the wider organizational systems context of the potential information system S_1.

A criticism that might be made of this view, however, is the relative position in the sequence of information systems planning and business analysis. The meanings given to these terms seem to suggest the wrong sequence, given the emphasis we have made in this book. We have conceived information as a component of control, and control as a component of management. It is difficult to conceive that planning an information system can precede an analysis of business needs. To be fair, this is not what Olle et al. are implying, but the use of terminology is confusing. It comes, I suspect, from the influence of Martin (1984) who saw innovative strategic planning and vigorous use of information systems as a driving force for organizational success. (But as we saw in Chapter 6, the 'driver', the information and control system, is not the central purpose system 'engine'.)

We will therefore look at a third view of the stages of systems development which I think best reflects the concepts of information systems in the context of control systems and hierarchy which we have followed in this book. This is the b-model of software development of Birrell and Ould (1988) shown in Fig 7.6.

In order to compare their view with the others we have considered, we should note two ways in which we are going to modify their uses of names:

1 They refer to software development, but their detailed review of methods and methodology shows that they are covering the wider field of information systems development which is our concern. From now on we will use the latter term for consistency.

2 They envisage the information systems development life cycle as being made up of phases which can be broken down into stages. Since their phases correspond to what our other views we have looked at call stages, we will use the term stages for consistency.

If we return to Fig 7.6 we can see why their view of information systems development fits into the context of control systems and hierarchy. What they call the development path is concerned with deciding what the system must be like, i.e. goal-setting. The system is then implemented, i.e. actuation. Having done this, the maintenance cycle assesses the performance of the working system, i.e. feedback. Where the system deviates from the goals laid down for it, maintenance either corrects this, i.e. first-order control, or carries out further development and modification, i.e. second-order control.

Birrell and Ould (B&O) see seven main stages to systems development. These are listed together with the pithy description which B&O give of what they do:

1. Project inception: decide to do something for some reason.
2. System definition: agree what is to be done.
3. System design: work out how to do it.
4. System production: do it.
5. System acceptance: have it accepted.
6. Post-acceptance development: look after it following delivery.
7. Project debriefing: look back on how it all went.

Besides describing the stages in this very effective way, they also raise the important issue of how stages can be delineated. How do we decide, for example, what is 'definition' and what is 'design'? We have already seen that in practice systems development includes a heurisitic function which results in iteration. This means that the stages can

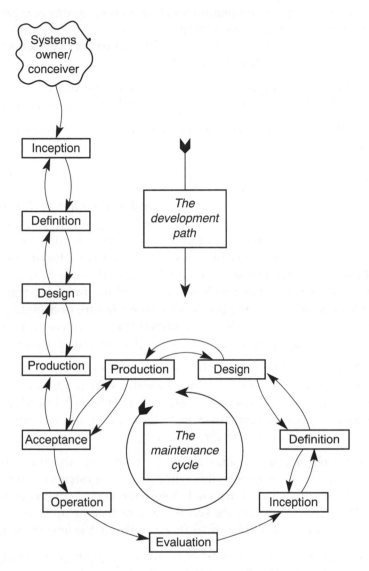

Fig 7.6 The 'b' model of Systems Development of Birrel and Ould (1985)
The role of the systems owner/conceiver is not part of the original, but
has been added to show the source of any system's weltanschauung.
Although quite old, I have yet to see a better control systems view of
systems development.

get blurred. We might find, for example, that we get some way through the production stage and then find there's something missing from the design. At this point
we've got to go back to fill in some detail. Are we now 'designing' or 'producing'?

Besides the kind of iteration which involves going back, there is another form
which involves looking forward. We don't start out on systems development without
having some initial, high-level view that the project is worth attempting. (I find this
broader view of what feasibility means more acceptable than the more detailed view

we criticized above.) This implies that some thought about design and production will already be taking place at the inception stage.

Given the practical necessity of iteration and the blurring of systems development stages, there are also dangers associated with it:

1 It becomes difficult to manage the systems development process through monitoring and control because we are not clear which goals have to be attained.

2 Systems development takes place on shifting foundations because the goal-setting itself is unclear.

We would see these two points as being a lack of clear first- and second-order control respectively.

There is a need therefore to define each stage and its boundaries. The answer to this need is seen by B&O in terms of *deliverables*. Each stage has to produce a specified output which in turn forms the input that the next stage needs before it can begin. Let's now look at the seven stages in terms of their deliverables or outputs, and the procedures or processes they must carry out to produce them.

Project inception is where we decide to do something for some reason. We have already discussed in detail the motivations based on failure or aspiration which provide reasons that make us decide to do something: i.e. move from S_0 to S_1. Our deliverable from this stage will therefore be some clear record or documentation of:

a *What the decision was.* This will include quite specific details like the name of the systems development project and its aims, as well as an analysis of its business or organizational context. What is it supposed to do? How is it intended to fit in with the wider management system? Answers to these questions will form a deliverable in the form of a requirements specification.

b *Who authorized the decision.* Besides defining down-to-earth aspects like who will pay for the systems development, this will define the systems owner(s). This more general responsibility is vital if we are to know whose system it is going to be. This knowledge is needed to resolve the soft issues which come up in the early stages of systems development. We shall look further into this in the next section.

c *The commitment.* This will identify what resources in terms of money, time, personnel and other resources are allocated to the project.

With the previous deliverables, the *system definition* process has to agree what is to be done. Given that we are committed, authorized and resourced to produce a system that will meet the requirements specification, we now need to translate this into:

a *A functional specification and logical systems model.* These will define what the system must do to be one that meets the specification. In practice this will be achieved using diagramming and other tools whose particular format will depend on the systems development method being used. The point here is the word what. It must be clear to the systems designer what the system is intended to achieve before it can be decided how it can be done.

b *A project management plan.* Once we have defined the system in terms of the previous deliverables, we are now in a position to draw up an initial management plan that defines two things. First, if we know what the system is intended to do, we can define quality standards for the system. Second, if we know what the system has to consist of, we can produce a scheduled breakdown of what has to be done in the later stages of design and production.

Following the completion of the previous stage, we now have a logical model of S_1. *System design* is the process of converting the logical model into a definition of how the system is constructed, a model of the physical S_1. We therefore see two deliverables from this stage:

a *A design specification.* The form of this will depend, like the functional specification and logical systems model, on the systems development method. The essential point about any design however is that it contains all the information needed to enable the systems builder to know how to construct the system.

b *A refined project management plan.* Having details of how the system is to be constructed, we are now in a position to clarify the project plan in terms of estimating time and other resource requirements. We can also now match the skills of people on the design team to the various construction tasks and get more informed estimates from them of what the job entails.

System production is the construction of the working system which corresponds to the design. If we are talking in terms of a mainly computerized information system with supporting manual procedures, then the major construction task is the creation of working software. The main deliverables will therefore be the software itself plus the necessary definition of its complete systems implementation:

a *Working software.* The computer implementation of the design specification.

b *Documentation.* Very little working software is entirely self-explanatory. Accompanying documentation will help both the users and new members of the computer systems team understand it, and how it fits into the whole of the new system.

c *Training schedules.* To support the implementation of the vital human component of the whole system.

d *Acceptance test description.* To provide an agreed set of procedures that will define that the job of the production team is complete.

e *Systems conversion schedule.* Once the system has been accepted, the users will need clear instructions for full implementation. The analogy here is with the acceptance of any product from a producer. In these circumstances you expect an instruction manual, or something similar, to tell you what you have to do and in what order. For information systems the main issue is usually how the new system is introduced or how the changeover from the old is made.

System acceptance is experiencing the system in action and accepting it. Notice that the implication of this statement is that there is once more a deliverer and a receiver involved, just as there was in the transition between all the previous stages. The important point here is that the deliverer is likely to be a specialist information system team, and the receiver is management. When we look at systems development as a system at the end of this chapter, we shall say more about the roles of the people involved. Meanwhile, we can identify the main deliverables as:

a *A record of acceptance.* Given the important change in the nature of those involved, acceptance is a likely area of political argument and apportionment of 'blame' if the system doesn't deliver. It therefore makes sense to formalize the acceptance that the system does indeed fulfil what was laid down by the initial stages of the systems development process.

b *Monitoring procedures.* The car might be working perfectly well when you drive it out of the dealer's showroom, but what do you do to keep it that way? So with systems acceptance: what are the procedures which enable both the producer and the user to agree what checks should be made to ensure that the system continues to work successfully?

Post-acceptance development is described by B&O as 'look after it following delivery'. I think that this is where our control systems view would make us modify their description of this stage in relation to the deliverables they define. Their main deliverables from this stage are:

a *Systems longevity.* The deliverable if, to quote B&O, you 'look after' a system should be a system that keeps going, or has longevity: but we would not call this process 'development'. Instead, we are describing the concept of a systems definition (goals) that continues to be implemented in the face of (environmental) disturbances. I think the term maintenance used by B&O in Fig 7.6 is more appropriate. It rightly implies the process of trying to ensure that the defined system (goals) is maintained (first-order control).

b *Record of systems performance.* Yes, the implication here is that we will wish to record how well the working information system conformed to the defined system (goals). Why should this be of interest? The answer is easily interpreted in terms of our hierarchical control model: a record of systems performance represents feedback on the implementation of the goals defined for the systems development process with a view to what the next stage, project debriefing, will require. When we go on to look at what this final stage involves, we shall see that it is concerned with higher-order control: goal-setting and the reasoning behind it.

The process of *project debriefing* is described by B&O as 'look back on how it all went'. This will mean that we review the experience of the systems development process and analyse the record of systems performance. When we do this we are not merely involved in a kind of spectator sport where we might say, 'OK, that wasn't too bad' or 'Didn't we do well!' There are deliverables from this process in the form of:

a *Critical evaluation of method.* We can now make informed comment on the pros and cons of the particular method we chose. This is second-order control feedback because it is feedback on our goal-setting in the form of the defined method.

b *Critical evaluation of methodology.* Our critical experience also allows us to review the principles that we used to choose the particular method that we did. This amounts to the study of method, i.e. methodology. Since we are now reviewing the process of goal-setting, we can see this as a form of higher-order control.

Both of these deliverables can be seen as a form of learning.

Given our critical analysis of three representative views of the systems development process, we now need to choose one we can refer to when discussing particular methods. Figure 7.7 represents a view virtually identical to B&O, but with modifications to emphasize:

Stage 1. The strategic context of information systems development.
Stage 2. The role of analysis in defining the logical S_1.
Stage 6. Concept of control by use of the term maintenance.
Stage 7. Concept of higher-order control by inclusion of the term methodology.

The mention of strategy leads us naturally to the subject of the next section. When we consider the strategic context of the information system and information systems development, we look at the management system and the whole business and organizational system itself. This will involve us in the soft human and policy components of these systems and the messes at the earliest stage of the systems development process. Since the process will not be able to pass this first stage until these soft aspects are covered, we need to consider how we deal with messes.

7.3.5 Dealing with messes

When we considered derivative and innovative methods earlier in this chapter, we found that both were dependent on the condition that 'we anticipate that our needs are definable in hard terms'. We know from our study of systemic properties in Chapter 3 and our consideration of problems and messes earlier in this chapter that this will not be the case for the needs of the wider management system, or the whole

```
1. Strategy and Inception
2. Definition and Analysis
3. Design
4. Production
5. Acceptance
6. Maintenance
7. Debriefing, Learning and Methodology
```

Fig 7.7 The Phases of Systems Development of Harry (1990)
A view which is very close to both Birrell & Ould (1985) and Olle et al. (1988). The main feature is the emphasis on setting information systems development in the context of the organizational or business need, rather than reference to existing systems.

business or organizational system itself. Needs at these higher systems levels bring us up against questions of value judgement, policy decision, conflict, and other soft issues that make for messes rather than clear-cut technical problems.

Modern views of the methods of systems development based on Fig 7.7 emphasize the strategic context of the information system and information systems development. They involve us in messes at their earliest stage. Failure to recognize that messes cannot be solved by methods intended for hard problems has been a common cause of failure in systems development. An example of how this lesson has been learned can be seen in Fig 7.8, taken from Cutts (1987). If we consider the terms well-structured and ill-structured, we can see that they closely correspond to the properties of a situation that lead us to describe it as a problem or mess respectively. The message of Fig 7.8 is that SSADM is not likely to be successful if applied mechanically to a messy situation for which it is not suitable.

This lesson will apply to any systems development method whose main concern is information systems development. Messes are a wider management systems issue, and need to be sorted before we start the process of information systems development. If dealing with messes has to take place at the beginning of the strategy and inception stage, and precede any further move with systems development, what can 'dealing with messes' involve?

We can investigate this issue by returning to the meliorist model of Fig 7.2 and relating it to the criteria of Fig 7.1. We said that the criteria of Fig 7.1 involved agreement as to the boundary, separation, responsibility, information requirements and description of the problem if it was not to be regarded as a mess. Hence the initial stage of systems development requires us to identify where we are now, S_0, and where we would like to be, S_1. The deliverable required by any such systems development method is *clarification* of S_0 and S_1.

For this reason, when we come to look at information system development methods later in this chapter, we need first to consider what approaches or methods are available to clarify the soft issues involved in any mess before we move on to information system development itself.

Parameter	Well-structured	Ill-structured
Objectives	Clear	Vague
Problem areas	Known	In dispute
Requirements	Defined	Intuitive
Communication	Reliable	Unreliable
Attitudes	Cooperative	Obstructive

Fig 7.8 Well-structured Conditions Needed for the Appropriate Application of SSADM
This derives from an early work by Cutts (1987), but is still relevant comment on the method.

7.3.6 Signposts for a problem–method road map

Our consideration of the terms problem, mess, approach, method and methodology has now led us to consider how:

a. Problems and messes: concerns with what we have, what we want and the differences between them (S_0 and S_1 in Fig 7.2)

can be related to:

b. Approaches and methods: concerns with how we hope to improve our position (the arrow in Fig 7.2).

To understand how such a relationship can be described, it is worth summarizing which attributes of problem, mess, approach, method and methodology we need to take account of.

The differences between problems and messes are summarized in Fig 7.1 and have been discussed in detail above. The essential distinction between them is that problems are seen as hard and messes as soft. Individual problems can be considered to lie somewhere in a range from being exclusively hard at the top end and exclusively soft at the bottom, with most real-life ones being somewhere in between. The vertical axis in Fig 7.9 represents such a range.

Approaches and methods essentially differ in terms of how formally they are structured. Methods have defined sequences of stages and the deliverables associated with them: they are structured and rational. Approaches use sets of principles to achieve final deliverables, but no fixed sequence of stages or actions is laid down for them. Approaches are therefore unstructured and empirical. In practice we saw that procedures like iteration meant that methods were not completely formal in their structure. We can also imagine that an overall informal approach might include the use of some

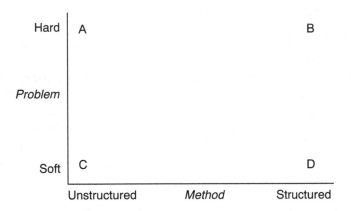

Fig 7.9 Combining Problems and Methods
Problems can have characteristics that place them on a spectrum of soft to hard. Methods may range from being tightly structured to being open, unstructured approached. In principle, combinations can occur anywhere in the range shown by the diagram, but the regions A, B, C, D are used to illustrate the major types of combination.

formal methods. For example, an informal talk introducing a new system to users might include a structured run through its main features. So in practice, approaches and methods can be thought to lie on a spectrum which ranges from the very informal and unstructured to the very formal and structured. This is the horizontal axis in Fig 7.9.

The whole of Fig 7.9, taken from Harry (1987), shows the range of possibilities that can occur in principle when we match the hard/soft range of possible problems to the structured/unstructured range of possible approaches. On the basis of this relationship, we can recognize four positions A, B, C and D. These represent the extremes of a range of combinations of problem and approach that we can conceive as being possible. While it will be rare to find combinations represented exactly by these corner positions in practice, we can use them and the whole of Fig 7.9 as part of a 'road map' to illustrate the features that tend to be shown by particular application of approaches to problems.

Position A represents the situation where an unstructured approach is applied to a hard problem. This means that the problem itself is clearly defined, has objectively measurable criteria for success and all the other hard properties of Fig 7.1. The approach, however, is unstructured and informal. Here we can imagine someone using inspiration, 'feel', guesses, trial and error, and many other unstructured ways of facing hard realities. Sometimes this approach will result in spectacular success, sometimes spectacular failure, and perhaps quite often rather mixed results.

A common example of this combination in the systems development field is the use of *prototyping*. Here the potential user and the systems developer work together in a relaxed and unstructured way to build up a usable system bit by bit. This can be done by using friendly software such as a 4GL (Chapter 5), with possible graphical support like that discussed later in this chapter.

Position B represents the situation where a structured approach or method is applied to a hard problem. This extreme position might be illustrated by the example of a qualified professional applying a body of well defined techniques in a situation where the problem is clear, and success or failure are clearly defined. An example of this in information systems development might be the normalization of data as part of the application of a tightly structured method like SSADM to an agreed system specification.

Position C represents the situation where an unstructured approach, as in position A, is now applied to a soft problem. Here we envisage a situation where there is dispute about what the problem actually is, conflicting values, and many of the other messy aspects of soft problems. An unstructured approach to such problems amounts to a very open situation. In practice it could include a very rich range of activities from inspired creation to muddle, or from political in-fighting to enjoying friendly cooperation. The main examples in practice of this position on our road map will come from the human activity component of systems development. We shall say more about this aspect when we look at systems development itself as a system towards the end of this chapter.

Position D is the last of our illustrative positions on the 'road map'. Here we consider the application of a structured approach or method to a soft problem. The situation represented is one where an attempt is made to deal with disputes about the nature of the problem, conflicting values and so on as in position C, but to approach the mess systematically. The idea of having a structured approach to a mess may seem instinctively wrong. If most messes have their origin in human activity, it seems unlikely that anything as elusive and subtle as a human being can be successfully dealt with like a machine. (I am reminded of a colleague who said that trying to organize academics was rather like trying to herd cats.) In practice we do use quite formal structures to organize how we deal with soft human issues like taste, opinion, etc. Courts, political elections and formal negotiations are all structured approaches to very messy issues.

In the systems development field we are most likely to be in position D when we are trying to deal with messes at the earlier strategy and inception, and definition and analysis, stages of systems development. Here, as we saw in the previous section, we are still likely to be concerned with the wider management system aspects of the problem which have to be clarified before proceeding to systems development.

This last reasoning means that in the next section we shall look at methods for dealing with messes in the management systems context before going on to the examples of information systems development methods.

One other important aspect now follows from the important issue of matching methods to problems, which does not appear in Fig 7.9. This is an analysis of what the term structured can mean in the context of systems methodology.

If we look back to see when we have used the word structure so far, there are two principal ways in which we have used the term:

1. The structure of a system
2. The structure of a method.

The structure of a system has been used to describe the form of the relationship between the interacting components of a system within the systems hierarchy. Structure of a method has been used to describe the organization of the actions needed for the process of systems development into the stages which make up the method. In this, and the previous section, we have been talking about the structure of the method.

If we look at the way in which individual methods are structured, we will find that the structure of a method is often determined by what view is taken of the system being developed. We know from Chapter 3 that there are many aspects of a system which may be important, but the relationship between structure and process is one which can have a major effect on the method of creating or modifying a system: i.e. systems development. We will find that the particular stages which occur in a method, and their sequential order, is influenced by the relative emphasis given to the structure or the processes of a system.

We can illustrate this issue with a simple example. If I look at my 'clothing' system while I am writing this, one of its structural features is the relationship between my socks and my shoes: like most other people I wear my socks inside my shoes. The fact that such a structural relationship exists also says something about the process of clothing myself. If my socks are inside my shoes, then when I dress in the morning I have to put my socks on before I put on my shoes. I can therefore describe my clothing system in two ways. I can either say 'I wear my socks inside my shoes', or I can say 'I put my socks on first and then I put on my shoes'. The first way defines my clothing system in terms of structure, the second in terms of process.

When we consider the structure of many of the methods for information systems development, we find that they tend towards one of two types:

1. Structure-oriented methods
2. Process-oriented methods.

Structure-oriented methods start from a viewpoint, which we first considered in Chapter 1, that information is data organized into a particular structure. When we look at how such methods approach systems development they take some form of detailing of this data structure as their starting point for describing an existing system or defining a new one. Once these structures have been established, the processes needed for their production can then be derived from them. Once we know that socks lie inside shoes we can derive the dressing procedure needed to produce such a structure.

Process-oriented methods start from a viewpoint, which we also first considered in Chapter 1, that a system does something, and what an information system does is to take raw data and process it in such a way that it produces the information we want. Methods based on this view take as their starting point a coordinated description or definition of what processes the existing system carries out, or what a new system will have to.

Structure and process are not mutually exclusive however. Instead we see them as complementary views which contribute to a holist view of a system. Similarly, when we talk of a structure- or process-oriented view of methods, we are not pretending that these are mutually exclusive categories. Good systems development methods will have to take account of both structure and process because systems themselves have both these properties. For this reason we use the word *oriented* to indicate emphasis rather than exclusive classification. When we come to look at examples of particularly oriented methods later in the chapter, we shall also explore how strong the particular orientation happens to be. When we do this, we shall find that real methods usually have some features which do not conform to their overall orientation.

If the previous paragraph has led you to look ahead in the chapter you will see that a third orientation is covered. *Object-oriented* approaches are based on the most recent of the three views we consider. The rise of object-oriented methods is an example of methodology in its true sense of 'the study of method'. As we saw in section 7.3.4, true methodology involves a learning process. What the pioneers of object-oriented methods found was that many of the problems of systems software implementation could be avoided or reduced in seriousness if systems builders learned from their experience. The design and implementation of modern software applications can be complicated enough without those involved re-inventing the wheel. The simplification and introduction of consistency into any task, including systems development, makes it easier to achieve and less prone to error while it is being carried out.

The important product of the learning that comes from an object-oriented approach is the recognition of how concepts of hierarchy and classification can be used for simplification and the introduction of consistency in systems development. We can return to our sock and shoe example to make the point. My method for dressing needs to cover other articles of clothing apart from my shoes and socks. Thus, in the winter I wear a vest next to my skin, a shirt outside that and a sweater on top. We notice that this structure of one item of clothing on top of another is another example of the relationship we've already seen between sock and shoe. It is no surprise therefore that the similarities between sock–shoe structure and the vest–shirt or shirt–sweater structures means that the methods I use to achieve these systems structures are also similar. I can say quite generally that if the structure is:

outer garment
containing
inner garment
containing
body

then the method is:

1. Put inner garment on body.
2. Put outer garment on inner garment.

Once I build up an understanding of structural relationships by using the concepts of hierarchy and classification, these simplify my future systems development and make it less prone to error by enabling me to recognize how I can re-use or adapt features of successful existing systems. If I decide to wear my underpants inside my trousers, I no longer need to develop a management from first principles. If like a particular popular female singer I decide to wear a corset on the outside, I only need to recognize it as an outer garment to automatically adapt the dressing method.

We can now see why object-orientation is a more recent approach to systems development because it depends on having had some experience to classify.

Two final concepts will help us make sense of the range of systems development methods. These are described by the terms *top-down* and *bottom-up*. The relationship between the concepts of systems hierarchy and emergent property is the key to our understanding of these terms. The words 'top' and 'bottom' refer to the systems hierarchy itself. Thus top-down means looking at the whole system before looking at the components as we descend the systems hierarchy; while bottom-up means starting with the lowest elements before looking at rising aggregations through subsystems to the whole system itself.

When systems development methods are referred to as top-down the implication is that the method begins by referring to the characteristics or needs of the whole existing (S_0) or desired (S_1) system before detailing what these will mean for its components. We can see that a top-down approach is implied by the view of typical stages of systems development we adopted at the end of section 7.3.4. In that section we noted that a modern view of analysis is that it involves breaking down the high-level, strategic specification for S_1, the desired system, into the implications of that specification for the goals of the system components. An example of this might be that we would decide that a system for dog registration ought to be difficult to avoid, before we decided how the subsystem file which recorded dog owners ought to be updated. Whats before hows is the essence of a systemic top-down approach.

At this point in our study of systems methodology we need to realize that 'top-down' is used colloquially to mean something very different. This other use of the term is emotionally pejorative. In everyday life, 'top-down' is frequently used to mean that a higher authority imposes its will on those below. 'Top-down' might mean, for example, that a local coucil would exterminate stray dogs whether the majority of its citizens liked it or not. The reason for the difference between our use of the term and the colloquial use is that a systems hierarchy is different from the organizational or political view. As we have emphasized since Chapters 3 and 4: a systems hierarchy is about levels of aggregation, not about 'who is the boss of who'.

This analysis then leads us to the question of what role the concept bottom-up has in a systemic view of systems development. Given that a system is a holist concept, trying to describe or define the properties of a system's components before identifying the system itself seems like a contradiction in terms. We don't know whether something is a component until we know what it is supposed to be a component of. For this reason a bottom-up approach is not normally applied to the initial stages of systems development as defined in Fig 7.7. The strategy and definition stages refer to the whole system, and it would not make sense to try and design the components of a system before having a design for the structure of the whole. Imagine going ahead with the design of an invoice document before even knowing whether the whole system was going to be concerned with order processing anyway!

A bottom-up approach does make sense however in the production and later stages of systems development. Systems, like anything else that is constructed, are built by creating and assembling components. The whole can only come into existence after the parts or components, since the whole cannot exist without them. We therefore see that the normal view of systems development is that we *design top-down* and we *construct bottom-up*.

I have twice used the term 'normal' to describe this view of the two approaches. When we come to look at Jackson Systems Development and prototyping, we shall see apparently different views, but I hope to show that this difference is only one of emphasis.

7.4 METHODOLOGY AND MANAGING SYSTEMS DEVELOPMENT

7.4.1 Systems development as an organizational system that has to be managed

Developing an information, or any other kind of system, is *an activity aimed at achieving something desirable*. I use italics for this last phrase because it is a direct quote from section 3.2.1. My aim is to recall the important concept of the relation between *management*, *control* and *information* we covered in Chapter 3 and is summarized in Fig 3.4.

We can then relate this to the *meliorist model* of Fig 7.2, by seeing systems development itself as a *system*. Systems development *transforms* any existing situation or system, S_0, into a desired system S_1, as in Fig 7.10. If we are concerned with the *management* of systems development, then this transformation process needs to be *controlled*.

So far, our interpretation of the role of control in systems development has focussed on the use of methods or approaches to deal with problems or messes. In section 7.3.1 we introduced the relationship of method to control, and in section 7.3.4 we went further to show how a model like that of Birrell & Ould in Fig 7.6 spelled out the role of *learning* in the goal-setting process.

If we now go on to consider the wider context of the *management* of systems development, then all our studies so far would tell us that management is more than just method. So what role does method play in management? Once we realize that systems development is itself a system that has to be managed, we can draw some simple analogies with other managed systems to understand the answer to this question. In Carry-Out Cupboards we would expect that there are methods for assembling the various components of a kit. In MX Marketing, Ben Lister will have an approach to selling his products. What is obvious in these examples is that we would not expect the kits to assemble themselves, or the products to sell themselves. As we saw in Chapter 6, a *systems* view of management recognizes that many different components have to work together in order that management of any organization can pursue its *central purpose*.

As we saw in Section 6.1, a systems view of organizations tells us that the term *organization* does not refer to the name on the company notepaper or on a manager's office door. Organizations as systems are seen in terms of what goes on behind the labels. In the case of systems development, this means that we look at *what* is involved in the transformation process of Fig 7.10, rather than labels like 'IT Manager' or 'Systems Analyst'. Hence the term *organization*, in the context of systems development, refers to the system of components involved in the *central purpose* of transforming the existing system or situation, S_0, into a desired system S_1. This might be a specialist firm of external consultants, or something more complex like the mixed team of the George Michaelson Mini-Case.

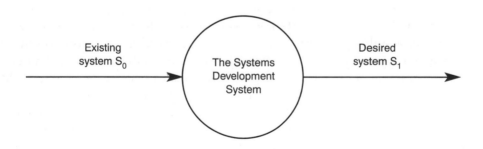

Existing system S_0 → The Systems Development System → Desired system S_1

Fig 7.10 Systems Development as a Transformation Process
The aim of systems development is to replace the existing system or situation, S_0, with the desired system, S_1.

Such a view enables us to look at systems development in terms of the information and management systems model of Figs 6.1 and 6.2. If we do this we can distinguish:

a A *central purpose subsystem* for systems development which is concerned with the process of transforming S_0 into S_1.

b *Central purpose support subsystems* concerned with enabling this transformation process by providing its various needs.

So systems development means much more than method. We know from Chapter 6 that the central purpose subsystem uses financial, human, and facilities components provided by the central purpose support subsystems, and that all these have to be co-ordinated by the corporate planning and control subsystem. There are, therefore, many aspects of the systems development process which it will share with other forms of *project management*.

The need for *financial* support will mean that any systems development project will have to be looked at as the allocation of money to an investment from which we expect a return. Standard financial techniques, such as investment appraisal using discounted cash flow analysis, will be as relevant to the installation of a new information system as they would be to building a new factory. The costs of systems development will need to be budgeted for and controlled just like any other form of management spending. Systems development does tend to be, however, a project area where lack of promised return and poorly controlled overspending are common. We have already identified that a major reason for this is lack of clear *systems definition and specification*. When we talk of 'poor financial control' in systems development we are often blaming the financial subsystem for something beyond its boundaries. If we have poor definition of the system we are trying to develop, it is hardly surprising that we can't determine and control the costs of creating it. The lesson is therefore that clear definition and specification of the central purpose of systems development will be a major influence on the success of its financial control.

The *human* or *personnel* support for systems development will also include most of the activities found in other forms of project management. Issues such as skills, training, motivation, equal opportunities, or whatever, are as likely to be present in the management of a systems development project as they are in the mounting of a major marketing programme or opening a new pub. What makes systems development different from these examples is the often complex *roles* of those involved. As we shall see in the next section, systems development can be a process in which the marketing manager is also the customer, or the pub drinker has to help brew his own beer.

The *facilities* subsystem will be called upon to provide much the same type of resources for systems development as it does for many other forms of project management. Systems development requires desks and chairs for its staff in well lit, heated and ventilated offices and all the other paraphernalia of late 20th-century organizational life. But the development of *information* systems brings a special feature. In Chapter 6 we saw that a banking system has to distinguish between the money which it processes in its central purpose subsystem and the money provided by its financial subsystem for its use. Similarly, information systems development needs to distinguish between the information system it uses to help manage its activities and the information which will be used by the developed system S_1.

If this seems a complex point, consider the example of George Michaelson. He needed all sorts of information in order to understand PROPS. Some of this information was about why PROPS didn't work. This wasn't part of the PROPS system, but it was relevant to the management of its further development. The information that George gained about the working relationship between the production and inspection functions at Technoturbines was an example of this kind of information. The other kind of information was information actually used by the information system itself. An example of this would be the information that the inspectors were supposed to key into the computer about the jobs processed in the factory.

As far as the facilities subsystem is concerned, the existence of these two kinds of information can lead to a potential confusion when considering the use of *computers* as a facility provided to support systems development. In this situation, besides being a facility, the computer is also a potential *component* of the desired system S_1. This happens when we use *prototyping* and *CASE* tools. We introduced methods and tools like these at the end of Chapter 5 and we shall say more about them in Chapter 8. They enable the desired system S_1 to be developed on the computer itself using software designed to help the development process. This can make systems development very quick and easy; and there is the danger that it is all to easy to blindly accept existing hardware as the basis for the new system, so that the facilities subsystem which is supposed to support the central purpose starts to control it instead. The facilities subsystem tail starts to wag the central purpose dog.

When considering the role of the *corporate planning and control* subsystem in systems development, I am still surprised how often the subject of project management is not seen as relevant. Final year and postgraduate students who are also following courses in project management can successfully learn techniques such as PERT or critical path analysis and use computer software for their application. Yet they seem not to realize that these techniques could be used to schedule an information systems development project as it can for a piece of civil engineering. But perhaps the students are not as unthinking as I imply. You notice I used the words *could be used*. The essential ingredient to using PERT or any other scheduling technique is that we have a complete and clear definition of the activities that have to be carried out to complete a project, and we know what sequence or order they can be done in. This is often not the case with information systems development, where the definition and specification of the central purpose is the major problem.

Our analysis of the role of the various central purpose support subsystems in systems development shows why *method* seems to be such an important issue when we think about managing the process. The major problem we are likely to face in systems development is not that we don't know how to do discounted cash flow calculations, calculate a budget, train people, light a room or draw a critical path network. These are all well established management activities. But we can only carry out these activities in *support* of the central purpose of systems development if we know what systems development is trying to achieve. In terms of the meliorist model of Fig 7.2, if we don't know what S_1 is, how can we aim the arrow?

If we therefore appear to concentrate on information systems development methodology, rather than the broader issues of the financial, human, and facilities components provided by the central purpose support subsystems, it is not because we are forgetting about holism. Instead, we are trying to focus on those particular issues which often make systems development management particularly complex.

7.4.2 Issues in the relationships between four major components of the systems development process

Figure 7.11 identifies four important components of the systems development process which are involved with the achievement of its central purpose, the production of the desired system S_1:

1. The client.
2. The systems developer.
3. The problem.
4. The method.

As we saw in the previous section, these four are just a small selection from the range of components that are involved. They are especially significant, however, in giving the systems development process its particular characteristics.

When interpreting Fig 7.11 it is important to note that it is a systems diagram and that it takes a *conceptual* view. Thus, following the approach of Chapter 6, the terms client and developer refer to *roles* rather than names of people or official jobs descriptions. Likewise, the terms *problem* and *method* reflect the views of problems, messes, approaches and methods found earlier in this chapter.

As components of a *system*, the client, developer, problem and method interact (section 3.1.5). Looking at the way they interact will help us understand some of the important management issues of systems development.

7.4.3 Issues of problem–method interaction

We have already looked at the relationship between problems and methods in section 7.3.6, but the interaction between these components in systems development raises three further important issues:

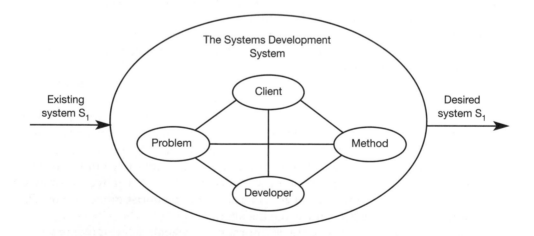

Fig 7.11 Components of the Systems Development System
The diagram shows roles rather than individuals. Thus, one person could play a part as Developer and Client. It is also important to note that the components interact, with effects on each other.

1. Are there particular methods which lend themselves to particular types of problem? Thus if we understand a problem, does this automatically mean that we will choose a particular method?
2. Does a bias towards a particular method mean that the problem will be defined in a particular way?
3. After we start to explore and understand a particular problem, are we likely to change the method?

The answer to the first of these questions seems to be yes, if we observe what happens in real life. If my computer software appears to have a bug in it, I am most likely to bring in a software expert who will use some very specific software methods to try and solve my problem. It is not likely that I would apply a method which analysed my whole business system or call in the methods of medical pathology.

Is it necessarily desirable to associate certain kinds of method with certain kinds of problem? Could it be that any association is more to do with laziness or inertia? Flood and Jackson consider the issue of the relationship between problems and methods when advocating the policy of 'Total Systems Intervention' or 'TSI'. They review six systems methods:

1. System Dynamics
2. Viable System Diagnosis
3. Strategic Assumption Surfacing and Testing
4. Interactive Planning
5. Soft Systems Methodology
6. Critical Systems Heuristics

They conclude that while particular methods may be associated with 'ideal-type' problem situations, this association depends on the perception of the problems themselves. Since different people may see different problems in the same situation, so different perceptions of an appropriate method are also possible.

While Flood and Jackson are concerned with broad systems methodology rather than specifically information systems development methodology, their conclusions agree with our studies too. In Chapter 3 we made clear the role of the information system as a component of the management system. We established that any system is someone's concept. Any links that are seen between problems and methods are therefore likely to reflect which particular personal concepts of the problem are actually involved. Later in this section we will see that the client and the developer are likely to be the most important sources of personal concepts of the problem, and we shall study the issues further when covering the problem–client and problem–developer relationships.

Our second question on the problem–method relationship was whether a bias towards a particular method means that the problem will be defined in a particular way? I think the answer to this question is also yes. Just as eyes tell us about light while ears tell us about sound, so particular methods of analysing problems will bring out those features of the problem which the method is best at dealing with. The problem is therefore very likely to reflect the methods applied to it. We shall say more of this when considering the use of the rich picture of the Soft Systems Methodology in Chapter 8.

Our final question was whether, once we start to explore and understand a particular problem, we are likely to change the method as we progress. Here again I think that the answer is yes. The concept of reflective goal-setting (section 3.2.4) tells us that feedback on the success of particular methods can lead to modifications or changes in their use. An example of this is SSADM (section 7.3.3). Despite being a 'standard' method, it has gone through four major modifications.

7.4.4 Issues of problem–client interaction

The client is a potential source of the values or weltanschauung on which the desired system S_1 is going to be based. To understand the problem–client interaction we therefore need to answer three important questions about the client:

1. Client *identity*. Who is the client?
2. Client *perception*. What does the client consider the problem to be?
3. Client *motivation*. What does the client want from the solution of the problem?

We begin to answer these questions by reminding ourselves that the term *client* refers to a *role*. Thus when my wife and I first developed a spreadsheet program to do our quarterly VAT accounts for our business, we discussed what sort of information we wanted from the program and how we wanted it presented on the screen. Both of us, as potential users, had inputs into deciding what was wanted from the system; and we were attempting to develop a system for both of us to use. Since the client role involved more than one person, the concept of client perceptions was an *emergent property* which came from the interaction of the individual components of the client role, i.e. my wife and myself.

For a small close partnership like this, and a simple problem like doing VAT on a spreadsheet, the problem–client relationship was pretty easy to deal with; but what of larger, more complex problems? An example of this might be the changes in UK taxation procedures known as 'self-assessment' which came into force in 1996. Potential clients of this system could be the Inland Revenue staff who have to work it, the accountants who may make money out of it, or the taxpayer who has to suffer it. It's hard to imagine them all assembled in Wembley Stadium informally agreeing their perceptions of the problem; both their large number and their different *motivations* prevent this.

In all situations where small-scale, informal procedures will not answer the questions of client identity, perception and motivation, a more *formal* or *structured* method is needed. This will have to incorporate the following criteria if it is to overcome the *mess* of a complex client role:

1. Clarification of the client role must *precede* definition of the problem
2. Definition of both client and problem must be a *deliverable* from the *inception* phase of the chosen method.

These criteria raise what are essentially management rather than information systems issues, and many so-called 'computer' or 'information systems' problems stem from failing to meet them. However, the problems of clarifying the client role cannot be dismissed as a problem that has nothing to do with information systems development methodology. As we shall see in Chapter 8, when exploring *soft systems methodology* and *integrated methods*, attempts have been made to recognize the human role in systems development.

7.4.5 Issues of problem–developer interaction

The developer role, like the client role, raises questions of subjectivity and values:

1. Can the developer be separated from the problem?
2. Does the developer distort the problem?

If the developer role is a *component* of the systems development *system*, then we know that the answer to the first question is no, and that the answer to the second question is yes.

The assertion that the developer role cannot be separated from the problem is a particular example of the principle that the components of a system *interact*. The developer will interact with other components of the systems development system, including the problem itself. Reference to the George Michaelson Mini-Case can be used to illustrate this, since it is based on a real experience. The existing system at Technoturbines was itself the product of systems developers. Also, the acceptance that there were problems with the existing system, and the particular view of those problems, was partly the result of the developer's contribution. If George had decided that it was purely a question of forcing production and inspection to keep to the formal system, the view of the problem would have been very different.

In practice, therefore, it is difficult to talk about problems without talking about developers. Developers, like clients, are part of any perception of the problem.

The George Michaelson Mini-Case example could also be interpreted to show how developers distort the problem. As we saw, after a few hours on the night shift, George decided that the problem was different from what had originally been alleged. His presence actually *disturbed* the original perception. As in Section 4.3, *measurement*, or any other form of observation, *disturbs*.

7.4.6 Issues of developer–method interaction

When considering the interaction of the developer and the method, we could say that the link is true by definition. Whatever actions the developer carries out to develop a system will be a manifestation of the method, however good or bad it is. Similarly, anyone who carries actions which are part of the systems development is fulfilling the role of developer. Hence the real question is not whether there is much significant connexion between developer and method, but what form this connexion takes. In practical systems development this raises two important questions:

1. What are the motives of the developer when choosing a method?
2. Should the developer change or modify a chosen systems method?

The motives of a developer when choosing a method are not likely to be confined to a straight technical decision about the links between problems and methods we covered in section 7.4.3. Not only is the perception of the problem influenced by who the developer is; the developer will also have views about choices of method even before knowing about the problem. For example, it isn't hard to imagine that once an organization has invested time, money and human skills to develop a team skilled in a particular systems development method, that it won't turn to this method first when confronted with a systems development problem.

Having a bias towards certain methods even before we understand the problem may not be as obviously wrong as it seems. If we take a systems view of systems development as in Fig 7.11, the effectiveness of the systems development process is an emergent property coming from the interaction of *all* the components, including the human ones. Thus the ideal method for a particular problem badly executed may not give such successful results as a less ideal method carried out well. A good driver in a Robin Reliant is more likely to be a successful motorist than a fool in a Rolls-Royce.

The danger of sticking to what you are good at, however, is that no *learning* or *adaption* takes place. Since the control component of management must adapt to environmental disturbance and learn from them, so good systems development methodology includes the ability to change or modify a chosen systems method: thus answering our second question.

7.4.7 Issues of developer–client interaction

We have already touched on one of the major issues of this relationship: that of *roles*.

Developer and client are the names of roles which different people can take at different times. Thus in the small-scale example of my wife and I developing a VAT system, sometimes I would make suggestions as to how the spreadsheet could be arranged to meet something my wife wanted, sometimes these roles were exchanged. Who was the developer and who the client? At various times we both played both roles, where one was client and said what they needed, and the other was developer trying to produce systems features to meet these needs. Even in larger organizations with more formal job definitions, this exchange still occurs. The kind of investigating that George Michaelson carried out is similar to what most developers have to do in the early stages of a project, when they try to understand the existing situation S_0 and its problems. Where the people who are questioned give replies and help out with information, they are contributing to the development process, and it would be a very arrogant and foolish systems professional who didn't recognize this.

The importance of *participation* in the development process is sometimes misinterpreted. Just as the concept of control can be misinterpreted as implying an authoritarian style of management, so participation can be misinterpreted as an assertion of democracy and fair play. In practice, a wide participation in the developer role is necessary for two reasons:

1. The knowledge of the existing situation S_0, which is essential for successful systems development, is likely to be spread well beyond those formally concerned with systems development.
2. Involvement of the client in the development process is a means of ensuring satisfaction, commitment and understanding of the product of systems development.

Recent developments in *prototyping* have helped to blur the client and developer roles further. As we shall see in Chapter 8, the use of *visual programming* enables a non-specialist to explore on a computer screen with the help of the specialist, or even unaided, different possibilities for the outputs from the desired system. Examples of this would include menus, pictorial screen models of how the system would work, or layouts for printed documents. Once decided, the software can automatically develop the programming procedures to produce them. The need for *expertise*, which separated the client and developer roles in the 1970s and early 1980s, is disappearing.

7.4.8 Issues of client–method interaction

Given the blurring of the client and developer roles it is worth considering when this is most likely to occur in whatever method is used in the development process.

In small-scale development, like my VAT example above, the blurring is likely to occur throughout the systems development process because a small number of people are involved, and they have to play multiple roles most of the time.

For *structured* methods applied to larger-scale projects, like the tax or George Michaelson examples, the client tends to be drawn into systems development at the initial and final stages. Thus in terms of the meliorist model, the client has to provide information to the developer about the existing situation or system S_0, as well as what needs and criteria should be applied to the desired system S_1. Referring to Fig 7.7, this means that the client is involved in Phases 1 and 2. Once the new system has been produced, however, it is the client who has to *accept* it and to subsequently use it. Hence Phases 5 onwards will involve the client in the method.

But what of the client as a client and nothing else? Suppose the client has no desire at all to be involved in the systems development process? People who buy baked beans or cars don't get involved in their production, so why should the client treat the acquisition of a new system as anything more than a purchasing operation? In situations like these the client may still be involved with the method in two ways:

1. As purchaser of the method through the choice of systems developer.
2. As quality controller of the method through systems acceptance.

To understand the first of these, consider someone who runs their own business like Ben Lister of MX Marketing or Harry Seaton in the BSW Mini-Case. They are unlikely to have either the interest or the time to become involved in systems development. What they are most likely to do is to talk to other business people they know and take recommendations for the choice of a systems developer. For Ben or Harry, this is most likely to be a specialist consultancy company which markets a particular approach or method to systems development. Hence the client chooses the method through the choice of developer, not because the problem itself implies a particular method.

Once a client has chosen a method via the choice of the developer, the client is likely to act as a quality controller. Thus it is hard to imagine the Bens or Harrys of the business world just sitting back and waiting for the system to arrive. They will want to check how well the systems development process is going. The form of the particular method, and especially whether it has clear stages and *deliverables*, will affect the relationship between the client and the method. From the client's viewpoint, a good method is one that allows him to check the progress of the product which he has purchased.

7.4.9 Conclusion

Just as the systems view of organizations shows that *what* happens in an organization is a better guide to the role of information in management than looking at labels, so regarding systems development as a system reveals a better practical understanding of its complexity. The old labels of 'expert', 'consultant' or 'analyst' hark back to the early days of information technology.

Box 7.1

ELECTRICITY 'FREE-MARKET-FOR-ALL' IN CRISIS

(*Investors Chronicle* 18/10/96)

There are fears that the kick-off for the final stage in the free market's penetration of the electricity market will not happen on time nationwide. . .

Every household in the country is scheduled to have the right to choose its electricity supplier from 1 April 1998 in what was billed, at privatisation in 1990, as the final stage in the free market's penetration of the electricity market.

However, with 18 months to go to when information on customers and billing systems need to be in place to offer choice to 21 million households, Nigel Hawkins, electricity analyst at Yamaichi Securities, cannot see how competition can kick off on time nationwide. Mr Hawkins is not alone in his view.

Not a single local or regional market trial has yet been fixed, to mirror the domestic gas trial under way in the South West. The two main players involved – the regional electricity companies (the Recs) and the industry regulator Offer – have been blaming each other for the lack of progress.

Rather than being obliged to develop common computer systems needed to make customer details easily available to new entrants supplying electricity, each Rec is, instead, developing its own computer systems. . .

Industry analysts say that the Recs are dragging their feet. But given the threat to the Recs' regional monopolies, why they should be expected to act voluntarily against the best interests of their shareholders is unclear.

One problem is Offer's legal remit. Offer has a duty to promote competition. But UK competition law is negative, in the sense that it is about stopping companies from abusing market position. Offer does not have the right to oblige the Recs to create competition because no such concept of obligation exists in UK competition law. . .

COMMENT

Sounds familiar? No doubt if things do turn out as badly as this article fears, we shall be treated to another 'it's-the-computer's-fault' story. Yet none of the problems which any new system will face has anything to do with software or information technology. The actual operations that the system will have to carry out have been successfully performed for nearly thirty years now. We do not need any further advances in hardware or software to keep up to date records of customer names and addresses, their suppliers or the calculation and monitoring of payment.

What we have instead is a classic lesson in the importance of the *management* context of any potential information system. Unless this context is determined in the systems specification stages, we merely end up computerizing the existing chaos.

The particular problem we have here is that the *client* role is ambiguous. The system could end up trying to satisfy the needs of different clients with different, even opposing goals. What control concept is it therefore trying to support in terms of management *weltanschauung*, policy or goal-seeking?

FURTHER STUDY

Follow the history of this case as it runs towards 1 April 1998. It could be a suitable subject for *soft systems methodology*, as in Chapter 8. It is also worth investigating how far different information systems development methods actually include recognition of client definition in their initial stages. This could turn out to be a good dissertation topic for anyone submitting from late 1997 onwards.

KEY WORDS

Analysis
Approach
Aspiration driven
Bottom-up
Business analysis
CASE tool
Client
Deliverable
Derivative method
Design
Desired system
Existing system
Failure
Failure driven
Feasibility study
HCI, human–computer interaction
Implementation
Innovative method
Issue
Iteration
Logical system

Maintenance
Meliorist model
Mess
Method
Methodology
Object-orientation
Physical system
Problem
Process orientation
Project debriefing
Prototyping
Specification
SSADM
Structure orientation
Structured method
Systems developer
Systems life cycle
Technique
Tool
Top-down
WIMP

SEMINAR AGENDAS, EXAM QUESTIONS AND PROJECT/DISSERTATION SUBJECTS

1 Are *iteration* and *structure* mutually incompatible in systems development methods?

2 Consider the history of the different versions of SSADM. Why were the changes made? Is the concept of a standard method a useful one?

3 What other major components would you have included in Section 7.4 in addition to the client, developer, problem and method?

4 Is the Internet an information system? If so, what management function does it support?

5 Is a specialist profession of systems developer no longer relevant?

FEEDBACK ON SELF-TESTING QUESTIONS

◆ STQ 7.1

If we look at the question of definition, the problem could be clearly defined in terms of document and other errors which could be clearly counted. Also it would take a very academic person to argue that such errors were anything other than undesirable. When it came to the detailed causes of the errors the problem was much messier. Both poor commitment from those operating the system, and criticism of the system and its implementers, were legitimate possible disputed ingredients to any definition of what the problem was. Deciding their relative importance was a soft issue, since it depended on individual perceptions rather than an agreed objective way of assessment.

Once we recognize the presence of soft issues in the causes of the problem then these blur the questions of boundary, since we can't define whether certain issues like operator commitment or modification of the system ought to be included or not. This then means that a clear separation of responsibility is unlikely until the definition and boundaries are sorted out. The information needed was obviously not clear because that is why the team was set up, but a description of what a solution would look like was possible in terms of hard, measurable error rates. How such a solution could be carried out was widely disputed and very messy, as the final discussions showed.

◆ STQ 7.2

The assumption that all the factories in the group were sufficiently similar in the way that they operated tended towards a standard view of the system with the implication that implementation too could be according to a formula. It was lack of flexibility that prevented the implementation at PST taking account of local conditions.

◆ STQ 7.3

Systemic, as introduced in Chapter 2, means having the properties of a system or based on systems, principles. Any approach or method that recognizes and uses systems principles will be systemic. An example of this would be any approach to developing an information system for an organization which viewed the organization and the role of its information system in terms of the view presented in Chapter 6.

For an approach to be systematic we imply that it is carried out in an orderly way with definable, logical connexions between the actions carried out. A systematic approach is therefore one which we would call a method. If a method was also based on a systems view of the problem or used systems principles, then it would also be systemic.

◆ STQ 7.4

See *Figure 7.12.*

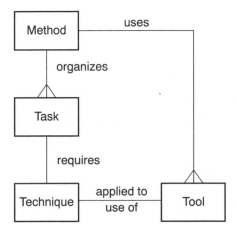

Fig 7.12 A Possible Relationship between Methods, Tasks, Techniques, and Tools

This is shown as an Entity Relationship Diagram. The STQ invited you to choose. Other choices may have been digraph or Venn diagrams, or many other ideas I have not listed. The important point is that the choice of the form of diagram should reflect the needed use.

REFERENCES/BIBLIOGRAPHY

Ackoff, R. & Hall, J.R. (1972). A Systems Approach to the Problems of Solid Waste and Litter. *Journal of Environmental Systems.* No. 2, pp. 531–64.

Avison, D.E. & Fitzgerald, G. (1988). *Information Systems Development.* Blackwell Scientific.

Birrell, N.D. & Ould, M.A. (1985). *A Practical Handbook for Software Development.* Cambridge University Press.

Cutts, G. (1987). *Structured Systems Analysis and Design Methodology.* Paradigm.

Cutts, G. (1991). *Structured Systems Analysis and Design Methodology.* Blackwell Scientific.

Flynn, D.J. (1992). *Information Systems Requirements: Determination and Analysis.* McGraw-Hill.

Gane, C. & Sarson, T. (1979). *Structured Systems Analysis.* Prentice-Hall.

Harry, M.J.S. (1990). *Information and Management Systems.* Pitman.

Kendel, P.A. (1987). *Systems Analysis and Design.* Allyn and Bacon.

de Marco, T. (1979). *Structured Analysis and Systems Specification.* Prentice-Hall.

Olle, T.W. et al. (1988). *Information Systems Methodologies.* Addison-Wesley.

Page-Jones, M. (1980). *The Practical Guide to Structured Systems Design.* Yourdon Press.

Yourdon, E. & Constantine, L.L. (1978). *Structured Design.* Yourdon Press.

George Michaelson's first redundancy package

The year 1993 began as a very bad year for George Michaelson at Technoturbines. The SC 322 aeroengine, which he had been involved with for over five years, didn't quite capture the initial orders that a potential world market should have implied. The product was not a failure, but its production seemed to require many less skilled people than George had thought when estimating his chances of not being made redundant. So George found himself taking his redundancy money and entering the various official state procedures that were designed to help people get back to work.

Then one Saturday morning a few weeks later, while George was still unemployed, he got a letter from an old friend from his days at university. Jill Farmer was one of three people that George had shared a house with during his last year on the degree course. For some reason that George had never really gone into, Jill had ended up failing her degree in mathematics and serving in a fast-food outlet. He was therefore quite interested to find that she had moved into his local area and had set up a company called 'Infosure'. Both Jill's letter, and the name she had chosen for the company, sounded more like a public relations handout than a letter from the person George remembered; but he decided to revive the old friendship. A weekend later, he found himself sitting in a restaurant eating chicken dhansak and being subjected to some hard questioning from Jill.

Although George had been mainly concerned with production management during his final time at Technoturbines, Jill was more interested in the work he had previously done in production information systems. This had involved him in cooperation with specialist consultants who had used the Structured System Analysis and Design Methodology, SSADM, to develop a new production planning and control system. Jill seemed to be very familiar with the methodology. She explained that before setting up her own company she had worked for a firm of consultants similar to the one George had worked with. It turned out that Jill herself had been made redundant about a year before George, and that it was this that had spurred her into going it alone.

'My first thought, when I was made redundant', she said, 'was to cash in on my knowledge and experience of structured systems development methods. I soon realized that PCs and networking were outdating many of those large-scale formal systems which you were involved with at Technoturbines. An awful lot of software can be developed into a practical working system without the application of very structured and formal approaches. New visual programming packages mean I can sit down with a user in front of a screen and present them with actual examples of potential outputs right from the start. It cuts out all the formal specification business.'

George wondered exactly what would be designed if people just sat in front of a computer without any specification, formal or otherwise, of what they were aiming at; but he didn't argue, because Jill was clearly warming to her subject. 'People working for organizations these days often find that their children are more in touch with modern software through home computing and the Internet than the management of the organization they work for.' At this point the arrival of the waiter bringing the coffee interrupted her lecture. By the time they had sorted out who took sugar or didn't take milk, she came to the point of their meeting.

What did George feel about global warming? George was amused. Jill was someone who drove a large fast car that looked like it was designed to consume all the oil in the world and every other motorist on the road. Was she really a sudden convert to conservation? She ignored his smile. 'The reason I ask is because I am going to make a tender to develop a Water Management Information System for the East Farthing Drainage Authority.' George looked blank, 'What's that, and who are they?' 'That's what I asked myself when I saw the invitation to tender. Apparently nearly a fifth of England is so low-lying that it would regularly flood if it were not protected and drained: and that includes a lot of the London area by the way. The people responsible for flood protection are a collection of drainage boards who cover the various areas. The East Farthing Drainage Authority is one of these. They are inviting tenders to develop a Windows-based system which will analyse data automatically radioed in from pumping stations and present it on screen to the engineers at headquarters. The aim is to give them the information they need to operate the pumping system effectively. Apparently this means preventing flooding whilst not wasting money on unnecessary pumping. Did you hear about that flood in Holland in 1993? If there really is global warming, we're on to a potential winner with this system.'

'But I don't know anything about water management, let alone Visual Basic', said George. 'That's not important', said Jill, 'the main thing is that you understand computer systems and constructing databases; and above all, you have experience of talking to users and finding out their needs. That's the important thing. If I get the contract, will you join us?'

George didn't accept immediately. It seemed like a big step to go from being someone who worked in a large international company, to being one of four members of a small business. When he did accept, however, he found that Jill was right. Sitting with her and discussing details of the new system with engineering staff at the East Farthing Drainage Authority did recall the same skills and experience he had used at Technoturbines. He also found that although managing water was very different from managing the production of aeroengines, there were many principles he was already familiar with. The modelling of the storage and flow of water did link to his own experience of inventory control, and many of the project scheduling techniques used by the authority were familiar to him. Within three months George felt he was back on course.

A systems methodology view

In the previous chapter, Chapter 7, we noted that the term *methodology* could be used in its original sense of the *study of method*. We found that systems development methods could be understood in terms of:

1. Their role in control and management of information systems.
2. The types of problem they might be suitably applied to.
3. The motives for choosing them.
4. Whether they are derivative or innovative in terms of their analytical approach.
5. Their structure and the role of iteration.
6. Whether they are process, structure or object-oriented.

I chose to continue George Michaelson's story because the history of his own career development has paralleled many of the changes which have taken place in the field of information systems development methodology from the late 1980s through to the present. The late 1980s saw highly structured methods like SSADM being widely advocated for the development of systems that would most likely be implemented on mini-computers systems of the type George would have been familiar with at Technoturbines. But the 1980s was much more the decade in which the personal computer (PC) by-passed many of the older mainframe and mini-computer based applications. As Jill Farmer said, 'many people working for organizations these days often find that their children are more in touch'.

Along with this expansion of PC use came a widening of the range of people who used computers. This led to a less technical interest in the *hows* of the workings of information technology, like writing programs, and more interest in just making it do *what* the user required. So-called WIMP (Windows, Icons, Menu, Pointer) software was then developed to meet this need. Microsoft Windows is an example of this.

By the mid-1990s networking software by firms such as Novell and Microsoft had enabled the personal computer expansion of the 1980s to be taken a stage further. There had been a conflict between an individual user's desire for personal computer-based information systems on the desktop, and the organization's need for coordination and compatibility. Local area networks, using networking software, resolved much of this conflict. A user could still use their machine in their own personal way, but in a software environment which enabled communication and sharing between different users within an organization.

Now, in the late 1990s, the days of systems methodology which were associated with mainframe and mini-computer systems seem to be over: as Jill Farmer implied.

The issues raised

The issues raised by our final mini-case should therefore be seen in the methodology context of Chapter 7. In particular:

> *Issue 1. Do recent information systems development innovations, like the networking of personal computer hardware and the emergence of user-friendly visual programming and systems development tools, mean that earlier methods, like structured systems development, are out of date?*

> *Issue 2. If some older methods are still relevant, how do we decide which ones to retain?*

Issue 1 is best answered by referring yet again to the distinction of *whats* and *hows*. New innovations, of the type quoted above, relate to particular ways of doing things in systems development. They are therefore concerned with new *hows* rather than new *whats*. We are still concerned with the same process of moving from S_0 to S_1 that we covered in Chapter 7. New methods should only replace older ones when they represent better ways of doing this.

Issue 2 then asks us how we decide whether this replacement is needed. I think that the answer to this question depends on two important criteria:

1. Do we have a *hard* information systems development problem with S_0 and S_1 clearly defined?
2. Is the *human* context of the systems development process, particularly in terms of the *developer* and *client roles*, small-scale and informal?

If the answer to either of these questions is negative, then more recent developments in prototyping and the use of visual programming will either be insufficient or even irrelevant.

The first criterion reminds us that any kind of information systems development, using whatever kind of software, on whatever kind of information technology, is not much use until we are clear about the problem. Some form of soft systems methodology is therefore as relevant as it was in the pre-1980s, when its early forms were first developed.

The second criterion leads back to the thought that George had in response to Jill's enthusiasm for cutting out 'all the formal specification business': what would be designed if people just sat in front of the computer without any specification?

The objectives of our final chapter should therefore be to understand enough of applied information systems development methodology to make choices that deal with what we find today, rather than the past or an imaginary other world.

LEARNING OBJECTIVES CHAPTER 8

1 **To understand soft systems methodology and its relevance to information systems development.**

2 **To understand structure, process and object-oriented information systems development methods.**

3 **To understand the study of the human–computer interface and human–computer interaction as important additions to the subject of information systems development.**

Information Systems Development: Methods

8.1 SOFT SYSTEMS ANALYSIS

8.1.1 The role of soft systems analysis in systems development

Before looking any further at methods designed to analyse the soft aspects of problems or messes, we need to answer three questions:

1. Why should consideration of soft issues be relevant to information systems development?
2. What is the relationship between soft systems analysis and information systems development methods?
3. Should methods applied to soft problems be seen as different or separate from those applied to hard problems?

The first of these questions has already been answered in section 7.3.4 where we saw that the initial strategy and inception stage involved us in looking at both the management system and the whole business or organizational system. We saw that this will involve us in sorting out soft human and policy issues *before* we can produce the deliverables of decision, authorization and commitment.

Once this question has been answered it leads naturally to the second question. If we have to sort out the soft issues at the initial stage of systems development and before we can produce the deliverables for that stage, then we would expect soft systems analysis to be carried out right at the beginning of systems development. This seems sensible when we refer back to Fig 7.1. As long as questions of the boundary or separation of the problem are unclear, or we don't know whose responsibility it is, or any of the other features of a mess exist, we shall not know just what system it is that we are supposed to be developing.

There is however a further answer to the question of how soft systems analysis might fit into the view of systems development presented in section 7.3.4. In later maintenance and debriefing stages, it is very likely that some of the causes of the need for maintenance and the lessons to be learned at debriefing have messy human origins as well as hard technical ones. In particular, any outright failure of a system is likely to have human implications in terms of motivation, communication or training.

◆ **STQ 8.1**
Is such failure therefore a holist phenomenon?

This leaves the final question of why should methods applied to soft problems be any different in principle from those applied to hard problems? If they are, then we must be accepting that the nature of the problem affects the nature of the method applied to it. This assertion then leads us to question whether all the range of combinations shown in Fig 7.9 are possible. The short answer is that if a problem is mainly a mess, then this does imply some differences in the deliverables of the approach compared with those applied to essentially hard problems. These differences however do not preclude the relevance of similar concepts such as stages, deliverables, iterations, tools and techniques, like those used by methods on hard problems. The main differences are likely to be that a soft systems method would need to recognize the soft complexity of messes as shown in Fig 7.1.

We can illustrate these differences in deliverables between methods applied to hard and soft problems by referring to the meliorist model of Fig 7.2. With a soft problem, the conflicts over what the problem is, or what might constitute a solution, mean that S_0 and S_1 are themselves issues of dispute. Any thought about the set of actions needed to move from S_0 to S_1 must therefore be irrelevant until it is clear where the arrow starts from and where it is intended to go. We have seen that the set of actions represented by this arrow will come from the chosen method, but with a very messy soft problem we first need a method to deal with S_0 and S_1 before going on to one dealing with the arrow itself. In the Technoturbines case for example, until it is decided whether the problem is the behaviour of the workforce, the inadequacies of the system at PST, or some messy mixture of both, there is little point in considering what is to be done to clear up the problem.

A soft systems method is likely therefore to have deliverables concerned with trying to define, or at least make more clear, the *nature of the problem* itself, rather than offering *solutions*. In particular this will mean trying to get some *clarification* and agreement of what constitutes S_0 and S_1. To do this it will be necessary to distinguish which areas of disagreement come from disputes over soft issues, and which come from disputes over hard fact. If this can be done, then appropriate methods can be applied to each. Disputes about hard facts can be resolved by processes such as measurement, computation, observation or other technical means. Disputes over soft issues will need to be resolved or defused by means like negotiation, persuasion or compromise. In our Technoturbines example, questions about the frequency with which products failed their first inspection are hard ones and can be resolved by reference to recorded data and statistical analysis. Disputes over the relative merits of redesigning the system or imposing greater discipline on the workforce at PST cannot be resolved by reference to some agreed standard; and are therefore soft. Resolution of issues like these will come through negotiation, politics and social action.

The difference between methods focussing on hard and soft problems will not therefore be absolute. Instead we would expect that methods would tend to vary in the emphasis they make. Generally we would expect soft systems analysis methods to put a strong emphasis in their early stages on identifying soft issues and trying to evolve a clarified, shareable view of the problem. Hard aspects of the problem can then be identified for subsequent treatment using the appropriate methods for solving hard problems.

The sequence of considering possible soft aspects of a problem first is a practical one. Any system which is subsequently developed as a result of the definition of the problems associated with S_0, or the requirements of S_1, is a concept which reflects the interests and values of those concerned, and can therefore only be defined after resolving the soft issues.

This necessity of having to deal with both hard and soft aspects when trying to create information systems for management has led to attempts at combining aspects of hard and soft methods into integrated methodologies. We shall look further into this below, once we have studied both soft and hard systems methodology. Meanwhile, we will look at the main features of the soft systems method which has probably held the field above all others for the last twenty years or so. This is the so-called *Soft Systems Methodology* of Checkland (1981), called SSM from now on.

In choosing to cover the SSM first, it is important that I pass on to you warnings that I give to my university students when I follow the same sequence in my lectures:

a SSM is a 'methodology that aims to bring about improvement in areas of social concern', Bulow (1989). It is not therefore an information systems development methodology per se.

b SSM is not covered first because it is the most important method we consider; but as we saw above, the resolution of messes should logically precede the solving of hard problems.

Given these caveats, we will now look at SSM in more detail.

8.1.2 The main features of soft systems methodology

SSM has developed over the years of application that separate Checkland (1981) and Checkland & Scholes (1990). The earlier 'conventional seven-stage' form is represented by Fig 8.1, and the later 'developed form' by Fig 8.2. The reasons given for this development in Checkland & Scholes (1990) will be familiar to us in terms of our study of methods and approaches earlier. They say, 'In the late 1980s the 1975 version seems rather bald, and in any case gives too much an impression that SSM is a seven-stage process to be followed in sequence...'.

We should not find it difficult to keep in mind this, and other, reservations of the authors about the mechanistic and undeveloping application of systems methods. Our analysis earlier in this chapter of messes, the role of structure in methods, and above all the higher-order learning which is true methodology, have prepared us for a wide-ranging view of what systems development might involve.

Given this background we will cover SSM in three stages:

1 We will use the rest of this section to investigate what the authors describe as the 'basic shape' of SSM shown in Fig 8.3, and see how it may be interpreted in terms of our meliorist model of Fig 7.2.

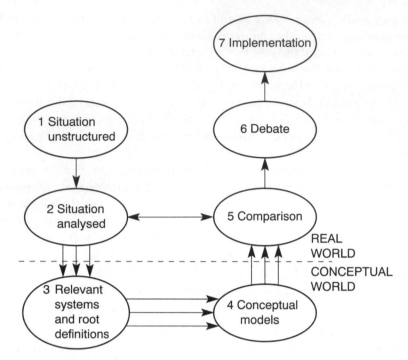

Fig 8.1 The Conventional Seven-Stage Soft Systems Methodology
The essence of the method (*see* also Fig 8.3) is the comparison of the relevant systems in the conceptual world with the existing analysed situation as a means of generating clarification and progress. In terms of Fig 7.2, S_1 is compared with S_0 as a means of specifying action for change.

2 Having got a feel for the methodological principles behind SSM, we will run through the conventional seven-stage form in detail, since this forms the basis of the later developed form.

3 Having acquired a more detailed view of conventional SSM, we can note what developments have been made to it and why.

We will therefore begin with the *basic shape* of SSM shown in Fig 8.3, before going on to its expression in the more sophisticated terms of the conventional and later models.

The first feature to note is the 'real-world situation of concern'. This is the S_0 or where we are now of our meliorist model of Fig 7.2. The use of the word concern makes it clear that this situation is not satisfactory and that we would therefore like to do something about it.

Since we are considering a mess rather than a clear-cut problem, we would expect the arrow or action for change of the meliorist model to be concerned with clarification or improvement of a mess rather than the solution of a problem. This is represented as 'Action needed to improve the situation' in SSM.

Having found the SSM equivalents of S_0 and the arrow in our meliorist model, we are left with seeing what might be representing S_1, where we would like to be. Answering this question brings in the essential feature of SSM in terms of how its stages fit together and what deliverable we should expect from applying them.

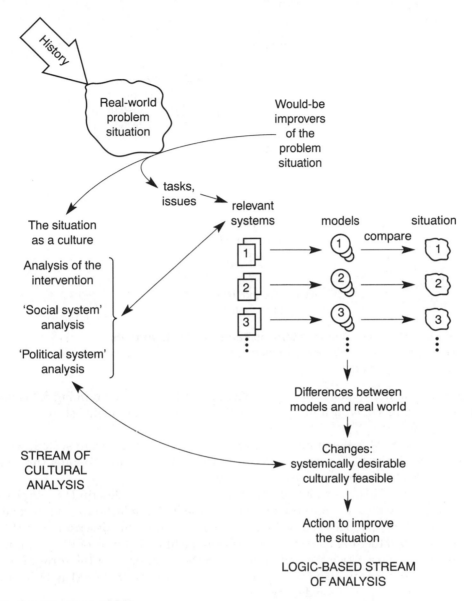

Fig 8.2 Developed SSM
This develops SSM by identifying more clearly the interaction of the cultural aspects of the human situation with the logic-driven seven-stage progress.

What SSM does is to set a relevant system against any particular aspect of the mess which is giving us concern. This relevant system is a model of the purposeful activity we would like to have, in contrast to the particular feature of the mess we have at the moment. It is this 'purposeful activity we would like to have' which is the SSM equivalent of S_1, where we would like to be.

The important feature we need to remember, however, is that we are dealing with clarification or improvement of a mess rather than the solution of a problem. Hence S_1 represents an aim we would like to strive for but we may not immediately, if ever,

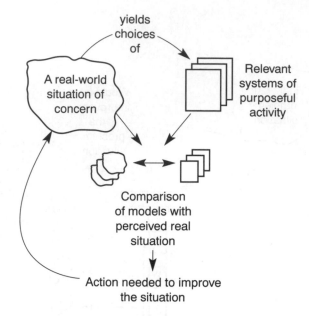

yields
choices
of

A real-world
situation of
concern

Relevant
systems of
purposeful
activity

Comparison
of models with
perceived real
situation

Action needed to improve
the situation

Fig 8.3 The Basic Shape of SSM as Perceived by its Authors
Comparison of models with the perceived real situation is the dialectic drive
behind the method.

fully achieve. The deliverable from the application of SSM as shown in Fig 8.3 is not therefore S_1, where we would like to be; but the arrow of the meliorist model, i.e. action for change.

The essence of SSM is therefore the comparing of an S_1, the relevant system we'd like to have, with the S_0, the mess we've got at the moment, to generate, through analysis and debate, the meliorist arrow or action for change.

Two final points. First, we should confirm that the use of the description 'purposeful' implying that we have a purpose or aim, and the belief in 'action ... to improve', are clear indications that SSM is based on meliorism. Second, the description of SSM as a methodology rather than a method is probably justified in terms of the meanings we established earlier. Since the deliverable of SSM is action, and the form of this action will differ according to the application, we may say that SSM is indeed a methodology whose application delivers a method.

8.1.3 The conventional seven-stage model

We can look at how the basic shape of SSM was first structured and applied. Before we do this, it is important to set out the current context of the seven-stage model.

Although the implication of Checkland & Scholes (1990) is that this version of SSM has been superseded, much of the popular literature and other developments outside the control of its originator have kept it going under its own momentum. When I see this happening, I wonder if Professor Checkland, like Tchaikovsky with his 1812 Overture, might be a victim of his own success. Patching (1990) is a good example of how someone outside the original school of SSM may take it up successfully for their own purposes, while perhaps not exciting enthusiasm in the hearts of its originators.

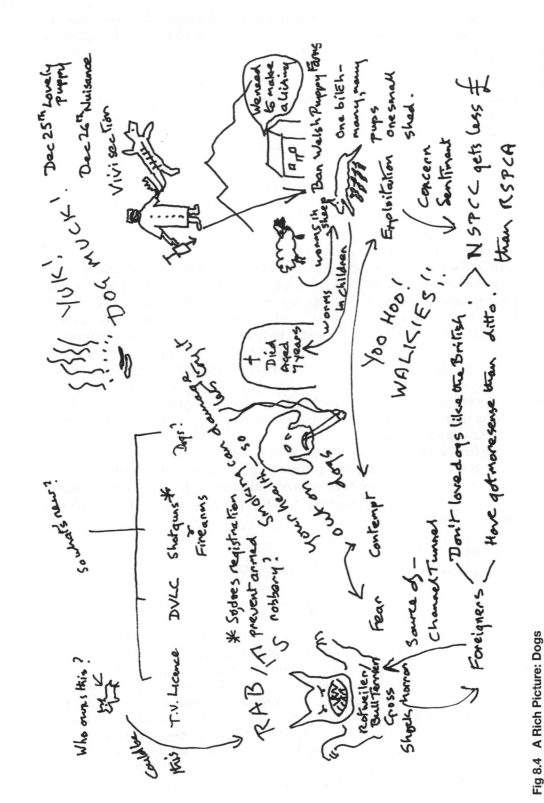

Fig 8.4 A Rich Picture: Dogs

The aim of a rich picture is to capture a holist view of the existing situation. The open, unstructured nature of this way of diagramming helps prevent the failure to record something just because it won't fit into a particular diagramming convention. Every rich picture will be *someone's* rich picture, rather than *the* rich picture.

Whatever the wider arguments about SSM, our attitude is empirical: where it has relevance to the understanding of information systems development methodology, we are interested. If we are to look back to our need to cover messes, or to look ahead to integrated methodologies, we shall find that the seven-stage model is relevant.

The seven-stages of the conventional model of SSM are shown in Fig 8.1. To illustrate their application to a messy problem we will use the Dogs Case of Appendix 4.

◆ **STQ 8.2**

What makes the Dogs Case messy in terms of the criteria of Section 7.1?

If the Dogs Case is a mess rather than a clear-cut problem, how does the conventional seven-stage model of SSM record the 'Problem situation considered problematic'. The answer to this is the *rich picture* we introduced in Chapter 3. Figure 8.4 is a rich picture of the Dogs Case. The important feature of the rich picture is that it prevents a predetermined view of the situation being forced into a particular mould.

We can understand why an open, unstructured record like a rich picture is used if we consider what normally happens when we seek to record something about a situation. If we go into a room with a camera, we end up recording what is visible; and if we go in with sound recording equipment, we only record sounds. If our aim however is to have a holist view of what is present in the room our aims are more complex. We might wish to learn not only about silent, invisible, physical things like smells; but also about abstract or emotional things like the social atmosphere between the people present. No one measuring or recording device or technique will be able to record all this. A rich picture, however, is not confined to a limited range of symbols or a definition of what it may include. As a result, it can convey a wide range of hard and soft information: hence the term rich.

Once we have captured our view of the existing situation, we can see what features it includes. Since we are talking about a mess, we are not assuming that there is any particular underlying structure or consistency. Instead we are concerned to identify themes or issues in the situation recorded which help us express why we consider the situation to be problematic.

◆ **STQ 8.3**

Suggest some themes and issues for the Dogs Case.

SSM has come to discriminate between those themes which it relates to *primary tasks* and those which are *issues*. This distinction is not meant to be an absolute one, but expresses the extremes of a range. We use an example from Checkland and Scholes (1990) to illustrate the two types. A charity organization which has been set up to relieve hunger is experiencing several committee disputes. Of the themes that come from analysing the situation, some relate to the actual processes directly connected with the activities of money raising and the provision of food. Other themes are more to do with debate or disagreement over the charity's attitudes, policies or philosophy. Primary task themes are those immediately related to the processes for which the organization exists, like a charity's money-raising efforts. Issue-based themes relate to the concerns which are generated in the wider activities surrounding the primary task, like deciding how open and communicative the committee should be to other members.

Once stage 2 has identified the themes of concern in the existing situation (Fig 8.5), stage 3 involves *conceiving* (hence *conceptual world*) *a relevant system* as a model of the purposeful activity we would like to have in relation to each theme. (It should be noted that the sequence of stages we are about to follow from stage 2 through to stage 6 would be carried out in turn for each theme identified at stage 2.)

In our Dogs Case we are concerned with several themes, but let us use the example of the issue of identification. In contrast this particular feature of the mess we have at the moment, the 'purposeful activity we would like to have', would be a Dog Identification System. It is called a relevant system because it is relevant to one of the themes in the real world identified in stage 2.

Once we have chosen a relevant system, then stage 3 requires us to define what properties such a system should have. We say 'should' here because we are talking about a system in the conceptual world that we would like to have, not one we can automatically expect to get. Remember, SSM is looking to deliver improvement or clarification of a mess, not automatic solutions to problems. The role of the relevant system concept is to help with this improvement or clarification. It would be nice to have it, but as we shall see at the later stages, it can still play an important role even if we don't.

The *root definition* of a relevant system, which we produce in stage 4, should be a definition of what the relevant system should be in terms of the qualities we would

---

Dogs: Themes and Issues

Danger: Dogs can bite and even kill. Shock pictures in the media of children with severely lacerated faces.

Irresponsible Owners: Dogs can be trained and controlled. Problems arise when this is not recognized or acted on. You don't get bad dogs; you only get bad owners.

Identification: If you can't identify a dog, how do you know which dog did it, or even whether it was a dog at all? Even if you know the dog, who is responsible for training, control or restitution for irresponsiblility?

Animal Welfare: Exploitation and cruelty to animals. 'A puppy isn't just for Christmas; it's a dog for life.' Breeding dogs for animal experiments.

Health: Dirty dogs fouling pavements and public places leads to concern about effects on human health; e.g. Hydatid disease, where dogs act as vehicle for cross-infection by tapeworm that kills seven people annually in England and Wales. Threats of rabies.

Sentimentality/Sensitivity/Humanity: As the composer Elgar was more concerned about the effects of World War I on the army horses than on the soldiers, so threats to burn a dog in protest at the Vietnam War almost seemed to raise as many protests as the napalming of human beings. W.C. Fields: 'Anyone who hates animals and children can't be all bad.' Animals' rights. The cruellest animal is man.

Fig 8.5 The Situation Analysed

Themes and issues that can be identified in the rich picture. There may be others. The iterative nature of SSM will almost certainly mean that these themes would be re-examined, added to and modified.

want it to possess. For any relevant system, like our Dog Identification System, a statement of the root definition should sound like an answer to the question 'what should a Dog Identification System be?' As an answer we could then say it should be:

'An officially enforced system to identify approved owners of dogs'

thus producing a root definition of the relevant system.

Now it happens that this root definition is not terribly good in terms of being either complete or clear about the qualities of the Dog Identification System, but how can we know? What makes a good root definition?

The answer to this last question is that SSM considers that six features of the relevant system either should be clearly stated in its root definition, or should be sufficiently inferrable from it to justify the omission. The six features are called the CATWOE criteria, where CATWOE is an acronym for the six features shown in Fig 8.6.

How does our root definition:

'An officially enforced system to identify approved owners of dogs'

stand up to the CATWOE test? Taking each criterion in turn:

The CATWOE Criteria

Customers: Those who would receive the immediate output from the relevant system. Not necessarily the customers of the company, organization, etc.

Actors: Those who would be directly involved in making the relevant system work as a *process*.

Transformation Process: What the relevant system does in terms of transforming *inputs* into *outputs*. The SSM uses the concept of process in much the same way as we have done in Chapters 2 and 3.

Weltanschauung: German word meaning 'world view' or fundamental set of values and assumptions implicit in the root definition. This is the criterion which newcomers to SSM and all other forms of systemic thinking tend to find difficult because it is seldom explicitly spelled out.

Owner: Person or body ultimately speaking for the nature and purpose of the relevant system based on their potential *control* over its existence or otherwise.

Environment: Defined exactly as we have done in Chapter 2. Those things which strongly affect or disturb the system, but over which the system has only limited influence or control.

Fig 8.6 Criteria for Assessing Root Definitions
CATWOE lists six elements that must either be specified by the root definition of the relevant system, or be clearly deducible from it.

Customers: Presumably meant to be the 'owners' who are identified. Possibly could be whoever is implied by 'officially' or even the dogs? Ambiguous because the root definition does not clearly state who will be the recipients or victims of the relevant system's output. Perhaps if we substituted 'impose identification on approved owners' it might be clearer.

Actors: Not at all clear. If it is 'officially enforced', the implication is that the enforcers will decide who should be acting out the system. We really need something in the definition to clarify whether this system is going to be carried out by a national government agency, subcontracted private enterprise or some other agent. In the practical application of SSM, this issue might be separated out, and would lead us back to rethinking the name of our relevant system in stage 3 or re-defining our themes at stage 2.

Transformation Process: A fairly clear implication that the system will transform unidentified dog owners into identified ones, but is there an implied 'approval' process? This is dangerous, since a root definition should have only one clear transformation process.

Weltanschauung: The phrase 'officially enforced' makes it pretty clear that this relevant system has a strong authoritarian world view. Nothing much optional or open to discussion about this system.

Owner: If the relevant system is to be 'officially enforced', that is a clear statement that it will be owned by officialdom. Any remaining ambiguity could be removed by using 'legally enforced'?

Environment: The definition is very weak on this point. The 'officially enforced' possibly implies that the relevant system will exist in the context of a defined legal environment, but there is nothing about, for example, the emotive social environment that this system will have to operate in.

The CATWOE criteria show that this root definition of the relevant system needs improving. We chose an only moderately successful root definition in order to illustrate the workings of CATWOE. In practice, such a CATWOE analysis would lead to an iteration back to stage 3 in order to clarify our view of the relevant system and then come up with a new root definition in stage 4. For the purpose of illustrating how a conceptual model follows from a root definition we will take a slightly improved version:

'A legally enforceable agency system to record dog ownership'

and see what model would follow from this latest definition.

We said that a root definition should define what a relevant system should be. Stage 5 of the SSM is concerned to construct a model of what the relevant system should *do* to *be* the system defined. Doing implies *actions* or *activities*. The *conceptual model* is a model which shows the sequence and coordination of the activities that must logically be carried out by the relevant system to meet the root definition.

Figure 8.7 shows how such a conceptual model of the relevant system might be diagrammed. Referring back to Chapter 3, we can see that since a conceptual model is concerned with defining what the system does, any diagram of such a model will focus on process. Its important constituents are therefore activities in a particular sequence. Our understanding of diagramming from Chapter 3 reminds us that any

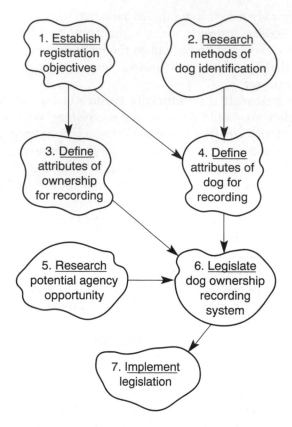

Fig 8.7 A Conceptual Model
What the relevant system must *do* to *be* what the root definition defines.
This example would need further detailing of the activities and the addition
of some coordinating activity of the whole.

shape of activity 'blob', or form of 'arrow' showing sequence, is acceptable provided it
is logically correct. Another important aspect which we might find in more detailed
studies of SSM is that blobs representing activities can themselves be broken down
into more detailed components. For the purposes of explaining SSM at this stage this
raises no more issues than those we covered when considering systems hierarchy.

Once the conceptual model of the relevant system has been defined we now have a
definition of S_1, the situation we would like to have. In practice we shall probably be
nowhere near this at all, since we are dealing with a mess. Given this situation, the
purpose of stage 6 is then to compare:

      a. What we do have, which is S_0 described by the analysed rich picture of stage 2
with:

      b. What we would like to have, which is S_1 in the form of the relevant system
          modelled in stage 5

to produce:

      c. Suggested action for change.

There are several ways of making this comparison and of producing *c*, which is the outcome or deliverable from stage 7 of the SSM. Reference to Checkland (1981), Checkland & Scholes (1990), or Patching (1990), will detail what the ways might be. We will choose what is probably the most common. This consists of a matrix, as in Fig 8.8, in which each of the activities in the conceptual model is checked to see if it exists in the real-world situation. The results of this check are then used to focus on the question as to what should be done about it. It may be that the absence of an activity is a clear indication that we need to go ahead and try to make it happen. It may be that we

	ACTIVITY	PRESENT	COMMENT
1.	Establish registration objectives.	No	Debate already started, so proceed.
2.	Research methods of dog identification.	No	Depends on resolution of Theme/Issue 1. Postpone.
3.	Define attributes of ownership for recording.	No	Depends on Theme/Issue1, but could also affect it. Integrate with 1?
4.	Define attributes of dog for recording.	No	Integrate with 3?
5.	Research potential agency opportunity.	Yes?	Some existing local authority or other nation's systems. Research further?
6.	Legislate dog ownership recording system.	No	Leave until last.
7.	Implement legislation.	No	Ditto.

Fig 8.8 An Agenda
There are several ways of approaching the comparison stage of SSM, and different forms of the output from it. The device shown here lists every activity in the conceptual model and checks to see how far it may be present in the real-world analysis. Suggestions for action or further analysis emerge from this.

can do nothing about the absence of one activity until another is carried out. It may be that trying to find out whether an activity in the conceptual model is present in the real-world merely reveals that we don't yet know. Whatever the outcome of the comparison, its main purpose is to produce an agenda for debate that will lead to action for change.

Figure 8.8 is intended to illustrate how stage 6 leads to stage 7 in the SSM. Our example is only an illustration, however. In practice, stages 3 to 6 would be carried out for all the major themes identified in stage 2. We would also expect much more iteration and refinement than we have shown here.

We warned in the previous sections that SSM should be seen in terms of our previous analysis of the issues involved in information systems development and the context of the meliorist model. We concluded that we would expect the SSM to clarify a way forward from the existing situation S_0 as represented by the arrow of the meliorist model. Although SSM is not an information systems development method, it might be useful in the initial inception or the later debriefing stages of systems development.

The usefulness of SSM at the inception stage has led to attempts at producing integrated methodologies. These attempt to use elements of the SSM in the initial stage of systems development where the focus is on sorting out messes, and lead through to incorporating tools and techniques from hard systems methods in the later stages where the problem has been more clearly defined. We shall look at an integrated methodology later in this chapter.

8.1.4 Developed SSM

Having covered the conventional seven-stage model of SSM, we are now in a position to understand its later development as in Checkland & Scholes (1990). We have already noted that although SSM is not specifically an information systems development methodology, we were interested in its possible application in some stages of systems development and its contribution to integrated informations systems development methods. The more recent developments in SSM have a further contribution to make to our understanding of systems development itself as a system, which we shall cover at the end of this chapter. Meanwhile, Fig 8.2 shows the more recent form of the process of SSM ('Developed SSM' or DSSM).

The main feature of DSSM is the recognition of two analysis 'streams' in the process. The logic-based analysis stream on the right of Fig 8.2 is the sequence of tasks, issues, relevant systems, root definitions, etc., which we find in SSM. The cultural analysis stream however recognizes that the process of applying SSM itself becomes part of the existing situation. The analysis process and those who carry it out cannot do anything about the mess without interacting with it. We might draw parallels with what we saw with Heisenberg's Uncertainty Principle in Chapter 4. Measurement or any other intervention in a situation disturbs that situation and makes it different from what it was before. Where intervention has this effect it makes sense to take account of it, rather than to pretend it doesn't exist.

The DSSM cultural analysis stream recognizes three particular areas of the problem situation as a culture:

1. The activity of intervention itself.
2. The 'social system' in the problem situation.
3. The 'political system' in the problem situation.

The authors put the terms 'social system' and 'political system' in quotes because they intend them to be used in the everyday colloquial sense.

The activity of intervention itself is seen in terms of three *roles*. The authors use the term role in each case to mean person or persons who may be:

1. The *client*: whoever caused the study to take place.
2. The *would-be problem solver*: whoever wishes to do something about the situation in question.
3. The *problem owner:* no one is intrinsically this. The problem solver should recognize that there will always be several useful sources for perceptions of what is important problematically.

The importance of this first activity of identifying roles should be obvious. If no one (client) has asked nobody (would-be problem solver) to be concerned with nobody's view (problem owner) of a situation, then we are hardly into 'action to improve the situation' as shown in Fig 8.2.

Although I have reservations about the details of these authors' views of the roles in analysis, we can see that a study of similar roles relationships would be relevant when considering information systems development. As promised, we will take this up at the end of the chapter.

The 'social system' in the problem situation is seen by the authors in terms of the rich mix of human relationships we would expect to find in any social situation including those in organizations. The authors see both formal roles, like 'shop steward' and informal roles, like 'licensed jester'; and they recognize the interplay of roles, norms and values. Having recognized right from the beginning of this book that information systems are to be seen as a component of management systems, we see no great surprise in recognizing that all human activities have a human dimension.

Likewise, the 'political system' in the problem situation seems to be no more than a recognition that since Rebekah manoeuvred Isaac's possession of the power of blessing, via her son's use of a gift, to topple the power that Esau possessed on account of his greater age, etc., human society has had its power possession, exchange, clash and resolution dimension. Thus in an institution where I recently worked the system of allocating money for staff development was made completely transparent: everyone could apply for it and everyone knew who got what and why. Needless to say the system was soon subverted and possessed by a small top management group. The allocation of the money represented power and could be used by its possessors as a lever to their own ends.

So why should the 'political system' in the problem situation be of any more or less interest to information systems development than to any other management activity? The answer to this question is to be found in Chapter 1, where we saw that information itself is a very strong political commodity. This is why information systems development should be seen as a management activity, not just a technical process.

We can conclude that although DSSM does not add anything new to our understanding of human nature, it does re-emphasize the human dimension and keep us on our guard from thinking that information technology is an information system.

8.2 PROCESS-ORIENTED DEVELOPMENT

8.2.1 Traditional process-oriented development

We saw how information systems development methods could be seen from the different views of process, structure and object-orientation in section 7.3.6.

The *process* view is the oldest of these three historically, and it dominated information systems development in the 1970s and early 1980s. Classic examples were the structured analysis methods of Gane & Sarson (1979) and de Marco (1979), often coupled with the structured design methods of Yourdon & Constantine (1978).

Combinations like these were traditionally called systems analysis and design, and covered stages 1–4 of our model of systems development in Fig 7.7. They also happened to share some common properties which did not in themselves have any special connexion with the fact that they were process-oriented methods:

a. They were structured, i.e. had clear stages with deliverables.
b. Their view of analysis was derivative in the sense described in section 7.3.3.
c. They were top-down methods which recognized the hierarchical view of systems. Their systems development procedures followed the top-down sequence of breaking down high-level specifications of what the system must be, into increasingly detailed logical models of what it should do, finally followed by the detail of how it should be constructed.

None of these three features, as we said, are specifically process-oriented. The important criterion of the process view is that an information system is seen as a process that takes components as inputs in the form of raw data, and transforms them into different outputs called information.

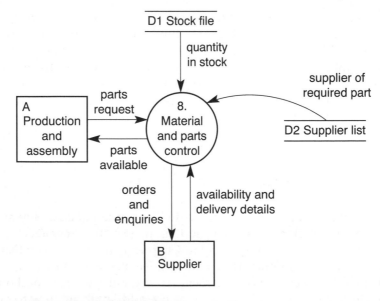

Fig 8.9 Data Flow Diagram (1)
This shows part of the highest-level diagram of a system.

This view had a very specific effect on the nature of the tools and techniques which typify these methods, and in particular the central role of the *data flow diagram*. We can understand how this came about if we note that the output from any definition and analysis based on a process view is a model of an information system. This being the case, then the ways available to us for describing it are the same as those for describing any kind of system.

Thus all the systemic features covered in Chapter 3, and the means of diagrammatically describing them, may be relevant to the analysis and definition stages of such methods. The principal features of any system, including an information system, that need to be defined are:

1. The identity of the system as defined by a structure showing its components, hierarchy, boundary and environment.
2. The behaviour of the system that emerges from transformation processes changing inputs into discernably different outputs.

We can illustrate how the tools used in process-oriented analysis methods fulfil these requirements by referring to Gane & Sarson (1979) as an example. The tools used are:

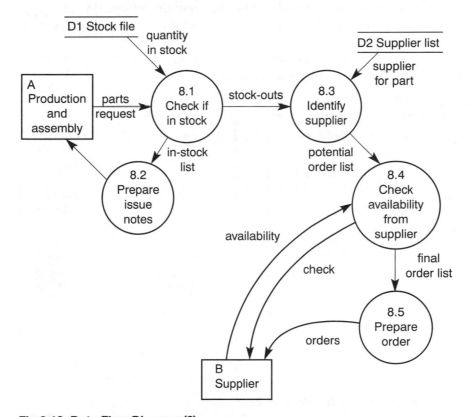

Fig 8.10 Data Flow Diagram (2)
An explosion of process 8 in Fig 8.9 to form a lower diagram which details the original process as a subsystem. This procedure of exploding processes into lower-level detailed components is called 'levelling'.

1 *A set of levelled data flow diagrams*, as in Figs 8.9 and 8.10 which cover:

- the components of the system: by identifying the processes, data flows, and data stores
- the hierarchy of the system: by showing how processes which are components in the higher-level diagram can be seen as subsystems and broken down into lower-level data flow diagrams in their own right
- the boundary and environment of the system: by identifying external entities which act as sources and destinations of the information system's inputs and outputs, as a result of its behaviour.

Once the data flow diagrams have been used to define the whole system, its components are detailed using:

2 *A data dictionary*, which describes:

- the structure of the data, either at rest in a data store, or moving as a data flow, as in Fig 8.11
- the forms of access required to store data, based on the principles of Fig 8.12
- the processes which transform the data into the information required by the wider management system, like some form of process description such as *structured English*, given in Fig 8.13
- details of the external entities in terms of their own identity and the identity of data flows for which they act as source or destination.

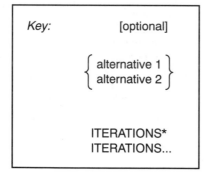
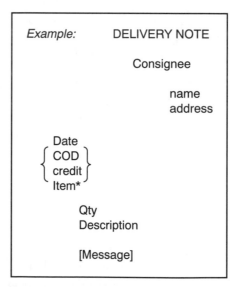

Fig 8.11 Entries in a Data Dictionary

For traditional process-based information systems development methods, the data dictionary defines the data structures which either flow through the system as shown in the data flow diagram, or are at rest as stored data in the data stores.

```
Key:

    A =  Attribute, e.g. Month
    E =  Entity, e.g. Product
    V =  Value, e.g. Value of sales

Possible forms of access

    A (E) = ?      Find value of sales for particular product in a particular month.
    A (?) = V      Find which products had certain value of sales in a particular month.
    ? (E) = V      Find which months sales of particular product had given value.
    ? (E) = ?      Find value of sales for all months for specified product.
    A (?) = ?      Find values of sales of all products in a specified month.
    ? (?) = V      Which products in which month had given sales value.
```

Fig 8.12 Data Access
Data which is at rest in the data stores has to be accessed by a process. The data
dictionary in a traditional process-based information systems development method will
define this.

A logical specification of the desired system S_1 produced as the result of such analy-
sis methods was then used as the input to a systems design method such as Yourdon
& Constantine (1978). A good example of this classic coverage is to be found in Page-
Jones (1980), or if you prefer a very elementary introduction, Harry (1990).

We are not going to look at this here for one simple reason. In an article entitled
'Auld Lang Syne', Yourdon (1990) abandoned his earlier position and embraced the
new faith of object-oriented analysis and design, which we shall consider in Section

```
IF (KNOWN CUSTOMER)
   THEN IF (IN STOCK)
           THEN (RECORD DETAILS)
         ELSE (NOT IN STOCK)
           SO IF (FILLABLE PART)
                 THEN (RECORD DETAILS)
               ELSE (NO FILLABLE PART)
                 SO IF (STOCK ITEM)
                       THEN (RECORD PENDING ORDER)
                     ELSE (NOT STOCK ITEM)
                       SO (ACTIVATE REVIEW PROCEDURE)

ELSE (NOT KNOWN CUSTOMER)
   SO (ACCEPTANCE PROCEDURE)
```

Fig 8.13 Structured English
Defines what a process should do in way that can be easily converted
into working computer code. There are many minor variants of structured English; this example is based on the convention for conditional
used by Gane & Sarson (1979).

8.4. He said, while dismissing the class of methods we have just considered, 'Object-orientation is the future ... the 1990s are likely to be a period of gradual acceptance of object-orientation... Meanwhile, just as there will always be a job somewhere on the planet for renegade assembly programmers, there will always be a home for those who want to draw data flow diagrams'.

While the last part of this quotation is hardly a recommendation for us to study Yourdon's earlier systems design methods, the death of process-oriented methods based on the data flow diagram has been greatly exaggerated. Two developments need noting in this respect:

1. Modern methods which inherit the process-oriented tradition have developed to take account of contributions from other methodologies.
2. The advent of CASE tools and automated support (*see* Section 8.7) has meant that the old view of a data flow diagram as something drawn by hand with a pencil and template is disappearing. Instead, the use of this and other tools can be coordinated and integrated to give greater flexibility and adaptability.

We shall now look at a process-oriented method which is very much alive.

8.2.2 Introduction to the application of SSADM

Before looking in more detail at a version of the method known as SSADM, which we introduced in section 7.3.3, it is necessary to answer three questions:

1. Why choose SSADM as an example of a process-oriented method?
2. Where and why has SSADM become a widely known and applied method?
3. Why has SSADM become so successful in the organizational context?

The first question point that needs to be answered is why SSADM has been chosen for our example of a modern method with a process, rather than some other, orientation. As we come to look at the method in more detail, we shall find that it also focusses on such concepts as logical data structure and entity life history. Since these could be taken to imply structure-oriented and object-oriented development respectively, why do we see SSADM as process-oriented?

This apparent contradiction can be resolved if we recall two things. The first is our assertion in section 7.3.6 that we saw the different orientations as complementary views rather than mutually exclusive categories of method. The second is that what determines the orientation is the view which acts as the basis for the method as a whole, and therefore coordinates the overall structure of the method. For SSADM the tool which is used for the overall view of both the existing system S_0 and the desired system S_1 is the data flow diagram. The essence of such a diagram is that it sees an information system as something which processes data. What we see before everything else, when we look at such a diagram, is a model of what happens to the data, i.e. process.

The second question is one we already began to answer when discussing systems analysis in section 7.3.3. There we saw that SSADM in its conventional form is based on a *derivative view* of systems development. Noting this point helps us to understand where and why it has become a popularly applied method. Thus in 1981 it was selected as the mandatory method for United Kingdom government projects, and its use by contractors has helped spread it widely in the private sector, as explained in the Preface to Ashworth & Goodland (1990). Again as we discussed in section 7.3.3, we would expect a derivative method to be popular in government and related organizations, since applications in these areas are likely to have many of their objectives clearly defined by legislation. In such cases the criteria of Fig 7.8 are likely to be applicable.

The third question could be answered by referring to the Preface of Ashworth & Goodland (1990) where they say of SSADM that 'It is a very comprehensive method and, although the techniques do not require a particularly high level of skill to learn, it is often difficult to apply them directly without guidance from an experienced user'. We can understand this weltanschauung or world view in terms of our hierarchical control model of information systems development. We built this up in Section 7.3, and we can now explain it further. If systems development itself is a process that has to be managed, then we can see it as the central purpose of a wider information systems development management system along the lines of the GMOS presented in Chapter 6.

With this view of systems development, we can assess SSADM in terms of the management of information systems development. In this context there are many reasons why large formal organizations would wish to have a 'very comprehensive method', that would 'not require a particularly high level of skill to learn', but would need 'guidance from an experienced user'; because such a method:

a Minimizes the need to 're-invent the wheel'. Thus, a 'very comprehensive method' means that the expensively disturbing effects of an innovative method on large organizations which aim at standardization are reduced.

b De-skills the human input. Reduces the dependence of the effective implementation of the method on particular individuals because it does 'not require a particularly high level of skill to learn'. Makes individuals more easily replaceable.

c Strengthens the implementation of the weltanschauung or world view of the organization by ensuring that the method of systems development conforms to the 'guidance from an experienced user'.

This analysis of the role of SSADM in systems development might be used to stereotype it as a 'conservative' or 'reactionary' methodology. Our view of problems, messes and methodology, which we covered in Sections 7.1 and 7.3.2, should prevent this simplification by reasserting the criterion that methods should be judged in terms of their objectives. On this basis, SSADM could be an excellent method to prevent destructive 'innovation' in such areas as democratic government or financial accountability.

Apart from choosing SSADM as an example of a widely applied process-oriented method, we shall also find that it provides a useful link with our other orientations for systems development methods. As we stated at the end of the previous section, SSADM incorporates tools and techniques from these other orientations, such as JSD in section 8.3.2, and therefore forms a useful lead into the next sections.

With this justification, we can now look at the method in more detail.

8.2.3 The tools, techniques and structure of SSADM

The tools used by SSADM are all ones which have come from existing methodology, since SSADM itself is at the end of a line of methodological development, rather than being a new, innovative method. This is not necessarily a criticism of the method itself; instead it shows its potential strength in using tested technical resources.

The chief tools used by the method are:

a *Data flow diagrams* (DFDs): which show the *data flows, data stores and processes* used by the information system, together with the *external entities* which act as sources and destinations for data outside the system (Fig 8.14).

b *Logical data structures* (LDS): which show how data is brought together to form the emergent property of information.

c *Entity life histories* (ELH): which show how information is changed during its lifetime in relation to the entity to which it refers (Fig 8.15).

To understand the structure of SSADM as a method, it is worth referring to:

    a. The stages of SSADM as shown in Fig 7.5.
    b. The inputs and outputs of these stages as shown in Fig 8.16.

We can note that the use of defined inputs and outputs for each stage of Fig 7.5 is close to that of our general model of the deliverables of the stages of systems development presented in Fig 7.7 and discussed in section 7.3.4.

It is also important to note that in the detailed application of SSADM, each *stage* is broken down into *steps*, which define the *tasks* needed to *transform* defined *inputs* into defined *outputs*. All the terms in the previous sentence which I have put into italics are those defined by the method itself, except the term transform. This latter term is one that I have deliberately chosen to show how the stages of the method can be seen as component processes of systems development seen as a system itself.

Our aim in subsequent sections is now to understand what these stages of SSADM seek to achieve. In doing so, we shall look at the main tasks, tools and techniques that are used. Our approach will concentrate on seeing how the workings of the method relate to the systems and information concepts we developed in earlier chapters and the view of systems development methodology found earlier in this chapter. Since there are over fifty tasks and sub-tasks in fully detailed SSADM, Cutts (1991) or Weaver (1993) should be referred to for a fully detailed run through.

8.2.4 Analysis

Stage 1: Analysis will take as its starting point the terms of reference for the whole project and, possibly, a feasibility study report. The need for terms of reference clearly puts SSADM into the category of a top-down approach which sees the information system in the role of meeting the needs of a wider management system of an organization. The Cutts (1991) criteria of Fig 7.8 make it clear that any soft, messy issues need to be sorted out before moving into a problem area with a clearly structured hard systems method like SSADM. In particular, the ownership of the system must be clear, otherwise we don't know whose view of S_1 we are trying to fulfil.

The feasibility study report is an optional requirement for Stage 1. As we saw in Fig 7.5, the first three stages of SSADM may be repeated in an attempt to gain an initial view of the potential system or choice of systems. Where this happens, the second pass through the analysis stage will include the input of the feasibility study output from stage 3.

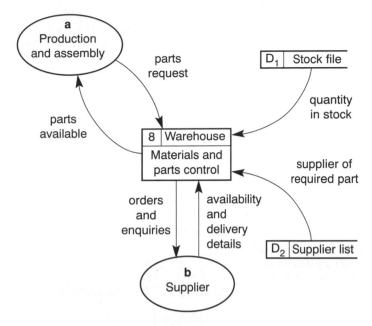

Fig 8.14 Data Flow Diagram (3)
An SSADM version of Fig 8.9.

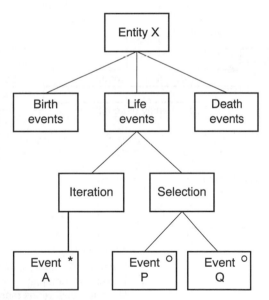

Fig 8.15 Entity Life History
However portrayed, this must show the event that results in the birth of an entity into the system, those events that happen to it during its life in the system, and the event that results in its removal from the system. Entity life histories in SSADM are portrayed in a similar manner to that used in the JSD method (*see* Section 8.3). This is because SSADM has inherited certain aspects of methodology from JSD, and is an example of how process and structure orientations interact.

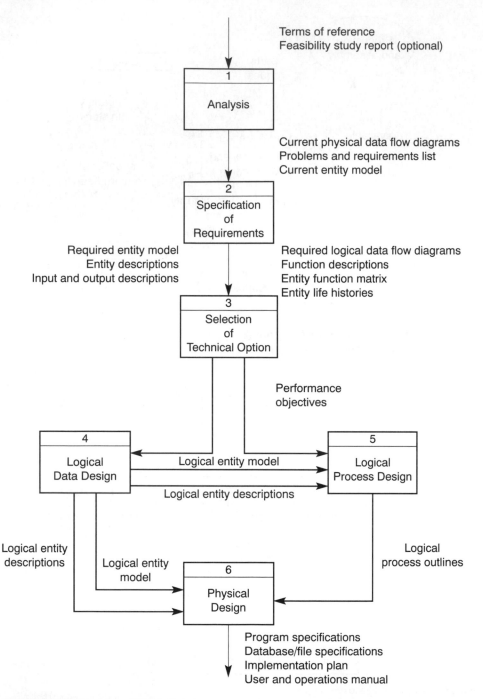

Fig 8.16 SSADM Tools and Techniques

The diagram shows how these are used in relation to the various stages of the method. Although this shows a particular sequence of stages for a particular method, the link between the tools and techniques and the methodological processes is much wider. Thus, for example, data flow diagrams are used to record or define physical and logical systems in many methods.

Where SSADM is being applied in an innovative situation, in the sense discussed in section 7.3.3, the analysis stage will essentially consist of documenting the new system requirements list alone. More typically however, the method will be used in derivative systems development. In this case, analysis (cf. Fig 7.4) will consist of gaining a thorough understanding of:

a. The current system and how it works.
b. What problems are associated with the current system.
c. What additional requirements do we have for the new system.

The outputs from this process will be:

a. Data flow diagrams of the current physical system (cf. section 7.3.3) and an entity model showing its LDS (cf. Section 5.1), to cover *a* above.
b. A problems and requirements list to cover *b* and *c* above.

8.2.5 Specification of requirements

Although the detailed input to this stage can be listed as current system physical DFDs, LDS and a problems and requirements list, what the Analysis Stage must essentially deliver, as the result of producing all these, is the potential for understanding the current system. This understanding enables those concerned with the systems development to see what is wrong with the present system S_0 and what any new system S_1 should deliver.

If this understanding has come from Analysis, then it makes possible the main tasks in the detailed operation of *Stage 2: Specification of Requirements*. These involve extracting and defining the logic which lies behind the existing physical system and setting this against the problems and requirements list. As a result of this comparison, *business system options* (BSOs) are identified which would represent improvements to the logic of the existing system which would meet user requirements. We would see this as analysing the shortcomings or failures of the logical S_0 and identifying possible candidates for a logical S_1.

Once a preferred BSO has been selected, the 'specification' referred to in the stage's title is that of the logical S_1. Hence the outputs from Stage 2, shown in Fig 8.16, are all essentially concerned with defining a logical view of the required system.

8.2.6 Selection of technical options

The first five stages of SSADM place the emphasis on logical analysis and design, and they follow the classic sequence of section 7.3.3 for a failure-driven, derivative method. The intrusion of *Stage 3: Selection of Technical Options* seems at first like a regression to a bottom-up 'I've got a computer; what shall I do with it?' type of approach.

In fact the inclusion of a preliminary consideration of the potential physical implementation before the completion of the detailed logical design is for a good reason. Subsequent choices of physical implementation can actually affect the range of logical choices open to the systems developers in Stages 4 & 5. Thus, for example, the logical design of the processes in *Stage 5: Logical Process Design* can be affected by the envisaged processing power and storage capacity of the computer system. A specific instance of this would be the dependence of the logical choices available on the decision to have real-time rather than batch processing procedures. The choice of a logical system that assumes real-time processing of files will normally imply large-scale processing power and data storage.

Stage 3 is not therefore concerned with detailed physical design choices, since these can only follow the complete logical data and process design of Stages 4 & 5, but it does detail those physical aspects which are needed to refine the specification of requirements sufficiently to allow detailed logical systems design to go ahead.

8.2.7 Logical data design and logical process design

We shall consider these two stages together. If we look at Fig 7.5, or its equivalent in any other specialist presentation of SSADM, we can see that Stages 4 & 5 are seen as parallel, or at least complementary. We can understand the reasoning behind this if we recall the complementary nature of structure and process views of a system which we discussed in section 7.3.6. It is also important to recall that we said in section 8.2.2 that SSADM is a latter-day process-oriented method which has taken on board elements of structure and object-oriented methods. The way that SSADM regards the interrelationship of Stages 4 & 5 is an illustration of this point.

Stages 4 & 5 are concerned with the detailed logical design of the requirements of S_1, as specified in Stage 2 and developed further in terms of the choice of expected technical implementation decided on in Stage 3. The complementary nature of these two stages of systems development in SSADM can be illustrated by the example of data access first discussed in Chapter 5. Defining the way we access data, which is about process, will depend on how that data is arranged, which is about structure. Hence the detailed tasks of Stage 4, which include creating a detailed logical data design, can be seen to be intimately involved with Stage 5 tasks such as defining logical enquiry processing.

Both stages of the method need to be complete before any unambiguous physical system can be developed in Stage 6. We can interpret this criterion in terms of the model of systems development that we put forward in section 7.3.4. We saw there that a design must essentially consist of all the information that the systems builder needs in order to create a system which conforms to the specified needs of the systems users.

8.2.8 Physical design

Stage 6: Physical Design is concerned with how logical views of the desired system, S_1, can be implemented into a physical working system conforming to the logical design of S_1 delivered by the previous stages. Our use of the word implemented reveals the need for a third type of model which can make the link between a very abstract, logical view of the data and processes, and the way in which it is physically done.

What is this link? SSADM does not see it as an automatic or standard move from a preceding stage of the method to the next. This is because the move forward from the definition Stages 4 & 5 to producing the deliverables of *Stage 6: Physical Design* depends on the implementation medium. The details of implementation will therefore depend on the type of systems software to be used in the practical application. Reference to Chapter 5 shows how this bridge between logical and physical views of the treatment of data, which makes up information, should be dealt with using a systemic view.

A final note about SSADM as a very tightly structured, hard information systems development method in the wider context of this book: SSADM can be, and in my experience of talking to users, is sometimes blindly applied to soft, messy situations in the hope that technical expertise will roll like a juggernaut over the soft mess. In practice, this results in either:

a. Truculent acceptance by potential actors, using this word in the sense of section 8.1.3, or:

b. Naive acceptance by systems owners, also in the sense of section 8.1.3, that if SSADM is 'official' it must be OK.

Either of these views detracts from the way in which SSADM can accommodate a wider, holist view of systems development. If we look at the details of the structure of the method in terms of its stages, Stages 3, 4, & 5 are all defined as contributing to the final stage of physical design. Our systems view of systems development should help us see that SSADM need not be 'derivative' or 'process-oriented' in any colloquial, pejorative sense. Indeed, the concept that the final implementation in *Stage 6: Physical Design* takes account of technical options, logical data and process views of the desired system S_1 makes it more holist than either its supporters or opponents may realize.

Box 8.1

MADNESS OF TOO MANY METHODS

(*Financial Times* 27/8/96: all the italics are mine)

The European Commission's zeal for standardisation has reached the software industry with the release this month of Euromethod, a pan-European standard for procuring computer systems, which the EC hopes will improve competitiveness in Europe's fragmented software market.

Euromethod started in 1989 as an attempt to overcome the problems caused by incompatible systems development 'methods'. . . A method defines the procedural and technical standards to be used in developing an information system. It provides a framework for developing and managing large complex information systems, *thus reducing risks*.

Methods are not foolproof, as the London Stock Exchange found out with *Taurus*, a paperless system which was plagued with delays and finally abandoned . . . at a cost of £50m. Taurus was supposedly developed using the Structured Systems Analysis and Design Method, but many SSADM guidelines were not followed. . .

Used properly, methods can *reduce misunderstandings* between *contractor and customer* by explicitly defining responsiblities and setting milestones. SSADM was originally developed as a standard for public projects in the UK . . . Italy's state-owned company Finsiel developed Dafne . . . France, Germany, the Netherlands and Spain also have their own methods.

The main problem is understanding the precise *meaning of concepts and terminologies* used in different methods. For example, is the 'preliminary study' of one method equivalent to the 'requirements analysis' of the other?

Also, the *vocabularies used are typically derived from software engineering* and can be *difficult to understand by non-specialists*.

. . . Euromethod aims to overcome these hurdles . . . It acts as a sort of *Esperanto*. . .

COMMENT

This article by Geoff Nairn includes some good examples of the issues raised when we seek to use *structured* methods and *standards* in information systems development.

A central information systems concept raised by this article is that systems development is itself a system whose processes we seek to control. Managing systems development will require us to identify and understand the *normative*, *reflective* and *automatic* components which may be present in the goal-setting implied by the term 'standard'.

With the Euromethod, the European Commission is attempting to control the software procurement process, where national attempts at standards have failed. The *normative* assumption behind this attempt at control is that a common European dimension, like the artificial language Esperanto, is desirable, and that 'fragmentation' is somehow bad. Note how the choice of language gives the normative spin. We could spin the language the other way by remembering that one person's 'fragmentation' can be another person's 'diversity'.

So is the Euromethod merely an unnecessary bureaucratic interference? The answer to this question comes from the arguments for and against structuring systems development which we covered in section 7.2. On a European scale, systems must be developed by large numbers of people across different organizations in different countries. In such a context, informal unstructured methods make consistency and control very difficult. Imagine delegates from across the EU assembling in the bar at Schipol airport to sort out a new computerized information system for cooperating European firms. It might work well as a human activity system, but consider the problems that come when some of the people who were at the original meeting move on, and new people with different opinions are incorporated into the decision-making and management process. I suspect it would be the longest party in history.

Hence structured methods and standards come into their own when we try to coordinate the activities of large numbers of people and organizations. But as in any control system, attempts at control by the European Commission must see that goal-setting is itself part of the control process. The process of setting standards must provide for feedback and modification. The weakness of many attempts at standardization is that much effort goes into setting the standards, but little effort is devoted to designing systems for their review and replacement. Euromethod is likely to be as successful and enduring (or otherwise) as the national standards which it replaces. Given that a so-called standard method like SSADM is in its *fourth* version, will we really be surprised if Euromethod has been changed or abandoned in 50 years' time?

FURTHER STUDY

Identify an organization which claims to use standard information systems development methods such as SSADM. Has the method ever been used without modification?

Consider how the concepts of *experience* and *learning* as in section 3.2.4 might be applied to information systems development. If you were responsible for advising the European Commission, what would you suggest about the implementation of Euromethod?

8.3   STRUCTURE-ORIENTED DEVELOPMENT

8.3.1 The main features of structure orientation

We saw in section 7.3.6 that structure-oriented methods use the view that information is data organized into a particular structure as their starting point. Once this structure has been established, the processes needed for its production can then be derived from the structure itself. Typically, the tasks which are performed when developing a system using a structure-oriented method are:

1. Identify the data structures that make up the information which the system must process.
2. Analyse the relationship between the components of the data structures in terms of sequence, conditionals and iteration.
3. Define the processes which will produce the components of the data structure.
4. Map the structural relationship of the data into a control hierarchy for the processes.

We can illustrate these general principles of structure-oriented methods by choosing the specific example of the method known as *Jackson Structured Programming* (JSP), *see* Jackson (1975). We choose this particular method because, although it is a *software* programming method rather than a systems development method, it fulfils two of our requirements at the same time. Besides illustrating structure-orientation, it also provides the background to a later systems development method which Jackson also developed. This latter method is known as *Jackson System Development* (JSD), *see* Jackson (1983), which we shall study in detail in the next sections. The stages of JSP require:

1. Analyse the data structure.
2. Convert the data structure to a program structure.
3. Define the program operations.
4. Insert the program operations into the data structure.
5. Convert the structured program operations into pseudo-code.

Comparison of the first four stages of JSP with our general view of structure-oriented method shows that JSP conforms closely to the principle of making the data structure the basis for determining the organization or structuring of the process.

We can now look at a simple example to illustrate JSP. Suppose we wish to develop a program which has to produce a monthly statement of account for a customer. The account statement has to show what they have bought on credit during the month and how much they owe at the end of the month. The logical structure of such an account can be illustrated with a diagram such as Fig 8.17. This is called a data structure diagram, and resembles many other similar forms of diagram used to show hierarchical structure.

Sequence in such a diagram is shown by the convention of reading from left to right, iteration by the use of an asterisk symbol for those components which may iterate, and an o-character for conditional components whose occurrence depends on a particular condition being true.

Hence we see that the Monthly Account will consist of:

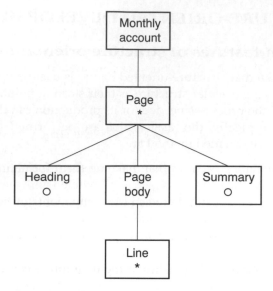

Fig 8.17 Data Structure Diagram
By defining the logical structure of the data it also defines the processess
which have to be carried out to produce its physical representation.

- one or more (i.e. iteration of) pages
- lines which may be (i.e. conditional) heading or summary
- one or more (i.e. iteration of) lines.

Presenting the logical structure of the Monthly Account in this way will fulfil the first
stage of JSP: Analyse the data structure, and conforms to what we said any structure-
oriented method would do in terms of analysing the relationship between the
components of the data structures in terms of sequence, conditionals and iteration.

```
open files
while not end of Monthly Account
do
        write page heading
        initialize line count
        while not end of page
        do

                write line
                increment line count
        end while
write summary line
end while
close files
```

Fig 8.18 Pseudo-Code
Just another example of a method of defining a process with sufficient rigour
for it to be unambiguously converted into working software, cf. Fig 8.13.

The second stage of JSP requires us to convert the data structure to a program structure. This is very easy. Once we have decided in what physical form the logical structure has to be manifested, we just have to put the appropriate verb or imperative action in front of each component. So, if we wanted the Monthly Account to be printed, we would put 'print Monthly Account', 'print page', etc., in front of each component in the structure diagram.

Stages 3 to 5 require us to define the program operations, to insert the program operations into the data structure, and to convert the structured program operations into pseudo-code. Figure 8.18 shows what the results of these three stages might look like in terms of our Monthly Account example. The sequence of operations is reflected by our movement down the listing. Iterations ('do while') and conditionals (true/false or 'not') are expressed in terms of do while/do while not type statements which we can find in any modern processing software.

The important feature that comes from this brief study of JSP is that specification of what the software should do, i.e. process, derives directly from the structure of the information it is intended to produce. In developing his systems development method JSD, Jackson applied the same principle. JSD builds a model of the desired system, and uses the structure of this model to derive specifications of what processes the software must carry out.

8.3.2 Introduction to JSD

We will try to justify our choice of Jackson System Development (JSD) as an example of structure-oriented development by asking some initial questions as we did when justifying the choice of SSADM as a process-oriented method:

1. Is JSD a structure-oriented method?
2. How does JSD fit into our view of methodology developed in section 7.3.6?
3. Are there any additional reasons to choose JSD?

The first question has already been partially answered in the previous section. Since JSD was developed after JSP by the same person and using a common weltanschauung, it would not be surprising to find similarities of approach. Indeed Jackson (1983) himself regards a system as a 'large program' and JSD as an extension of JSP. As we go further into JSD, I think we shall see that its initial emphasis on the structural make-up of entities and the relationship between them give the method a strong structure orientation.

Other authors come close to our view. Pressman (1987) describes JSD as 'data structure-oriented' rather than 'data flow-oriented' or 'object-oriented'. Booch (1991) categorizes JSD as 'data-driven' rather than 'top-down structured', i.e. design methods linked with data flow orientation, or 'object-oriented'. Sutcliffe (1988) says , 'JSD guides the analyst to model the system's basic *structure* rather than some of its more obvious manifestations as *functions* ...Most of JSD's rivals fall into the functional school of methods which concentrate on the process communication model'. (The emphases in the quotations are mine.)

Having shown why I think JSD can be described as structure-oriented, we shall also see that, as with SSADM or any other method, the orientation is not exclusive. The concept of making the system model entities in the real-world gives it certain characteristics which link it to object-oriented methods, as we shall see below.

In answering our first question above we have already run naturally into the second question: how does JSD look in relation to our view of methodology developed in Section 7.3? We have already seen it as a structure-oriented method, but what of the methodological questions of:

- approaches and methods
- the stages of systems development
- top-down and bottom-up approaches?

The answers to these methodological questions show JSD to be a very individualistic method, so we shall look at them each in turn.

JSD is certainly a structured method rather than an unstructured approach because its earlier and later versions are structured in the sense that they have steps and stages respectively. Figure 8.19 shows the steps of the earlier version of JSD, to be found in Jackson (1983); and the stages of the more recent version in Sutcliffe (1988). Figure 8.19 also shows how the stages of the more recent version represent a partial amalgamation of the earlier steps.

The next methodological question is how JSD compares with the view of the stages of systems development we set out in section 7.3.4. But if we look at this question, reference to Jackson (1983) shows that it cannot be separated from the third question of top-down and bottom-up approaches.

Jackson sees JSD as a bottom-up approach which ignores the conventional view of 'the systems life cycle' or 'analysis' followed by 'design'. His explicit statement in Jackson (1983) that his method is bottom-up thus appears to reject the top-down view implicit in Birrell & Ould (1985) which we developed in section 7.3.4. His reasoning is that high-level decisions about what S_1 should be are decided 'at the time of greatest ignorance'; i.e. when we begin the systems development process.

Harry (1990)	Jackson (1983)	Sutcliffe (1988)
Definition & Analysis	Entity/Action	Modelling
	Entity/Structure	
	Initial Model	Network
Design	Function	
	Systems Timing	
Production	Implementation	Implementation

Fig 8.19 JSD: Steps and Stages
The table shows the approximate correspondence between the *steps* of the original form of JSD with the *stages* of the later form. These are both related to the overall methodological view of the stages of systems development given in Fig 7.7.

However, I think that we can see that JSD does have features that follow our view of the top-down nature of systems development. First we notice that the implementation follows those stages concerned with modelling the system. Hence 'whats' come before 'hows'. Second, no attempt to model a system can proceed without some concept of the whole that enables us to decide what is and what is not part of the system to be modelled. When JSD refers to a 'model' we only have to ask 'model of what?' to realize that somewhere a high-level concept has already been decided on, even if not made explicit by the method, which is being realized top-down as we build the model up. Figure 8.19 therefore shows how the steps or stages of JSD correspond to our methodological view.

Finally, it is worth noting that several authors, like Avison & Fitzgerald (1988), point out that JSD is not a complete method. While its activities run right through to systems implementation, it omits detailed guidance on such topics as database design.

Having set JSD in its context, we will now look at its main features. To do this we will go through the sequence of steps to be found in the earlier version, but set them in the combinations which make up the stages of the later version, as in Fig 8.19.

8.3.3 The modelling stage

The concept of a model plays a central role in JSD. We introduced the concept in Chapter 3, where we saw that the purpose of a model was to represent something. That 'something' could be an existing physical, concrete system or an abstract concept.

The particular concept of modelling used in JSD fits our general view. In this case what is being modelled is what goes on in the real-world. A strong emphasis is placed on the correct modelling of the way things change over time in the real-world so that the information system we develop will accurately reflect the dynamics of the real-world system it seeks to control.

We also need to note the concept which we introduced in the previous section. JSD uses a bottom-up approach in much of its detailed application.

With these two fundamentals of the JSD approach to modelling we are ready to understand the first, *entity-action*, step of the method. As its name implies, this step is concerned with identifying entities and actions in the real-world which are relevant to the information system which JSD seeks to develop. Once identified, these entities will be used to build a model of the real-world.

Identifying entities is not an automatic procedure. It requires skill and judgement. The most commonly recommended way of doing it is to identify the nouns in any description of the real-world situation that we seek to model. If we take the example of Carry-Out Cupboards we find the following entities mentioned or implied:

> Customer
> Supplier
> Supplier list
> Order
> Stock record
> Cupboard.

Not all of these are entities in the JSD sense. The use of the term entity in JSD is not the same as that we described in Chapter 5. Entities as defined in Chapter 5 could include entities which were part of the computerized information system such as a supplier list or a stock record. JSD would not include these as entities in the entity-action step because they are part of the way in which the existing information system describes the real-world rather than being part of it.

Sutcliffe (1988) says that 'Discovering entities within a system is one of the more difficult tasks in JSD'. I think that our control systems view of businesses and organizations which we established in Chapter 3 and developed in Chapter 6 makes this task easier. We saw that a control system sought to control a process, with its inputs and outputs, by means of an information system, which provided the sensor, feedback, etc. JSD is concerned with developing a new information system which will control the processes of a business or organization. Any entities which are part of that existing information system are not part of the real-world process which JSD seeks to model and control. Hence entities within the existing information system, or outputs from it, are not included in the entity-action step.

Entities which are included must be uniquely named and must retain their individuality or type throughout their life. A specifically important property relevant to this step of JSD is that they perform actions, or have action performed on them ('suffer' actions), in a set order. Actions must:

a *Take place at a point in time.* Actions are not continuous. Thus 'selling' would not be an action in JSD, since it is a continuous activity; but 'concluding a sale' would be, because it occurs as an event at a point in time.

b *Take place in the real-world.* This requirement is a repetition of the need, we identified above, to distinguish between the real-world system and the information system which seeks to control it. Thus 'print supplier list' is not an action but 'engage supplier' is.

Having identified the relevant entities of the real-world system and the actions which they perform or suffer, we are ready for the next, *entity structure*, step. This seeks to establish the structural relationship between an entity and its associated actions. The tool used for this can be either a *structure diagram* or a *structure text*.

Figure 8.20 shows a structure diagram, sometimes called a *process structure diagram* (PSD), for the entity 'supplier' as it might be for Carry-Out Cupboards. Notice the dia-

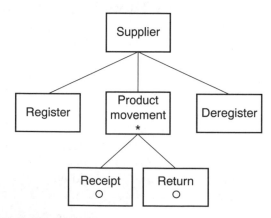

Fig 8.20 JSD; Entity Life History
The similarity to Fig 8.13 comes from the inheritance of the tool by SSADM.

gramming convention is identical to that for the structure diagrams used in JSP, *see* Fig 8.17. Structure text in JSD also follows on from the principles established in JSP. JSD structure text is very similar to the pseudo-code of JSP, with conventions for showing sequence, iteration and conditionals.

8.3.4 The network stage

The conclusion of the modelling stage has left us with a detailed structured view of individual real-world entities and their actions, which concern us as systems developers. We now seek to specify an information system which will enable us to model and, by means of this model, control these real-world entities and their actions.

This talk of 'models' and 'modelling' may seem confusing. Haven't we just been 'modelling' in the previous stage? What 'model' are we talking about now? Answering these questions leads us naturally into the first, *initial model*, step of the network stage.

In the previous stage we were concerned with identifying and describing the entities and their actions which we wished to model. We need therefore to distinguish between the real-world entities themselves which we have identified, and the description of them that we wish to use in our model of the real-world.

JSD recognizes the need for this distinction and has a convention to deal with it. When representing any entity, JSD uses a suffix to the name of the entity to distinguish the real-world entity itself from its representation in the model. The suffix '-0' is placed after the name of a real-world entity, and the suffix '-1' after the process which we use to represent it, and its actions in the model. Thus Supplier-0 refers to an actual supplier to, say, Carry-Out Cupboards; while Supplier-1 refers to a process in the model which specifies the information system.

At this point we should note two things. First, the 0 and 1 in the suffixes have nothing to do with our use of them in S_0 and S_1. Second, our use of the word 'process' in the previous paragraph needs further explanation.

The aim of the initial model step is to begin the specification of the information system. It does this using a *systems specification diagram* (SSD), which acts as a simulation model (*see* Chapter 3) of what happens in the real-world. Since the model simulates the real-world, every entity in the real-world will be represented by a process in the SSD. What each process does will be defined by the structure text which we developed for the corresponding entity at the previous entity structure step.

The representation of real-world entities as processes in a model was already prepared for by the previous step of JSD. If the SSD is to be a simulation model of a system however, we now need to consider how these potential *components* are *connected* into a *whole*. (The use of italics here is aimed to point us back to the important properties of any system, as per Chapter 3.)

Reference to the diagramming components of Fig 8.21 shows how systemic connexion can be made. JSD SSDs represent the connexions both between model processes, and between them and the corresponding real-world entities, by defining how they communicate. JSD distinguishes two kinds of communication:

1 A *data stream connexion* is one which where a stream of sequential messages, such as text being keyed into a microcomputer, connects two processes as between materials and parts control and purchasing and supply as in Fig 8.21.

2 A *state vector connexion* represents the situation where one process inspects the state of another process at a particular point in time like the checking of stock availability in Fig 8.21.

The deliverable of the initial model step is a simulation model of the real-world which the information system is designed to control. This model still lacks a description of how it will be in communication with this real-world system. Since the model needs to communicate in order to function, the next step of the network stage which defines this communication is called the *function step*. It covers the omission of communication in the SSD by adding a specification of the function processes which produce the required outputs and those which receive defined inputs. These processes will be defined by structure text and connected through data streams or state vectors like other model processes. Since JSD is a structure-oriented method, the definition of these function processes will derive directly from the structure of the data involved as for JSP in section 8.3.1.

At the end of the function step we have a SSD showing:

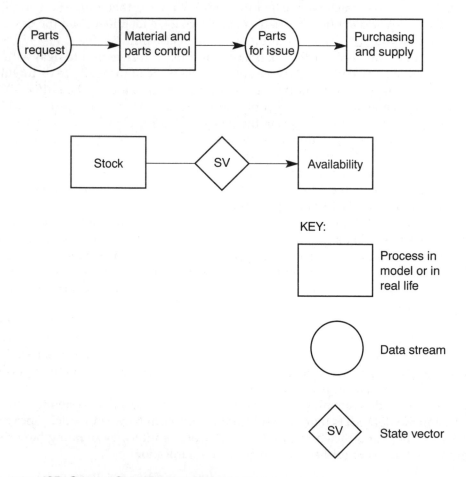

Fig 8.21 JSD: System Specification Diagrams
These are used to form the initial model before merging in the network stage. The diagram shows the two forms of process connexion used in the modelling.

- all the model and function processes
- the connexion of all processes to each other and the real-world via data streams and state vectors
- structure text reflecting the structure of a modelled entity for model processes
- the structure of input or output data for function processes.

Although the function step leaves us with a complete logical model in terms of connexion, we still have not considered when information is needed and therefore when processes should run. This is very much in line with what Jackson considers to be a bottom-up approach, which avoids unnecessarily early decisions made at a time of ignorance. The *systems timing step* continues with this philosophy. It only builds timing constraints into the SSD where these are needed to define a process itself. Thus if a vendor rating system for Carry-Out Cupboards required a regular printout of supplier performance, the timing or frequency of this process would only be settled in the SSD if it had been specifically defined to produce an output, such as a 'monthly average', whose actual nature has a specific timing implication. Where the SSD is not affected, the timing constraints are left until the final implementation stage.

8.3.5 The implementation stage

The *implementation step* of earlier JSD and the later version's implementation stage are the same. The aim is to convert the system specified by the SSD into working software. Given the tight nature of structure code and its virtual similarity with many high-level programming languages, this conversion could be virtually automatic. As Birrell & Ould (1985) amusingly point out, we could allocate a separate microprocessor to each process and use shared memory for communication between them. A logically possible but hardly efficient implementation!

The final stage of JSD is therefore concerned with deciding how to:

a. Share processors amongst processes
b. Schedule processes
c. Share memory amongst parts of processes.

However, making these decisions is essentially one of allocation and arrangement. The essence of JSD is that the code is seen as a semi-automatic derivative from the SSD and its structure text. Code is never written directly or changed: it is only generated from higher-level descriptions.

(We might note, finally, that the use of the term higher-level in the previous paragraph means that we are right to have reservations about Jackson's 'bottom-up' assertions for JSD?)

8.4 OBJECT-ORIENTED DEVELOPMENT

8.4.1 The main features of object-orientation

Object-orientation is the most recent of our views of systems development. Placing it last in our study of systems development methodology is not just a question of historical sequence. Given our earlier distinction of method and methodology in Section 7.2, it makes sense that our study or learning about method, i.e. methodology, should place object-orientation last. This is because object-orientation is a view that comes as the result of experience and learning in systems development, as we shall see later. Meanwhile it is worth referring to some of the initial concepts relating to object-orientation which we covered in Chapters 3–5: in particular hierarchy, classification and object-oriented databases.

To begin understanding object-oriented systems development we need to answer similar questions about object-orientation to those we asked about process- and structure-oriented methods. Important questions we should answer are:

1. Is object-orientation actually a systems development method?
2. How does object-orientation fit into our view of methodology developed in section 7.3.6?
3. What is the relationship between object-orientation, other orientations we have studied, and systems thinking?
4. Why does object-orientation appear to be a present fashion or vogue in the field of information systems and computing?

I think that the answer to our first question is likely to be very messy. To explain this opinion further we need to recall that in section 7.3.6 we distinguished between structured methods and unstructured approaches. Methods we saw as having a clear-cut, definable sequence of stages, each with its specific deliverables. Approaches we saw as less structured but still based on a clear set of principles. We can find references to 'method', 'milestones' and 'products' in major authors like Booch (1991). This sequence of terms sounds suspiciously like methods, stages and deliverables respectively; but I think we should treat this similarity with caution. Booch himself emphasizes the strongly iterative nature of object-oriented design, and many practitioners of object-orientation advocate that one of its major advantages is that it is not tied to a rigid development sequence. (At a recent major conference on object-oriented design I heard one very experienced delegate maintain that anyone offering object-oriented methods would, by definition, not know what object-orientation was actually about!) We shall say more of this issue when considering prototyping below.

Meanwhile, a clue to how I think object-orientation ought to be viewed comes from the devious way I switched from object-oriented to object-orientation earlier in this section. I think that what we are considering in this section is object-oriented approaches or an object-orientation in our view of systems development, rather than a structured method. As we shall see, an object-oriented approach brings very specific definitions, procedures and deliverables with it; but it does not bring anything as detailed as stages like we find them in SSADM or even JSD.

Answering this first question then leads naturally to an answer for the second. If object-oriented systems development is an approach rather than a method, but it involves specific definitions, procedures and deliverables, then we can see it as unstructured but hard. We would place it more towards region A of Fig 7.9 rather than region B.

What of the other methods we have considered? What is the relationship between object-orientation and other method orientations we have studied? This is the third question we raised above.

We can use JSD as the link here that helps our understanding of the answers to these questions. JSD saw modelling of real-world entities as a central task. The model which was then developed was used to inform us of the state of the real-world, so that we could make decisions as to how to control it.

Examples of this method of control are very common outside the field of business or organizational information systems. Thus a modern railway signal box has an electronic screen diagramming the track layout, and the position and movement of trains. Changes in the real-world situation are reflected by changes of what is shown on the screen. Thus, as a train moves along the track, so a light representing the train moves along the diagram of the track on the screen.

◆ **STQ 8.4**
What difference would you see between the railway model and those used in systems development?

Object-orientation uses modelling in a similar way. It also creates a systemic software model of the real-world situation which we wish to control, but this model is made up of objects. The concept of an object was first used in the Simula programming language. In that, and subsequent object-oriented applications, objects existed in programs to simulate some aspect of real-life.

Thus the components of an object-oriented model will include clusters of program language code that enable us to do this.

Thus far, we can see a close similarity with JSD. We are concerned with simulating some particular thing, which exists in the real-world and which we can apparently call either an entity or an object. However, real-world entities are not the only objects which an object-oriented approach will consider in developing the software which implements the information system through the model. An object can be any concrete or abstract identifiable element or component of what Booch (1991) calls 'the problem domain'.

We can further develop the concept of an object in systems terms by quoting Halbert & O'Brian (1988), as edited by Booch (1991): 'Other important kinds of objects are inventions of the design process whose collaborations with other objects serve as mechanisms that provide some higher-level behaviour.'

There are three important phrases or words used here, which will enable us to understand how an object-oriented approach can be seen in systems terms:

    a. The use of the word 'invention'.
    b. The phrase '*process* [my italics] whose collaborations'.
    c. The term 'higher-level behaviour'.

We will now look at each of these in turn to see how an object-oriented approach to information systems development relates to the other orientations we have presented.

The use of the word invention implies that an object is someone's concept: inventions do not come into being without the existence of inventors. The quotation describes objects as inventions of 'the design process', but any implication that this is an abstract impersonal procedure is nonsense. People make design processes work and they set the weltanschauung for them. The false implication that objects are somehow objective is something we shall look at more deeply later in this chapter.

Process and collaboration have strong systemic implications. Together, these words not only imply that objects do something, but that they do it in an ordered and connected way. Thus the systemic concepts of process, connexion and structure are clearly present when modelling the world in object terms.

Behaviour is a holist concept of an emergent property which the definition places in the context of hierarchy by its use of the term higher-level.

Given this set of systems concepts and the systems thinking behind the definition, is object-orientation no different from the kind of systems view we have considered so far? I think that the answer to this question is best understood if we begin by rejecting the false implication that somehow a systems view and object-orientation are somehow opposites or alternatives between which we have to choose. An object-oriented model of real-life, with its components, connexion, interaction, structure, hierarchy, etc., can easily be seen as systemic. What gives it an object-orientation, rather than any other orientation, is the particular way it views:

- The components (i.e. the objects) and their interactions through the passing of messages.
- The nature of hierarchy and how types of hierarchy can be classified.

In formal terms, the essential concepts that give object-orientation this view are:

- Abstraction
- Encapsulation
- Modularity
- Hierarchy

Abstraction focusses on the essential characteristics of an object which clearly define it relative to the perspective of the viewer. Thus in Carry-Out Cupboards, someone interested in order processing would see a cupboard as a sales item in terms of characteristics like sales-to-date or stock levels; while someone interested in assembly and packing might see a cupboard as a physical product in terms of its components and their structural relationship within the finally assembly.

We are very familiar with this concept as a result of our study of systems. What a system is and is not seen to be, will depend on whose values and purposes we are referring to. Similarly, 'the essential characteristics' of an object will depend on whose 'perspective' we are taking. The concept of *abstraction* is particularly important in developing the further concept of hierarchy, which we discuss below.

Encapsulation is not something we have explicitly met with before, but I think it is not entirely new to us. It is the process of specifying what essential characteristics an object has, while 'hiding' how it produces them. I think that the concept of a black box (Chapter 3) is similar to encapsulation. In both cases we know what kinds of input will produce what outputs, but we don't know what goes on to produce them. The difference between the two concepts is that encapsulation involves deliberately hiding how an object carries out operations or methods. This is done to protect the object from unnecessary modification or interference during systems development, implementation and use.

Understanding encapsulation is an important prerequisite to the understanding of the concepts of *message passing* between objects and their behaviour, which we study later. For the moment we should note that the concept of encapsulation enables us to see objects as 'an encapsulation of a set of operations or methods which can be invoked externally and of a state which remembers the effects of the methods', Blair (1991). We might illustrate this by considering an object like a packing machine in the central assembly and packing facility of Carry-Out Cupboards. Such a machine can assemble and pack a specified quantity of one of the cupboards in response to 'requests' from another object, like a production scheduler.

Modularity 'packages abstractions into discrete units', Booch (1991); or, 'with the introduction of objects, a system has a natural modular *structure* (my emphasis) consisting of a number of objects *interacting* (my emphasis again) via message passing'. We can therefore see the object model as showing the same characteristics we have always emphasized for any system. It just happens to be a particular form of system where the components are exclusively objects, where the structure is expressed as modularity, and in which interaction between components takes the form of passing messages.

Object-orientation uses the term *hierarchy* in both the 'kind of' and 'part of' senses which we introduced in Chapter 3. For most of this book our control model view of management has led us to emphasize the aggregation or 'part of' view. In object-orientation the classification or 'kind of' view gets much more attention. It enables us to classify objects according to shared characteristics, at increasing levels of abstraction. This in turn enables the re-use of implemented software for commonly shared characteristics. We will now say more of this while answering our final question.

The final question we posed at the beginning of this section was why object-orientation appears to be a present fashion or vogue.

My approach to answering this comes from the view of systems development presented in section 7.3.4 where we saw methodology in its true sense as involving learning in the context of higher-order control. We now have had several decades during which computer-based information and other systems have been developed, used, modified and discarded. We have gained a large amount of experience, including the kind of which Oscar Wilde said 'experience is the name we give to our mistakes'.

A major feature of object-orientation is that the emphasis on hierarchy and classification we introduced above enables us to build on our existing experience. In systems development terms, object-orientation enables us to avoid having to re-invent the wheel, if all we want is a new wheel with a different diameter. But to pursue this analogy further, object-orientation enables us to cash in on the fact that a wheel is a circular object, to avoid the need for designing a manhole cover from scratch. In the software context this principle leads to the feature of 're-usable code' as an important product of an object-oriented approach. It means that once a particular software need is seen as an instance of a wider category of application for which we already have working software, the new software is generated from what exists, rather than being built from scratch.

This important feature then brings others with it. Re-usable software, or even whole designs, reduce the risks which come from starting with something completely new and untried. It also allows for evolutionary systems development based on learning.

Given this 'plug' for object-oriented systems development, let us now look at some of its main principles in more detail.

8.4.2 Objects and their properties

An object has three important properties which we need to understand:

1. State
2. Behaviour
3. Identity

and when considering these for more than one object, we can develop the further concept of:

4. Class.

Booch (1991) says that the state of an object encompasses 'all of the (usually static) properties of the object plus the current (usually dynamic) values of each of these properties'.

We can explore this view of the *state of an object* by developing the example of one specific cupboard from the Carry-Out Cupboards range. One of the properties of such a cupboard is the total quantity sold. This property is static because it is unlikely to be changed to anything else like the total quantity bought. As long as Carry-Out Cupboards are in the business of selling cupboards, this property will be one of continued interest. The value of the property is dynamic however, because the total quantity sold will take up different values through time.

Although properties and values are referred to as being 'usually' static and dynamic respectively, they can be otherwise. The value for the property surface finish will be static, since it will remain unchanged as long as the cupboard exists as part of the Carry-Out Cupboards range. The property of VAT Code is likely to be fixed for the commercial life of the cupboard, but it is not impossible that VAT could be changed or abolished.

The value of a property can denote another object rather than a simple quantity. Thus the state of a Carry-Out Cupboards retail outlet will include references to individual cupboards stocked.

Like many other concepts in object-orientation, the concept of the state of an object is not as new or as unusual as may sometimes be claimed. Just one example of what we are already familiar with is that of an attribute of an entity taking on a particular value. This will not seem terribly different from the concept that a property of an object will take on a particular value. A difference does begin to appear when we go on to consider the additional concepts that can be applied to thinking about objects. When we have considered them we shall find that an object is a richer concept than that of an entity in terms of how it is applied.

The *behaviour of an object* is described in terms of the changes of state it undergoes as the result of passing and receiving messages to and from other objects.

The concept of message passing was introduced in the previous section. We can now see an object (Fig 8.22) as being an encapsulation of:

a. A *set of operations or methods* which can be invoked by a message from another object. (Since a message is an operation which one object performs on another, the terms are 'two sides of the same coin'.)
b. A *state* which remembers the effect of the methods.

Behaviour is therefore an emergent property describing the whole of what an object suffers and does as a component with these properties.

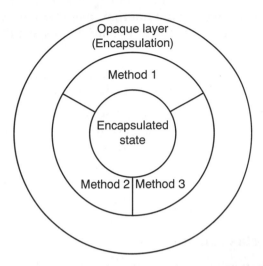

Fig 8.22 Object-Orientation: an Encapsulated Object
An object is an encapsulation of a set of operations or methods which can be invoked externally, and of a state which remembers the effect of the methods.

Recalling the concept of emergent property is also a useful way of understanding *object identity*. A mistake which is easily made is to confuse the name of an object and the object itself. As long as we recall the holist thinking behind the concept of emergent property, then we can see that the identity of an object is not just a name or a label, but the emergent whole of the properties that make the object what it is.

This view of identity goes beyond the use of keys, labels or variable names, and an object keeps its identity even when its state is completely changed.

Once we have the concepts of state, behaviour and identity to help us understand the nature of individual objects, we can then move on to understand something of the *relationships* between them. We can use this understanding to build an object-oriented model of the real-life situation we seek to control.

Object-oriented approaches describe the forms of such relationships in terms of the concept of *class*. These relationships can be:

    a. Using-relationships
    b. Containing-relationships

which we look at in turn.

Using-relationships are those where objects are principally seen in terms of how they affect one another. We could see, for example in Fig 8.23, that any object that had a control function might send a message to another object in order to check on some value of its state in order to receive feedback information from that object.

Containing-relationships are those which we can see in terms of our view of the aggregation of components within a systemic hierarchy, as in Chapter 3. In the Carry-Out Cupboards case we would therefore see a cupboard as consisting of components like container unit, doors, etc., as in Fig 8.23.

I think that our systems view would interpret these two forms of object-oriented relationship in terms of process and structure contributions that they each make to the object-oriented model. Thus:

- Using-relationships are principally concerned with *process*.
- Containing-relationships are principally concerned with *structure*.

We can now consider how the concept of class enables us to understand how an object-oriented approach goes beyond the view of objects and their properties being the same as that of entities and attributes. We said that a difference would appear when we considered additional concepts that can be applied to our thinking about objects. *Class* and *Class Hierarchy* are the additional concepts that enable us to see that an object is a richer concept than that of an entity.

8.4.3 Class and class hierarchy

To understand how object-orientation sees the concept of a class, we need to look back to the important role of modelling in an object-oriented approach. We said above that an object in our object-oriented model represents 'any concrete or abstract identifiable element or component ... of the problem domain'. The concept of *class* then leads us to seeing how a set of objects can share a *common structure* and a *common behaviour*. When we do this, we see a class as an abstraction of the properties that enable us to relate and distinguish objects in terms of their characteristics.

Four kinds of class hierarchy relationships can be found in object-orientation:

1. Inheritance
2. Using
3. Instantiation
4. Meta-class relationships.

We can explore the idea of class and class relationships by referring to a usefully stupid question which I know was once set in an IQ test:

Which of the following three things is the odd one out: a dog, a cat, a television set?

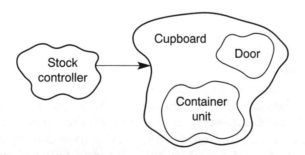

Fig 8.23 Object-Orientation: Using- and Containing-Relationships
The stock controller *uses* the object cupboard when it sends a message in order to check its availability. The cupboard itself has a *containing* relationship with its hierarchical components, container unit and door.

The question was set at a time when both dogs and TVs required licences and a cat didn't. So the official answer was that a cat was the odd one out. Presumably that meant that people like me, who thought a TV was the odd one out because it wasn't an animal, had low IQs! Anyway, when I learnt the answer to this, I sarcastically suggested that a dog was the odd one out because a cat and a TV are both working components of the Harry family dogless household. However, we are indebted to whoever set this question for simply illustrating some important points.

The first point is about classification itself. Although the 'obvious' answer to the IQ question may have been to see a TV as the odd one out, in practice it would depend on what purpose we had in attempting to classify the three types of objects. Thus the viewpoint of a vet would be different from that of an object-oriented systems developer trying to create a national system for licensing TVs, dogs, shotguns, etc. An object, we saw earlier, is someone's concept; and this concept is in turn dependent on the standpoint and aims of the person whose concept it is.

An important practical systems development point follows from this. Although it is likely that the implementation of object-oriented systems development will lie in the hands of a systems programmer, the weltanschauung or world view built into the system by the assumptions behind any classification should reflect the management perspective. We again see the importance of systems specification as in section 7.3.4.

Once we do decide on a form of classification, we find that the four types of relationship listed above are possible between classes.

Inheritance relationships are those where one class shares the structure or behaviour defined in one (single inheritance) or more (multiple inheritance) other classes (superclasses). Inheritance comes from 'kind of' relationships.

Figure 8.24 illustrates these concepts. Both dogs and cats inherit behaviour, like suckling their young, from being members of the mammal superclass. This is an example of single inheritance because the behaviour of suckling the young derives

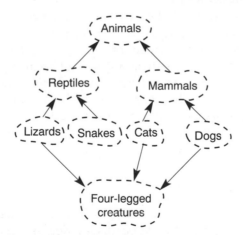

Fig 8.24 Object-Orientation: Inheritance Relationships
Classes *inherit* behaviour from superclasses. Thus mammals inherit behaviour from the fact that they are animals. *Multiple Inheritance* occurs where a class inherits from more than one superclass. Thus lizards inherit some behaviour from the fact that they are reptiles, and other behaviour from being four legged.

from that defined by the one superclass. However, there are many other ways we might classify animals. To classify in terms of how-many-legs divides animals in a different way. Hence the structure and behaviour of being a four-legged animal that suckles its young is a multiple inheritance.

◆ **STQ 8.5**
Suggest some examples of inheritance shown by the Carry-Out Cupboards range of products.

When we saw dogs and cats as different from TVs in our IQ question above, we were using the concept of *inheritance* as the basis of our classification. *Using-relationships* arise when we classify in terms of *aggregation*. Using-relationships are 'part of' relationships. Thus cats and TVs are classes of objects which are part of the superclass 'used by the Harry household', while dogs are not.

The concept of a using-relationship can be extended to build on the idea of the *instantiation* of any set of relationships. Thus the 'instantiation of licensable household objects' (according to 1960s UK laws) would include dogs and TVs, but not cats.

Understanding *meta-class relationships* follows from realizing that classes themselves may be regarded as objects. We can then see that we may have *classes of classes*. To understand the way in which classes may be classified means we can then use the same criteria of inheritance, using and instantiation as before.

This concept of meta-class relationships leads to two other important points that we can consider as being important for an object-oriented approach:

1. Understanding that classes are objects but objects are not classes.
2. Clarifying the possible confusion of objects and classes.

Our systems view of hierarchy helps us with understanding the first point. We understand how a system can be a component (or subsystem) of a wider system. Thus a system can have components and also be a component itself. We used the term element to distinguish the lowest level of component in the systems hierarchy. What this level would be depends on our view of the system. Thus in a retailing operation, an individual TV might be seen as an element of a stock control system. To a TV technician however, the TV itself might be seen as a system of electronic components.

The relationship between classes and objects has similarities to our systems hierarchy view. We have already seen that what constitutes an object depends on our motives for modelling a system. Thus whether we saw a particular dog as an object or a class would be different if we were designing a dog licensing system (individual dog is object) from if we were modelling canine physiology (dog is using class of body-part objects).

Although this comparison with our systems hierarchy view is a help, we need also to clarify the possible confusion of objects and classes. In its common generic use, 'dog' means a kind of animal, not one particular animal. In this sense dog is a class. If by 'a dog' we mean one particular instance of a dog, then we are referring to an object. So if we are thinking of dog licensing (as in Appendix 4), 'dog' is a class and Fido or Rover are the values of the property name of individual instances of objects in that class.

When we build an object-oriented software model, we normally see classes as static, with their form and relationships fixed before execution of the model. Objects however are created and destroyed during the lifetime of the model's application. Thus the class dog remains throughout the life of our licensing system, but individual objects like 'Fido' or 'Rover' come and go.

8.4.4 Developing an object-oriented model

We saw in section 7.7.1 that an object-oriented model will take the form of computer code able to represent the real-world we seek to control in terms of objects interacting by the passing of messages. Now we understand some of the basic object-oriented concepts like object, class, inheritance and instantiation, we can look further into the tasks, tools and deliverables involved in developing such an object-oriented model. To do this we will consider three things:

1. The processes involved in object-oriented systems development and their deliverables
2. Possible roles for diagramming
3. Object-oriented software.

We introduced the issue of whether object-oriented systems development was a method or an approach in section 8.4.1. We decided that the issue was a messy one. We found references to 'method', 'milestones' and 'products' in major authors like Booch (1991); but we also saw that claims to see object-orientation as a method can be dismissed by statements like 'object-oriented design may seem to be a terribly unconstrained and fuzzy process'.

The information systems methodology which we introduced in section 7.3.6 should not give us any problems with these supposed contradictions. We see object-oriented systems development as an approach which has clear concepts which have to be delivered, but which are not tied to a rigid development sequence. In this context we can consider four tasks:

1 *Identifiying classes and objects.* What we see in the problem situation as objects and classes will depend on the purpose of our systems development, so no structured or systematic method is generally available here. What may be useful as a general guide is the recognition that names of things or nouns in any description of the problem situation could be indicators for object or classes of interest.

2 *Defining the semantics of classes and objects.* Here we seek to establish the activities and behaviour of the classes and objects so that we know exactly what they are (and are not). Again no rigid method is available, but consideration of the verbs in any description of the problem situation could be good indicators of behaviour. Life cycles can be constructed for objects heuristically by assembling all they do and suffer (cf. JSD section 8.3.3).

3 *Identifying relationships between classes and objects.* Once our definitions have made clear the nature of the classes and objects themselves, we can then try to clarify how things interact within the system. For classes this means identifying inheritance, using and other relationships. For objects it means establishing their static and dynamic properties.

4 *Implementing the classes and objects.* This involves creating the object-oriented software model itself. Besides the software implementation of classes and objects, it will involve their allocation to modules within the program, and the allocation of programs to processors.

Consideration of these tasks shows why object-oriented systems development is unlikely to be a structured method. Identification of classes and objects can easily come after observing behaviour. Identifying class relationships can often be mixed with identifying classes themselves. In these and other ways, we can see that a set sequence of task 1 to task 4 is unlikely in practice.

Tasks 1–3 above imply that we will have some means of exploring, recording and defining various characteristics of classes, objects and their relationships and behaviour. This leads naturally to our second subject of possible roles for *diagramming*. The need for diagramming is not so obvious in object-oriented systems development as in other methods for two reasons.

First, object-orientation aims to model the world directly. There is a close correspondence between model objects and the real-world items that they represent. In this situation there is much less of a clear division between the logical model and the physical model as in other methods. In these methods a detailed system in terms of data flow diagrams, logical data structures, etc. is converted into working software at the systems production stage. In object-orientation the modelling is the production phase of Fig 7.7.

Second, even where some documentation is needed as a prelude to software implementation, diagrams are not necessarily the best choice. Much of the definition of behaviour and relationships for classes and objects is better done using templates or formal tables. These can list their properties and values, message synchronization, etc.

Booch (1991) does detail a number of object-oriented diagram types. The four most important are shown in Figs 8.25 to 8.28. These are:

a *Class diagrams* (Fig 8.25). To specify what classes exist and how are they are related. Their symbols are chosen to reflect forms of class relationships and cardinality.

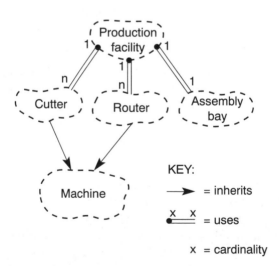

Fig 8.25 Object-Orientation: Class Diagrams
These specify what classes exist and how they are related. The symbols used here are a selection from Booch (1991). Thus one Production facility uses many (= n) Cutters. Both Cutters and Router inherit behaviour from being machines.

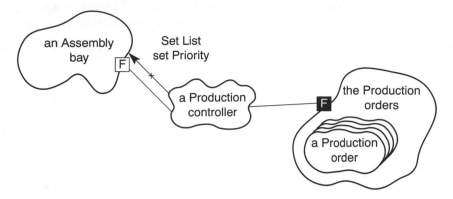

Fig 8.26 Object-Orientation: Object Diagrams
These specify what mechanisms are used to regulate how objects collaborate. The symbols are again from Booch (1991).

b *Object diagrams* (Fig 8.26). To specifiy what mechanisms are used to regulate how objects collaborate. These have symbols for objects and messages, and message synchronization.

c *State transition diagrams* (Fig 8.27). To specify how the time ordering of external events can affect the state of each instance of the class. These have symbols for start state, state, stop state, events and actions.

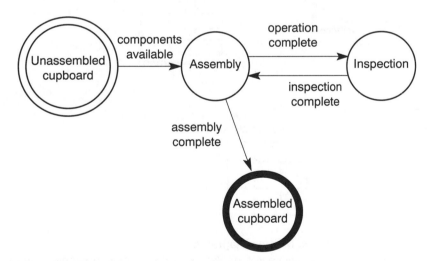

Fig 8.27 Object-Orientation: State Transition Diagrams
These specify how the time ordering of external events can affect the state of each instance of the class. The symbols are again from Booch (1991). Here: Unassembled cupboard is a start state, Assembly and Inspection are states, and Assembled cupboard is a stop state. Labels for events and actions are added to the linking arrows.

d *Module diagrams* (Fig 8.28). (Often called Booch diagrams by other authors.) These illustrate the physical packaging of classes and objects into software modules.

Diagram types a–c might be used throughout tasks 1–3 above. Module diagrams however apply to task 4.

Our final subject is that of *object-orientated software*. Theoretically we could adapt or bend most kinds of programming language to be object-oriented, since object-orientation is a principle not a method. However, in practice, computer programming languages need

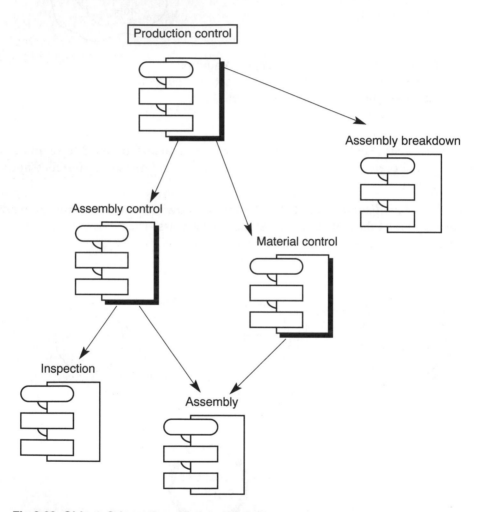

Fig 8.28 Object-Orientation: Module Diagrams
These illustrate the physical packaging of classes and objects into software modules. The symbols are again from Booch (1991). The relationship between the object and its software representation bears a close conceptual relationship to the way real-life entities are represented by models in JSD. Thus, just as process-oriented methods like SSADM incorporate structure-oriented concepts like entity life histories (*see* caption for Fig 8.15), so the concepts of object-oriented methods have links with structure-oriented methods.

to deal conveniently with the main object-orientation concepts of abstraction, encapsulation, modularity and hierarchy which we introduced in section 8.4.1.

Five principal languages do this:

1. Object-oriented forms of Pascal, e.g. Turbo Pascal (Borland).
2. C++, an object-oriented development of the C language.
3. CLOS (Common Lisp Object System), an object-oriented development of the LISP language.
4. Smalltalk, e.g. Smalltalk V or Smalltalk 80. Unlike the previous examples, this was created as an object-oriented language from the beginning.
5. Eiffel, another specifically created object-oriented language.

A detailed comparison of these and other languages is in Booch (1991). For the other references try Schmucker (1986), Faison (1991), Keene (1989), Mével (1987), and Meyer (1988).

8.5 PROTOTYPING

The concept of a prototype is probably familiar to us from its use in manufacturing and engineering. It is usually used to mean the first of something to be produced, like a protoype car or aircraft, which is then used for further research and development. The usual assumption is that the prototype will probably be modified as the result of testing, before the model goes into final production.

Prototyping has a similar meaning in systems development, except that instead of being the first of many copies, a prototype is more likely to be either:

- the first version of a complete system which will be modified after testing, or:
- a component of a system whose creation may subsequently act as a guide to the creation of others in the complete system.

Another slight difference between the engineering and systems uses of the word lies in the form of the development and testing. Testing a prototype engineering product like an aircraft usually takes place with the finished product and focusses on physical performance. With systems prototyping, testing is likely to be a continuous process as the system is built up, and is usually done in cooperation with the user. Much of the testing of a systems prototype is concerned with not so much 'does it work?', but with 'does it work the way you (the user) want it to?' Prototyping is the term then used to describe the whole process of building bottom-up, bit by bit, and continually consulting with the user in the process.

Prototyping is the other side of the argument that led to the need for structured methods. When systems development gets into a mess because objectives are not agreed or are changed, or people join and leave the development team and continuity is lost, or there is no definition of what should be delivered at various stages of development, we then feel the need for order. This is when we call for clearly structured methods with defined stages and deliverables. But structured methods also have their disadvantages. Rules and structure can be suppressive of imagination and creative activity. Furthermore, the frequent use of iteration in structured methods in practice shows that systems development is not a serial activity. It does not consist of separate individual activities which follow one another a step at a time. Human creativity is a rich, holist activity that cannot be done to a formula, so where creativity is required in systems development, a structured approach can be a disadvantage.

In total however, systems development is no different from any other practically applied creative process in that it requires the freedom that stimulates imagination and the order that leads to deliverable results. To understand the role of prototyping, we therefore need to identify its relationship with structured systems development, rather than see the two approaches as mutually exclusive. Prototyping is most likely to be appropriate:

> a. For small intimate systems that can be developed informally by a small intimate band of analysts and potential users.
> b. For clearly identifiable *components* of a wider system where it is possible to delegate detailed development without conflicting with the whole.

A house building analogy can help us here. We could hardly prototype a house in the systems development sense. Imagine standing around throwing out ideas about the materials to be used, the location of the building, the numbers of the rooms, etc.; and then frequently changing our minds so that part-built structures were demolished and rebuilt. The only practical way to coordinate such a project is to agree the design with the architect before we start. As we have seen above, the systems design stage of systems development produces much the same deliverable for the systems builder of the production stage, as the architect does for the house builder. All but the smallest systems, like all but the smallest buildings, need a structured approach to development.

We can take our analogy further however. Although we would want the architect to design the house, I doubt if we would need his services to help us with arranging the pictures on the walls or deciding where to put the TV. Most people decide such details by trial and error. So even if a structured method has been used to design a system, it is possible to see prototyping as an excellent way of designing such intimate things as screen presentations and sequences for users, or formats for printouts. Note, however, that just as our choice about the TV is limited by where the architect puts the electricity points, so our choice on systems details will be determined by the overall systems design. For a detailed account of incorporating prototyping within structured systems development, *see* Crinnion (1991).

However, even if the context of protoyping has been fixed within a wider plan, there are other reasons why it may not be appropriate. In our house building analogy we considered a house dictated by one client. In all but the smallest organizations, the client is more likely to be a client set. In these circumstances the idea of having two or more people all shouting instructions to the house builder would be a recipe for chaos. This might be overcome by coordinating the demands of the various prototypers, but if we do this we are back to forming some agreed model of the overall system that is being aimed at. This then implies the potential for a more formal approach.

Another restriction on prototyping comes when the costs of trial and error become high. If the client is in need of large amounts of time and support in order to make the prototyping software effective, then its cost could be much more than handing over much more of the systems development process to a professional.

Finally, prototyping may be so client-centred that its results can be very conservative and colloquial. This can occur because attempts to talk about the new system often relate its development to the existing physical one. The use of analogies can then carry through bad features of the old system into the new. This is especially the case where some form of computerized graphical user-interface is used as a systems development tool. As we shall see in Section 8.7, these tools often interpret systems concepts in terms of older physical analogies by showing files as filing cabinets or inputs and outputs as particular documents, etc.

However, given these cautions, prototyping is a vigorous and often swiftly effective way to sweep aside red tape and get a working system.

Having set a context for prototyping, it is worth noting two major ways in which it has been implemented:

1. The use of fourth-generation programming languages (4GLs) for prototyping.
2. Prototyping using object-oriented programming languages.

4GLs, as we saw in Chapter 5, are declarative languages. Users state what they want from, say, a database, rather than having to specify how the software should obtain it. As we also saw in Chapter 5, these languages use English-like statements whose meaning is easy to understand.

A further step forward in making software easy to use has been the advent of graphical user interfaces (GUIs), with pull-down menus, icons, use of the mouse and an overall removal of the need to know a programming language. It is now possible for users to develop personal systems by showing what they want rather than telling the computer how to do it.

Object-oriented systems development lends itself to a prototyping approach because of its iterative, building-block approach as we saw in section 8.3.4. Direct prototyping with object-oriented languages is an expert's job however. While most people would find little difficulty with a 4GL, C++ code looks much less friendly. It is worth noting that object-orientation does lie behind the development of many of the user-friendly graphical interfaces (including most video games) used by the non-expert.

The power which prototyping places in the hands of the non-expert developer raises one vital issue of systems development. If it is now increasingly 'possible for users to develop personal systems by showing what they want rather than telling the computer how to do it', this throws a strong emphasis on knowing what you want. For management of business or organizations this leads to the central theme of this book that information systems should be seen in the context of management systems.

8.6 INTEGRATED METHODS

We have now almost completed our survey of information systems methodology, or study of method. We began this chapter by emphasizing that information systems development can only hope to be successful once we have sorted out the messes in the wider management system.

We justified our study of soft systems methodology (SSM) in Section 8.1 as a way of coping with messes. We also saw in Section 7.3 that the initial strategy and inception stages of information systems development involved us in looking at both the management system and the whole business or organizational system. This involvement required sorting out the soft human and policy issues before the deliverables of decision, authorization and commitment could be produced.

The need for that 'sorting out' explains why an integrated methodology of information systems development has begun to appear since the mid-1980s. Our previous studies show that we can identify a soft systems methodology which will deal with the messes of the wider management system. We have also studied specialist information systems methodology which will deliver working information systems in response to a defined problem. We can now ask if these two components can be brought together to produce ideas about how we can have an integrated information systems methodology which combines the functions of soft and hard systems methods.

The publication of details of the *Multiview* (MV) method of Wood-Harper et al. (1985) was the first attempt that I have identified of this synthesis. It was followed by Avison & Wood-Harper (1990).

The Multiview synthesis envisages five stages:

1. Analysis of human activity systems
2. Analysis of entities, functions and events
3. Analysis and design of socio-technical system
4. Design of human computer interface
5. Design of technical subsystems.

Figure 8.29 shows the details of the method.

Analysis of human activity systems essentially involves the SSM we covered in Section 8.1, in the conventional seven-stage model of section 8.1.3. The stages used by MV go as far as stage 4 of SSM: the specification of the conceptual model. As we saw, this model defines what the system we would like to have, S_1, should do to be the desired system. In terms of our model of systems development in section 7.3.4, this produces the conceptual model as a high-level form of the eventual deliverable from the definition and analysis stage of systems development.

Analysis of entities, functions and events takes the high-level definition of S_1 in the form of the conceptual model and models the detailed breakdown of the desired information system. The terms entity, function and event are used in the conventional ways which you will find earlier in this chapter and in Chapter 5. This stage is sometimes called *information systems modelling* to reflect that it follows mainstream information systems development components and process in this field.

Analysis and design of socio-technical systems recognizes that 'all change involves conflict of interest' Mumford (1983). This is a reference to a weltanschauung of a systems development method which assumes that working information systems are 'both technically efficient and have social characteristics which lead to high job satisfaction'. The implication of this weltanschauung is that there is a need for:

- a knowledge fit because employees (we would call them actors in the SSM context?) should believe that their skills and worth are being adequately used
- a psychological fit which conforms to the employee's view of their aspirations
- an efficiency fit which covers the balancing of financial rewards to employees against the requirements of the employer in terms of job performance
- a task structure fit which reflects the success in making the job appropriately demanding and fulfilling for the employee
- an ethical fit between the values of the employee and the employer.

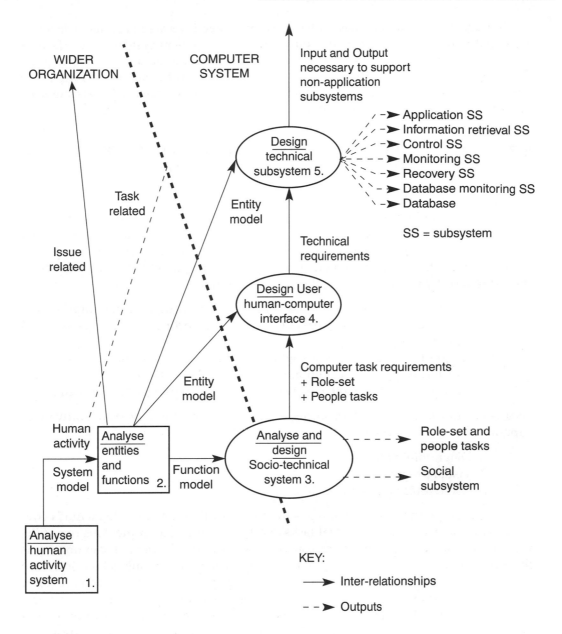

Fig 8.29 Multiview
Since details of this method were first published as a book by Wood-Harper et al. (1985), this has probably been the leader in integrating hard and soft methodology.

Design of human computer interface takes a holist view of the design process by looking at the design of how humans and computers may work together before detailing the final stage: design technical subsystems. Thus if we have different technical alternatives like choices of hardware and software, these are detailed after consultation and consideration as to how they would work in the wider human–computer system context. (One way of doing this could be the use of prototyping.)

Although MV is the only major attempt at integrated information systems development that I am aware of, I think that our view of management systems would lead us to expect continued attempts at developing some form of integrated approach. Real-life management systems always have their hard, technical components interacting with soft, human ones. Practical information systems development will therefore need to take account of this holist situation.

8.7 AUTOMATED SUPPORT FOR SYSTEMS DEVELOPMENT: DIAGRAMMING AND CASE TOOLS

Most modern information systems development is carried out knowing that a computer system is likely to be a major component of the information system being developed. It would very strange if the process of information systems development were then to ignore the existence of the computer as a tool for its own use.

The potential for using the computer in systems development has been increased in the last decade by two important and related developments:

a. The proliferation of personal computers with internal memory beyond 640K, advanced processors, VGA monitors and very-high-capacity hard disk storage.

b. A parallel development of sophisticated graphical user-interface software which can support diagramming, data modelling, object hierarchy and classification, and many other activities and tools of systems development.

As a result of these technical advances, we can now find three types of software to support the systems developer:

1. Diagramming tools
2. Visual programming
3. CASE tools and Workbenches.

The need for diagramming tools comes from the fact that many of the methods covered in this chapter, and individual tasks and techniques used in previous ones (like Chapter 5), use diagrams for the reasons we discussed in Chapter 3. Diagramming is therefore an important systems tool but drawing by hand is not only labour intensive but also repetitive. Conceiving what must be included in a data flow diagram requires great skill, but drawing the same symbols with a pencil and template is very tedious. We take the term diagramming tool to mean software that enables us to draw diagrams, and nothing more than that. Some diagramming tools which are designed specifically to draw data flow diagrams, structure charts and other diagrams specifically used in information systems development are sometimes called CASE tools. If all they do is draw diagrams, this is a false description. We shall see below that a CASE tool does more than just draw diagrams.

Visual programming uses graphical devices like easy-to-recognize symbols called (upsettingly for some of us) icons, tabular structures or preset document formats. These enable the less specialist systems developer to define the high-level procedures carried out by the desired system S_1. This use of a visual programming 'language' compares with the way that 4GLs have made programming easier for the less expert by the use of English-like language.

Some of the different ways that this kind of visual support can be given are:

1. Graphical environment to assist:
   visualization of information about data
   visualization of programs and execution
   visualization of software design
   general visual coaching
2. Symbol languages for:
   handling visual information
   supporting visual interactions
   programming with visual expressions:
   diagrammatic systems
   iconic systems
   form systems.

This classification is close to Shu (1988).

When discussing diagramming above, we contrasted the skill needed to decide a diagram's contents, with the routine process of drawing from a small set of symbols. If we are designing a whole system, even with the support of a diagramming tool, there are still other routine tasks remaining that can make the process tiresome; and therefore open to errors and inconsistencies.

Thus if we considered developing a system using a process-oriented method, typical tools might include data flow diagrams, data modelling, structured English and entity life histories. Using these tools would involve the analyst in some quite laborious paperwork. It would involve drawing data flow diagrams by hand, with carefully and systematically numbered processes, data stores, external entities, etc. Details of all these features would then have to be recorded in some form. Again, consider the procedure when using a diagram for modelling entities, attributes and relationships. Deciding what the entity is, and what form of data should be used for the attributes, is only one of the tasks. It is also necessary to check that a particular name for an entity has not been used before, and if so, where it occurs in data stores. For these actions we again require some record to back up the diagramming.

Unless the analyst was superhuman, there would be much redrawing and modification involved with the diagrams, which in turn would require renumbering of entities and changes to whatever record is kept of them. A good deal of time would be spent erasing and copying. The situation would be further complicated by the fact that several members of the team would be working on the project, so that coordination and consistency would be needed to prevent conflicting versions of the system appearing.

It would be nice to have a tool that would help not only with the diagramming, but also with recording and checking these routine cross-references across the various diagrams. Such an overall record (usually called a data dictionary or encyclopedia) would keep track of the processes, entities, attributes, structural relationships, etc., used in developing an information system.

Tools like these are usually called CASE tools or Workbenches. CASE is an acronym for Computer-Aided Systems (or sometimes Software) Engineering. A CASE tool makes it possible to avoid many of the problems of carrying out and coordinating the systems development process. Typical CASE tools enable diagrams to be drawn on a computer screen using a mouse and a menu of diagram symbols. When additions are made to the diagram, an entry is automatically opened for it in the data dictionary. The CASE tool will automatically check the naming and numbering of entities to avoid duplication and omission, and to keep the entries in the data dictionary in line with the diagram and vice versa. CASE tools are also able to check the logic of diagrams. All these facilities are combined with the more general ones associated with word processing and graphics editing.

The typical diagramming components of a CASE tool are shown in Fig 8.30. The actual components in any particular CASE tool will depend on the method it is intended to work with. This particular example illustrates a workbench designed to support systems development for a process-oriented method. Its main components are:

a *Six types of diagram or tabular representations:*

1. Data flow diagram. Conventional data flow diagramming with choice of symbol conventions for process, data flow, external entity and data store.
2. Structure or decomposition diagram. Hierarchical diagram using digraph (*see* Chapter 3) convention to show relationship between system, subsystem and components.
3. Entity relationship diagram or model. To show entities and their interrelationship, including cardinalities.
4. Action diagram or structured English table. Diagrammatic or verbal definition of processes in terms of sequence, conditionals and iterations.
5. Entity description table. Defining the attributes of the entities, and their relationship type.
6. Data flow table. Identifies data flows and details the data structures that make them up.

b *Encyclopedia reports for:*

1. Lists of objects and their properties. Enables us to list all the processes, entities, or any other object recorded anywhere by the CASE tool for the project.
2. Consistency and propriety. Enables us to check for omissions or inconsistencies in the record at any stage of development, e.g. processes with no output or data that gets 'lost'. Generally a good CASE tool will prevent illogical entries or omissions from being made. Thus you cannot enter a data flow without it having both a source and a destination, or you may not give two different data flows the same name.

The properties of a typical CASE tool described so far are mainly designed to support the analysis and design stages of systems development. However, modern tools can support a much greater range of the stages of systems development. More recently CASE tools are making links between the definition, design and production phases by incorporating program generators. These are able to take the process specifications and turn them into working programs. A set of such tools are available to work with ORACLE (*see* Chapter 5). With facilities like these, it is not surprising that, for example, a famous British brewery is retraining its programmers as analysts to avoid them being made redundant.

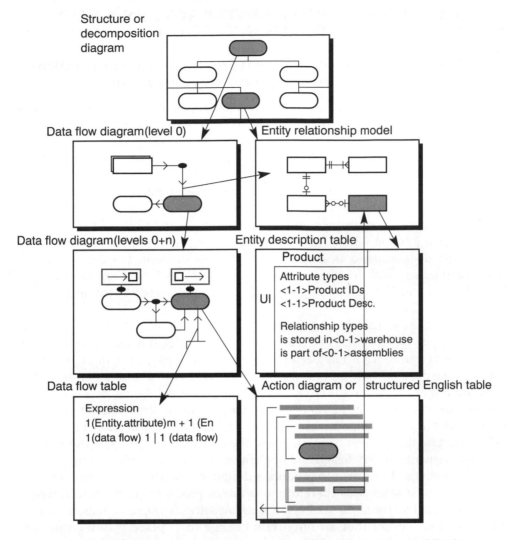

Fig 8.30 CASE (Computer-Aided Systems or Software Engineering) Tools and Techniques
CASE tools are not just diagramming tools: they coordinate both the tools and techniques used and the users themselves.

The availability of such tools leads to an important management lesson. Since a CASE tool aims to automate most of the later stages from analysis through to production, it places even more emphasis on the importance of resolving initial soft issues and the high-level systems definition stage. Otherwise we are using a powerful tool to automate conflict and ambiguity. The emphasis of the future is likely to move away from the mechanics of software towards the management and strategic issues of systems development.

8.8 HUMAN–COMPUTER INTERACTION AND THE HUMAN–COMPUTER INTERFACE

8.8.1 The changing role of the human–computer relationship in information systems development

If we stand back from the details of the various information systems development methods in this chapter to see a general picture, it is possible to see a historical theme. Thus process-oriented methods were the earliest to be developed and object-oriented are the most recent. We then dealt with prototyping, CASE tools and visual programming as some of the latest things to arrive in the late 1980s.

The important factor that lies behind this historical sequence is the change in the role of the computer. The early forms of process-oriented systems development like de Marco (1979) made clear distinctions between the *logical* and *physical* systems in analysis and design (section 7.3.3). This was because design and implementation could be quite clearly distinguished as stages in systems development. The design was something specified *separately* from the computer using such tools as diagrams on paper. In the mid-1970s, much programming still took the form of handwritten documents that were later encoded.

The major change that has taken place in the last ten years is the involvement of the computer as *facility* for systems development (section 7.4.2), not just a potential component of the system once it has been implemented. The idea of using CASE tools to automate the development process was the first step forward. Instead of drawing diagrams on paper or working out data models by filling out forms, this could now be done on the computer. The advantage was not just one of replacing paper with computer screens or filing cabinets with disks; a CASE tool could also check for consistency and coordinate the various components of the development process. But notice that this improvement still left design and implementation as two separate things: the computer was helping the human to produce a design, not to actually implement the new system. The next stage was therefore to produce programs that could convert the design produced by the CASE tool into a working software implementation.

It was at this point that an important change took place in the nature of the human–computer relationship. Why use a computer to help develop a separate design which the computer then has to implement? This may have been logical in the days when the user knew little about computers. At that time it was sensible for the systems developer to help the user to define his needs away from the computer. Once agreed, a design that met these needs could then be implemented by the specialists. But if the user could actually try out ideas directly on the computer system, using easily understood graphics instead of complex computer code, then there would be less need for a systems developer to help translate the user's ideas into practice.

It was the advent of *visual programming* linked to *object-orientation* and *prototyping* that brought about this final change. Software such as Microsoft Visual Basic makes it possible for the potential user to be directly involved in the *creation*, not just the design, of such outputs as screen presentations, menus or printouts directly in the Windows environment in which they will be used. In such a situation, there is a

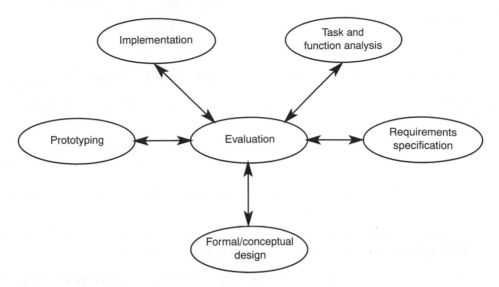

Fig 8.31 The Star Life Cycle of Hix and Hartson

blurring of the logical and physical requirement concepts, as well as of the developer–client roles (Section 7.4). Essentially *sequential* models of systems development like Fig 7.6 are not the best way of describing what goes on in such circumstances. Instead, an interactive model like Fig 8.31 is more appropriate. Here we see the same type of activities as before, but much less of a sequence. The model in Fig 8.31 could be seen as Fig 7.6 in conditions where a high degree of *iteration* has finally removed any significant degree of sequence.

This new relationship brings out the importance of the *interface* between the computer and the human users. It emphasizes the ease with which the human users can *interact* with the computer through such means as:

- entering commands and responding to dialogues
- navigating menus
- adopting ready-made templates, spreadsheets and form layouts
- manipulation of graphical, and other toolbox components.

The examples I have quoted in this list all refer to visual, screen-based communication between human and computer via keyboard and mouse; but speech and other media are already becoming available. The central issue, however, is that success in information systems development is depending more and more on successful direct interaction between human and computer through the human–computer interface. The acronym *HCI* is frequently used to refer to *human–computer interaction* through the human–computer interface.

8.8.2 Human aspects of HCI

When we use the term 'human' in the context of HCI, we are referring to a rich range of situations. One way of making sense of the different forms of human activity involved in HCI is that of Preece (1994) who identifies:

- cognitive psychology
- social knowledge, and
- organizational knowledge

as sources of understanding how human beings interact with computers.

Cognitive psychology can help us to improve the workings of the human–computer interface in three particular ways:

1. By correctly *assessing* what humans can, and cannot, be expected to do
2. By giving a greater *understanding* of why humans fail to deal with some kinds of problem
3. By supplying models, methods and tools which *enable* human beings through appropriately built interfaces.

Assessing what humans can do, first requires us to identify what sorts of activity the word 'do' refers to. In the HCI context the most important of these are:

- perception, especially visual perception, of what is represented by the computer system
- attention to, and memory of, what is presented
- understanding and knowledge of what is presented, by the use of model and metaphor.

The identification of *social knowledge* as an aspect of HCI recognizes that human beings interact with computers as groups as well as at an individual level. This will include group interaction with a computer system, like a team using a common piece of software, or individuals becoming a group through their interaction via the software. A popular example of the latter would be discussion groups on the Internet.

The questions we need to answer in order to promote social knowledge are:

1. What is the social context?
2. How do people work together?

Organizational knowledge refers to the formal conditions in which individual human beings come together as a social group. The rules, job titles, responsibilities and other aspects of being an employee, member or other component of a formal system will affect what kind of human–computer interface we have to deal with.

KEY WORDS

Abstraction	JSD, Jackson systems development
Action diagram	JSP, Jackson structured programming
Analysis	LISP
Approach	Logical system
Aspiration driven	Maintenance
Bottom-up	Meliorist model
Business analysis	Mess
C++	Meta-class
CASE tool	Method

CATWOE
Class
CLOS
Conceptual model
Conceptual world
Containing relationship
Data dictionary
Data flow diagram
Data stream
Data structure diagram
Decomposition diagram
Deliverable
Derivative method
Design
Desired system
Encapsulation
Entity life history
Entity-action step
Existing system
Failure
Failure driven
Feasibility study
HCI, human–computer interface/interaction
Implementation
Inheritance
Innovative method
Instantiation
Issue
Iteration
Methodology

Modularity
Object
Object-orientation
Physical system
Primary task
Problem
Process orientation
Project debriefing
Prototyping
Pseudo-code
Relevant system
Rich picture
Root definition
Smalltalk
Socio-technical system
Soft systems methodology
Specification
SSADM
State vector
Structure orientation
Structured English
Structured method
Systems life cycle
Technique
Tool
Top-down
Using hierarchy
Using relationship
WIMP

SEMINAR AGENDAS, EXAM QUESTIONS AND PROJECT/DISSERTATION SUBJECTS

1 We saw in Section 8.1 that SSM is a broad systems method applicable to a wider field than information systems development. What other broad systems methodologies are available? How might they be classified? Can they be used in conjunction with specific information systems methods? Try Flood & Jackson (1991), Wilson (1990), Wolstenholme (1990) and Roberts et al. (1983), as references.

2 Are all systems-based methods coercive? Try Flood & Jackson (1991).

3 In Section 7.3 we used the analogy of building a house to explain the stages of information systems development. In STQ 7.9 we drew an analogy between object-oriented approaches to information systems development and the use of hierarchical classification of products for manufacture. Is systems development just a particular form of a manufacturing or production system? What differentiates systems development from any other form of development? Can other analogies be used to mutually enrich development methodology?

4 In the late 1980s I gave some students the task of developing a registration system for a specialist sheep breed society. Students soon realized that any such system could then be adapted for any breed of sheep with hardly any modifications. Small modifications could then extend it for any farm animal, racehourse, pedigree dogs, etc.

Choose an established and apparently specialist system like car registration, and consider how it might be broadened in its application with minimum modification. (You may choose to use the principles of object-orientation.)

5 I stated in Section 7.5 that SSADM was at the end of an established line of methodological development. What are the origins and ancestry of SSADM? What changes have been made to it?

6 'All professions are conspiracies against the laity' (George Bernard Shaw: The Doctor's Dilemma). Can this be asserted about professionals in the field of computerized information systems development? Is it a big issue? What remedies are available?

7 Can the analogy of systems development with product manufacture tell us what changes are likely to occur in systems development methods? Will there be a 'Henry Ford' for systems development? Will an appropriate/intermediate information technology movement arise? Will there be a violent information systems Luddite movement?

8 Is there a case for an official standard for graphical user-interface iconic symbols? What principles would you use to devise such a system?

9 'Computer programmers are a dying breed'. Discuss.

FEEDBACK ON SELF-TESTING QUESTIONS

◆ STQ 8.1

We first recall from Chapter 3 that it is not the presence of human components that makes something holist. Rather it is the presence of emergent properties that shows the whole to be more than the sum of its parts. To say that failure is 'therefore' holist just because humans are involved is incorrect.

However I think that failure is a holist phenomenon in its true sense since failure itself is an emergent property. If we think of any failure, it is inevitably the result of at least two contributory components coming together. The failure of the system at Technoturbines came about not only because the workforce were lazy about making the correct entries, but also because supervision allowed them to get away with it. In control systems terms, environmental disturbances alone do not make failures. It also requires the absence of effective feedback and corrective actuation or knowledge of goals. In the Technoturbines case these would be represented by poor supervision and poor training respectively.

◆ STQ 8.2

There is no clear definition of the problem. Is it a dog problem or an owner problem? Is there any problem at all, or is it a media invention?

The question of boundary and separation is then blurred by these soft issues. If there is a health problem, then the vets ought to be involved. If it involves money then perhaps we are into local government finance. Questions like these raise issues of responsibility.

As to information, until we can decide on such questions as owners or dogs, health, danger or media hype, the information we ought to be seeking is also debatable.

What would a solution look like? Well, if we could agree what the problem was, or whether there is a problem, we might be able to answer that, but for the moment any description eludes us.

◆ STQ 8.3

There are both high-level themes and more specific issues. We can see general themes like fear, hysteria and sentimentality as well as more specific issues like fouling footpaths, attacks by dogs, incidence of various diseases or the number and identity of dogs.

Since we are concerned with a soft messy problem, it is not surprising that there is no 'correct' list of themes.

◆ STQ 8.4

In terms of Section 3.4, many practically applied models like the signalling example make use of iconic and analogue modelling. For systems development, symbolic models, and particularly diagrams, tend to dominate. Note that, as we saw in Section 3.4 also, many so-called 'icons' used in graphical user-interfaces are symbolic models.

◆ STQ 8.5

All cupboards (as opposed to some other class of furniture) inherit the property of having a container unit. Within the class of cupboards, members of the subclass of standing cupboards inherit the property of having four feet, and so on.

Note that the production system of Carry-Out Cupboards is using the concepts of classification to simplify its production of cupboards for the same reasons of principle that object-orientation uses them to simplify information systems development.

REFERENCES / BIBLIOGRAPHY

Ackoff, R. & Hall, J.R. (1972). A Systems Approach to the Problems of Solid Waste and Litter. *Journal of Environment Systems.* No. 2, pp. 351–64.

Ashworth, C. & Goodland, M. (1990). *SSADM: A Practical Approach.* McGraw-Hill.

Avison, D.E. & Fitzgerald, G. (1995) *Information Systems Development.* Blackwell Scientific.

Avison, D.E. & Wood-Harper, A.T. (1990). *Multiview.* Blackwell Scientific.

Birrell, N.D. & Ould, M.A. (1985). *A Practical Handbook for Software Development.* Cambridge University Press.

Blair, G. et al. (1991). *Object-oriented Languages, Systems and Applications.* UCL Press.

Booch, G. (1991). *Object Oriented Design.* Benjamin/Cummings.

Bulow, I. von. (1989). The bounding of a problem situation and the concept of a system's boundary in soft systems methodology. *Journal of Applied Systems Analysis.* 16, 35–41.

Checkland, P.B. (1981). *Systems Thinking, Systems Practice.* Wiley.

Checkland, P.B. & Scholes, J. (1990). *Soft Systems Methodology in Action.* Wiley.

Crinnion, J. (1991). *Evolutionary Systems Development.* Pitman.

Cutts, G. (1987). *SSADM.* Paradigm.

Cutts, G. (1991). *SSADM.* Blackwell Scientific.

Faison, T. (1991). *Borland C++3 Object-Oriented Programming.* SAMS.

Flood, R.L. & Jackson, M.C. (1991). *Creative Problem Solving.* Wiley.

Flynn, D.J. (1992). *Information Systems Requirements: Determination and Analysis.* McGraw-Hill.

Gane, C. & Sarson, T. (1979). *Structured Systems Analysis.* Prentice-Hall.

Halbert, D. & O'Brian, P. (1988). Using Types and Inheritance in Object-Oriented Programming. *IEEE Software.* 4, 73.

Harry, M.J.S. (1990). *Information and Management Systems.* Pitman.

Jackson, M. (1975). *Principles of Program Design.* Academic Press.

Jackson, M. (1983). *System Development.* Prentice-Hall International.

Keene, S.E. (1989). *Object-Orientated Programming in Common LISP.* Addison-Wesley.

de Marco, T. (1979). *Structured Analysis and Systems Specification.* Prentice-Hall.

Mével, A. & Guguen, T. (1987). *Smalltalk-80.* Macmillan Education.

Meyer, B. (1988). *Object-Orientated Software Construction.* Prentice-Hall.

Mumford, E. (1983). *Designing Participatively.* Manchester Business School.

Olle, T.W. et al. (1988), *Information Systems Methodologies.* Addison-Wesley.

Page-Jones, M. (1980). *The Practical Guide to Structured Systems Design.* Yourdon Press.

Pressman, R.S. (1987). *Software Engineering.* McGraw-Hill.

Robson, W. (1994). *Strategic Management and Information Systems: an integrated approach.* Pitman.

Roberts, N., Andersen, D.F., Deal, R.M., Garet, M.S. & Schaffer, W.A. (1983). *Introduction to Computer Simulation.* Addison-Wesley.

Schmucker, K.J. (1986). *Object-Orientated Programming for the Macintosh.* Hayden.

Shu, N.C. (1988). *Visual Programming.* Van Nostrand.

Sutcliffe, A. (1988). *Jackson System Development.* Prentice-Hall International.

Warnier, J.D. (1974). *Logical Construction of Programs.* Van Nostrand Rheinhold.

Weaver, P.L. (1993). *Practical SSADM Version 4: a complete tutorial guide.* Pitman.

Wilson, B. (1990). *Systems: Concepts, Methodologies, and Applications.* Wiley.

Wolstenholme, E.F. (1990). *System Enquiry.* Wiley.

Wood-Harper, A.T., Antill, L. & Avison, D.E. (1985). *Information Systems Definition: The Multiview Approach.* Blackwell Scientific.

Yourdon, E. & Constantine, L.L. (1978). *Structured Design.* Yourdon Press.

Yourdon, E. (1990). Auld Lang Syne. *Byte.* 15 (10).

APPENDIX 1

•••••••••••••••••••

Carry-Out Cupboards

1 COMPANY AND PRODUCT OUTLINE

Carry-Out Cupboards design their products for those who require variety in their choice of cupboards and some related household furniture such as tables, chairs and work-tops; but at a reasonable price. Instead of being sold as expensive completed products ready for use, each Carry-Out Cupboards product is sold as a packed *kit* which can be easily assembled by the customer. The only skill needed is to clip and screw things together according to the instructions supplied.

Carry-Out Cupboards sell their products through a chain of retail outlets (RO). All of these retail outlets are supplied with kits by the central assembly and packing facility (CP) of Carry-Out Cupboards. The CP mainly uses materials and components bought from a range of suppliers to produce the kits, and uses only limited production processing like cutting and finishing off of materials.

When customers come to a retail outlet, they can see catalogues and assembled examples of the products on display. Customers may then buy their own choice of product in kit form to take home and assemble.

At any one time Carry-Out Cupboards sell up to about a dozen different surface finish designs. This is done by keeping the basic structure of units and parts the same, but making the products from chipboard 'veneered' with a glue bonded surface design. (A 'veneer' is a thin skin of wood or other substance with a decorative appearance.) The surface design, colour and other minor details of the product can thus be changed without major production or overall structural upsets.

A particular *kit* is usually an *assembly* made up of one or more *parts*. Each kit is used to make up a particular product like a cupboard, but the products themselves can be variations on a basic idea. Thus cupboards may:

   a. be freestanding with worktops or hung on the wall
   b. have swing or sliding doors
   c. have internal shelves or drawers

or various combinations of these possibilities can make up the different assemblies which form the product range. Figure A1.1 gives an example of how differing combinations and selections of common components can produce six different cupboard types. Combined with six different surface designs, for example, there is the possibility of three dozen different cupboards for a range of applications from kitchen to bedroom.

Since Carry-Out Cupboards perform relatively few manufacturing processes of their own, much of the activity at the CP is concerned with assembly and packing of components. All of these components, plus the small proportion of raw materials used in

	COMPONENT QUANTITIES										
KITCHEN UNIT TYPES	Unit Container	Feet	Wall Fittings	Single Worktops	Door	Full Drawers	Half Drawers	Slide Guides	Hinges	Handles	Inside Shelves
STANDING UNIT											
Single –sliding door	1	4	0	1	2	0	0	4	0	2	2
–hinged door	1	4	0	1	2	0	0	0	4	2	2
–two drawer	1	4	0	1	0	1	1	4	0	2	0
–three drawer	1	4	0	1	0	0	3	6	0	3	0
HANGING UNIT											
Single –sliding door	1	0	4	0	2	0	0	4	0	2	2
–hinged door	1	0	4	0	2	0	0	0	4	2	2

Fig A 1.1 Details of the Breakdown of Some Carry-Out Cupboards Products
The thinking behind this structure of permutations of common components is explained in the text.

manufacturing processes, have to be ordered from a range of outside suppliers. This situation means that the cost of components represents a relatively high proportion of the final product. Carry-Out Cupboards therefore ensure competitive pricing and reliability of supply by usually having more than one supplier for each component. The performance of suppliers, in terms of product quality and delivery, is regularly reviewed.

The ROs depend on being able to offer the customer kits off the shelf. They therefore aim to have all kits in the range available from stock, and to be able to obtain easy replenishment from the CP.

The context in which both the CP and the ROs operate means that they are therefore very concerned with various forms of *stock control* as a major subsystem of their central purpose operations. Holding stocks is necessary when we wish to *buffer* different patterns of supply and demand, or more generally, *inputs* and *outputs* to a *transformation process* (*see* Chapter 3). There are many examples of this in Carry-Out Cupboards because it makes sense in terms of processing and organization (first- and higher-order control) for:

- a. Suppliers to deliver their products in particular numbers that reflect the sizes of such things as containers and lorryloads.
- b. Manufacturing, assembly and packing at the CP to do so in batch sizes that reflect the *setup costs* to perform a particular operation against the *holding costs* which result from long runs of that operation in terms of stock levels.
- c. Retailers at the ROs to hold stocks of all the product range because they cannot control or accurately predict when customers will come to buy which product.

2   DESIGNING STOCK CONTROL SYSTEMS

There are many different forms of detailed working stock control systems in organizations and business practice; but all of them are based on attempting to answer two questions:

1. *How much* should the actuator make the *input* to the *transformation process* in order to achieve the desired *output*? For a stock control system this means 'how much should we order?'
2. *When* should we implement the value of the input to allow for the time taken by the transformation process to achieve the desired outputs? For a stock control system this means 'when should we place an order?'

These two questions are not independent of each other. Although the purpose of holding stock is to enable different *patterns* of input and output to be coordinated, the total inputs and outputs have to be equal in the long term if they are to balance. Without such a long-term balance, stock would either eventually run out for good, or grow without limit, depending on whether the long-term output exceeded the long-term input or vice versa.

In practice therefore the average input, or deliveries, must equal the average output, use or sales. If the average sales of a particular cupboard are 10 per week, then the average delivery rate must be the same. An answer to question 1 above that decided to order in quantities of 20 at a time would therefore lead to delivery orders being placed every two weeks on average. Thus a decision that 'how much' should be 20 would automatically result in 'when' being every two weeks in order that the average demand be met. Similarly, a decision in answer to question 2 above to order on a regular four-weekly basis would require an order size of 40 if the average demand were to be met. In this case a decision to make the 'when' four weekly automatically resulted in a 'how much' of 40.

Although any stock control has to answer both the questions above, in the face of a known average demand, answering one of the questions automatically answers the other. In practice therefore, individual stock control systems tend to work on the basis of dealing with one of the two questions above. They focus either on *quantity* or on *how much* as the criterion for reordering, or else on *timing* or *when* to reorder. Figures A1.2 and A1.3 show examples of each approach.

Figure A1.2 shows the behaviour of a *reorder level* (ROL) system. The amount in stock is shown following a typical 'saw tooth' shape. The down slopes of the shape show demand depleting the stock. The particular form I have shown in the figure is the situation for stocks of finished products being sold to the customer. Here the curve falls irregularly, reflecting the variation of individual customer demand around the long-term average. For stocks of parts or materials used in production, the down slope would consist of clearer steps, as individual set batch sizes were issued into the manufacturing and assembly process.

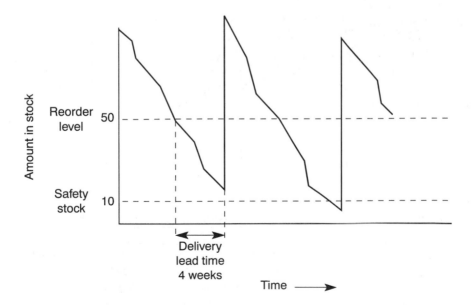

Fig A1.2 Stock Control (1): A ROL System
When to reorder is determined by *how much* is in stock.

Whatever the pattern of stock depletion, this system uses a particular level of stock, called a *reorder level*, as a trigger for reordering. When stock reaches this level, a replenishment order is placed. In all real business situations it will take time for the order to be processed and the new stock to be delivered, and the reorder level must leave enough in stock to cover the demand for the product over this *lead time*. Since demand for stock will be a *stochastic* (*see* Chapter 3) figure, the demand used to determine the reorder level will be an estimate of the maximum that the system wishes to cope with.

In the example of Fig 3.2, a lead time of 4 weeks and a reorder level of 50 implies that Carry-Out Cupboards don't think that it is worth trying to cope with a demand in excess of an average of 12.5 packs per week at a particular RO.

Most of the time however, the reordering of stock has only to cope with a demand closer to the average. The *minimum* or *buffer level* shown in Figs 3.2 and A1.2 represents the lowest level that the stock would be expected to reach on average. Any occasion when the stock fell below this level could indicate an above average demand or exceptional circumstances such as delayed delivery. Whatever the reason, depletion below this level usually calls for additional action to ensure restocking takes place before running out altogether.

The characteristics of a *reorder period* (ROP) system are illustrated by Fig A1.3. Again we see the saw toothed shape of stock levels as they deplete and are then replenished. The difference here is that the reordering takes place on a regular periodic basis. The quantity ordered is whatever is needed to 'top up' stocks to a maximum level. This is calculated as the level needed to cover the *maximum* demand expected over the reorder period.

The ROL system makes sense where it is more economic or convenient to have regular deliveries, rather than the irregular pattern generated by a ROL system. This regularity may work in well with *batch processing* in the information system. If, for example, we carry out stock level checking in coordination with doing such things as calculating and updating financial accounts, this may be a convenient time to generate and send off a replenishment order to a supplier. A ROP system makes particular sense where the *cost of*

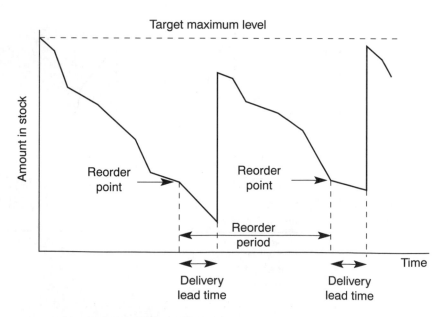

Fig A1.3 Stock Control (2): A ROP System
How much to reorder is determined by *when* the order is placed.

checking is high, since we do not need to keep a *real time* record of stocks. We can therefore see that the reasons for preferring ROL or ROP systems are examples of the issues covering *control frequency* discussed in Section 3.3.

3 UNSTABLE BEHAVIOUR IN COMPLEX STOCK CONTROL SYSTEMS

Everything we have discussed so far applies to the control of stock at one particular point in the sequence from supplier, through manufacturing and assembly, to retail outlet and sales to customers. Extra issues of *systems behaviour* come into play when designing the coordination of the stock held at different points along the sequence.

The old way of ordering and stock control at Carry-Out Cupboards is shown in Fig A1.4. The retail outlets each sent a weekly order to the CP which took a week to process and deliver to the ROs. Thus each retail outlet expected its orders to arrive the week after they had been ordered.

The CP also worked on a weekly basis, both for sending replenishment orders to the ROs and for placing its own orders on its various suppliers of materials and components. The turn-round time from suppliers however was four weeks because these were usually manufacturing components, not just assembling and packing like most of the Carry-Out Cupboards operations.

Such a sequential system of processing and stock control systems was inherently unstable. Figure A1.5 gives an example of how such instability could arise. The figures are deliberately simplistic to keep the illustration easy, but the principles they illustrate are important and realistic.

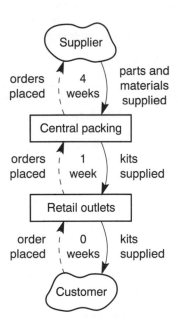

Fig A1.4 A Sequential Reordering System for Carry-Out Cupboards
Each component of the system operates a need/request and provision/response sequence as in Fig 6.4.

We start by considering the decision facing a RO manager who has regularly dealt with a demand of 10 for a particular cupboard. When a demand of 11 occurs in week 2 he might carry out one of three actions depending on different assumptions about the significance of the increase in demand:

1. Ignore the rise in demand on the assumption that it is a 'one-off' exception, and continue to reorder 10 per week as in the past. Such an action would leave his stock permanently depleted by one unit. If further increased demands were experienced, this policy would eventually exhaust the stock and make it impossible to fulfil the demand. So this action will only work in a long-term stable market.
2. Reorder 11 on the assumption that the average demand was still 10 but an extra 1 was needed to replenish the stock level. This is acceptable for RO stock control, but does not alter the principles that we will establish on the basis of any assumption of increased orders on the CP, as in action 3.
3. Reorder 12 on the assumption that the average demand has risen to 11. Hence a reorder figure of 12 would be made up of 11 for the anticipated next week's demand, plus 1 to replenish the stock.

Given the danger that action 1 postpones the potential problems associated with eventual changes in the demand, we will consider the effects of taking action 3. As we shall see, any assumption of increased demand will have the same effects in principle as action 3, so action 2 can be seen as being similar but less intensive in its effects.

The CP management has to deal with the orders from all the ROs. If we consider the effect of 10 ROs taking action 3, the CP will find itself faced with a demand that moves from 100 to 120. In real life such exact figures would be unlikely, since different ROs would experience different increases in a rising market, but we can take some particular figures to illustrate the principle of the effects of increased demand.

The CP management is therefore faced with a similar set of potential actions as that of a RO manager. The only difference is that the CP management has to interpret an apparent

	Retail Outlet (RO)			Deviation from desired stock level	Central Packing (CP)			Deviation from desired stock level
Week	Demand	Supply	Ordered	level	Demand	Supply	Ordered	level
1	10	10	10	nil	100	100	100	nil
2	11	10	12	−1	120	100	200	−20
3	11	12	11	nil	110	100	70	−30
4	11	11	11	nil	110	100	110	−40
5					110	100	110	−50
6					110	200	110	+40
7					110	70	110	nil
8					110	110	110	nil

Fig A1.5 The Effects of a Simple Disturbance on the System of Fig A1.4
The form of the disturbance and the associated data are simple, but the results illustrate important principles covered in the text.

increase from 100 to 120, rather than an increase from 10 to 11. The logic however is the same. If a demand of 100 has gone to 120, with a lead time of 4 weeks, CP management has to reorder 200. This figure is made up of the old order of 100, plus the 20 increase, and the other four lots of 20 increases that have to be covered until the new order arrives in four weeks time.

In week 3 however, the total orders received by the CP management drop back to 110. Using the same logic as before, the CP management now finds itself faced with a potential delivery of 200 which looks excessive in terms of the new assumption of a demand of 110. Allowing for the potential depletion and refurbishment of stock that is 'in the pipeline', an order of 70 should eventually put stock levels back to where they were before the changes in demand.

At this point Fig A1.5 stops. It has illustrated with simple data the effects of a simple change in the inputs to a sequential stock control system like that of Fig A1.4. These effects are illustrated by Fig A1.6. The important principles that this analysis establishes are:

    a. Any complex stock control system in which the components' feedback loops interact sequentially on a demand-response basis is potentially unstable when disturbed.

    b. The effects of the disturbance are increased by increased lags in the demand-response between components.

    c. Both the complexity and amplitude of the disturbances increases with increasing numbers of components in the sequence.

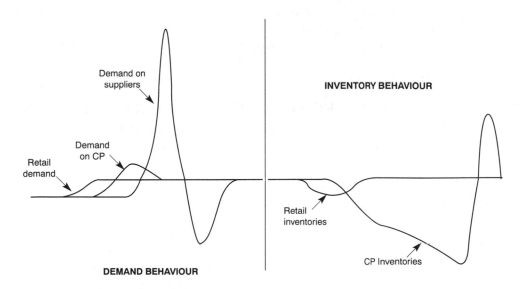

Fig A1.6 Examples of the Reaction of the Old System of Reordering and Stock Control at Carry-Out Cupboards to a Disturbance
An apparently theoretical illustration of a principle which has been illustrated by a wide range of actual examples cited in the text.

4   A POTENTIAL STABILIZING ROLE FOR INFORMATION SYSTEMS

We have illustrated some principles which explain potential instability in stock control systems. In fact, *any* system whose components are individual control systems responding to each other in this sequential way, with lags, is potentially unstable. As in Chapter 3, since all real-life processes take time, lags are inevitable in practice. This means that any real-life system with a demand-response sequence of this type will exhibit the instability features illustrated by our Carry-Out Cupboards example. Since, in turn, virtually all real-life systems will have such a feature in some form, the principles of instability we have just explored are nearly universally applicable.

The key to removing such instability is to remove or at least reduce the lags. A very effective way of doing this is to enable *all* the component control systems to have access to information at the same time. Thus in our Carry-Out Cupboards example, we would attempt to give the CP and the suppliers direct access to the latest figures on RO demand, without waiting for it to be fed sequentially through the system. The effect of this would be to remove the guesswork in interpreting fluctuating demand figures like the 100–120–110 for the CP, or the horrendous 100–200–70–110 sequence sent to the supplier.

The principle that would enable common and virtually simultaneous access to important information, like that of RO demand in the Carry-Out Cupboards case, is that of *information as a common organizational resource*. The concept that can deliver this resource to management is that of a *database*. If, instead of the individual control systems running their own separate system of physical files and data processing, the whole organization can integrate its information system through a database: great improvements in stability are possible.

So why does this not happen? Systems thinking also tells us that systems are *holist* concepts, and that therefore we know that there are strong human reasons why, for example, individual RO managers at Carry-Out Cupboards would not wish to share their data with others. A practical application of a database would have to take account of this. For Carry-Out Cupboards one answer might be that, if individual RO managers could trade stock with each other, they would have a self-interested motive to reveal their stock surpluses and shortages.

5   CENTRAL PURPOSE SUBSYSTEM INFORMATION FLOWS FOR CARRY-OUT CUPBOARDS

Customers–Marketing

Information to establish what kind of product Carry-Out Cupboards can sell to what kind of customer, where and when. For the product defined in terms like function (type of cupboard and components), appearance, finish, quality and price. For the customer defined in terms like income/social class, sex, age and geography. Trends and forecasts.

Most likely to occur in the form of a professional market research report carried out by the marketing department of Carry-Out Cupboards or from a professional agency.

Marketing–Customers

Investigations and requests to potential customers as part of the market research activity. Projecting information of existing products and Carry-Out Cupboards' image.

Verbal interview questions, questionnaires, media stimulation inviting potential customers to communicate their needs and ideas. *Example:* Competition in DIY magazine to choose 'my idea of a favourite cupboard'. Image through advertising media and actual view of Carry-Out Cupboards given by premises and personnel.

Marketing–Sales & order processing

Details of the current product range: what kits we are currently offering, official description, code numbers, price, etc. Advance notice of modifications, deletions and additions. Possible help with sales targets and forecasts.

Catalogues: printed. Product lists: either printed or on computer file. Notification of changes: either a document or could be Email.

Sales & order processing–Marketing

Sales statistics which will enable Marketing to monitor and modify their evaluation of the market for the various products offered by Carry-Out Cupboards.

It would most likely be Marketing's job to acquire the data and analyse it. In a manual system this would involve a very tiresome physical sifting through documents containing sales data, recording them, and performing the necessary statistical analysis. In a computerized system, programs could be included which would automatically update a file of sales data and provide Marketing with a sales analysis either periodically or on demand. (A statistical package like Minitab could do this.)

Customer–Sales & order processing

Orders or enquiries from customers, concerning type, quantity, price, availability, quality and sales conditions.

For Carry-Out Cupboards these will be mostly verbal, as customers place orders in retail outlets. If Carry-Out Cupboards do a credit card service, the orders could be by phone or by letter.

Sales & order processing–Customers

Informing the customer whether their order can be fulfilled, with or without modification, or whether it has to be delayed or rejected as confirmation of acceptance or notification of delivery. Also stimulating sales talk.

Since most Carry-Out Cupboards customers come personally to the retail outlets, this is likely to initially be verbal communication, but confirmation of the order as recorded on an order form will either be given to the customer or be sent as a delivery note with the goods. A receipt, although mainly a financial document, could fulfil this role in confirming physical collection by customer at RO.

Sales & order processing–Finished product inventory

Either enquiries as to product availability, or instructions as to the delivery of the order. As far as most customer orders are concerned, these go to those who get the stuff off the shelf and hump it to the customer's car! Where an order is delivered to the customer's address, the information would go on from the lifters and carriers to the van driver.

Sales staff enquiries would probably involve quizzing a printed or screen-based stock record. If stock was available, sales staff at the retail outlets would pass on a filled-in copy of the standard order form, sometimes called a picking list, which would tell helpers or deliverers what to load.

Finished product inventory–Sales & order processing

Information about what stocks are available or have been dispatched. The former in response to the customer's original order; the latter in response to subsequent enquiry, nagging and complaint: both received by Finished Product Inventory via Sales and Order Processing.

The medium for this information flow is likely to be the same as the previous flow. Thus if this flow were a picking list, it could be the same document with the items ticked off or signed. If it involves someone at a Carry-Out Cupboards retail outlet looking at what is physically in stock or at a record (manual or computer) in response to a request, the return of this information is the flow.

Marketing–Design & engineering

A specification of what qualities the product should possess in the context of market research. This could be the results of the market research interpreted by Marketing in terms of appearance, finish, quality, price, etc. and passed to the design people as a set of detailed instructions. Alternatively, it could be in the form of higher-level concepts like 'convenience' or 'hygienic appearance' which the designers would creatively realize in the form of their own product design. Which it was would depend on whether Carry-Out Cupboards saw marketing as serving design, or the other way around.

Since this flow would probably combine iteratively with the next flow, I suspect it would initially be mainly verbal leading to a final product specification document. The discussions would probably be carefully minuted and would finally centre around detailed concepts revealed next. (*See* Chapter 4 Mini-Case.)

Design & engineering–Marketing

Proposals by Design and Engineering to meet the requirements of the previous flow, plus information on Carry-Out Cupboards' productive capability and capacity to produce the concept. Design and Engineering may also initiate proposals for product modification based on production experience.

Verbal feedback as part of the previous iterative discussion. May be a formal minuting if there is distrust between engineering design and marketing, accompanied by designs or prototype/mockup/model. CAD/CAM helps here too.

Design & engineering–Production planning & control

All the details of the design of the various cupboard kits produced by Carry-Out Cupboards which are necessary to enable the kits to be assembled and packed correctly. This will include information on components, methods and machinery used.

Design drawings, parts/component breakdowns, lists of assembly operations. Can be screen or paper based.

Production planning & control–Design & engineering

Information on the feasibility and success of working to the instructions issued by Design and Engineering as in Production to Purchasing. This would also include details of quality performance. Design and Engineering would use this to build up their experience in judging what could be achieved by Production Planning and Control.

Documented data, manually or computer collected, probably used in connexion with meetings held to discuss strategic production plans.

Sales & order processing–Production planning & control

Total orders for each of the product range over the order period used by Carry-Out Cupboards. Could also include forecasted orders, if Carry-Out Cupboards have learned the lesson of the effect of lags in a process on the control system. Could be a standard reorder quantity if the retail outlets use a ROL stock control system.

Either standard paperwork or electronic data communications: depends on what degree of computerization is at work in Carry-Out Cupboards. The paperwork or order screen used will probably consist of a product table or list, with details of scheduled times and quantities for the kits.

Production planning & control–Sales & ordering processing

Information on the estimated ability, in advance of actual production, to meet the scheduled needs transmitted in the previous flow; or the actual performance of production planning and control in trying to meet the order needs.

For a manual/paperwork system this could be the original or a duplicate of the product table or list mentioned for flow 13 with the extra performance information added. For electronic data communications, the order screen could be added to in a similar fashion. If production was falling behind, both this and the previous flow could take the form of some lively verbal exchanges!

Production planning & control–Manufacturing & assembly

A schedule detailing how many of each kit must be assembled and packed by various target dates, plus instructions on assembly and packing methods.

Both manual and computerized systems would normally produce the schedule as a document, although in a computerized system this would be also available on screen. The schedule could be broken down into individual tasks or collections of tasks defined by a job ticket issued to the worker or section of the workforce responsible for its execution, or a separate operations sheet or list can sometimes be used in conjunction with the job ticket.

Manufacturing & assembly–Production planning & control

Details of actual production performance against the schedule. These would include quantities and dates of completion for the various kits scheduled, plus excuses for failure.

Most likely to be recorded as entries on the original schedule document/screen. Excuses formally encapsulated in quality control reports.

Design & engineering–Logistics & supply management

Parts and materials requirements and specification which includes details of quality standards and also possibly how manufactured. *Example:* design details of the hinges used in Carry-Out Cupboards' cupboards.

Almost certainly a documented record with drawings and a detailed quality specification, so that standards are clear and can be monitored. Modern CAD/CAM packages could integrate drawings and assembly breakdowns with quality specs.

Logistics & supply management–Design & engineering

Details of the availability of products and materials from suppliers, including the quality and delivery performance of suppliers. Could include suggestions for alternatives and new products.

Logistics and Supply Management will almost certainly have a formal hard copy/computer file record of these details for existing suppliers, of which Design and Engineering can be given copies. There are also trade reference books which list suppliers in a particular field. Look in the reference section of the library.

Logistics & supply management–Purchasing

Details of suppliers of materials and parts, which Materials and Parts Inventory need to know about when ordering supplies. Besides details like their addresses and who to contact, information would also include specifications of what is supplied, order quantities and procedures.

Specification of the product supplied is likely to be held as a document agreed with the supplier, of which both parties have a copy. Details of supply, like reorder quantity or supplier's address, could be on a supplier's file and/or on a stock record. Both of the latter could be screens and printout for a computer-based system, or paper records for a manual system.

Purchasing–Logistics & supply management

Analysis of supplier performance in terms of quality, quantities, costs and lead times.

Sometimes called 'Vendor Rating', for Carry-Out Cupboards it is most likely to be a combination of informal verbal feedback by Purchasing management and an analysis of data extracted from stock and financial records of delivery, quality conformance and payment. These will subsequently be combined in a report with a summary of supplier performance statistics by Logistics and Supply Management.

Production planning & control–Purchasing

Similar to the flow between Sales and Order Processing and Production Planning and Control, this could be a list of total quantities of material and parts needed to make up the kits actually ordered by the retail outlets, or a list of total quantities of material and parts needed to meet the *forecast* requirements of the retail outlets.

If the purchasing function in Carry-Out Cupboards is physically separate from production planning and control, the latter would break down quantities of kits (ordered or forecasted) into quantities of material and parts. These would be forwarded as paperwork or via a computer system order screen, and purchasing would use these to generate orders to suppliers.

Purchasing–Production planning & control

Notification of the supply of parts and materials against the order schedule generated by the previous flow.

If the purchasing function in Carry-Out Cupboards is physically separate from production planning and control, the latter would inform the former of quantities of material and parts delivered and available (or not!). These would be available as an updated paperwork list or via a computer system on screen, supplemented by more informal verbal communication at times of crisis.

Purchasing–Materials & parts inventory

Enquiries about stock availability. Instructions to purchase (for a reorder level type of stock control system), or purchasing schedules.

This information flow is likely to involve someone at Carry-Out Cupboards wanting to know the contents of a stock record (manual or computer). So the information flow is likely to be some form of manual/electronic/verbal communication.

Materials & parts inventory–Purchasing

What is in stock, has been supplied, or details of delivery time and quality conformance.

Since this information flow is likely to involve someone at Carry-Out Cupboards looking at a stock record (manual or computer), the information flow is the visual/verbal communication. However, if instructions are sent for someone else to do it, the medium for the flow of these instructions is likely to be a physical copy or extract from the stock record.

Logistics & supply management–Suppliers

For new parts and materials this could be both invitations to tender to new suppliers and notification of needs to existing suppliers. In either case, requirements specifications which included details of quality standards and also possible methods of manufacture might be included in the information sent.

Although initial enquiries might be verbal, the contractual nature of the eventual request implies that this would be a formal document, possibly with drawings attached, copies of which would be held by both parties.

Suppliers–Logistics & supply management

Tenders, directly communicated information on products, information gained from adverts and other indirect communication.

Tenders and directly communicated information on products are most likely to come from suppliers in written, possibly fax, form. Information gained from adverts is likely to come via trade magazines or directories. Personal contact through sales reps or visits could result in the use of samples and other forms of visual communication of product qualities.

Purchasing–Suppliers

Individual orders for materials and parts sent to the appropriate supplier, giving details of identity, quantity and delivery.

The order might begin as an informal telephone or personal enquiry, but an order form generated by Carry-Out Cupboards would be needed to confirm it.

Suppliers–Purchasing

Confirmation of orders placed and/or notification of delivery.

Notice of Supply, Delivery Notes or Goods Received Notes (GRNs) are typical examples.

APPENDIX 2

The East Farthing Drainage Authority

1 INTRODUCTION

The East Farthing Drainage Authority is a fictitious body, but its background, duties, operations and problems are similar to those of real 'drainage boards' operating under the 1991 Land Drainage Act.

2 HISTORICAL BACKGROUND

Much of the land on the East Coast of England from London to East Yorkshire is flat. Until the 17th century most of this flat land was a mixture of wild marsh and slow flowing rivers. Any agriculture was mainly confined to the grazing of sheep and cattle on the marshes during the summer months when water levels fell and the grass grew.

From the end of the 17th century onwards however, various drainage schemes were carried out. Many of these were instigated by the large landowners who sought the profits that came from the major improvements in British agriculture during the 18th century. The work was often done by Dutch engineers or used skills acquired from them.

By the late 19th century most of this East Coast land was as it is today: fully drained by a complex network of drainage channels (known as 'dykes') and rerouted rivers. What has changed however is the kind of farming carried out. British food needs during World War II, developments in agricultural technology, and the effects of British membership of the European Community, have transformed this land into areas of large-scale arable farming.

In the last ten years the results of another trend have started to appear. The growth in large-scale, capitally intensive arable farming has had a depopulating effect; but this has been counteracted by other factors. Increased British ties with Europe have pushed the 'centre of gravity' of England eastwards, with an expansionary effect on ports and the location of industries. The decay of some inner cities has also pushed population out into the countryside. Hence many of the towns and areas of the East Coast have grown in population and wealth. As we shall see below, all these changes have affected the workings of the drainage boards, including the East Farthing Drainage Authority.

3   CONTEMPORARY CONTEXT

The result of the various drainage schemes described above has been to leave much East Coast agriculture, industry and habitation dependent on successful drainage. Yet the word 'drainage' has often been associated with the mundane and amusing. It has overtones associated with sewerage, and popular phrases like 'down the drain', which have nothing to do with the activities of the drainage boards.

Recent developments are removing such ignorant prejudice. Increase in the interest in 'green issues' and publicity for the potential effects of global warming are drawing attention to the possibility of increased risks of flooding for low lying areas like the East Coast. This concern has revived the accounts of 1953, when a combination of wind and tide led to serious flooding in the area, with dramatic damage and death.

Another green issue has been the effect of the kind of agriculture that drainage has encouraged and its effect on wildlife. Before the 17th century, the East Coast marshes were a rich environment of birds, fish and flora. Now only the dykes remain as limited habitats for fish and hunting grounds for water birds, in areas dominated by the results of modern arable farming.

Various ecologically conscious political groups are now in place criticizing this situation, with farmers and politicians increasingly sensitive to the criticism.

4   STATUTORY DUTIES

The Land Drainage Act of 1991 is an attempt to consolidate previous legislation governing the operation of land drainage. It focusses on the *operational* need to avoid the dangers of flooding by containing sections on 'control of watercourses' or 'restoration and improvement of ditches': ditches being the official term for dykes. It also recognizes the wider *environmental* role of drainage by referring to 'duties with respect to the environment and recreation'.

A view of a wider system, of which the drainage boards form a component, would recognize the role of the NRA or National Rivers Authority and local councils. The NRA is concerned with the issues of drainage, pollution and ecology associated with natural rivers, and has powers to intervene in drainage board affairs. The local councils are not only represented on drainage boards, but may also be assigned powers by the NRA.

Within this context however, a drainage board has to carry out the operational and environmental duties above in the area over which it has been granted statutory powers. For the East Farthing Drainage Authority, this area is the East Farthing itself.

5   TECHNOLOGY

The technology used by drainage boards falls into three general categories:

1. Civil engineering equipment used to create drainages systems and ensure that they work. This would include machines for excavation, clearing out dykes, pumping, etc.
2. Surveying and planning equipment used to draw up plans and maintain records. Historically this would be equipment such as theodolites, measuring lines and paper maps. Modern surveying now also uses electronic devices that can accu-

rately locate positions using satellites, and computer aided design (CAD) software that can automatically produce maps from surveyors' measurements.

3. Conventional business computer systems for maintaining accounts and payment of employees.

The East Farthing Drainage Authority is well equipped with modern forms of all of the
above. The fact that its operations are similar at least to other boards, and often to a whole
range of other industries, means that existing sources of equipment from diggers to computer software are available to the authority.

6   FINANCE

Drainage boards are financed by a 'drainage rate' levied on all property in its area.
Properties are valued by an official body which is independent of the boards. The boards
then set a 'rate' which is a fixed charge for every £'s worth of the property's value:

Total drainage charge = property value × drainage rate

For agricultural land the charge is collected directly from individual landowners by the
board. For residential property, the local council is charged a single sum by the board for
the combined value of all the residential properties in its area. The council then recovers
this money from individual residential property owners as part of the local Council Tax.

7   POLITICS

Politics comes into the East Farthing Drainage Authority both with a big and a small 'p'.
Each kind of politics stems from the way the authority is governed. This is done by a board
of elected and nominated members designed to reflect the interests of those who finance its
operations. Thus the agricultural landowners are entitled to elect members directly to the
board, and the local council may nominate members to represent the domestic and industrial property owners, who in turn elect the council.

The membership of the board brings in 'small p' politics through members directly
elected to the board by agricultural landowners. The voting system laid down by the statutory legislation gives power to electors roughly in proportion to the amount of land that
they own: but this is only approximate. At a detailed level, owners of small areas of land
are disproportionately more powerful. This means that if such owners are determined
enough, they can outvote the large 'agribusiness' farmers hectare for hectare.

The membership of the board brings in 'big p' party politics through the members nominated by the local council. Where one form of party politics dominates the local council,
then the members nominated to the board reflect this party political bias.

In the past, both forms of politics have been low key. Most agricultural landowners
have been content to allow well known figures in the agricultural community to be
elected to the board, sometimes unopposed. The local council, in turn, has mainly consisted of independent members with no official party allegiance, so that nominated
members were an individualistic, heterogeneous group. However, in the early 1990s the
situation began to change.

First, educated middle class people who moved into the area from the towns and cities
began to occupy some of the smaller agricultural holdings. Their views of agriculture were

often less commercial than those of the large agribusiness farmers, with more emphasis on opposing high-tech farming and concern for 'the environment', by which they usually meant more consideration for natural vegetation and wildlife.

Second, many of both the previous and the new population who were hit by the recession and unemployment of the late 1980s and early 1990s began to question both the political and economic effects of the East Farthing Drainage Authority's policies on development and growth. There was an element of 'a plague on both your houses' from some council members who felt that the 'agribusiness' and the 'ecological' influences on the board were enemies to industrial development.

A particular butt of such criticism was the East Farthing Ecology Group. The group consisted mainly of educated middle class. It was set up in 1987 in response to concerns about the effects of modern agriculture on the environment, and a belief that the East Farthing Drainage Authority was essentially a tool of the large farmers. Whether they were incoming smallholders, young idealists or retired people, they were all concerned about pollution or the protection of wildlife. Since they were set up, the group has had the intention to field candidates in board elections.

Another political factor which seemed to creep into the public debate was the concept of 'privatization'. Since so many services provided by official and local government authorities had been contracted out to private enterprise, the feeling throughout the members of the governing board was that the East Farthing Drainage Authority itself might soon become essentially a subcontracting organization rather than a direct operator in the drainage of East Farthing.

Some thought the fashion for privatization could work the other way, with the East Farthing Drainage Authority becoming the 'East Farthing Drainage Company', with an obligation to earn more of its income from bidding for private work that would use its special skills and equipment.

A major catalyst to a debate of all these issues was the 'Cross-link Channel Scheme'. This was a proposal to build a new drainage dyke which would connect two of the major channels leading to the sea. As a result, one of the existing main channels would become redundant, and this would leave the beautiful conservation area of South Farthing free from the kind of regular maintenance operations which the East Farthing Conservation Group considered a threat to wildlife. The agribusiness element were concerned that this would imply that the area was no longer of major agricultural importance, and that conventional farming might eventually be made impossible by the increasing imposition of conservation-based restrictions. The supporters of industrial development were not sure if this meant a victory for the 'no development' conservationists or an opportunity for development.

The main result of the proposal seems to be that drainage is no longer a dull subject in East Farthing.

APPENDIX 3

· ·

MX Marketing

Late in 1988, information systems students at XYZ University attended an introductory talk and demonstration to some local business people in their area. It covered the main features of a typical office microcomputer-based system and included some simple demonstrations of data retrieval, word processing and spreadsheet software. An important aspect of the presentation was to caution against the automatic assumption that 'computers were a good thing', regardless of situation or need. The systems students took the initiative to suggest that they were available as a group for more detailed investigations of potential office systems computer applications. They explained that this would be on the basis that they could make tentative recommendations in exchange for an opportunity to apply their skills to a practical problem.

They were subsequently approached by Ben Lister who was present at the demonstration. Ben owned a small merchandising business, which he ran from an office attached to his home, and of which he and his wife were the owning partners.

The students made the following notes from initial conversations with Ben:

a. Civil/rural/farm products selling organization, essentially one man (the owner) travelling, exhibiting, visiting and selling.

b. Small office block (extension to private residence) with secretarial support consisting of wife and partner plus temporary, part-time secretary. Use of 24 hour answering machine.

c. Rented storage for products 20 miles away from office. Subcontracted delivery by transport company owner of rented storage.

d. Five categories of product:
   1. GRP/Cement animal feeding troughs. (GPR = glass-reinforced plastics)
   2. Drainage materials.
   3. Plastic storage bags, nets, etc., for animal feed.
   4. Farm animal feed supplements.
   5. Crop storage additives.

e. Customers in the hundreds.

f. Turnover in five figures.

g. Cautious about computers: seen too many dusty and unused machines in farm offices.

h. Main attractions towards computers are word processing and data retrieval for correspondence and ability to produce selected customer lists. Overdue need to produce computerized accounts.

The XYZ systems students received the following reply to their offer:

MX Marketing
(B. & A. Lister)
Reg.in Gt.Britain. No. 1234567

The Orchard,
Southcotes,
Lincs LN99 2ZX.

Tel: Southcotes (0107) 666000
Fax: Southcotes (0107) 675432

Dear XYZ University Systems Students,

Thanks for your interesting remarks during our chat on Thursday. I've thought over some of the things you mentioned and I suppose the main things that come to mind (not in any particular order) are:-

1. We are going to need new typewriting, copying, calculating and other office equipment soon to modernize for our new extension office building, so the whole question of word processing and choice of equipment is bound to come up anyway. It makes sense also to consider a computer system whilst we are about it.
2. There are a number of filing operations that need doing, some of which we cover already using paper:
   Storage of customer details.
   List of users of each product we sell.
   List of prospects (i.e. potential buyers) for each product we sell.
   Addresses for mailing each product at intervals in the year.

It would be useful to be able to do our own literature (e.g. leaflets) with diagrams or illustrations.

I would be interested in a system at a reasonable price, say not much beyond £5000?

Best regards,
Ben Lister

APPENDIX 4

Dog Registration

Until the late 1980s I suspect that most people in the UK had not heard of a breed of dog known as a Rotweiler. Now, following some highly publicized attacks on children during the late 1980s, the term 'Rotweiler' has entered into colloquial language to express the concept of aggression and danger.

A recent addition to the gallery of dogs reputed to share these characteristics has been the Pit Bull Terrier. Adverse publicity about this dog in the UK has actually led to the introduction of measures for ownership control and the culling of dangerous or unregistered dogs of the breed. Many dog owners and sympathizers feel that this attitude is not only exaggerated and misleading, but also actually results in the culling of harmless dogs due to hysterical over-reaction.

These reservations about current legislation on dangerous dogs does not mean that all dog sympathizers are against the concept of registration. Many organizations and individuals who support the interests and welfare of dogs favour the idea of compulsory registration of all dog ownership. Their view is that bad dog behaviour is the result of irresponsible owners, and that compulsory registration would help to control ownership and enable convicted bad owners to be banned from keeping dogs at all.

People and organizations holding this opinion cite many examples of how registration of ownership would protect dogs. Breeders of dogs above a certain quantity already have to be registered, but there are some small breeders who exploit bitches by keeping them and their offspring in dirty conditions and do the bare minimum to keep them alive until they become a marketable product. An important example of this market is the breeding of dogs for medical research.

Throughout the economic recession in European agriculture at the end of the 1980s and into the early 1990s, some farmers have identified an opportunity for using their buildings and facilities profitably, by breeding dogs for medical experiments.

Pet shops and dealers have often been too eager to concentrate on the sale of lovable puppies without drawing the buyer's attention to the assertion that 'a dog is not just for Christmas: it's for life'.

Professional and official bodies also have views on the issues. Besides the question of welfare, vets are concerned about animal health. Loose or stray dogs represent a potential health threat both to themselves and to humans. Increased international travel and the opening up of free trade areas has exacerbated this problem. At a more local level, some councils are concerned at the health and safety aspects of footpath fouling and the danger of stray dogs in traffic.

A less common view amongst official bodies is that, if dogs are a popular commodity, they represent a potential source of tax revenue. Registration could be a source of income for either local or central government.

Many politicians, knowing dogs to be an emotive issue, wish to avoid the subject of dog registration altogether.

INDEX
· · · · · · · · · · ·

An index is not intended to be a list or a catalogue. Instead, it is designed to help you find the most important occurrences of the words or terms you may seek in a book. Remember that the Contents pages at the beginning of the book can often give a better idea of how all these various words and terms fit together in the whole picture than an alphabetical list like this.